Soups, Stews and Chilies . Poultry . Beef, Pork and Lamb

eads . Desserts . An Introduction to Healthier Eating .

eef, Pork and Lamb . Fish and Seafood . Meatless Entrees

althier Eating . Appetizers . S [barcode: D0536752] Stews and

. Meatless Entrees . Side Dishes . Breads . Desserts .

Soups, Stews and Chilies . Poultry . Beef, Pork and Lamb

eads . Desserts . An Introduction to Healthier Eating .

eef, Pork and Lamb . Fish and Seafood . Meatless Entrees

althier Eating . Appetizers . Salads . Soups, Stews and

. Meatless Entrees . Side Dishes . Breads . Desserts .

Soups, Stews and Chilies . Poultry . Beef, Pork and Lamb

eads . Desserts . An Introduction to Healthier Eating

An Introduction to Healthier Eating . Appetizers . Salads

. Fish and Seafood . Meatless Entrees . Side Dishes .

Appetizers . Salads . Soups, Stews and Chilies . Poultry

. Side Dishes . Breads . Desserts . An Introduction to

Chilies . Poultry . Beef, Pork and Lamb . Fish and Seafo

An Introduction to Healthier Eating . Appetizers . Salads

. Fish and Seafood . Meatless Entrees . Side Dishes .

Appetizers . Salads . Soups, Stews and Chilies . Poultry

. Side Dishes . Breads . Desserts . An Introduction to

Chilies . Poultry . Beef, Pork and Lamb . Fish and Seafo

An Introduction to Healthier Eating . Appetizers . Salads

. Fish and Seafood . Meatless Entrees . Side Dishes .

Pillsbury Fast AND Healthy COOKBOOK

Pillsbury Fast AND Healthy COOKBOOK

350 Easy Recipes for Every Day

WILEY

Wiley Publishing, Inc.

For general information on our other products and services or to obtain technical support please contact our Customer Care Department within the U.S. at 800-762-2974, outside the U.S. at 317-572-3993 or fax 317-572-4002.

Wiley also publishes its books in a variety of electronic formats. Some content that appears in print may not be available in electronic books. For more information about Wiley products, visit our web site at www.wiley.com.

Library of Congress Cataloging-in-Publication Data is available upon request.

ISBN-13: 978-0-7645-8862-1 (cloth)
ISBN-10: 0-7645-8862-1 (cloth)

Manufactured in Japan

10 9 8 7 6 5 4

First Edition

GENERAL MILLS
Director, Book and Online Publishing: Kim Walter
Manager, Cookbook Publishing: Lois Tlusty
Recipe Development and Testing: Pillsbury Kitchens
Photography and Food Styling: General Mills Photography Studios and Image Library

WILEY PUBLISHING, INC.
Publisher: Natalie Chapman
Executive Editor: Anne Ficklen
Manufacturing Manager: Kevin Watt

Design by Susan DeStaebler

Home of the Pillsbury Bake-Off® Contest

Pillsbury

Our recipes have been tested in the Pillsbury Kitchens and meet our standards of easy preparation, reliability and great taste.

For more great recipes, visit pillsbury.com

Contents

A Guide to Healthier Eating

The *Fast and Healthy*® Philosophy

■ ■

At *Fast and Healthy* magazine, we believe that your daily diet can affect your well-being—how you look, how you feel, how much energy you have. An increasing amount of scientific evidence suggests that a varied diet high in complex carbohydrates and low in fat is best and can help protect against serious illnesses such as cancer and heart disease.

At the same time, today's fast-paced lifestyles often don't leave time for cooking elaborate, multistep meals. Home cooks want foods that go from stove to table quickly, so most of our recipes require no more than 30 minutes of active preparation time and call for a short list of readily available ingredients.

Underlying all the considerations for health and ease of preparation is the most basic concept of all: food must taste good. "Healthy" doesn't have to mean "deprivation"; you shouldn't have to worry about "forbidden" foods. Within the context of healthy eating, you can enjoy all foods—in moderation, as part of a varied diet. There's nothing wrong with offsetting a rich indulgence one day with a lighter choice the next, or choosing a smaller portion of a special treat or, best of all, selecting a recipe from our pages to satisfy that craving in a lighter way. In each chapter, we seek to provide satisfying, healthy versions of well-loved, high-fat favorites, as well as delicious new creations destined to become favorites.

You may notice that sometimes we call for lower-fat or lower-sodium products, such as egg substitute or reduced-sodium tomato sauce, and other times we call for the regular item. We try to use the regular ingredients whenever possible. But when necessary, we make substitutions to keep nutrition in line. For example, we may reduce the amount of oil needed and call for egg substitute in a chocolate dessert so that we can "afford" the amount of real chocolate necessary for best flavor.

The Food Guide Pyramid

In 1992, the U.S. Department of Agriculture, in cooperation with the Department of Health and Human Services, unveiled the "Food Guide Pyramid" to illustrate guidelines for a healthy diet. The pyramid replaced the older notion of the "Basic Four Food Groups" (later the Basic Five), which had been in use since the 1950s.

In a shift from decades past, the pyramid does not use meat as the centerpiece of a healthy diet. Instead, it emphasizes grain products, fruits and vegetables. Meat and dairy products are still important, but play more of a supporting role. The tip of the pyramid serves as a reminder that sugars and fats should be used sparingly.

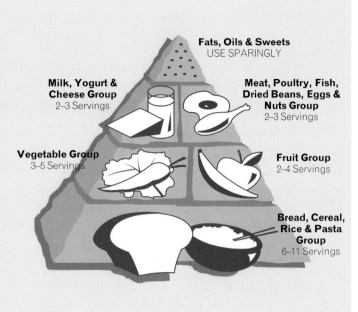

What's a Serving?

Serving sizes vary depending on the nutrients a food provides. Here is a basic guide for what counts as a serving in the Food Guide Pyramid. You may be surprised that you're getting several servings of a food group with one food—a large bowl of cereal, for example, may actually be three or four servings from the bread group.

Bread, Cereal, Rice and Pasta Group
- 1 slice of bread
- 1 oz. of ready-to-eat cereal
- ½ cup of cooked cereal, rice or pasta

Vegetable Group
- 1 cup of raw leafy vegetables
- ½ cup of other vegetables, cooked or chopped raw
- ¾ cup of vegetable juice

Fruit Group
- 1 medium apple, banana or orange
- ½ cup of chopped, cooked or canned fruit
- ¾ cup of fruit juice

Milk, Yogurt and Cheese Group
- 1 cup of milk or yogurt
- 1½ oz. of natural cheese
- 2 oz. of processed cheese

Meat, Poultry, Fish, Dry Beans, Eggs and Nuts Group
- 2 to 3 oz. of cooked lean meat, poultry or fish
- ½ cup of cooked dry beans, 1 egg or 2 tablespoons of peanut butter count as 1 oz. of lean meat

How Many Servings Do You Need Each Day?

	Many Women, Older Adults	Children, Teen Girls, Active Women, Most Men	Teen Boys, Active Men
Calorie level	1,600	2,000	2,800
Bread group	6	9	11
Vegetable group	3	4	5
Fruit group	2	3	4
Milk group	2–3*	2–3*	2–3*
Meat group	5 oz.	6 oz.	7 oz.

Women who are pregnant or breast-feeding, teenagers and young adults to age 24 need 3 servings.

Seven Steps to a Healthy Diet

Fast and Healthy recipes are designed to help you meet the Dietary Guidelines for Americans. Issued jointly by the U.S. Department of Agriculture and the Department of Health and Human Services, the guidelines offer advice for healthy Americans about food choices that help promote health and prevent disease.

1. Eat a variety of foods to get the energy, protein, vitamins, minerals and fiber you need for good health. No single food can provide everything you need; it's important to vary your choices. Use the Food Guide Pyramid (page 9) to help you plan your choices.

2. Balance the foods you eat with physical activity to maintain or improve a healthy weight. Weight gain increases your risk of developing high blood pressure, heart disease, stroke, diabetes, certain cancers and other illness.

3. Choose a diet low in fat, saturated fat and cholesterol to reduce your risk of heart disease and certain types of cancer. Because fat contains more than twice the calories of an equal amount of carbohydrates or protein, a diet low in fat can help you maintain a healthy weight.

4. Choose a diet with plenty of vegetables, fruits and grain products. Most of the calories in your diet should come from these foods, which provide needed vitamins, minerals, fiber and complex carbohydrates and can help you lower your intake of fat.

5. Use sugars in moderation. A diet with lots of sugar probably has too few nutrients for most people and can contribute to tooth decay.

6. Use salt and sodium in moderation to help reduce your risk of high blood pressure. While sodium occurs naturally in foods, the amount in fresh fruits and vegetables is usually very small. Read the Nutrition Facts panel of prepared foods to identify those lower in sodium.

7. If you drink alcoholic beverages, do so in moderation, with meals and only when consumption does not put you and others at risk. Alcoholic beverages supply calories, but little or no nutrients. Moderate consumption has been associated with a lower risk for heart disease, but too much alcohol may cause many health problems and accidents and can lead to addiction.

Healthy Convenience

A growing number of fresh foods simplify life for the health-conscious cook who just doesn't have the time or energy to face a lot of chopping and peeling at the end of a long day.

■ *Salad bars in the grocery store.* Skip the potato salad and other ready-made items and concentrate on the prepared fresh produce such as cleaned lettuce and grated carrots. You'll pay a higher price per pound, but you'll spend less time making dinner and probably still come out ahead of takeout or eating out. Salad bars also offer a good solution for single people and small families when they need a few celery stalks or a cup of melon chunks, for example, but wouldn't use up a whole head of celery or an entire watermelon before it spoiled.

■ *Prepared vegetables in the produce section.* The increasing array of ready-to-use vegetables includes prewashed lettuce, coleslaw mix with no dressing (great for stir-fries as well as slaw), peeled baby carrots, precut broccoli and cauliflower florets, mesclun salad (colorful mixture of several baby lettuces) and sprouts.

■ *Single ingredients from the deli or seafood counter.* Roasted fresh chicken, slices of roast beef and cooked shrimp can all streamline preparation of main courses.

Healthier Cooking Techniques

■ ■ ■ ■ ■ ■ ■ ■ ■ ■ ■ ■ ■ ■ ■ ■ ■ ■ ■

Deep-fat frying, even panfrying, adds calories and fat to foods. The following techniques, on the other hand, require no added fat:

Poaching

Boiling

Steaming

Baking

Roasting

Grilling

Broiling

Microwaving

Stir-frying or sautéing in a nonstick pan with nonstick cooking spray

Dreamy Steamers

A steamer, an inexpensive and underappreciated piece of cookware, is ideal for healthy cooking. Foods retain vitamins and minerals and require no added fat for cooking. In addition, vegetables usually retain superb color and texture. Vegetables can be placed directly on the steamer rack; delicate items such as fish can be cooked on a heat-proof plate set inside a bamboo steamer.

■ Bamboo steamers, available in housewares departments and Asian cookware shops, resemble short round baskets. The flat bottom fits inside a wok or over an ordinary skillet filled with simmering water. Steamer baskets can be stacked, allowing you to cook items such as broccoli, which takes longer, at the same time as shorter-cooking ingredients, like snow pea pods. The longer-cooking ingredient should be placed in a steamer basket closer to the heat.

■ Collapsible metal steamers expand to fit a variety of pots or skillets and take up little storage space.

Nonstick Skillets

Nonstick skillets are a key item in the healthy cook's cupboard. Many foods can be cooked with no added fat or just a spritz of nonstick cooking spray or a small amount of regular oil. Treat the pans gently and they will reward you with long service:

■ Use only plastic or wooden utensils.

■ Clean them only with a sponge or plastic scrubber, never with steel wool or abrasives.

■ Don't store other cookware directly on top of them. If you must "nest" pans, protect the nonstick skillet with a layer of paper toweling or a dishcloth.

Make the Most of Your Microwave

Microwave cooking is perfect for the healthy cook because many dishes require no added fat. Speed is a definite advantage. With a microwave, it's easy to incorporate acorn squash into a quick supper, for example, because it cooks in 8 to 10 minutes instead of an hour in the conventional oven. Starches such as rice can be cooked in the microwave, too. You won't save time, but the microwave oven stops cooking after a designated number of minutes so you don't have to worry about scorching.

Fast and Healthy Glossary

As health news has become a regular part of the headlines, the use of certain nutrition terms has become commonplace. This glossary defines some of the frequently used terms.

Antioxidants Vitamins E and C and beta-carotene (which the body can convert to vitamin A) are antioxidants. Antioxidants are believed to be an important defense against free radicals—substances that can damage cells through oxidation. Free radicals can alter a cell's genetic structure, promoting the growth of cancer. **Good sources:** Orange and yellow vegetables, such as carrots, sweet potatoes and winter squash; dark green vegetables like Swiss chard, broccoli, Brussels sprouts, spinach and kale.

Calcium An essential mineral for strong bones and teeth as well as for the functioning of cells, muscles and nerves. Too little calcium in the diet can contribute to osteoporosis, or brittle bones, as you age. Women are more susceptible than men; slender women with small bones are especially at risk. **Good sources:** Dairy products, especially milk; fish, especially sardines and shellfish; green leafy vegetables.

Cholesterol Cholesterol, despite its bad reputation, is in fact a key component of the nervous system and plays a role in the body's production of several hormones. Cholesterol is found only in animal foods, such as meat, poultry, dairy products and eggs. It is not found in plant foods, even high-fat ones such as peanut butter. Cholesterol's bad reputation stems from the fact that too much saturated fat, and to a lesser extent cholesterol, in the diet can increase the risk of heart disease by raising blood cholesterol levels. Excess fat can also contribute to obesity and pos-

sibly cancer. Health professionals recommend limiting daily cholesterol intake to 300 milligrams.

Complex carbohydrates
Complex carbohydrates, or starches, are important sources of energy, and foods that contain them provide a wide variety of vitamins, minerals and fiber. Despite what many people have believed over the years, carbohydrate foods are not fattening in and of themselves. Fat provides 9 calories per gram, while carbohydrates contribute just 4 calories per gram. Of course, topping carbohydrates with butter, rich sauces or dressings changes the story. **Good sources:** Breads, cereals, pasta and rice, as well as fruits and vegetables.

Cruciferous vegetables The cruciferous family includes broccoli, cauliflower, Brussels sprouts, turnips, cabbage and kale. These vegetables contain certain chemicals thought to reduce the risk of some cancers.

Fat Fat is the most concentrated source of energy and can be stored in the body for later use. Fats provide 9 calories per gram, compared with 4 calories per gram from carbohydrates or protein. Health experts recommend limiting fat to 30 percent of daily calories. That doesn't mean eliminating individual foods that may contain more than 30 percent of calories from fat, but rather balancing these foods with lower-fat choices over the course of a day or week.

Fiber   Fiber is a type of complex carbohydrate that's not digested by the body. It comes in two forms: insoluble and soluble. Insoluble fiber is thought to help reduce the risk of colorectal cancer. Soluble fiber helps reduce blood cholesterol and, therefore, to lower the risk of coronary heart disease. Both types of fiber aid digestion and regularity. Experts recommend 20 to 35 grams of fiber daily. **Good sources:** Fruits and vegetables, especially with the skins; whole-grain products; canned and packaged dried beans; nuts and popcorn.

Folic acid   Also known as folate or folacin, folic acid is a vitamin especially important for women who may conceive or are in the early stages of pregnancy to reduce the risk of several serious birth defects. **Good sources:** Green leafy vegetables, organ meats, dried peas, beans and lentils. Many cereal products are now fortified with folic acid; check nutrition labels.

Iron   Iron is important for the formation of hemoglobin, the substance in the blood that carries oxygen throughout the body. If you don't consume enough iron, you may develop iron-deficiency anemia. During their menstruating years women require more iron then men (15 milligrams daily compared to 10 milligrams for men). Pregnant women have even higher needs (30 milligrams). **Good sources:** Red meat, especially liver and other organ meats; poultry, fish, eggs. Cooking in cast-iron cookware can boost iron content of foods slightly, too. Vitamin C helps the body absorb iron, so it's a good idea to have a glass of orange juice with an iron-rich meal or along with iron tablets if your doctor recommends them.

Niacin   A vitamin that plays a role in carbohydrate, protein and fat metabolism. **Good sources:** Meat, poultry, fish, enriched cereals, peanuts, potatoes, dairy products, eggs.

Nutraceuticals   A term coined (to combine "nutrition" and "pharmaceuticals") to indicate foods that provide health benefits beyond their contribution of "traditional" nutrients.

Phytochemicals   Natural compounds found in foods that may help protect against cancer and other diseases.

Protein   A substance that's a necessary building block for cells. **Good sources:** Meat, poultry, fish, eggs, milk, legumes and soy products such as tofu.

Saturated fat   Saturated fat, one of the three major types of fats, is found predominantly in animal products, such as meat, fish, poultry, dairy products and eggs, as well as animal-source fat products such as butter and lard. It is also found in tropical oils, including palm, palm kernel and coconut oils. Excessive saturated fat in the diet can contribute to heart disease. The daily diet should include no more than 30 percent of its calories from fat, and in turn, the fat quota should include no more than one-third of its calories from saturated fats.

Simple carbohydrates (sugars)   Like complex carbohydrates, simple carbohydrates provide 4 calories per gram.

Sodium   Sodium is a mineral that occurs naturally in most of the foods we eat and in sodium chloride—ordinary table salt. Sodium in the diet helps to regulate the body's fluid balance and is also necessary for normal muscle and nerve function. In some individuals, however, high sodium intake is thought to contribute to hypertension (high blood pressure). Health experts recommend a daily intake of no more than 2,400 milligrams of sodium—the amount in about $1\frac{1}{4}$ teaspoons of salt.

Unsaturated fat   Health experts recommend that two-thirds of the daily fat intake come from polyunsaturated and monounsaturated fat, which generally decrease blood cholesterol levels. Examples of monounsaturated fats include olive oil and canola oil. Polyunsaturated fats include corn, safflower and sunflower oils. Other fats, such as sesame, soybean and peanut oils, contain a combination of polyunsaturated and monounsaturated fats.

Vitamin A   Necessary for maintaining healthy tissue in the body, bone and tooth growth and night vision, vitamin A comes directly from animal sources and is converted in the body, when necessary, from beta-carotene in plant sources. **Good sources:** Yellow or orange fruits and vegetables, fortified oatmeal, liver, dairy products.

Vitamin B₁ (thiamine)   Helps the body release energy from carbohydrates during metabolism; growth and muscle tone. **Good sources:** Fortified cereals and oatmeals, meats, rice and pasta, whole grains, liver.

Vitamin B₂ (riboflavin)   Helps the body release energy from protein, fat and carbohydrates during metabolism. **Good sources:** Whole grains, green leafy vegetables, organ meats, milk and eggs.

Vitamin B₆ (pyroxidine)   Helps build body tissue and aids in metabolism of protein. **Good sources:** Fish, poultry, lean meats, bananas, prunes, dried beans, whole grains, avocados.

Vitamin B₁₂ (cobalamin)   Aids cell development, functioning of the nervous system and the metabolism of protein and fat. **Good sources:** Meats, milk products, seafood.

Vitamin C (ascorbic acid)   Vital for the structure of bones, cartilage, muscle and blood vessels. Also helps maintain capillaries and gums, aids in the absorption of iron and may reduce the risk of some cancers. **Good sources:** Citrus fruits, berries and vegetables, especially peppers.

Vitamin D   Aids in bone and tooth formation; helps maintain heart action and the nervous system. **Good sources:** Fortified milk, sunlight, fish, eggs, butter, fortified margarine.

Vitamin E   Protects blood cells, body tissue and essential fatty acids from destruction in the body; may reduce the risk of coronary heart disease. **Good sources:** Fortified and multigrain cereals, nuts, wheat germ, vegetable oils, green leafy vegetables.

Vitamin K   Necessary for blood clotting functions. **Good sources:** Green leafy vegetables, fruit, dairy and grain products.

How to Use Our Nutrition Information

▪ ▪ ▪ ▪ ▪ ▪ ▪ ▪ ▪ ▪ ▪ ▪ ▪ ▪ ▪ ▪ ▪ ▪ ▪

The nutrition information provided with each recipe can help you estimate how the recipe fits your overall meal plan. At the end of each recipe, we list calories, fat, cholesterol, sodium, carbohydrate, dietary fiber, sugars, protein, vitamins A and C, calcium and iron.

Each recipe also lists Percent Daily Values (%DVs), which tell you how much the nutrients in one serving of food contribute to a 2,000-calorie diet. For example, if the daily value for total fat is 10%, this means one serving of this food contributes 10% of the daily total fat suggested for a person on a 2,000-calorie-a-day diet. (When the labeling guidelines were developed by the government, 2,000 calories was designated as an average level. It's about right for most moderately active women, teenage girls and sedentary men. Older adults, sedentary women and children need less; many men, teenage boys and active women may need more.)

In addition, you'll find dietary exchanges, the nutritional accounting system commonly used by people with diabetes. This information is based on *1995 Exchange Lists for Meal Planning* by the American Diabetes Association and the American Dietetic Association. (They are not the same as Weight Watchers exchanges.) For many recipes, two lists of exchanges are provided: the first option is based on the traditional method of figuring dietary exchanges; the second option reflects the newer system of carbohydrate counting. (If the recipe contains no carbohydrate exchanges, just one set of exchanges will be listed.) If you use the exchanges, consult your doctor or registered dietitian if you have questions, or call the American Dietetic Association at 1-800-366-1655.

How We Determine Nutrition Information

When the recipe gives options, we base the analysis on the *first* ingredient mentioned. For example, if "egg substitute or eggs" is listed, egg substitute would be calculated.

- When there's a range for amounts of an ingredient, we use the *larger* amount.

- When garnishes or "if desired" ingredients are included in the ingredient list, we *include* them in the nutritional analysis.

- When a recipe uses a marinade, the nutritional analysis includes the estimated amount *absorbed* into the final dish.

Your Daily Nutritional Requirements

This chart outlines average daily nutritional needs for healthy adults age 25 to 50. Since your age, size, activity level and health all affect dietary considerations, your requirements may be different.

	Men	Women
Calories	2,400	1,850
Total fat	80 g or less	62 g or less
Saturated fat	27 g or less	20 g or less
Cholesterol	300 mg or less	300 mg or less
Sodium	2,400 mg	2,400 mg
Total carbohydrate	360 g	275 g
Dietary fiber	20–30 g	20–30 g
Protein	63 g	50 g
Calcium	1,000 mg	1,000 mg
Iron	10 mg	15 mg

Source: National Academy of Sciences, National Research Council, Recommended Dietary Allowances (10th edition, 1989).

Menus

Springtime Sunday Brunch for 4

Canadian Bacon and Potato Frittata (page 188)

Carrot Zucchini Muffins (page 293)

Deli tropical fruit salad

English Brunch for 8

Moist Spiced Apple Scones (page 306)

Miniature Quick Cherry Pecan Scones (page 305)

Sliced broiled Canadian bacon

Scrambled eggs with tomatoes

Grapefruit and orange slices

Hearty Pancake Breakfast for 4 ▼

Oat and Wheat Pancakes with Cherry-Berry Sauce (page 300)

Low-fat turkey sausage links or patties

Yogurt and juice beverage

After Shopping Luncheon for 4

Cobb Salad Shells (page 46)

Cantaloupe and honeydew melon wedges

Whole wheat rolls

Chocolate Cinnamon Flans (page 335)

Garden Party Luncheon for 10 ▲

Crunchy Broccoli Party Dip (page 22) with cut-up fresh vegetables

Colorful Shrimp Rice Salad (page 51)

Low-fat bran muffins or sliced quick bread

Luscious Berry Lemon Tart (page 332)

Card Party Luncheon for 8

Italian Vegetarian Lasagna (page 252)

Fresh Spinach, Orange and Red Onion Salad (page 61)

Crisp breadsticks

Chocolate frozen yogurt

Busy Day Soup Supper for 6

Southwestern Turkey Chili Soup (page 84)

Buttermilk Cornmeal Biscuits (page 288)

Sliced fresh fruit

Cookies

Patio Burger Bash for 6

All-American Lean Burgers (page 173) on onion buns

Tomato slices, lettuce, dill pickles, mayonnaise, ketchup, mustard

Potato salad

Low-fat brownies

Elegant Supper for 6

Turkey Scaloppine with Vegetables (page 135)

Wilted Spinach Vinaigrette (page 62)

Garlic bread

Biscotti

Dinner on the Grill for 4

Grilled Lamb Chops with Rosemary and Black Pepper (page 190)

Italian Parmesan Potatoes (page 270)

Antipasto Onion-Tomato Salad (page 62)

Fresh raspberries or strawberries with low-fat whipped topping

Steak Sandwich Supper for 4 ▲

Easy Steak Sandwiches (page 170)

Farmers' Market Salad (page 69)

Low-fat potato chips

Low-fat cookies

Easy Spaghetti Supper for 4

Herbed Spaghetti (page 156)

Tossed green salad with low-fat Italian or ranch dressing

Soft breadsticks

Low-fat Neapolitan ice cream

◄ Chinese Supper for 4

Easy Pork Chow Mein (page 179)

Hot cooked rice

Asian Slaw (page 64)

Fortune cookies

Orange sherbet

Italian Soup and Salad Supper for 6

Italian Turkey Soup (page 83)

Napoli Bread Salad (page 68)

Low-fat chocolate pudding

Down-Home Dinner for 4

Peppered Cube Steaks with Mashed Potatoes and Gravy (page 161)

Steamed broccoli

Gelatin salad

Double Chocolate Chip Cookies (page 316)

French Stew Supper for 4

White Burgundy Coq au Vin (page 115)

Mixed greens salad

Sliced French or sourdough bread

Chocolate Almond Mousse (page 336)

After Skiing Pizza Party for 6

Barbecued Chicken Pizza (page 120)

Caesar salad

Low-fat brownies or chocolate cake

Southwestern Fiesta Supper for 6

Fiesta Quesadillas (page 34)

Creamy Hot Black Bean Dip (page 22) with low-fat tortilla chips

Southwest Pork and Black Bean Stir-Fry (page 180)

Hot cooked rice or Spanish rice

Frosty Margarita Pie (page 329)

Appetizer Buffet for 8

Smoked Salmon Toast (page 35)

Artichoke and Cheese Crostini (page 32)

Spicy Cajun Dip (page 20) with cut-up fresh vegetables

Assorted sliced cheeses with assorted low-fat crackers

Assorted olives and/or pickles

Fresh fruit platter (fresh whole strawberries, grapes, melon balls, kiwi fruit slices, orange segments)

Holiday Supper for 6

Cornish Game Hen with Mustard-Orange Glaze (page 148)

Wild Rice with Apples (page 266)

Pearl Onion, Carrot and Zucchini Sauté (page 280)

Whole wheat dinner rolls

Pumpkin pie

Fast Family Supper for 4

Creamy Basil Chicken Pasta (page 110)

Cantaloupe and honeydew melon wedges

Soft breadsticks

Low-fat vanilla yogurt with toppings

Meatless Soup and Salad for 6

Easy Vegetable Minestrone (page 76)

Spring Salad with Honey-Mustard Dressing (page 71)

Red and green grape clusters

Low-fat chocolate cookies

Last-Minute Omelet Supper for 2

Creamy Seafood Omelet (page 222)

Crisp green salad with French dressing

Low-fat orange or banana muffins

Harvesttime Get-Together for 4

Summer Harvest Chicken-Potato Salad (page 44)

Cut up fresh vegetables with low-fat dip

Tomato Basil Dinner Bread (page 304)

Ginger Apple Crisp (page 323)

Candlelight Supper for 6

Smoked Salmon Toast (page 35)

Chicken Piccata (page 112)

Herb Vegetable Couscous (page 268)

Whole wheat dinner rolls

Phyllo Cheesecakes with Raspberry Sauce (page 338)

Appetizers

2

Spinach and Feta Quesadillas (page 34)

Creamy Shrimp Dip

■ ■ ■ ■ ■ ■ ■ ■ ■ ■ ■ ■ ■ ■

PREP TIME: 10 MINUTES

1 (8-oz.) pkg. ⅓-less-fat cream cheese
  (Neufchâtel), softened

3 to 4 tablespoons skim milk

1 teaspoon salt-free lemon-herb seasoning

1 (4¼-oz.) can tiny shrimp, drained

1 tablespoon sliced green onions

1 tablespoon chopped green bell pepper

1. In small bowl, combine cream cheese, milk and lemon-herb seasoning; beat until smooth. Add shrimp, onions and bell pepper; mix well.

2. Serve with cut-up fresh vegetables, low-fat crackers or sliced cocktail bread. Store in refrigerator.

YIELD: 1⅔ CUPS

Nutrition Information Per Serving
Serving Size: 1 Tablespoon

Calories 20		Calories from Fat 10	
		% Daily Value	
Total Fat 1g		............................2%	
Saturated 1g		............................5%	
Cholesterol 10mg		............................3%	
Sodium 50mg		............................2%	
Total Carbohydrate...........1g		............................1%	
Dietary Fiber 0g		............................0%	
Sugars 1g			
Protein...........................2g			
Vitamin A 2%		Vitamin C 0%	
Calcium 0%		Iron..............................0%	

Dietary Exchanges: Free

double-duty Dips

■ ■ ■ ■ ■ ■ ■ ■ ■ ■ ■ ■ ■ ■

Leftover dips can make a great savory spread for all kinds of hot or cold sandwiches. Spread dips on bread and pair with lean roast beef, a grilled hamburger or leftover chicken.

Caution: Reuse only dips that have been kept refrigerated. At a party, put dip out a little at a time and always spoon the next batch into a clean bowl rather than refilling a bowl that's been sitting out a while. If the dip's been at room temperature for several hours, don't save it.

Spicy Cajun Dip

■ ■ ■ ■ ■ ■ ■ ■ ■ ■ ■ ■ ■ ■

PREP TIME: 20 MINUTES

½ cup dry-pack sun-dried tomatoes

1 (8-oz.) pkg. ⅓-less-fat cream cheese
  (Neufchâtel), softened

½ cup nonfat plain yogurt

¼ cup chili sauce

¼ cup chopped green bell pepper

¼ cup chopped green onions

1 garlic clove, minced

½ teaspoon celery seed

⅛ teaspoon ground red pepper (cayenne)

1. In small bowl, pour 1 cup boiling water over tomatoes. Let stand at room temperature for 5 to 10 minutes. Drain and chop tomatoes.

2. Meanwhile, in another small bowl, combine cream cheese, yogurt and chili sauce; mix well. Add tomatoes and all remaining ingredients; mix well. Refrigerate until serving time.

3. Just before serving, stir dip. Serve with cut-up fresh vegetables or garlic-flavored bagel crisps.

YIELD: 2 CUPS

Nutrition Information Per Serving
Serving Size: 2 Tablespoons

Calories 45		Calories from Fat 25	
		% Daily Value	
Total Fat 3g		............................5%	
Saturated 2g		..........................10%	
Cholesterol 10mg		............................3%	
Sodium 150mg		............................6%	
Total Carbohydrate...........3g		............................1%	
Dietary Fiber 0g		............................0%	
Sugars 2g			
Protein...........................2g			
Vitamin A 6%		Vitamin C 4%	
Calcium 2%		Iron..............................0%	

Dietary Exchanges: 1 Vegetable, ½ Fat

Spicy Cajun Dip/Fiesta Quesadillas (page 34) ▶

■ ■ ■ ■ ■ ■ ■ ■ ■ ■ ■ ■ ■ ■ ■ ■ ■

To dress up a dish of dip, especially one that has a dull or neutral color, garnish with one or more of the following:

Minced chopped herbs

Finely shredded carrots

Minced red, yellow and/or green bell pepper

Chopped green onions

Dollop of nonfat sour cream sprinkled with chili powder or paprika, or decorated with a small herb sprig

Minced tomato and red onion

Crunchy Broccoli Party Dip

■ ■ ■ ■ ■ ■ ■ ■ ■ ■ ■ ■ ■ ■ ■ ■ ■

PREP TIME: 10 MINUTES

½ **cup reduced-calorie mayonnaise or salad dressing**

1 **(8-oz.) container nonfat plain yogurt**

1 **teaspoon sugar**

½ **teaspoon salt**

¼ **teaspoon garlic powder**

¼ **teaspoon hot pepper sauce**

2 **cups finely chopped fresh broccoli**

2 **tablespoons finely chopped green onions**

1 **(8-oz.) can water chestnuts, drained, chopped**

1 **(2-oz.) jar diced pimientos, drained**

1. In medium bowl, combine mayonnaise, yogurt, sugar, salt, garlic powder and hot pepper sauce; mix well. Stir in all remaining ingredients.

2. Serve with baked pita crisps or cut-up fresh vegetables. Store in refrigerator.

YIELD: 3 CUPS

Nutrition Information Per Serving
Serving Size: 2 Tablespoons

Calories	30	Calories from Fat	15
		% Daily Value	
Total Fat	2g		3%
Saturated	0g		0%
Cholesterol	5mg		1%
Sodium	85mg		4%
Total Carbohydrate	3g		1%
Dietary Fiber	0g		0%
Sugars	1g		
Protein	1g		
Vitamin A	4%	Vitamin C	15%
Calcium	2%	Iron	0%

Dietary Exchanges: 1 Vegetable

Creamy Hot Black Bean Dip

■ ■ ■ ■ ■ ■ ■ ■ ■ ■ ■ ■ ■ ■ ■ ■ ■

PREP TIME: 25 MINUTES

1 **(15-oz.) can black beans, drained, rinsed**

1 **(8-oz.) pkg. ⅓-less-fat cream cheese (Neufchâtel), softened**

⅓ **cup chopped red onion**

2 **tablespoons chopped fresh cilantro**

½ **teaspoon chili powder**

¼ **teaspoon cumin**

¼ **teaspoon dried oregano leaves**

¼ **teaspoon hot pepper sauce**

1 **garlic clove, minced**

½ **jalapeño chile, chopped**

2 **tablespoons chopped fresh parsley or cilantro**

1. Heat oven to 375°F. In food processer bowl with metal blade, combine all ingredients except parsley; process until well blended. Spread mixture in ungreased 9-inch pie pan.

2. Bake at 375°F. for 15 minutes or until hot. Sprinkle with parsley. Serve with cut-up fresh vegetables or baked tortilla chips.

YIELD: 2 CUPS

Nutrition Information Per Serving
Serving Size: 2 Tablespoons

Calories 60	Calories from Fat 25
	% Daily Value
Total Fat 3g	.........5%
Saturated 2g	.........10%
Cholesterol 10mg	.........3%
Sodium 120mg	.........5%
Total Carbohydrate 5g	.........2%
Dietary Fiber 1g	.........4%
Sugars 0g	
Protein 3g	
Vitamin A 4%	Vitamin C 0%
Calcium 2%	Iron 2%

Dietary Exchanges: ½ Starch, ½ Fat OR ½ Carbohydrate, ½ Fat

low-fat **Dippers**

Breads
French bread slices
Cocktail bread
Pita chips (cut pita bread into wedges and bake until crisp)

Crackers/Chips
Melba rounds
Crisp bread
Reduced-fat and nonfat crackers
Mini rice cakes
Baked (not fried) tortilla or potato chips

Vegetables
Carrots, celery, zucchini, jicama or green, red or yellow bell pepper sticks
Thick slices of cucumber
Whole mushrooms, radishes, cherry tomatoes, snow pea pods, sugar snap peas
Broccoli, cauliflower or broccoflower florets

Molded Herbed Cheese Spread

PREP TIME: 20 MINUTES
(READY IN 2 HOURS 20 MINUTES)

1 (12-oz.) container (1½ cups) nonfat cream cheese, softened

2 oz. feta cheese, crumbled (½ cup)

1 oz. blue cheese, crumbled (¼ cup)

½ teaspoon dried basil leaves

½ teaspoon dried rosemary leaves, crushed

1 tablespoon finely chopped chives or green onion tops

2 red or green apples, cut into 16 slices each, or assorted fat-free crackers

1. Line 2-cup ring mold or small decorative mold with cheesecloth or plastic wrap.

2. In medium bowl, combine cream cheese, feta cheese, blue cheese, basil and rosemary; beat with electric mixer or spoon until well mixed.

3. Spoon cheese mixture into mold, spreading evenly. Cover with plastic wrap. Refrigerate about 2 hours or until firm.

4. To serve, unmold onto serving platter; sprinkle with chives. Serve with apple slices.

YIELD: 8 SERVINGS

Nutrition Information Per Serving
Serving Size: ⅛ of Recipe

Calories 110	Calories from Fat 25
	% Daily Value
Total Fat 3g	.........5%
Saturated 2g	.........10%
Cholesterol 15mg	.........5%
Sodium 330mg	.........14%
Total Carbohydrate 12g	.........4%
Dietary Fiber 1g	.........4%
Sugars 9g	
Protein 8g	
Vitamin A 15%	Vitamin C 6%
Calcium 20%	Iron 0%

Dietary Exchanges: 1 Fruit, 1 Lean Meat OR 1 Carbohydrate, 1 Lean Meat

▲ Cracker Bread Rolls

Cracker Bread Rolls

∎ ∎ ∎ ∎ ∎ ∎ ∎ ∎ ∎ ∎ ∎ ∎ ∎ ∎ ∎ ∎ ∎ ∎ ∎

PREP TIME: 15 MINUTES
(READY IN 35 MINUTES)

**1 (16-inch) soft cracker bread, room
    temperature***

**4 oz. 1/3-less-fat cream cheese (Neufchâtel),
    softened**

**1 tablespoon chopped fresh basil or 1 teaspoon
    dried basil leaves**

**1 tablespoon chopped fresh oregano or
    1 teaspoon dried oregano leaves**

4 oz. thinly sliced deli cooked ham

12 large spinach leaves, stems removed

1/2 red bell pepper, cut into thin julienne strips

1. Cut cracker bread in half. In small bowl, combine cream cheese, basil and oregano; mix well. Spread half of cream cheese mixture on 1 cracker bread half to within 1/4 inch of edges.

2. Arrange half of ham slices over cream cheese to within 1 inch of rounded edge. Top with 6 spinach leaves. Starting about 1 inch from straight edge, arrange half of bell pepper strips in rows parallel to straight edge. Starting at straight edge, roll up tightly, jelly-roll fashion. Wrap roll tightly in plastic wrap.

3. Repeat with remaining ingredients to form second roll. Refrigerate at least 20 minutes or until firm enough to slice. Cut rolls into 1-inch-thick slices.

YIELD: 28 APPETIZERS

Tip: * Cracker bread, also called lahvosh, can be found in the deli section of most supermarkets or in Middle Eastern markets. Four 7- or 8-inch flour tortillas can be substituted for the cracker bread. Spread 1/4 of cream cheese mixture on each tortilla. Arrange ham slices, spinach and bell pepper strips over top of each. Roll up tightly. Continue as directed above.

YIELD: 32 APPETIZERS

Nutrition Information Per Serving
Serving Size: 1 Appetizer

Calories	35	Calories from Fat	10
		% Daily Value	
Total Fat	1g		2%
Saturated	1g		5%
Cholesterol	4mg		1%
Sodium	115mg		5%
Total Carbohydrate	5g		2%
Dietary Fiber	0g		0%
Sugars	0g		
Protein	2g		
Vitamin A	4%	Vitamin C	8%
Calcium	0%	Iron	0%

Dietary Exchanges: 1/2 Starch OR 1/2 Carbohydrate

make-ahead **Appetizers**

∎ ∎ ∎ ∎ ∎ ∎ ∎ ∎ ∎ ∎ ∎ ∎ ∎ ∎ ∎ ∎ ∎ ∎ ∎

Cracker Bread Rolls (left)
Creamy Shrimp Dip (page 20)
Crunchy Broccoli Party Dip (page 22)
Italian Cheese Balls (opposite)
Spicy Cajun Dip (page 20)

Appetizer Pie

PREP TIME: 25 MINUTES

1 (8-oz.) pkg. fat-free cream cheese, softened

2 tablespoons skim milk

½ cup nonfat sour cream

2 tablespoons sliced green onions

2 tablespoons chopped green bell pepper

⅛ teaspoon pepper

1 (2½-oz.) jar sliced dried beef, rinsed, drained and finely chopped

¼ cup chopped fresh parsley

Oven Directions: 1. Heat oven to 350°F. In medium bowl, combine cream cheese and milk; beat until smooth. Stir in all remaining ingredients except parsley; mix well. Spoon and spread mixture in ungreased 9-inch pie pan or small shallow baking dish.

2. Bake at 350°F. for 15 minutes or until thoroughly heated. Sprinkle with parsley. Serve immediately with sliced cocktail bread or French bread.

Microwave Directions: 1. Prepare mixture as directed above; spoon into 9-inch microwave-safe pie pan or small shallow dish.

2. Microwave on MEDIUM for 5 to 8 minutes or until thoroughly heated, rotating dish once halfway through cooking. Sprinkle with parsley. Serve immediately with sliced cocktail bread or French bread.

YIELD: 2 CUPS

Nutrition Information Per Serving
Serving Size: 1 Tablespoon

Calories	10	Calories from Fat	0
		% Daily Value	
Total Fat	0g		0%
Saturated	0g		0%
Cholesterol	2mg		1%
Sodium	130mg		5%
Total Carbohydrate	1g		1%
Dietary Fiber	0g		0%
Sugars	1g		
Protein	2g		
Vitamin A	4%	Vitamin C	0%
Calcium	4%	Iron	0%

Dietary Exchanges: Free

Italian Cheese Balls

PREP TIME: 10 MINUTES
(READY IN 40 MINUTES)

1 (8-oz.) pkg. ⅓-less-fat cream cheese (Neufchâtel), softened

4 oz. (1 cup) shredded mozzarella cheese

⅓ cup sliced green onions

½ teaspoon dried Italian seasoning

½ teaspoon crushed red pepper flakes

1 (2-oz.) jar sliced pimientos, drained

½ cup chopped fresh parsley

1. In large bowl, combine all ingredients except pimientos and parsley; blend well.* Stir in pimientos. Cover; refrigerate 30 minutes for easier handling.

2. Shape mixture into 2 balls; roll each in parsley. Serve immediately, or wrap each ball in plastic wrap and refrigerate until serving time. Serve with low-fat crackers or crisp breadsticks.

YIELD: 1¾ CUPS; 2 CHEESE BALLS

Tip: * Mixture can be prepared in food processor. Combine all ingredients except pimientos and parsley in bowl with metal blade. Cover; process until smooth. Add pimientos; process just until combined. Place in large bowl. Continue as directed above.

Nutrition Information Per Serving
Serving Size: 1 Tablespoon

Calories	30	Calories from Fat	20
		% Daily Value	
Total Fat	2g		3%
Saturated	1g		5%
Cholesterol	5mg		2%
Sodium	60mg		3%
Total Carbohydrate	1g		1%
Dietary Fiber	0g		0%
Sugars	1g		
Protein	2g		
Vitamin A	4%	Vitamin C	8%
Calcium	4%	Iron	0%

Dietary Exchanges: ½ Fat

Maple-Glazed BBQ Meatballs

PREP TIME: 30 MINUTES

1 lb. lean ground turkey

½ cup finely chopped unpeeled apple

¼ cup corn flake crumbs

¼ teaspoon onion powder

¼ teaspoon dried thyme leaves

1 tablespoon real maple syrup or maple-flavored syrup

1 egg

1 cup barbecue sauce

⅓ cup real maple syrup or maple-flavored syrup

1. Heat oven to 400°F. Line 15 × 10 × 1-inch baking pan with foil; spray foil with nonstick cooking spray.

2. In medium bowl, combine ground turkey, apple, corn flake crumbs, onion powder, thyme, 1 table-spoon syrup and egg; mix well. To quickly form turkey mixture into meatballs, firmly press mixture into 8 × 4-inch rectangle. Cut into 32 (1-inch) squares; if desired, roll each into ball. Place on foil-lined pan.

3. Bake at 400°F. for 15 to 20 minutes or until no longer pink in center.

4. In medium saucepan, combine barbecue sauce and ⅓ cup syrup. Bring to a boil. Add baked meat-balls; stir until coated. Serve hot.

YIELD: ABOUT 32 MEATBALLS; 8 SERVINGS

Nutrition Information Per Serving
Serving Size: ⅛ of Recipe

Calories	170	Calories from Fat	45
			% Daily Value
Total Fat	5g		8%
Saturated	1g		5%
Cholesterol	65mg		22%
Sodium	340mg		14%
Total Carbohydrate	18g		6%
Dietary Fiber	1g		3%
Sugars	11g		
Protein	13g		
Vitamin A	8%	Vitamin C	4%
Calcium	4%	Iron	8%

Dietary Exchanges: 1 Fruit, 2 Lean Meat OR 1 Carbohydrate, 2 Lean Meat

Tomato–Red Pepper Crostini

PREP TIME: 25 MINUTES

½ cup dried sun-dried tomatoes

16 (¼-inch-thick) slices French bread

Olive oil nonstick cooking spray

1 (7.25-oz.) jar roasted red peppers, drained

1 teaspoon olive oil

¼ teaspoon minced garlic

¼ teaspoon dried basil leaves

Dash salt

Fresh basil or parsley leaves, if desired

1. Place sun-dried tomatoes in medium bowl; cover with boiling water. Let stand 3 minutes or until soft.

2. Meanwhile, place bread slices on ungreased cookie sheet; spray bread lightly with nonstick cook-ing spray. Broil 4 to 6 inches from heat for 1 to 2 minutes or until golden brown.

3. Drain tomatoes. Coarsely chop tomatoes and red peppers with knife or in food processor; place in medium bowl. Add oil, garlic, basil and salt; mix well.

4. Just before serving, spoon about 2 teaspoons tomato-pepper mixture onto toasted side of each bread slice; spread evenly. Garnish with fresh basil.

YIELD: 16 APPETIZERS; 8 SERVINGS

Nutrition Information Per Serving
Serving Size: ⅛ of Recipe

Calories	60	Calories from Fat	20
			% Daily Value
Total Fat	2g		3%
Saturated	0g		0%
Cholesterol	0mg		0%
Sodium	150mg		6%
Total Carbohydrate	9g		3%
Dietary Fiber	1g		4%
Sugars	2g		
Protein	2g		
Vitamin A	15%	Vitamin C	60%
Calcium	0%	Iron	4%

Dietary Exchanges: ½ Starch, 1 Vegetable OR ½ Carbohydrate, 1 Vegetable

Molded Herbed Cheese Spread (page 23)/Tomato–Red Pepper Crostini/Maple-Glazed BBQ Meatballs ▶

Microwave Dill Tater Snacks

PREP TIME: 20 MINUTES

10 small new red potatoes, unpeeled, halved

½ cup light sour cream

2 tablespoons sliced green onions

½ teaspoon dried dill weed

Dash pepper

¼ cup grated Parmesan cheese

3 slices lean turkey bacon, crisply cooked, crumbled

Microwave Directions: 1. Place potatoes, cut side down, in 12 × 8-inch (2-quart) microwave-safe dish; add 2 tablespoons water. Cover tightly with microwave-safe plastic wrap.

2. Microwave on HIGH for 9 to 12 minutes or until tender, rotating dish ¼ turn halfway through cooking. Let stand 3 minutes; drain. Cool slightly.

3. In small bowl, combine sour cream, onions and dill; mix well. Turn potatoes over. If necessary, trim thin slice off rounded bottom of each potato half to make potatoes stand upright. Sprinkle each with pepper and Parmesan cheese. Top each with dollop of sour cream mixture; sprinkle with bacon. If desired, garnish with fresh dill or parsley. Serve warm.

YIELD: 20 APPETIZERS

Tip: If 12 × 8-inch dish will not fit in microwave oven, use microwave-safe pie pan and cook half of potatoes at a time. Microwave on HIGH for 6 to 8 minutes or until tender.

Nutrition Information Per Serving
Serving Size: 1 Appetizer

Calories	70	Calories from Fat	10
		% Daily Value	
Total Fat	1g		2%
Saturated	1g		5%
Cholesterol	4mg		1%
Sodium	60mg		3%
Total Carbohydrate	13g		4%
Dietary Fiber	1g		4%
Sugars	1g		
Protein	2g		
Vitamin A	0%	Vitamin C	8%
Calcium	4%	Iron	4%

Dietary Exchanges: 1 Starch OR 1 Carbohydrate

▼ Microwave Dill Tater Snacks/Appetizer Chicken Saté

Appetizer Chicken Saté

PREP TIME: 25 MINUTES

Kabobs

24 bamboo skewers

3 boneless, skinless chicken breast halves

1 medium green bell pepper, cut into 1-inch squares

1 medium red bell pepper, cut into 1-inch squares

Sauce

½ cup creamy peanut butter

½ cup low-fat vanilla yogurt

¼ cup water

2 tablespoons lite soy sauce

¼ teaspoon ground red pepper (cayenne)

1. Heat oven to 375°F. Soak bamboo skewers in water for 15 minutes. Spray 15 × 10 × 1-inch baking pan with nonstick cooking spray.

2. Cut chicken diagonally into strips ½ inch wide and 3 to 4 inches long. On each skewer, thread 1 piece each of green and red bell pepper and 1 or 2 strips of chicken. Place on sprayed pan.

3. In medium saucepan, combine all sauce ingredients; blend well. Brush some of sauce on chicken pieces.

4. Bake at 375°F. for 10 to 12 minutes or until chicken is no longer pink.

5. Meanwhile, bring remaining sauce to a boil over medium heat, stirring constantly. Boil 1 minute. Serve sauce with kabobs.

YIELD: 24 APPETIZERS

Nutrition Information Per Serving
Serving Size: 1 Appetizer

Calories	60	Calories from Fat	25
			% Daily Value
Total Fat	3g		5%
Saturated	1g		5%
Cholesterol	10mg		3%
Sodium	90mg		4%
Total Carbohydrate	2g		1%
Dietary Fiber	0g		0%
Sugars	1g		
Protein	5g		
Vitamin A	4%	Vitamin C	10%
Calcium	0%	Iron	0%

Dietary Exchanges: 1 Lean Meat

Pork Tenderloin Canapés

PREP TIME: 15 MINUTES
(READY IN 45 MINUTES)

1 (½-lb.) pork tenderloin

¼ teaspoon salt

¼ teaspoon pepper

¼ cup soft cream cheese with chives and onion (from 8-oz. tub)

24 (¼-inch-thick) slices French bread

24 thin slices red or green apple

1 tablespoon apple juice

Chopped fresh chives

1. Heat oven to 425°F. Line cookie sheet with foil. Place pork tenderloin on foil-lined cookie sheet, tucking small end under to prevent overcooking. Sprinkle all sides with salt and pepper.

2. Bake at 425°F. for 20 to 30 minutes or until no longer pink in center and juices run clear. Remove from oven; cover with foil. Let stand 10 minutes.

3. Meanwhile, spread ½ teaspoon cream cheese on each slice of bread. Cut pork into 24 thin slices; place 1 slice on each slice of bread. Toss apple slices with apple juice to prevent browning. Arrange apple slices over pork. Sprinkle with fresh chives. Serve immediately, or cover and refrigerate until serving time.

YIELD: 24 APPETIZERS

Nutrition Information Per Serving
Serving Size: 1 Appetizer

Calories	90	Calories from Fat	20
			% Daily Value
Total Fat	2g		3%
Saturated	1g		5%
Cholesterol	10mg		3%
Sodium	190mg		8%
Total Carbohydrate	14g		5%
Dietary Fiber	1g		3%
Sugars	1g		
Protein	4g		
Vitamin A	0%	Vitamin C	0%
Calcium	2%	Iron	4%

Dietary Exchanges: 1 Starch OR 1 Carbohydrate

▲ Crisp-Coated Mushrooms

Crisp-Coated Mushrooms

■ ■

PREP TIME: 25 MINUTES

¼ **cup refrigerated or frozen fat-free egg product, thawed, or 1 egg**

½ **teaspoon onion salt**

8 to 10 drops hot pepper sauce, if desired

¼ **cup all-purpose flour**

¾ **cup crushed melba round snacks (about 18 snacks)**

1 (8-oz.) pkg. fresh whole mushrooms

Olive oil nonstick cooking spray, if desired

1. Heat oven to 450°F. Line 15 × 10 × 1-inch baking pan with foil.

2. In small bowl, combine egg product, onion salt and hot pepper sauce; blend well. Place flour in resealable plastic bag or another small bowl. Place snack crumbs on sheet of waxed paper or in another small bowl.

3. Place mushrooms in bag with flour; shake to coat. For each mushroom, shake off excess flour. Dip each into egg product mixture; coat well with snack crumbs. Place in foil-lined pan. For crispier mushrooms, spray all sides of mushrooms with nonstick cooking spray.

4. Bake at 450°F. for 8 to 12 minutes or until hot and crisp.

YIELD: 8 SERVINGS

Nutrition Information Per Serving
Serving Size: ⅛ of Recipe

Calories 50	Calories from Fat 0
	% Daily Value
Total Fat 0g	...........................0%
Saturated 0g	...........................0%
Cholesterol 0mg	...........................0%
Sodium 180mg	...........................8%
Total Carbohydrate 10g	...........................3%
Dietary Fiber 1g	...........................4%
Sugars 1g	
Protein 3g	
Vitamin A 0%	Vitamin C 0%
Calcium 0%	Iron............................6%

Dietary Exchanges: ½ Starch, ½ Vegetable OR ½ Carbohydrate, ½ Vegetable

Hot Chicken Wings

PREP TIME: 25 MINUTES

12 chicken drumettes (1¼ lb.), skin removed

½ cup lite soy sauce

⅓ cup lemon juice

2 tablespoons hot pepper sauce

½ to 1 teaspoon crushed red pepper flakes

Grill Directions: 1. In medium bowl, combine all ingredients; toss gently to coat chicken. Cover; let stand at room temperature for 10 minutes to marinate. **2.** Meanwhile, heat grill. When ready to grill, oil grill rack. Remove chicken from marinade; reserve marinade. Place chicken on gas grill over medium-high heat or on charcoal grill 4 to 6 inches from medium-high coals. Cook 10 to 15 minutes or until chicken is fork-tender and juices run clear, turning frequently and brushing occasionally with reserved marinade. Discard any remaining marinade. If desired, serve with purchased blue cheese salad dressing.

Broiler Directions: 1. Prepare and marinate chicken as directed above. Oil broiler pan. Remove chicken from marinade; reserve marinade. Place chicken on oiled pan. **2.** Broil 4 to 6 inches from heat for 10 to 15 minutes or until chicken is fork-tender and juices run clear, turning once and brushing occasionally with reserved marinade. Discard any remaining marinade. If desired, serve with purchased blue cheese salad dressing.

YIELD: 6 SERVINGS

Nutrition Information Per Serving
Serving Size: ⅙ of Recipe

Calories	50	Calories from Fat	20
		% Daily Value	
Total Fat	2g		3%
Saturated	0g		0%
Cholesterol	15mg		5%
Sodium	240mg		10%
Total Carbohydrate	1g		1%
Dietary Fiber	0g		0%
Sugars	0g		
Protein	7g		
Vitamin A	0%	Vitamin C	0%
Calcium	0%	Iron	0%

Dietary Exchanges: 1 Lean Meat

about Chicken Wings

While chicken wings were once considered an inferior part of the bird, they've become popular in recent years as an appetizer. Consequently, guess what's happened to the price per pound?

The wing consists of three parts: the drumette (found closest to the "shoulder" of the bird) and the two-part, V-shaped wing sections that follow. The drumette resembles a miniature drumstick and is the meatiest section in the wing. The tip has no meat worth bothering with and is often cut off prior to cooking; you can accumulate wing tips in the freezer for soup stock. In between the tip and the drumette lies a bony little section with a morsel of sweet meat.

Buffalo Chicken Wings, which has established itself as a casual appetizer standard over the past ten years or so, consists of spicy-hot wings served with palate-cooling blue cheese dressing accompanied by celery sticks. Legend has it that the now classic combination came about by accident, when a restaurant patron in Buffalo, New York, tried to quench the "burn" from spicy wings by dunking them into the nearest thing available, which happened to be blue cheese dressing.

Artichoke and Cheese Crostini

16 (½-inch-thick) diagonal slices French bread (about 2¾ × 1¾ inches)

Garlic powder

1 (14-oz.) can artichoke hearts, drained, chopped

1 (7.25-oz.) jar roasted red bell peppers, drained, chopped

2 (7 × 3½-inch) slices mozzarella cheese, each cut into 8 pieces

1. Place bread slices on ungreased cookie sheet. Broil 4 to 6 inches from heat for 1 to 3 minutes or until light golden brown.

2. Heat oven to 400°F. Turn bread slices over; sprinkle lightly with garlic powder.

3. In medium bowl, combine artichoke hearts and peppers; mix gently. Top bread slices with artichoke mixture and cheese slices.

4. Bake at 400°F. for 8 to 10 minutes or until cheese is melted and artichoke mixture is hot.

YIELD: 16 APPETIZERS

Nutrition Information Per Serving
Serving Size: 1 Appetizer

Calories 70	Calories from Fat 10
	% Daily Value
Total Fat 1g	.............................2%
Saturated 1g	.............................5%
Cholesterol 0mg	.............................0%
Sodium 140mg	.............................6%
Total Carbohydrate 12g	.............................4%
Dietary Fiber 1g	.............................4%
Sugars 1g	
Protein 3g	
Vitamin A 10%	Vitamin C 20%
Calcium 4%	Iron..............................4%

Dietary Exchanges: 1 Starch OR 1 Carbohydrate

Orange-Ginger Shrimp Snacks

½ cup oil

¼ cup vinegar

¼ cup frozen orange juice concentrate, thawed

1 tablespoon chopped red onion

2 teaspoons grated gingerroot

¾ teaspoon crushed red pepper flakes

1 lb. shelled, deveined, uncooked medium shrimp

5 (12-inch) bamboo skewers

1. In blender container, combine all ingredients except shrimp and skewers; process until blended.

2. Place shrimp in resealable plastic bag; pour oil mixture over shrimp. Let stand at room temperature for 15 minutes to marinate. Soak bamboo skewers in water while shrimp are marinating.

3. Drain shrimp; discard marinade. Thread shrimp onto bamboo skewers; place on cookie sheet.

4. Broil 6 inches from heat for 3 to 5 minutes or until shrimp turn pink, turning once. Before serving, cut each skewer into 3 pieces with kitchen scissors.

YIELD: 15 SERVINGS

Nutrition Information Per Serving
Serving Size: 1/15 of Recipe

Calories 40	Calories from Fat 20
	% Daily Value
Total Fat 2g	.............................3%
Saturated 0g	.............................0%
Cholesterol 45mg	.............................15%
Sodium 50mg	.............................2%
Total Carbohydrate 1g	.............................1%
Dietary Fiber 0g	.............................0%
Sugars 0g	
Protein 5g	
Vitamin A 0%	Vitamin C 2%
Calcium 0%	Iron..............................4%

Dietary Exchanges: 1 Very Lean Meat

Fiesta Quesadillas

■ ■

PREP TIME: 25 MINUTES

1 (10-oz.) can diced tomatoes with green chiles, drained

1 (7-oz.) can vacuum-packed whole kernel corn, drained

1 tablespoon chopped fresh cilantro

16 (6-inch) flour tortillas

1 cup fat-free refried beans (from 16-oz. can)

8 oz. (2 cups) shredded Mexican blend natural cheese

1. In medium bowl, combine tomatoes, corn and cilantro; mix well.

2. Spread each of 8 tortillas with 2 tablespoons refried beans. Top each of remaining 8 tortillas with ¼ cup cheese and scant 2 tablespoons corn mixture; spread evenly. Cover each with 1 bean-covered tortilla, bean side down.

3. In large nonstick skillet over medium heat, heat 1 quesadilla for 1 to 2 minutes on each side or until cheese is melted and tortilla is toasted.* Remove quesadilla from skillet; repeat with remaining quesadillas.**

4. To serve, cut each quesadilla into 4 wedges. If desired, serve with nonfat sour cream and salsa.

YIELD: 32 APPETIZERS

Tips: * A griddle heated to 400°F. can be used to heat 3 or 4 quesadillas at a time.

** At this point, quesadillas can be wrapped in foil and placed in a warm oven until serving time.

Nutrition Information Per Serving
Serving Size: 1 Appetizer

Calories 80		Calories from Fat 25	
		% Daily Value	
Total Fat 3g		.........5%	
Saturated 2g		.........10%	
Cholesterol 5mg		.........2%	
Sodium 160mg		.........7%	
Total Carbohydrate 9g		.........3%	
Dietary Fiber 1g		.........4%	
Sugars 1g			
Protein 3g			
Vitamin A 2%		Vitamin C 0%	
Calcium 8%		Iron 4%	

Dietary Exchanges: ½ Starch, ½ Fat OR ½ Carbohydrate, ½ Fat

Quesadillas (*keh-sah-DEE-yahs*) take their name from the Spanish word for cheese, *queso*. At its simplest, this Mexican-inspired snack is nothing more than cheese melted between two tortillas and cut into wedges, but it's easy to add more ingredients to vary the flavors. For a bite-sized variation, roll up a tortilla with some shredded cheese and a slice of ham and heat in the microwave for about 30 seconds. Slice the roll into 1-inch pieces and serve.

Spinach and Feta Quesadillas

■ ■

PREP TIME: 25 MINUTES

1 (8-oz.) container (tub) fat-free cream cheese

¼ teaspoon garlic powder

¼ teaspoon pepper

8 (8-inch) flour tortillas

1 (9-oz.) pkg. frozen spinach in a pouch, cooked, squeezed to drain

1 medium red bell pepper, finely chopped (1 cup)

4 oz. (1 cup) crumbled feta cheese

1. In small bowl, combine cream cheese, garlic powder and pepper; blend well. Spread 2 tablespoons cream cheese mixture on each tortilla. Sprinkle about 2 tablespoons each of spinach, bell pepper and cheese on half of each tortilla; fold tortillas in half.

2. Heat large nonstick skillet over medium-high heat until hot. Place 2 folded tortillas in skillet; cook about 2 minutes on each side or until golden brown.

3. Remove quesadillas from skillet; place on platter. Cover with foil to keep warm. Repeat with remaining folded tortillas. Cut each quesadilla into 4 wedges. Serve warm.

YIELD: 32 APPETIZERS

Nutrition Information Per Serving
Serving Size: 1 Appetizer

Calories 45	Calories from Fat 10
	% Daily Value
Total Fat 1g	..................2%
Saturated 1g	..................5%
Cholesterol 4mg	..................1%
Sodium 150mg	..................6%
Total Carbohydrate.............6g	..................2%
Dietary Fiber 0g	..................0%
Sugars 1g	
Protein 3g	
Vitamin A 10%	Vitamin C......................8%
Calcium 6%	Iron...........................2%

Dietary Exchanges: ½ Starch OR ½ Carbohydrate

Smoked Salmon Toast

■ ■ ■ ■ ■ ■ ■ ■ ■ ■ ■ ■ ■ ■ ■ ■ ■

PREP TIME: 20 MINUTES

4 oz. smoked salmon, minced

2 oz. (½ cup) shredded reduced-fat mozzarella cheese

½ cup fat-free mayonnaise or salad dressing

¼ cup finely chopped red onion

2 tablespoons drained capers, rinsed

32 melba toast rounds

Chopped fresh parsley, if desired

1. Heat oven to 350°F. In medium bowl, combine salmon, cheese, mayonnaise, onion and capers; mix well. Spread 1 heaping teaspoon salmon mixture on each toast round to cover; place on ungreased cookie sheet.

2. Bake at 350°F. for 8 to 10 minutes or until thoroughly heated. Sprinkle with parsley. Serve warm.

YIELD: 32 APPETIZERS

Nutrition Information Per Serving
Serving Size: 1 Appetizer

Calories 45	Calories from Fat 10
	% Daily Value
Total Fat 1g	..................2%
Saturated 0g	..................0%
Cholesterol 3mg	..................1%
Sodium 210mg	..................9%
Total Carbohydrate.............6g	..................2%
Dietary Fiber 1g	..................3%
Sugars 1g	
Protein 3g	
Vitamin A 0%	Vitamin C......................0%
Calcium 2%	Iron...........................0%

Dietary Exchanges: ½ Starch OR ½ Carbohydrate

Vietnamese Shrimp Toast

■ ■ ■ ■ ■ ■ ■ ■ ■ ■ ■ ■ ■ ■ ■ ■ ■

PREP TIME: 25 MINUTES

½ lb. shelled, deveined, uncooked shrimp, chopped

1 tablespoon cornstarch

1 tablespoon purchased fish sauce,* if desired

1½ teaspoons sugar

½ teaspoon grated gingerroot or ¼ teaspoon ground ginger

¼ teaspoon salt

⅛ teaspoon pepper

6 shallots, minced (about ⅓ cup)

4 garlic cloves, minced

16 (½-inch-thick) slices French bread, 2½ inches in diameter

16 fresh cilantro leaves

1. In medium bowl, combine all ingredients except bread and cilantro; mix well. Set aside.

2. Place bread slices on ungreased cookie sheet. Broil 4 to 6 inches from heat for 1 to 2 minutes or until golden brown.

3. Turn slices over; spread evenly with shrimp mixture. Return to broiler; broil an additional 1 to 3 minutes or until shrimp turn pink. Garnish with fresh cilantro.

YIELD: 16 APPETIZERS

Tip: * Fish sauce can be found in the Asian food section of most supermarkets.

Nutrition Information Per Serving
Serving Size: 1 Appetizer

Calories 90	Calories from Fat 10
	% Daily Value
Total Fat 1g	..................2%
Saturated 0g	..................0%
Cholesterol 20mg	..................7%
Sodium 280mg	..................12%
Total Carbohydrate.............15g	..................5%
Dietary Fiber 1g	..................4%
Sugars 2g	
Protein 5g	
Vitamin A 15%	Vitamin C......................0%
Calcium 2%	Iron...........................6%

Dietary Exchanges: 1 Starch, ½ Very Lean Meat OR 1 Carbohydrate, ½ Very Lean Meat

Tangy Turkey Meatballs

■ ■ ■ ■ ■ ■ ■ ■ ■ ■ ■ ■ ■ ■ ■ ■ ■ ■ ■ ■

PREP TIME: 30 MINUTES

Meatballs

½ lb. lean ground turkey

2 tablespoons unseasoned bread crumbs

2 tablespoons finely chopped green bell pepper

1 garlic clove, minced

1 egg white

2 drops hot pepper sauce

1 tablespoon oil

Sauce

½ cup light ketchup

3 tablespoons brown sugar

3 tablespoons water

3 tablespoons light molasses

2 tablespoons lemon juice

2 tablespoons red wine vinegar

½ teaspoon chili powder

½ teaspoon dry mustard

⅛ teaspoon ground red pepper (cayenne)

1. In medium bowl, combine all meatball ingredients except oil; mix well. Shape into 16 (1¼-inch) balls.
2. In medium skillet, heat oil over medium-high heat until hot. Add meatballs; cook until browned. Drain; return meatballs to skillet.

3. In small bowl, combine all sauce ingredients; mix well. Pour over drained meatballs. Cover; simmer 10 minutes. Serve with cocktail toothpicks.

YIELD: 8 SERVINGS

Nutrition Information Per Serving
Serving Size: ⅛ of Recipe

Calories	130	Calories from Fat	45
		% Daily Value	
Total Fat	5g		8%
Saturated	1g		5%
Cholesterol	20mg		7%
Sodium	150mg		6%
Total Carbohydrate	15g		5%
Dietary Fiber	0g		0%
Sugars	12g		
Protein	6g		
Vitamin A	4%	Vitamin C	4%
Calcium	4%	Iron	6%

Dietary Exchanges: 1 Starch, ½ Medium-Fat Meat OR 1 Carbohydrate, ½ Medium-Fat Meat

how **Snacks** *stack up*

Snack	Calories	Fat
Corn chips (1 oz.)	160	10 g
Melba rounds (5)	50	0 g
Potato chips, regular (1 oz.)	150	10 g
Potato chips, baked (1 oz.)	110	1.5 g
Pretzels (1 oz.)	110	0 g
Rice cake (1 cake)	35	0 g
Round buttery crackers (5)	80	4 g
Saltine crackers (5)	60	1.5 g
Tortilla chips, regular (1 oz.)	130	6 g
Tortilla chips, baked (1 oz.)	110	1 g
Whole wheat wafers (7)	140	5 g

Source: USDA Handbook 8 and package labels.

3 Salads

Warm Lime-Chicken Salad (page 42)

Ham Tossed Salad with Honey-Lime Dressing

PREP TIME: 20 MINUTES

Salad

2 cups torn iceberg lettuce or other salad greens

2 cups torn prewashed fresh spinach

1 cup cooked ham strips (1½ × ¼ × ¼ inches)

½ cup shredded carrot

2 tablespoons sliced green onions

2 tablespoons raisins

Dressing

1 tablespoon oil

3 tablespoons lime juice

3 tablespoons honey

½ teaspoon dry mustard

1. In large bowl, combine all salad ingredients; toss gently.

2. In small jar with tight-fitting lid or small bowl, combine all dressing ingredients; shake or beat with wire whisk until well blended. Pour dressing over salad; toss gently.

YIELD: 4 (1-CUP) SERVINGS

Nutrition Information Per Serving
Serving Size: 1 Cup

Calories................................160	Calories from Fat...........45
	% Daily Value
Total Fat 5g	.........8%
Saturated 1g	.........5%
Cholesterol 15mg	.........5%
Sodium 530mg	.......22%
Total Carbohydrate 21g	.........7%
Dietary Fiber 2g	.........8%
Sugars............................17g	
Protein 8g	
Vitamin A..........................120%	Vitamin C 35%
Calcium 4%	Iron 8%

Dietary Exchanges: 1 Fruit, 1 Vegetable, 1 Lean Meat, ½ Fat OR
1 Carbohydrate, 1 Vegetable, 1 Lean Meat, ½ Fat

Oriental Beef and Noodle Salad

PREP TIME: 25 MINUTES

Salad

2 (5oz.) pkg. Japanese curly noodles*

2 lb. deli-sliced cooked roast beef, cut into strips

6 cups chopped Chinese (napa) cabbage

3 cups fresh bean sprouts

1 large red bell pepper, cut into thin 1-inch strips

6 green onions, sliced

2 (8-oz.) cans sliced water chestnuts, drained

Dressing

⅓ cup oil

¼ cup rice wine vinegar

2 tablespoons sugar

1 tablespoon grated gingerroot

3 tablespoons lite soy sauce

2 garlic cloves, minced

1. Cook noodles as directed on package. Drain; rinse with cold water. In very large bowl, combine cooked noodles and remaining salad ingredients; mix well.

2. In small bowl, combine all dressing ingredients; blend well. Pour dressing over salad; toss gently.

YIELD: 14 (1½-CUP) SERVINGS

Tip: * Ten ounces of Chinese noodles, ramen noodles (omitting seasoning packet) or fine egg noodles can be substituted for Japanese noodles.

Nutrition Information Per Serving
Serving Size: 1½ Cups

Calories................................310	Calories from Fat..........100
	% Daily Value
Total Fat...........................11g	.........17%
Saturated 1g	.........5%
Cholesterol 60mg	.........20%
Sodium 850mg	.........35%
Total Carbohydrate 27g	.........9%
Dietary Fiber 3g	.........12%
Sugars 6g	
Protein 26g	
Vitamin A..........................15%	Vitamin C 50%
Calcium 4%	Iron 20%

Dietary Exchanges: 1½ Starch, 1 Vegetable, 3 Lean Meat OR
1½ Carbohydrate, 1 Vegetable, 3 Lean Meat

Italian Chef Salad

4 cups (6 oz.) purchased Italian blend salad greens or torn romaine lettuce

½ small yellow bell pepper, cut into thin strips

½ small cucumber, sliced

1 small tomato, cut into wedges

2 thin slices red onion, separated into rings

3 oz. deli-sliced cooked peppered roast beef, cut into strips

2 oz. sliced mozzarella cheese, cut into strips

1 tablespoon chopped fresh basil

6 tablespoons purchased fat-free Italian Parmesan or Italian salad dressing

1. On 2 individual plates, arrange salad greens, bell pepper, cucumber, tomato and onion.

2. Arrange roast beef and mozzarella strips over salads; sprinkle with basil. Drizzle salad dressing over salads.

YIELD: 2 SERVINGS

Nutrition Information Per Serving
Serving Size: ½ of Recipe

Calories	220	Calories from Fat	80
		% Daily Value	
Total Fat	9g		14%
Saturated	4g		20%
Cholesterol	55mg		18%
Sodium	930mg		39%
Total Carbohydrate	12g		4%
Dietary Fiber	2g		8%
Sugars	5g		
Protein	22g		
Vitamin A	60%	Vitamin C	60%
Calcium	20%	Iron	10%

Dietary Exchanges: 2 Vegetable, 2 Medium-Fat Meat

▼ Italian Chef Salad

Rio Grande Beef Salad

PREP TIME: 25 MINUTES

6 ½ oz. (2 cups) uncooked wagon wheel pasta

¼ cup chopped onion

1 garlic clove, minced

1 tablespoon oil

1 (10-oz.) can diced tomatoes and green chiles, undrained

½ teaspoon dried oregano leaves

¼ teaspoon cumin

½ lb. deli-sliced cooked roast beef, chopped (1½ cups)

1 (9-oz.) pkg. frozen corn in a pouch, cooked, drained

1 medium tomato, chopped

½ cup chopped green bell pepper

1 tablespoon chopped fresh cilantro

1. Cook pasta to desired doneness as directed on package.

2. Meanwhile, in small nonstick saucepan, cook onion and garlic in oil until tender. Stir in tomatoes, oregano and cumin. Bring to a boil over medium-high heat. Boil 4 minutes or until slightly thickened, stirring frequently to prevent sticking. Remove from heat.

3. Drain pasta; rinse with cold water. Drain well. In large bowl, combine cooked pasta, roast beef, corn, chopped tomato, bell pepper and cilantro; mix gently.

4. Add tomato mixture; toss gently until well mixed. Serve immediately, or cover and refrigerate until serving time. If desired, serve on lettuce-lined plates and garnish with tortilla chips and additional cilantro.

YIELD: 4 (2-CUP) SERVINGS

about Cilantro

Also known as fresh coriander or Chinese parsley, cilantro lends its distinctive flavor to dishes with Chinese, Indian, Mexican and Southwestern inspiration. It resembles a more delicate version of fresh parsley but has a brighter, almost citrusy flavor. Those who dislike this assertive herb describe it as metallic or soapy tasting.

Nutrition Information Per Serving
Serving Size: 2 Cups

Calories	400	Calories from Fat	80
		% Daily Value	
Total Fat	9g		14%
Saturated	2g		10%
Cholesterol	55mg		18%
Sodium	800mg		33%
Total Carbohydrate	52g		17%
Dietary Fiber	4g		16%
Sugars	7g		
Protein	27g		
Vitamin A	10%	Vitamin C	25%
Calcium	4%	Iron	25%

Dietary Exchanges: 3 Starch, 1 Vegetable, 2 Lean Meat, ½ Fat OR
3 Carbohydrate, 1 Vegetable, 2 Lean Meat, ½ Fat

▼ Rio Grande Beef Salad

tempting **Tomatoes**

The way you store tomatoes can mean all the difference in their taste and texture. Do *not* ripen tomatoes in the sun or in the refrigerator. Instead, ripen tomatoes by placing them in a cool spot out of sunlight or in a closed paper bag or fruit-ripening bowl. Use tomatoes once they are ripe or refrigerate them for a day or two to retard spoilage.

Beefsteak tomato Large, bright red, "beefy" variety with a slightly squatty shape; excellent for slicing in sandwiches.

Round red tomato Common garden variety; good for stuffing and cutting into wedges for salads. Bright red color, very juicy.

Round yellow tomato Sweeter than red because of its higher sugar content; can be bright orange or yellow. Good in salads, soups, salsas.

Plum tomato Also called Italian tomato; recognizable by its oval or egg shape. Less juicy than other tomatoes. Its higher pulp content makes a thicker sauce; best off-season choice for sauces.

Cherry tomato Small, round, yellow or red tomato with intense sweet flavor. Delicious in sauces or salads.

Pear tomato Pear-shaped variety about the size of a cherry tomato; also called teardrop tomatoes. Yellow or red, very sweet flavor. Good in salads or on a relish or vegetable tray.

Green tomato Underripe red tomatoes are favored by some cooks for the tang they add to salsa, chutney and pasta sauces. The firm fruit are somewhat citrusy in flavor.

Tomatillo Also called a Mexican green tomato; resembles a small green tomato with a papery husk. Can be used in place of a green tomato. Remove the husk and wash the tart fruit before using.

Grilled Chicken Salad with Raspberries

▪ ▪ ▪ ▪ ▪ ▪ ▪ ▪ ▪ ▪ ▪ ▪ ▪ ▪ ▪ ▪ ▪

PREP TIME: 30 MINUTES

¼ cup seedless raspberry jam

3 tablespoons raspberry vinegar

2 tablespoons honey

1 tablespoon olive oil

4 boneless, skinless chicken breast halves

½ teaspoon coarse ground black pepper

1 (10-oz.) pkg. mixed salad greens (about 8 cups)

1 cup raspberries

Grill Directions: 1. Heat grill. In medium bowl, combine jam, vinegar, honey and oil; mix well. Reserve ¼ cup for dressing. Add chicken breast halves to remaining mixture; toss to coat. Let stand at room temperature for 5 to 10 minutes to marinate.
2. When ready to grill, remove chicken from marinade; discard marinade. Place chicken on gas grill over medium heat or on charcoal grill 4 to 6 inches from medium coals. Cook 10 to 12 minutes or until chicken is fork-tender and juices run clear, turning once. Sprinkle with pepper.
3. Meanwhile, in large bowl, combine mixed greens and reserved ¼ cup dressing; toss to coat. Arrange on 4 individual plates.
4. Cut each chicken breast half crosswise into slices; do not separate slices. Arrange 1 chicken breast half on each salad, fanning slices. Garnish with raspberries.

Broiler Directions: 1. Marinate chicken breast halves as directed above.
2. Place chicken on broiler pan. Broil 4 to 6 inches from heat for 10 to 12 minutes or until chicken is fork-tender and juices run clear, turning once. Sprinkle with pepper.
3. Assemble salads as directed above.

YIELD: 4 SERVINGS

Nutrition Information Per Serving
Serving Size: ¼ of Recipe

Calories	240	Calories from Fat	50
		% Daily Value	
Total Fat	6g		9%
Saturated	1g		5%
Cholesterol	75mg		25%
Sodium	85mg		4%
Total Carbohydrate	19g		6%
Dietary Fiber	3g		12%
Sugars	13g		
Protein	28g		
Vitamin A	35%	Vitamin C	20%
Calcium	2%	Iron	6%

Dietary Exchanges: 1 Fruit, 1 Vegetable, 4 Very Lean Meat OR
1 Carbohydrate, 1 Vegetable, 4 Very Lean Meat

Warm Lime-Chicken Salad

▪ ▪ ▪ ▪ ▪ ▪ ▪ ▪ ▪ ▪ ▪ ▪ ▪ ▪ ▪ ▪ ▪

PREP TIME: 25 MINUTES

Dressing
1 teaspoon grated lime peel

¼ cup fresh lime juice

3 tablespoons sugar

½ teaspoon white wine vinegar

¼ teaspoon Dijon mustard

Chicken
2 tablespoons frozen limeade concentrate, thawed

¼ to ½ teaspoon pepper

1 lb. boneless, skinless chicken breast halves, cut into thin strips

1 tablespoon olive oil

Salad
8 cups torn leaf lettuce

1 (11-oz.) can mandarin orange segments, drained

¼ cup golden raisins

¼ cup chopped walnuts

1. In small jar with tight-fitting lid, combine all dressing ingredients; shake until well blended. Set aside.
2. In another small bowl, combine limeade concentrate and pepper. Add chicken strips; toss to coat. Heat oil in small nonstick skillet over medium-high heat until hot. Add chicken mixture; cook and stir 4

to 6 minutes or until chicken is lightly browned and no longer pink.

3. Line 4 individual plates with lettuce. Top each with orange segments, raisins and walnuts. Top lettuce mixture with cooked chicken. Drizzle with dressing.

YIELD: 4 SERVINGS

Nutrition Information Per Serving
Serving Size: 1/4 of Recipe

Calories	350	Calories from Fat	100
		% Daily Value	
Total Fat	11g		17%
Saturated	2g		10%
Cholesterol	65mg		22%
Sodium	80mg		3%
Total Carbohydrate	34g		11%
Dietary Fiber	4g		16%
Sugars	27g		
Protein	28g		
Vitamin A	50%	Vitamin C	50%
Calcium	10%	Iron	15%

Dietary Exchanges: 2 Fruit, 1 Vegetable, 4 Very Lean Meat, 1 1/2 Fat OR 2 Carbohydrate, 1 Vegetable, 4 Very Lean Meat, 1 1/2 Fat

Hot Barley and Chicken Salad

• • • • • • • • • • • • • • • • •

PREP TIME: 30 MINUTES

Dressing

1 tablespoon sugar

1 tablespoon balsamic vinegar

2 teaspoons red wine vinegar

2 teaspoons soy sauce

Dash pepper

Salad

1 cup water

1/2 cup uncooked quick-cooking barley

1 boneless, skinless chicken breast half, cut into bite-sized pieces

1 garlic clove, minced

2 cups frozen mixed vegetables, thawed*

Fresh spinach leaves

1. In small bowl, combine all dressing ingredients; mix well. Set aside.

2. In medium saucepan, bring water to a boil. Add barley; return to a boil. Reduce heat to medium-low;

cover and simmer 10 to 12 minutes or until barley is tender and only about 1/4 of liquid remains.

3. Add chicken and garlic; mix well. Cover; cook an additional 5 minutes. Stir in vegetables. Cover; cook over medium heat until chicken is no longer pink and vegetables are tender. Add dressing; cook until thoroughly heated.

4. Arrange spinach leaves on 2 individual plates. Spoon salad onto spinach leaves.

YIELD: 2 (1 1/2-CUP) SERVINGS

Tip: * To quickly thaw mixed vegetables, place in colander or strainer; rinse with warm water until thawed. Drain well.

Nutrition Information Per Serving
Serving Size: 1 1/2 Cups

Calories	350	Calories from Fat	20
		% Daily Value	
Total Fat	2g		3%
Saturated	1g		5%
Cholesterol	35mg		12%
Sodium	440mg		18%
Total Carbohydrate	61g		20%
Dietary Fiber	12g		48%
Sugars	9g		
Protein	23g		
Vitamin A	60%	Vitamin C	15%
Calcium	6%	Iron	20%

Dietary Exchanges: 3 Starch, 3 Vegetable, 1 Very Lean Meat OR 3 Carbohydrate, 3 Vegetable, 1 Very Lean Meat

purchasing Prepared Greens

• • • • • • • • • • • • • • • • •

If you're one of those well-meaning shoppers who purchases a proliferation of greens at the market, only to have them rot in the refrigerator before you get around to cleaning them for a salad, you're in luck. Many greens are now available washed, torn and ready to dress, either in grocery store salad bars or in an increasing number of prepackaged options including romaine, coleslaw mix, mesclun (mixed young salad greens) and spinach. When purchasing packaged greens, look for bright color and crisp leaves with no signs of browning or wilting.

Strawberry-Orange Chicken Salad

PREP TIME: 20 MINUTES

Dressing
¼ cup strawberry syrup

1 tablespoon red wine vinegar

Salad
2 cups torn prewashed fresh spinach*

2 cups torn lettuce*

¾ cup sliced cooked chicken, cut into strips

⅔ cup sliced or halved fresh strawberries

1 seedless orange, peeled, cut up

1. In small bowl, combine dressing ingredients; mix well.

2. In medium bowl, combine all salad ingredients; toss well. Spoon salad onto 2 individual plates. Drizzle with dressing.

YIELD: 2 SERVINGS

Tip: * If desired, 4 cups prepackaged mixed salad greens can be substituted for the spinach and lettuce.

Nutrition Information Per Serving
Serving Size: ½ of Recipe

Calories	270	Calories from Fat	35
		% Daily Value	
Total Fat	4g		6%
Saturated	1g		5%
Cholesterol	45mg		15%
Sodium	95mg		4%
Total Carbohydrate	40g		13%
Dietary Fiber	5g		20%
Sugars	35g		
Protein	18g		
Vitamin A	80%	Vitamin C	140%
Calcium	10%	Iron	15%

Dietary Exchanges: 2 Fruit, 1 Vegetable, 2 Lean Meat OR 2 Carbohydrate, 1 Vegetable, 2 Lean Meat

Summer Harvest Chicken-Potato Salad

PREP TIME: 30 MINUTES

4 medium red potatoes (1 lb.), cut into ¾-inch cubes

½ lb. fresh green beans, trimmed, cut into 1-inch pieces (about 2 cups)

½ cup nonfat plain yogurt

⅓ cup purchased fat-free ranch salad dressing

1 tablespoon prepared horseradish

¼ teaspoon salt

Dash pepper

2 cups cubed cooked chicken breast

⅔ cup thinly sliced celery

Torn salad greens, if desired

1. In large saucepan, bring 6 cups lightly salted water to a boil. Add potatoes. Return to a boil. Reduce heat; simmer 5 minutes. Add green beans; cook an additional 8 to 12 minutes or until potatoes and beans are crisp-tender.

2. In small bowl, combine yogurt, salad dressing, horseradish, salt and pepper; blend well. Set aside.

3. Drain potatoes and green beans; rinse with cold water. Drain well. Place in large serving bowl. Add chicken and celery. Pour dressing over salad; toss gently to coat. Line 4 individual plates with salad greens. Spoon salad onto lettuce.

YIELD: 4 (1¾-CUP) SERVINGS

Nutrition Information Per Serving
Serving Size: 1¾ Cups

Calories	270	Calories from Fat	25
		% Daily Value	
Total Fat	3g		5%
Saturated	1g		5%
Cholesterol	40mg		13%
Sodium	410mg		17%
Total Carbohydrate	41g		14%
Dietary Fiber	5g		20%
Sugars	8g		
Protein	19g		
Vitamin A	8%	Vitamin C	30%
Calcium	10%	Iron	15%

Dietary Exchanges: 2½ Starch, 1 Vegetable, 1 Very Lean Meat OR 2½ Carbohydrate, 1 Vegetable, 1 Very Lean Meat

Summer Harvest Chicken-Potato Salad ▶

appealing Sald Presentations

- Stuff hollowed-out tomatoes or roasted or raw whole red or yellow bell peppers.

- Nestle the salad in the curve of two or three endive leaves.

- Mound the salad on a bed of shredded greens.

- Scoop the salad onto a pile of mild alfalfa sprouts or peppery radish sprouts.

- Spoon some salad into a few jumbo pasta shells or roll it up in cooked, cooled lasagna noodles for a spiral treat.

Cobb Salad Shells

PREP TIME: 40 MINUTES

12 uncooked jumbo pasta shells

1 cup chopped cooked turkey or chicken breast

2 medium tomatoes, chopped

1 hard-cooked egg, chopped

1 slice bacon, crisply cooked, crumbled

1 tablespoon chèvre (goat) cheese

3 cups shredded romaine lettuce

3 tablespoons purchased reduced-calorie French salad dressing

1. Cook pasta shells to desired doneness as directed on package.

2. Meanwhile, in large bowl, combine turkey, tomatoes, egg, bacon and cheese; mix gently.

3. Drain pasta shells; rinse with cold water. Drain well.

4. Add lettuce to turkey mixture; toss gently. Fill each cold cooked pasta shell with $1/4$ to $1/3$ cup turkey mixture. If desired, line 4 individual salad plates with additional romaine lettuce. Place 3 shells on each plate; drizzle with salad dressing.

YIELD: 4 SERVINGS

Nutrition Information Per Serving
Serving Size: $1/4$ of Recipe

Calories	240	Calories from Fat	60
			% Daily Value
Total Fat	7g		11%
Saturated	2g		10%
Cholesterol	90mg		30%
Sodium	180mg		8%
Total Carbohydrate	27g		9%
Dietary Fiber	2g		8%
Sugars	7g		
Protein	18g		
Vitamin A	30%	Vitamin C	35%
Calcium	6%	Iron	15%

Dietary Exchanges: $1\frac{1}{2}$ Starch, 1 Vegetable, 2 Lean Meat OR $1\frac{1}{2}$ Carbohydrate, 1 Vegetable, 2 Lean Meat

Caribbean Turkey Salad

Dressing

1 (8-oz.) container low-fat lemon yogurt

1 tablespoon frozen orange juice concentrate, thawed

½ teaspoon cinnamon

Salad

8 oz. cooked turkey breast, cut into strips (about 2 cups)

2 cups strawberries, halved

1 cup cubed cantaloupe

1 banana, sliced

2 (8-oz.) cans pineapple chunks, drained

Lettuce leaves

¼ cup coconut, if desired

1. In small bowl, combine all dressing ingredients; mix well.

2. In large bowl, combine turkey, strawberries, cantaloupe, banana and pineapple; toss gently.

3. Line 4 individual salad plates or large platter with lettuce. Spoon turkey mixture onto lettuce. Spoon dressing over salads. Sprinkle with coconut.

YIELD: 4 (2-CUP) SERVINGS

Nutrition Information Per Serving
Serving Size: 2 Cups

Calories	280	Calories from Fat	25
			% Daily Value
Total Fat	3g		5%
Saturated	2g		10%
Cholesterol	50mg		17%
Sodium	80mg		3%
Total Carbohydrate	40g		13%
Dietary Fiber	4g		16%
Sugars	33g		
Protein	22g		
Vitamin A	30%	Vitamin C	130%
Calcium	15%	Iron	10%

Dietary Exchanges: 3 Fruit, 3 Very Lean Meat OR 3 Carbohydrate, 3 Very Lean Meat

Turkey Salad with Fresh Vegetables

1½ cups lean smoked or cooked turkey breast strips (2½ × ¼ × ¼ inches)

½ cup thinly sliced radishes

⅓ cup sliced green onions

⅓ cup chopped celery

1 cup seedless red or green grapes

1 (8-oz.) can pineapple chunks in unsweetened juice, drained

¼ cup fat-free mayonnaise or salad dressing

¼ cup nonfat plain yogurt

2 tablespoons purchased mango chutney

4 cups torn Bibb or other lettuce leaves

1. In large bowl, combine turkey, radishes, onions, celery, grapes and pineapple; mix well.

2. In small bowl, combine mayonnaise, yogurt and chutney; blend well. Pour dressing over salad; toss gently to coat. Line 4 individual plates with lettuce. Spoon salad onto lettuce.

YIELD: 4 SERVINGS

Nutrition Information Per Serving
Serving Size: ¼ of Recipe

Calories	150	Calories from Fat	20
			% Daily Value
Total Fat	2g		3%
Saturated	0g		0%
Cholesterol	15mg		5%
Sodium	560mg		23%
Total Carbohydrate	23g		8%
Dietary Fiber	3g		12%
Sugars	15g		
Protein	9g		
Vitamin A	10%	Vitamin C	30%
Calcium	8%	Iron	4%

Dietary Exchanges: 1 Fruit, 2 Vegetable, 1 Very Lean Meat OR 1 Carbohydrate, 2 Vegetable, 1 Very Lean Meat

Turkey and Melon Pasta Salad

■ ■ ■ ■ ■ ■ ■ ■ ■ ■ ■ ■ ■ ■ ■ ■

PREP TIME: 30 MINUTES

Salad

4 oz. (2 cups) uncooked bow tie pasta (farfalle)

1½ cups cubed cooked turkey breast (½ lb.)

1½ cups seeded small watermelon balls or cubes

½ cup sliced celery

2 tablespoons sliced green onions

Dressing

¼ cup nonfat plain yogurt

2 tablespoons reduced-calorie mayonnaise or salad dressing

2 tablespoons frozen limeade concentrate, thawed

1. Cook pasta to desired doneness as directed on package. Drain; rinse with cold water.

2. In large bowl, combine cooked pasta and all remaining salad ingredients; toss gently.

3. In small bowl, combine all dressing ingredients; blend with wire whisk until smooth. Add to turkey mixture; toss gently to coat.

YIELD: 4 (1½-CUP) SERVINGS

Nutrition Information Per Serving
Serving Size: 1½ Cups

Calories	230	Calories from Fat	35
		% Daily Value	
Total Fat	4g		6%
Saturated	1g		5%
Cholesterol	25mg		8%
Sodium	830mg		35%
Total Carbohydrate	32g		11%
Dietary Fiber	1g		4%
Sugars	11g		
Protein	17g		
Vitamin A	6%	Vitamin C	15%
Calcium	6%	Iron	8%

Dietary Exchanges: 1½ Starch, ½ Fruit, 2 Very Lean Meat OR
2 Carbohydrate, 2 Very Lean Meat

Louis Salad Niçoise

■ ■ ■ ■ ■ ■ ■ ■ ■ ■ ■ ■ ■ ■ ■ ■

PREP TIME: 20 MINUTES

4 (2-inch) new red potatoes

1 head Boston lettuce, torn (about 4 cups)

4 cups loosely packed torn prewashed fresh spinach

½ medium red onion, halved, thinly sliced (½ cup)

2 (6-oz.) cans water-packed white tuna, drained, flaked

⅓ cup sliced celery

1 (2¼-oz.) can sliced ripe olives, drained

¼ teaspoon coarse ground black pepper

¾ cup purchased fat-free Thousand Island salad dressing

1. Scrub potatoes; pierce with fork. Arrange on paper towel in microwave. Microwave on HIGH for 3 to 5 minutes or until very tender when pierced with fork. Cool under cold running water. Halve potatoes and slice. Set aside.

2. In large bowl, combine lettuce, spinach and onion; toss gently. Arrange on 4 individual plates. Top with potato slices, tuna, celery and olives. Sprinkle each with pepper. Serve with salad dressing.

YIELD: 4 SERVINGS

Nutrition Information Per Serving
Serving Size: ¼ of Recipe

Calories	300	Calories from Fat	25
		% Daily Value	
Total Fat	3g		5%
Saturated	0g		0%
Cholesterol	20mg		7%
Sodium	890mg		37%
Total Carbohydrate	45g		15%
Dietary Fiber	7g		28%
Sugars	12g		
Protein	23g		
Vitamin A	90%	Vitamin C	50%
Calcium	10%	Iron	25%

Dietary Exchanges: 2 Starch, 3 Vegetable, 2 Very Lean Meat OR
2 Carbohydrate, 3 Vegetable, 2 Very Lean Meat

Italian Bean and Tuna Salad

■ ■

PREP TIME: 30 MINUTES

1 (15½-oz.) can navy beans, drained, rinsed

1 (6-oz.) can water-packed white tuna, drained, flaked

⅔ cup finely chopped celery

⅓ cup finely chopped red bell pepper

⅓ cup fresh or frozen cut (1-inch) green beans, cooked, rinsed with cold water

3 tablespoons chopped fresh chives

2 tablespoons chopped fresh parsley

½ cup purchased reduced-calorie or fat-free Italian salad dressing

½ teaspoon dried oregano leaves

Lettuce leaves, if desired

1. In medium bowl, combine all ingredients except lettuce; mix well. Refrigerate 10 minutes to blend flavors.

2. Line 4 individual salad plates with lettuce. Spoon salad onto lettuce.

YIELD: 4 (1-CUP) SERVINGS

Nutrition Information Per Serving
Serving Size: 1 Cup

Calories.................................220	Calories from Fat 35	
	% Daily Value	
Total Fat 4g	....6%	
Saturated 1g	....5%	
Cholesterol 15mg	....5%	
Sodium 630mg	....26%	
Total Carbohydrate 26g	....9%	
Dietary Fiber 1g	....4%	
Sugars 1g		
Protein 19g		
Vitamin A 20%	Vitamin C 40%	
Calcium 8%	Iron 20%	

Dietary Exchanges: 1½ Starch, 1 Vegetable, 2 Very Lean Meat OR
1½ Carbohydrate, 1 Vegetable, 2 Very Lean Meat

▼ Italian Bean and Tuna Salad

Mango Shrimp Salad

PREP TIME: 20 MINUTES

Salad

3 ripe mangoes (about 2½ lb.), peeled, cut into cubes and seeded (about 3½ cups)

1½ lb. shelled, deveined, cooked large shrimp

Dressing

½ cup fat-free mayonnaise or salad dressing

¼ cup skim milk

2 teaspoons chopped fresh mint leaves

1 teaspoon sugar

1 teaspoon fresh lemon juice

Dash coarse ground black pepper

Garnish

Lettuce leaves

1 small green or red bell pepper, cut into 1½ × ¼-inch strips

1. Place mango cubes in serving bowl; add shrimp.

2. In small bowl, combine all dressing ingredients; mix well. If necessary, season to taste by adding additional lemon juice or pepper. Pour dressing over salad; stir gently to mix.

3. Arrange lettuce on large platter. Spoon salad onto lettuce. Sprinkle bell pepper strips over salad.

YIELD: 8 (1-CUP) SERVINGS

Nutrition Information Per Serving
Serving Size: 1 Cup

Calories	170	Calories from Fat	20
		% Daily Value	
Total Fat	2g		3%
Saturated	0g		0%
Cholesterol	165mg		55%
Sodium	390mg		16%
Total Carbohydrate	20g		7%
Dietary Fiber	3g		12%
Sugars	15g		
Protein	19g		
Vitamin A	80%	Vitamin C	60%
Calcium	6%	Iron	15%

Dietary Exchanges: 1 Fruit, 3 Very Lean Meat OR 1 Carbohydrate, 3 Very Lean Meat

---

a little Shrimp Savvy

Canned shrimp are relatively inexpensive and easy to use for many dips and appetizers, especially if the shrimp will be minced or pureed with other ingredients.

For salads and other recipes that call for cooked whole shrimp, it's better to start with uncanned shrimp. Most "fresh" shrimp at the fish market or fish counter have actually been shipped frozen and thawed for sale. Cooked, shelled, deveined shrimp are a convenience, but also a luxury. The price per pound may be nearly double that of the cook-it-and-peel-it-yourself variety.

Don't be afraid to cook shrimp yourself—it's easy. Bring a large pot of water to a boil and add the shrimp, stirring to distribute evenly. Watch the pot carefully. As soon as the shells turn pink (within 1 to 3 minutes), remove one shrimp with a slotted spoon and immediately run it under cold water. Cut it in half. If the meat looks slightly grayish and slightly translucent in the center, throw the shrimp back into the pot and try again in a few seconds. As soon as the meat is white and opaque, immediately drain the whole pot and run cold water over the shells. Cooling the shrimp immediately will prevent overcooking from retained heat.

To peel the shrimp, loosen the shell along the belly with a small knife or your finger and peel it off. The next step, deveining, is customary but optional, since the dark material running along the back just under the skin is both harmless and tasteless. Many people find its appearance unappetizing, however, especially when shrimp are large. To devein, make a shallow slit along the back (outside curve) of the shrimp with a small, sharp knife. Pick out the "vein" with the tip of the knife. Rinse the shrimp if neccessary to remove any little particles.

▲ Colorful Shrimp Rice Salad

Colorful Shrimp Rice Salad

PREP TIME: 30 MINUTES

Salad

6 cups cooked rice (cooked as directed on package, omitting margarine and salt)

2 lb. shelled, deveined, cooked medium shrimp

2 lb. fresh asparagus spears, cooked, cut into 1-inch pieces (5 cups)

1 large yellow or red bell pepper, chopped

½ cup chopped fresh basil

Dressing

¼ cup oil

¼ cup white wine vinegar

1 tablespoon grated orange peel

¼ cup orange juice

¼ teaspoon salt

1. In large serving bowl, combine all salad ingredients; mix well.

2. In small jar with tight-fitting lid, combine all dressing ingredients; shake until well blended.

3. About 15 minutes before serving, pour dressing over salad; toss gently. Serve immediately, or cover and refrigerate until serving time. If desired, garnish with orange slices.

YIELD: 10 (1⅔-CUP) SERVINGS

Nutrition Information Per Serving
Serving Size: 1⅔ Cups

Calories	280	Calories from Fat	60
		% Daily Value	
Total Fat	7g	11%	
Saturated	1g	5%	
Cholesterol	175mg	58%	
Sodium	270mg	11%	
Total Carbohydrate	31g	10%	
Dietary Fiber	2g	8%	
Sugars	2g		
Protein	24g		
Vitamin A	15%	Vitamin C	50%
Calcium	6%	Iron	25%

Dietary Exchanges: 2 Starch, 2 Very Lean Meat, 1 Fat OR 2 Carbohydrate, 2 Very Lean Meat, 1 Fat

Pasta Shell Salad with Salmon and Peas

PREP TIME: 30 MINUTES

8 oz. (3 cups) medium shell pasta

⅓ cup fat-free mayonnaise or salad dressing

⅓ cup nonfat plain yogurt

1 to 2 tablespoons chopped fresh dill

1 tablespoon skim milk

¼ teaspoon coarse ground black pepper

1 (7½-oz.) can red sockeye salmon, drained, skin and bones removed

1 cup fresh or frozen peas, cooked, drained

8 large lettuce leaves

Sprigs of fresh parsley or dill

1. Cook pasta to desired doneness as directed on package.

2. Meanwhile, in small bowl, combine mayonnaise, yogurt, dill, milk and pepper; mix well.

3. Drain pasta; rinse with cold water. In large bowl, combine cooked pasta, salmon and peas; mix gently. Pour dressing over salad; toss gently to coat.

4. Arrange lettuce on 5 individual plates. Spoon salad onto lettuce. Garnish with parsley. Serve immediately, or cover and refrigerate until serving time.*

YIELD: 5 (1-CUP) SERVINGS

Tip: * If stored in refrigerator, an additional 2 to 3 tablespoons skim milk may need to be added to moisten salad before serving.

Nutrition Information Per Serving
Serving Size: 1 Cup

Calories	260	Calories from Fat	25
		% Daily Value	
Total Fat	3g		5%
Saturated	1g		5%
Cholesterol	15mg		5%
Sodium	440mg		18%
Total Carbohydrate	42g		14%
Dietary Fiber	4g		16%
Sugars	5g		
Protein	16g		
Vitamin A	8%	Vitamin C	20%
Calcium	6%	Iron	15%

Dietary Exchanges: 2½ Starch, 1 Lean Meat OR 2½ Carbohydrate, 1 Lean Meat

Crab Salad

PREP TIME: 10 MINUTES

1 cup (about 6 oz.) chopped imitation crabmeat (surimi)

¼ cup chopped green onions

¼ cup chopped celery

⅛ teaspoon garlic powder

⅛ teaspoon pepper

½ cup nonfat cottage cheese

¼ cup nonfat sour cream

1 teaspoon Dijon mustard

2 leaf lettuce leaves

1 medium tomato, cut into wedges

1. In small bowl, combine imitation crabmeat, onions, celery, garlic powder, pepper, cottage cheese, sour cream and mustard; mix well.

2. Line 2 individual salad plates with lettuce. Spoon salad onto lettuce. Garnish with tomato wedges.

YIELD: 2 SERVINGS

Nutrition Information Per Serving
Serving Size: ½ of Recipe

Calories	180	Calories from Fat	20
		% Daily Value	
Total Fat	2g		3%
Saturated	0g		0%
Cholesterol	20mg		7%
Sodium	1,040mg		43%
Total Carbohydrate	20g		7%
Dietary Fiber	1g		4%
Sugars	7g		
Protein	21g		
Vitamin A	20%	Vitamin C	30%
Calcium	15%	Iron	6%

Dietary Exchanges: ½ Starch, 2 Vegetable, 2 Very Lean Meat OR ½ Carbohydrate, 2 Vegetable, 2 Very Lean Meat

▲ Crab Salad

Thai-Style Pasta Salad

PREP TIME: 30 MINUTES

7 oz. uncooked spaghetti

2 tablespoons peanut or vegetable oil

¼ cup chopped onion

½ teaspoon finely chopped jalapeño chile

1 garlic clove, minced

3 tablespoons soy sauce

¼ teaspoon grated gingerroot

1½ cups fresh snow pea pods or sugar snap peas*

1 cup sliced celery

1 cup chopped carrots

1 (8-oz.) can sliced water chestnuts, drained

¼ cup chopped fresh parsley or 2 tablespoons chopped fresh cilantro

1. Cook spaghetti to desired doneness as directed on package.

2. Meanwhile, heat oil in small nonstick saucepan over medium heat until hot. Add onion, chile and garlic; cook and stir until tender. Stir in soy sauce and gingerroot. Remove from heat; set aside.

3. Drain spaghetti; rinse with cold water. Drain well. In large bowl, combine cooked spaghetti, pea pods, celery, carrots, water chestnuts and parsley; mix gently. Add soy sauce mixture; stir gently until well mixed. Serve immediately, or cover and refrigerate until serving time. If desired, garnish with orange slices and additional parsley.

YIELD: 4 (2-CUP) SERVINGS

Tip: * If desired, for greener and more tender pea pods, add to spaghetti during last minute of cooking time.

Nutrition Information Per Serving
Serving Size: 2 Cups

Calories	340	Calories from Fat	70
		% Daily Value	
Total Fat	8g		12%
Saturated	1g		5%
Cholesterol	0mg		0%
Sodium	820mg		34%
Total Carbohydrate	56g		19%
Dietary Fiber	5g		20%
Sugars	8g		
Protein	10g		
Vitamin A	180%	Vitamin C	50%
Calcium	6%	Iron	20%

Dietary Exchanges: 3 Starch, 2 Vegetable, 1 Fat OR 3 Carbohydrate, 2 Vegetable, 1 Fat

Easy Greek Pasta Salad

PREP TIME: 25 MINUTES

6 oz. (1 cup) uncooked orzo or rosamarina (rice-shaped pasta)

¾ teaspoon grated lemon peel

⅓ cup lemon juice

1 tablespoon olive oil

1 tablespoon Dijon mustard

4 teaspoons honey

1 medium cucumber, seeded, chopped (1¼ cups)

2 Italian plum tomatoes, chopped

½ cup chopped red onion

12 medium pitted ripe olives, halved

¼ cup chopped fresh mint leaves

4 lettuce leaves

¼ cup crumbled feta cheese

1. Cook orzo to desired doneness as directed on package.

2. Meanwhile, in small bowl, combine lemon peel, lemon juice, oil, mustard and honey; beat with wire whisk until well blended. Set aside.

3. Drain orzo; rinse with cold water. Drain well. In large bowl, combine cooked orzo, cucumber, tomatoes, onion, olives and mint. Pour dressing over salad; toss gently until well mixed.

4. Line 4 individual salad plates with lettuce. Spoon salad onto lettuce. Sprinkle with cheese.

YIELD: 4 (1¼-CUP) SERVINGS

Nutrition Information Per Serving
Serving Size: 1¼ Cups

Calories	280	Calories from Fat	60
			% Daily Value
Total Fat	7g		11%
Saturated	2g		10%
Cholesterol	5mg		2%
Sodium	250mg		10%
Total Carbohydrate	45g		15%
Dietary Fiber	3g		12%
Sugars	10g		
Protein	8g		
Vitamin A	10%	Vitamin C	40%
Calcium	8%	Iron	15%

Dietary Exchanges: 2½ Starch, 2 Vegetable, 1 Fat OR 2½ Carbohydrate, 2 Vegetable, 1 Fat

noodles for Pasta Salads

Bow tie pasta Known in Italian as *farfalle* ("butterflies"), the bow ties are usually a bit more expensive than ordinary macaroni but offer a fanciful alternative.

Curly noodles Available in Asian markets or in the Asian ingredient aisle of large supermarkets, curly noodles cook up into a pleasant tangle. If you can't find plain curly noodles, substitute ramen soup noodles but omit the seasoning packet.

Fettuccine and linguine Flat noodles work well with saucy salads. Fettuccine noodles are about ³⁄₈ inch wide; linguine noodles are about half that width.

Orzo Small, rice-shaped pasta that's a favorite in Greek cooking and is often used in soups. Also called rosamarina.

Rotini Alias corkscrew pasta, these bite-sized spirals offer a fun twist.

Shell pasta Available in varying sizes, the cowry-shaped noodles have little pockets to catch a bit of sauce or dressing. Jumbo shells are good for stuffing.

Spaghetti The name means "strings" in Italian. Spaghetti noodles range from thin angel hair strands that cook extremely quickly to slightly thicker spaghettini or vermicelli to standard spaghetti #8. In general, the higher the number on the package, the thinner the strands.

Wagon wheel pasta Also called *ruote,* these circular noodles have spokes that form little nooks that are great for catching toppings.

salad *Shortcuts*

- **Slice carrots, celery and radishes** for use over several days. Wrap the cut vegetables in a dampened paper towel and refrigerate them in a self-sealing plastic bag.

- **Extend salads** and add a novel touch with canned ingredients from your pantry shelf. Good candidates include water chestnuts, pineapple chunks, olives, artichoke hearts, pickles and baby corn.

- **Transform the humble can of tuna** into an easy gourmet delight with the addition of chopped red onion, carrot, cucumber and other vegetables in season.

- **Take advantage of leftovers:** cooked potatoes, grilled chicken, steamed green beans and corn on the cob are just a few of the ingredients that gracefully make the switch from last night's star to tonight's supporting role in a salad.

- **When cooking rice or pasta,** cook more than you need and use the rest tomorrow in a cool salad that doesn't even require you to boil water.

- **If you feel like coleslaw** but dread shredding all that cabbage, consider paying slightly more and buying coleslaw mix, a packaged blend of shredded fresh cabbage and carrots sold in the produce aisle.

Pronto Pesto Pasta

PREP TIME: 20 MINUTES

Salad

4 oz. (1½ cups) uncooked rotini (spiral pasta)

1½ cups halved zucchini slices

4 Italian plum tomatoes, sliced

1 cup sliced fresh mushrooms

2 tablespoons chopped red onion

Dressing

½ cup purchased reduced-calorie Italian salad dressing

3 tablespoons chopped fresh basil

1 tablespoon crumbled blue cheese

⅛ teaspoon coarse ground black pepper

1. Cook rotini to desired doneness as directed on package.

2. Meanwhile, in large bowl, combine zucchini, tomatoes, mushrooms and onion; mix gently.

3. Drain rotini; rinse with cold water. Drain well. Add to zucchini mixture.

4. In blender container, combine all dressing ingredients; blend until well mixed. Pour over salad; toss gently. Serve immediately, or cover and refrigerate until serving time. If desired, garnish with fresh basil leaves and grated Parmesan cheese.

YIELD: 4 (1½-CUP) SERVINGS

Nutrition Information Per Serving
Serving Size: 1½ Cups

Calories	190	Calories from Fat	50
		% Daily Value	
Total Fat	6g		9%
Saturated	1g		5%
Cholesterol	0mg		0%
Sodium	280mg		12%
Total Carbohydrate	29g		10%
Dietary Fiber	2g		8%
Sugars	5g		
Protein	5g		
Vitamin A	10%	Vitamin C	25%
Calcium	4%	Iron	10%

Dietary Exchanges: 1½ Starch, 1 Vegetable, 1 Fat OR 1½ Carbohydrate, 1 Vegetable, 1 Fat

Pronto Pesto Salad ▶

Pick up a head of iceberg lettuce with two hands and give the stem end a good whack on a sturdy surface; you'll be able to remove the core easily with your fingers. Lettuces torn by hand usually keep their color longer than those chopped with a knife, which become rusty looking along the cut edges.

Avocado, Grapefruit and Orange Salad

PREP TIME: 30 MINUTES

Dressing

¼ cup frozen orange juice concentrate, thawed

¼ cup water

2 tablespoons Dijon mustard

1 teaspoon grated orange peel

⅛ teaspoon salt

Dash coarse ground black pepper

1 tablespoon olive oil

Salad

2 large grapefruit

4 large oranges

1 small avocado

4 cups shredded lettuce

2 tablespoons chopped fresh parsley

1. In medium bowl, combine all dressing ingredients except oil; beat with wire whisk until blended. Add oil; beat until well blended. Set aside.

2. To section grapefruit and oranges, cut or peel each fruit down to the flesh, leaving no white pith. Between walls of membrane, cut segments straight down with sharp knife. Gently remove segments. Peel, halve and pit avocado; cut into slices about

same size as grapefruit and orange sections.

3. To assemble salad, place shredded lettuce on large platter. Arrange grapefruit and orange segments over top. Toss avocado slices in dressing to prevent darkening. Place avocado on top of fruit. Spoon dressing over salad. Sprinkle with parsley.

YIELD: 12 (¾-CUP) SERVINGS

Nutrition Information Per Serving
Serving Size: ¾ Cup

Calories	100	Calories from Fat	35
		% Daily Value	
Total Fat	4g		6%
Saturated	1g		5%
Cholesterol	0mg		0%
Sodium	90mg		4%
Total Carbohydrate	14g		5%
Dietary Fiber	3g		12%
Sugars	10g		
Protein	2g		
Vitamin A	8%	Vitamin C	90%
Calcium	4%	Iron	2%

Dietary Exchanges: 1 Fruit, 1 Fat OR 1 Carbohydrate, 1 Fat

▼ Avocado, Grapefruit and Orange Salad

accent on **Avocados**

Two varieties of avocados are most commonly available in the United States. The Hass avocado, grown mostly in California and available year-round, is oval shaped with pebbly textured green skin that turns black upon ripening. The Fuerte avocado is pear shaped, larger and has thin, smooth skin that remains green as it ripens. It's in season late fall to spring and is grown primarily in Florida.

Look for unblemished avocados that are heavy for their size. Judge ripeness by pressing the avocado between your palms; it will yield to gentle pressure if it's ripe. If it's not ripe, let it stand at room temperature for a few days. Or speed the process up by placing the avocado in a paper bag and letting it stand on the counter; check it daily for ripeness. Refrigerate ripe avocados if you won't use them right away.

◀ Fuerte

Haas ▶

Tropical Rice Salad

PREP TIME: 25 MINUTES

3 cups cooked regular long-grain white rice (cooked as directed on package, omitting margarine and salt)

1 large tomato, finely chopped

1 small ripe papaya, peeled, seeded and coarsely chopped

2 medium jalapeño chiles, seeded, chopped (2 tablespoons)

½ cup loosely packed chopped fresh cilantro

2 tablespoons finely chopped red onion

1½ teaspoons sugar

1 teaspoon cumin

¼ teaspoon salt

⅛ teaspoon coarse ground black pepper

1. In large bowl, combine all ingredients; toss gently to combine.

2. Serve immediately, or cover and refrigerate until serving time. Bring to room temperature before serving.

YIELD: 8 (¾-CUP) SERVINGS

Nutrition Information Per Serving
Serving Size: ¾ Cup

Calories	100	Calories from Fat	0
		% Daily Value	
Total Fat	0g		0%
Saturated	0g		0%
Cholesterol	0mg		0%
Sodium	75mg		3%
Total Carbohydrate	23g		8%
Dietary Fiber	1g		4%
Sugars	3g		
Protein	2g		
Vitamin A	6%	Vitamin C	30%
Calcium	0%	Iron	8%

Dietary Exchanges: 1 Starch, ½ Fruit OR 1½ Carbohydrate

Cuban Black Bean and Rice Salad

PREP TIME: 15 MINUTES
(READY IN 45 MINUTES)

Salad

2 cups cooked instant white rice (cooked as directed on package, omitting margarine and salt)

3 tablespoons finely chopped onion

½ medium green bell pepper, chopped

1 (15-oz.) can black beans, drained, rinsed

1 (2-oz.) jar diced pimientos, drained

Dressing

1 teaspoon dried oregano leaves

¼ teaspoon salt

⅛ teaspoon pepper

1 to 2 garlic cloves, minced

3 tablespoons cider vinegar

3 tablespoons olive oil

1. In large bowl, combine all salad ingredients; mix well.

2. In small bowl, combine all dressing ingredients; blend well. Add to salad; mix well. Cover; refrigerate at least 30 minutes to blend flavors.

YIELD: 8 (½-CUP) SERVINGS

Nutrition Information Per Serving
Serving Size: ½ Cup

Calories	130	Calories from Fat	45
		% Daily Value	
Total Fat	5g		8%
Saturated	1g		5%
Cholesterol	0mg		0%
Sodium	180mg		8%
Total Carbohydrate	18g		6%
Dietary Fiber	3g		12%
Sugars	1g		
Protein	4g		
Vitamin A	4%	Vitamin C	15%
Calcium	2%	Iron	6%

Dietary Exchanges: 1 Starch, 1 Fat OR 1 Carbohydrate, 1 Fat

Lite Layered Vegetable Salad

PREP TIME: 20 MINUTES

1 head lettuce, torn into bite-sized pieces (about 10 cups)

½ cup chopped green onions

½ cup low-fat plain yogurt

½ cup light sour cream

½ cup sliced celery

½ cup chopped green bell pepper

1½ cups fresh or frozen peas, cooked, drained

3 oz. (¾ cup) grated fresh Romano or Parmesan cheese

5 slices low-sodium bacon, crisply cooked, crumbled

1. In large bowl or 13 × 9-inch (3-quart) baking dish, layer lettuce and onions.

2. In small bowl, combine yogurt and sour cream; blend well. Spoon ½ cup yogurt mixture evenly over onions.

3. Layer celery, bell pepper and peas over yogurt mixture. Spread remaining yogurt mixture over top. Sprinkle with cheese and bacon. If desired, toss before serving.

YIELD: 12 SERVINGS

Nutrition Information Per Serving
Serving Size: ¹/₁₂ of Recipe

Calories	80	Calories from Fat	30
		% Daily Value	
Total Fat	2g		10%
Saturated	2g		10%
Cholesterol	10mg		3%
Sodium	140mg		6%
Total Carbohydrate	7g		2%
Dietary Fiber	2g		8%
Sugars	4g		
Protein	6g		
Vitamin A	10%	Vitamin C	15%
Calcium	10%	Iron	4%

Dietary Exchanges: 1 Vegetable, ½ Medium-Fat Meat, ½ Fat

Fresh Spinach, Orange and Red Onion Salad

8 cups torn prewashed fresh spinach, stems removed

4 medium seedless oranges

Orange juice

⅓ cup honey

3 tablespoons raspberry vinegar

2 tablespoons olive oil

½ teaspoon salt

1 medium red onion, cut into ¼-inch-thick slices

1. Arrange spinach on serving platter or line 8 individual salad plates with spinach leaves.

2. With vegetable peeler, peel off eight $2\frac{1}{2} \times 2$-inch strips of orange peel, being careful to remove only orange part. Cut strips lengthwise into thin slivers.

3. With sharp knife, cut remaining peel and white pith from oranges. Remove segments of orange by cutting between membranes, catching juice in small bowl; set orange segments aside. Squeeze membranes of oranges into bowl to remove all of juice; if necessary, add orange juice to make $\frac{1}{2}$ cup. Add honey, vinegar, oil and salt; beat well with wire whisk.

4. Place onion slices in single layer on cookie sheet; brush with orange juice mixture. Broil 2 to 3 inches from heat for 4 to 5 minutes or just until edges begin to darken.

5. Arrange orange segments on top of spinach. Separate onion slices into rings; scatter over oranges. Drizzle with remaining orange juice mixture. Garnish with strips of orange peel.

YIELD: 8 SERVINGS

Nutrition Information Per Serving
Serving Size: ⅛ of Recipe

Calories	140	Calories from Fat	35
		% Daily Value	
Total Fat	4g		6%
Saturated	1g		5%
Cholesterol	0mg		0%
Sodium	180mg		8%
Total Carbohydrate	24g		8%
Dietary Fiber	3g		12%
Sugars	19g		
Protein	2g		
Vitamin A	80%	Vitamin C	90%
Calcium	8%	Iron	10%

Dietary Exchanges: 1 Fruit, 1 Vegetable, 1 Fat OR 1 Carbohydrate, 1 Vegetable, 1 Fat

▼ Fresh Spinach, Orange and Red Onion Salad

Wilted Spinach Vinaigrette

PREP TIME: 10 MINUTES

1 tablespoon oil

2 garlic cloves, minced

1 (10-oz.) pkg. prewashed fresh spinach, stems removed

⅓ cup raisins

¼ cup shelled sunflower seeds or pine nuts

2 teaspoons sugar

2 tablespoons white wine vinegar

1. Heat oil in nonstick Dutch oven over medium heat until hot. Add garlic; cook 1 minute.

2. Add spinach and raisins; cook and stir about 1 minute or just until spinach is barely wilted. Remove from heat; stir in sunflower seeds, sugar and vinegar.

YIELD: 6 (½-CUP) SERVINGS

Nutrition Information Per Serving
Serving Size: ½ Cup

Calories................................100	Calories from Fat 45
	% Daily Value
Total Fat 5g	.................8%
Saturated 1g	.................5%
Cholesterol 0mg	.................0%
Sodium 40mg	.................2%
Total Carbohydrate.............10g	.................3%
Dietary Fiber 2g	.................8%
Sugars 7g	
Protein..............................3g	
Vitamin A...........................60%	Vitamin C 15%
Calcium 6%	Iron 10%

Dietary Exchanges: ½ Fruit, 1 Vegetable, 1 Fat OR ½ Carbohydrate, 1 Vegetable, 1 Fat

about **Sunflower Seeds**

Hulled sunflower seeds, available in health food stores, make a crunchy, nutty addition to salads, trail mixes and baked goods. They're available raw or roasted, plain or salted.

Antipasto Onion-Tomato Salad

PREP TIME: 10 MINUTES

Dressing
2 teaspoons red wine vinegar

2 teaspoons olive oil

½ teaspoon dried basil leaves

¼ teaspoon pepper

⅛ teaspoon salt

Salad
1 cup thinly sliced sweet onions, separated into rings

2 large tomatoes, thinly sliced

2 to 3 tablespoons sliced ripe olives

4 lettuce leaves

1. In small jar with tight-fitting lid, combine all dressing ingredients; shake until well blended.

2. In large bowl, combine onions, tomatoes and olives. Shake dressing and pour over salad; toss gently.

3. Line 4 individual salad plates with lettuce. Spoon salad onto lettuce.

YIELD: 4 SERVINGS

Nutrition Information Per Serving
Serving Size: ¼ of Recipe

Calories..................................60	Calories from Fat 25
	% Daily Value
Total Fat 3g	.................5%
Saturated 0g	.................0%
Cholesterol 0mg	.................0%
Sodium 135mg	.................6%
Total Carbohydrate.............8g	.................3%
Dietary Fiber 2g	.................8%
Sugars 4g	
Protein..............................1g	
Vitamin A...........................15%	Vitamin C 35%
Calcium 0%	Iron 4%

Dietary Exchanges: 1 Vegetable, 1 Fat

Artichoke Tabbouleh Salad

PREP TIME: 30 MINUTES

- **1 cup uncooked bulgur**
- **1 cup boiling water**
- **1 (6½-oz.) jar marinated artichoke hearts**
- **2 medium tomatoes, chopped**
- **¼ cup chopped green onions**
- **⅓ cup chopped fresh parsley**
- **3 tablespoons finely chopped fresh mint leaves**
- **2 tablespoons lemon juice**
- **⅛ teaspoon coarse ground black pepper**

1. In medium bowl, combine bulgur and boiling water. Let stand 15 to 20 minutes or until bulgur has doubled in size and water is absorbed.

2. Meanwhile, drain artichoke hearts, reserving marinade in small bowl; cut artichokes in half. Add halved artichokes, tomatoes, onions, parsley and mint to bulgur.

about Tabbouleh

Tabbouleh, a favorite Middle Eastern grain salad made with cracked wheat, usually uses fresh lemon and mint as seasoning.

3. Add lemon juice and pepper to reserved marinade; mix well. Add marinade mixture to bulgur mixture; toss gently to coat. Serve immediately, or cover and refrigerate until serving time.

YIELD: 6 (1-CUP) SERVINGS

Nutrition Information Per Serving
Serving Size: 1 Cup

Calories................170	Calories from Fat..........50	
	% Daily Value	
Total Fat................6g	................9%	
Saturated................1g	................5%	
Cholesterol................0mg	................0%	
Sodium................115mg	................5%	
Total Carbohydrate............24g	................8%	
Dietary Fiber................6g	................24%	
Sugars................3g		
Protein................4g		
Vitamin A................10%	Vitamin C................35%	
Calcium................4%	Iron................8%	

Dietary Exchanges: 1 Starch, 2 Vegetable, 1 Fat OR 1 Carbohydrate, 2 Vegetable, 1 Fat

Olive Oil *Guide*

Olive oils are graded according to acidity. The highest quality (and most expensive) are those with the lowest acidity. Store olive oil in a cool, dark place for up to two years.

Extra virgin Made with the first pressing of the olives, this oil has a full-bodied, fruity flavor and the lowest acidity (less than 1%); color can range from dark yellow to green. Flavor evaporates quickly under heat, so this oil is best on salads or as a marinade.

Virgin First-pressing oils with a higher acidity (usually 1 to 3%) are called virgin.

Fino Italian for "fine"; these olive oils are blends of extra-virgin and virgin.

Olive oil Oils simply labeled "olive oil" are a combination of processed lower-grade olive oil and virgin or extra-virgin olive oil. It makes a good all-purpose cooking oil with a smaller price tag.

Light Pure olive oil with less than 5 percent extra-virgin content. The "light" refers to color and flavor, which is bland, making this oil suitable for cooking and baking where the more distinctive olive oil flavor isn't desired. Because light olive oil has a higher smoke point than regular olive oil, it's a good choice when frying at high temperatures.

Asian Slaw

Salad
1½ **cups purchased broccoli coleslaw blend***

½ **cup fresh bean sprouts**

½ **cup chopped red bell pepper**

½ **cup sliced fresh mushrooms**

Dressing
2 **tablespoons cider vinegar**

1 **tablespoon oil**

1½ **teaspoons sugar**

1½ **teaspoons soy sauce**

about Bean Sprouts

Fresh mung bean sprouts, available at Asian markets and in the produce aisle of the grocery store, add crunch and mild flavor to salads and stir-fries. Sprouts are usually very inexpensive.

1. In medium bowl, combine all salad ingredients; mix well.

2. In small jar with tight-fitting lid, combine all dressing ingredients; shake until well blended. Pour over salad; toss to coat. Serve immediately, or cover and refrigerate until serving time.

YIELD: 4 (²/₃-CUP) SERVINGS

choosing and using Cooking Oils

With the wide variety of cooking oils available, choosing one has become a complex decision. It doesn't have to be.

- *What all oils have in common.* Every cooking oil contains about 14 grams of fat and 120 calories per tablespoon. Substituting one type of oil for another will not lower your fat intake nor reduce the number of calories you consume.

- *What differentiates oils.* Cooking oils have different levels of saturated, monounsaturated and polyunsaturated fatty acids. Monounsaturated and polyunsaturated fatty acids appear to be the most beneficial healthwise; they may help lower blood cholesterol. Saturated fats are the ones you want to keep to a minimum; they raise cholesterol. The other key differentiating factor between oils is flavor.

- *The bottom line.* All oils are 100 percent fat and should be used in moderation.

Canola oil is high in monounsaturated fats and is the lowest in saturated fats of all oils. It is clear, light and neutral tasting, making it a good all-purpose oil. First developed in Canada, its name is derived from "Canada Oil." Also called rapeseed oil, it is pressed from the seeds of rape, a green, leafy vegetable.

Olive oil has the highest level of monounsaturated fatty acids of all oils. It lends distinctive flavor to foods, which varies depending on whether the oil is a top-quality extra-virgin oil (intense flavor) or a milder "light" olive oil.

Peanut oil is made up primarily of monounsaturated and polyunsaturated fats. Use it in stir-fries when its peanut flavor would complement other ingredients.

Safflower, sunflower and corn oil are high in polyunsaturated fat. Their neutral flavors make them good all-purpose oils.

Sesame oil, made up almost equally of mono- and polyunsaturated fatty acids, gives distinctive flavor to many Asian dishes. Its flavor is strong; use it in very small amounts to season a dish in conjunction with another oil.

Walnut oil, primarily a polyunsaturated fat, has a nutty flavor that's good in salad dressings.

Tip: * If broccoli coleslaw blend is unavailable, 1¹/₂ cups finely chopped broccoli can be used.

Nutrition Information Per Serving
Serving Size: ²/₃ Cup

Calories	60	Calories from Fat	35
		% Daily Value	
Total Fat	4g		6%
Saturated	1g		5%
Cholesterol	0mg		0%
Sodium	150mg		6%
Total Carbohydrate	6g		2%
Dietary Fiber	1g		4%
Sugars	4g		
Protein	1g		
Vitamin A	15%	Vitamin C	70%
Calcium	0%	Iron	2%

Dietary Exchanges: 1 Vegetable, 1 Fat

Creamy Caesar Salad with Feta Cheese

■■■■■■■■■■■■■■■■■■■■

PREP TIME: 25 MINUTES

Dressing

¹/₃ cup fat-free mayonnaise or salad dressing

2 tablespoons grated Parmesan cheese

2 tablespoons lemon juice

1 garlic clove, minced

2 tablespoons skim milk

Croutons

4 whole wheat English muffins, split

Olive oil nonstick cooking spray

¹/₂ teaspoon garlic powder

Salad

6 cups torn mixed salad greens

12 cherry tomatoes, halved

1 large green bell pepper, chopped

4 oz. feta cheese, crumbled (¾ cup)

1. In small bowl, combine all dressing ingredients except milk; beat with wire whisk until smooth. Stir in milk. Set aside.

2. Heat oven to 400°F. Spray cut surfaces of muffin halves with nonstick cooking spray. Sprinkle with garlic powder. Cut into ¹/₂-inch pieces; place on ungreased cookie sheet. Bake at 400°F. for 8 to 10 minutes or until crisp.

3. Meanwhile, in large salad bowl, combine all salad ingredients. Add dressing; toss until well coated. Arrange salad on 4 individual salad plates. Top with croutons.

YIELD: 4 SERVINGS

Nutrition Information Per Serving
Serving Size: ¹/₄ of Recipe

Calories	290	Calories from Fat	90
		% Daily Value	
Total Fat	10g		15%
Saturated	5g		25%
Cholesterol	25mg		8%
Sodium	830mg		35%
Total Carbohydrate	37g		12%
Dietary Fiber	2g		8%
Sugars	7g		
Protein	12g		
Vitamin A	50%	Vitamin C	60%
Calcium	30%	Iron	10%

Dietary Exchanges: 2 Starch, 1 Vegetable, 1 High-Fat Meat OR 2 Carbohydrate, 1 Vegetable, 1 High-Fat Meat

■ PRODUCE POINTERS
cleaning Greens

Grit may be great when it comes to character, but it's not something you want to run across in your salad. Most greens benefit from careful cleaning, especially spinach, which grows in sandy soil and can be particularly dirty.

Fill a large bowl with cold tap water and submerge the torn greens for at least 10 minutes. Grit from the leaves will settle to the bottom of the bowl. Carefully lift out the greens and set them in a colander while you rinse the bowl clean and refill it. Repeat the process until you find no grit at the bottom of the bowl. Dry the greens by whirling them in a salad spinner or by rolling them in clean paper towels.

Celery root is not the lower portion of the common green celery stalk, but rather a plant also known as celeriac, the bulb of which does grow underground. Its gnarled brown skin covers crisp, creamy white flesh that's good grated raw into salads.

Apple–Celery Root Slaw

PREP TIME: 20 MINUTES

⅔ cup nonfat sour cream

3 tablespoons chopped green onions

1 tablespoon lemon juice

2 cups shredded unpeeled red apple

2 cups shredded peeled celery root (celeriac)

½ cup raisins

¼ cup chopped celery

2 tablespoons shelled sunflower seeds

1. In medium bowl, combine sour cream, onions and lemon juice; mix well.

2. Stir in all remaining ingredients. Serve immediately, or cover and refrigerate up to 2 hours before serving. (Shredded apple will discolor if stored for a longer period of time.)

YIELD: 8 (½-CUP) SERVINGS

Nutrition Information Per Serving
Serving Size: ½ Cup

Calories	100	Calories from Fat	10
		% Daily Value	
Total Fat	1g		2%
Saturated	0g		0%
Cholesterol	0mg		0%
Sodium	85mg		4%
Total Carbohydrate	19g		6%
Dietary Fiber	2g		8%
Sugars	13g		
Protein	3g		
Vitamin A	4%	Vitamin C	10%
Calcium	6%	Iron	4%

Dietary Exchanges: 1 Fruit, 1 Vegetable OR 1 Carbohydrate, 1 Vegetable

Chopped Garden Salad with Curry-Tarragon Dressing

PREP TIME: 20 MINUTES

Dressing

½ cup nonfat cottage cheese

¼ cup water

2 tablespoons fat-free mayonnaise or salad dressing

1 tablespoon honey

½ teaspoon curry powder

1 teaspoon finely chopped fresh tarragon

Salad

3 cups chopped mixed lettuce (iceberg, Bibb and/or romaine)

1 cup chopped green cabbage

⅓ cup golden raisins

⅓ cup diced carrot

⅓ cup thinly sliced radishes

1 small tart apple, chopped

1. In blender container, combine all dressing ingredients except tarragon; blend until smooth. Stir in tarragon.

2. In large salad bowl, combine all salad ingredients. Pour dressing over salad; toss gently to coat.

YIELD: 7 (1-CUP) SERVINGS

Nutrition Information Per Serving
Serving Size: 1 Cup

Calories	80	Calories from Fat	0
		% Daily Value	
Total Fat	0g		0%
Saturated	0g		0%
Cholesterol	0mg		0%
Sodium	125mg		5%
Total Carbohydrate	17g		6%
Dietary Fiber	2g		8%
Sugars	14g		
Protein	3g		
Vitamin A	40%	Vitamin C	15%
Calcium	4%	Iron	4%

Dietary Exchanges: 1 Fruit, 1 Vegetable OR 1 Carbohydrate, 1 Vegetable

Apple–Celery Root Slaw ▶

A **Vinegar** *Primer*

Balsamic vinegar In Modena, Italy, sweet white grape juice is fermented in wooden barrels for at least ten and up to seventy years to create balsamic vinegar. The final product is dark, rich, sweet and as complex as a fine wine. Splash it on salads or vegetables.

Cider vinegar Made from apple cider, this golden brown vinegar is one of the most pungent. Use it to pickle vegetables or add it to a hearty stew.

Distilled white vinegar A handy pantry item, this colorless vinegar is made from grain alcohol. Because of its high acidity, use it only for pickling, and household chores such as cleaning windows and to keep drains running free.

Fruit vinegar Cider or white wine vinegar combined with assorted fruits and berries produces a flavorful vinegar for vinaigrettes.

Herb or chile vinegar Add garlic, rosemary, dill or any other herb to wine vinegar and use it to flavor a salad, vegetable or main dish (or purchase one of the many preflavored varieties available). In the Caribbean and the American South, fresh chiles are steeped in vinegar and set on tables as a zesty condiment.

Malt vinegar A must in England for fish and chips, this caramel-colored vinegar is made from malted barley and has a sharp, jarring flavor.

Rice vinegar Japanese rice vinegar, made from sake, has a mild, sweet flavor. (China and Thailand also have their versions of rice vinegar, usually heavier and darker.) Use rice vinegar to pickle vegetables or season rice, in Asian dishes, or as a dipping sauce for egg rolls.

Wine vinegar Like wine, wine vinegar is available in red, white, sparkling, sherry and rosé, and by law must be 6 to 7 percent acidic. Indispensable in the kitchen, wine vinegar can dress a salad, perk up a main dish, even flavor berries.

Napoli Bread Salad

PREP TIME: 20 MINUTES

6 oz. (about 7 inches) plain or herb-flavored Italian bread, cut into ½-inch-thick slices

1 medium tomato, chopped

1 cup red or yellow cherry tomatoes, halved

1 cup sliced celery

3 tablespoons chopped fresh parsley

2 tablespoons grated Parmesan cheese

¼ cup purchased Caesar salad dressing

1. Grill or toast bread slices until lightly browned. Cut into ½-inch squares (about 5 cups).

2. In medium bowl, combine bread and all remaining ingredients; mix gently. If desired, serve with additional grated cheese.

YIELD: 8 (½-CUP) SERVINGS

Nutrition Information Per Serving
Serving Size: ½ Cup

Calories................110	Calories from Fat..........45
	% Daily Value
Total Fat 5g	..........8%
Saturated 1g	..........5%
Cholesterol 3mg	..........1%
Sodium 270mg	..........11%
Total Carbohydrate 13g	..........4%
Dietary Fiber 1g	..........4%
Sugars 2g	
Protein..................3g	
Vitamin A 6%	Vitamin C 15%
Calcium 6%	Iron..................6%

Dietary Exchanges: 1 Starch, 1 Fat OR 1 Carbohydrate, 1 Fat

Farmers' Market Salad

■ ■ ■ ■ ■ ■ ■ ■ ■ ■ ■ ■ ■ ■ ■ ■ ■ ■

PREP TIME: 20 MINUTES

¼ lb. fresh green beans, cooked (1 cup)*

3 Italian plum tomatoes, cut into wedges

1 cup frozen artichoke hearts (from 9-oz. pkg.), cooked, drained

¼ cup coarsely chopped fresh basil

2 tablespoons honey

1 tablespoon lemon juice

Dash salt

3 cups torn Boston lettuce

½ small avocado, peeled, thinly sliced

2 tablespoons crumbled chèvre (goat) cheese, if desired

1. In large bowl, combine green beans, tomatoes, artichokes and basil; mix well.

2. In small bowl, combine honey, lemon juice and salt; mix well. Drizzle over vegetables; toss lightly to coat.

3. Arrange lettuce on large platter. Spoon vegetable mixture over lettuce. Garnish with avocado slices. Sprinkle with cheese.

YIELD: 4 (1½-CUP) SERVINGS

Tip: * To cook green beans, combine beans and ½ cup water in medium saucepan. Bring to a boil. Reduce heat; cover and simmer 5 to 10 minutes or until beans are crisp-tender. Drain; rinse with cold water. Drain well.

Nutrition Information Per Serving
Serving Size: 1½ Cups

Calories	140	Calories from Fat	45
		% Daily Value	
Total Fat	5g		8%
Saturated	1g		5%
Cholesterol	2mg		1%
Sodium	80mg		3%
Total Carbohydrate	19g		6%
Dietary Fiber	5g		20%
Sugars	12g		
Protein	4g		
Vitamin A	25%	Vitamin C	35%
Calcium	4%	Iron	8%

Dietary Exchanges: ½ Fruit, 2 Vegetable, 1 Fat OR ½ Carbohydrate, 2 Vegetable, 1 Fat

Mixed Potato Salad

■ ■ ■ ■ ■ ■ ■ ■ ■ ■ ■ ■ ■ ■ ■ ■ ■ ■

PREP TIME: 25 MINUTES
(READY IN 1 HOUR)

Salad

3 lb. red potatoes

2 lb. sweet potatoes

1 cup chopped celery

1 medium cucumber, peeled, seeded and chopped

Dressing

1 (8-oz.) container nonfat plain yogurt

¼ cup chopped fresh dill or 1 tablespoon dried dill weed

¼ cup reduced-calorie mayonnaise or salad dressing

1 tablespoon lemon juice

¼ teaspoon salt

1. Place whole red and sweet potatoes separately in 2 Dutch ovens or large saucepans; cover with water. Bring to a boil. Reduce heat; simmer until tender. Simmer red potatoes 20 to 25 minutes; simmer sweet potatoes 30 to 35 minutes.

2. Drain potatoes; rinse with cold water to cool. Peel potatoes; cut into cubes.

3. In large serving bowl, combine potatoes, celery and cucumber; mix well.

4. In medium bowl, combine all dressing ingredients; blend well. Pour dressing over salad; toss gently. Serve immediately, or cover and refrigerate until serving time.

YIELD: 24 (½-CUP) SERVINGS

Nutrition Information Per Serving
Serving Size: ½ Cup

Calories	80	Calories from Fat	10
		% Daily Value	
Total Fat	1g		2%
Saturated	0g		0%
Cholesterol	0mg		0%
Sodium	55mg		2%
Total Carbohydrate	16g		5%
Dietary Fiber	2g		8%
Sugars	5g		
Protein	2g		
Vitamin A	90%	Vitamin C	15%
Calcium	4%	Iron	2%

Dietary Exchanges: 1 Starch OR 1 Carbohydrate

a guide to **Greens**

Arugula (*ah-ROO-guh-lah*) Unless you like a bit of bite with every bite, this peppery green, also called rocket or roquette, is best mixed with milder lettuces.

Belgian endive Because it's cultivated in the dark, and photosynthesis is blocked, this "green" is actually mostly white, shading to pale yellow or light green at the tip. It has a pleasantly bitter flavor. Mix slices of it with other greens or trim off the bottom and separate the leaves to line a salad bowl.

Bibb or Boston lettuce Bibb and Boston are two of the most common varieties of butterhead lettuce. Buttery tasting and delicate, this hothouse lettuce is perfect for fruit salads.

Chicory or curly endive The pleasingly bitter taste makes this an interesting "mixer" for other lettuces. It also makes an attractive platter liner.

Iceberg lettuce Popular with kids and fast-food establishments, iceberg heads are pale green outside and almost white inside with crisp, very mild leaves.

Napa or Chinese cabbage Mild in flavor and heavily ribbed, this cabbage is equally good lightly stir-fried or raw in salads with crunchy Oriental vegetables, meats and chicken.

Radicchio Radicchio tends to be more expensive than other salad ingredients, but a little goes a long way. Its red-and-white leaves have an assertive, somewhat bitter flavor

that complements milder greens very well and is especially good in salads with lots of garlic and marinated vegetables.

Red cabbage Substitute red cabbage for green in any favorite salad or slaw; the maroon-purple leaves make a nice color contrast.

Red leaf lettuce As mild as the green leaf variety, this lettuce has a very tender texture. Use it with light dressings and fruits or mix with other greens.

Romaine Long a Caesar salad staple, this hearty lettuce has mild, heavily ribbed leaves that shade from dark green on the outside of the head to progressively paler, sweeter and crisper inside. Now you can buy just the hearts in some supermarkets. Tear it up into any salad.

Savoy cabbage The frilly texture of this mild cabbage makes its leaves perfect as a salad bowl liner, as a cradle for a salad mixture or as a shredded green.

Sorrel (*SOR-uhl*) Similar in shape to spinach leaves, young sorrel leaves can be used as you would spinach. Its flavor has a lemon tang.

Spinach Substitute fresh spinach for lettuce in any of your favorite green salads. Or try it as a base for curried chicken or fruit salads.

Watercress This delicate-looking, somewhat spicy green mixes well with spinach, Belgian endive or strong cheeses like blue or feta; it can stand up to the most tangy vinaigrette.

Orange-Carrot Slaw

PREP TIME: 15 MINUTES

Salad

3 cups shredded carrots

1 (11-oz.) can mandarin orange segments, drained

1 cup halved seedless green grapes

Dressing

½ cup low-fat orange yogurt

1 teaspoon cider vinegar

¼ teaspoon ginger

1. In serving bowl, combine all salad ingredients; mix well.

2. In small bowl, combine all dressing ingredients; blend well. Pour dressing over salad; mix thoroughly. Serve immediately, or cover and refrigerate until serving time.

YIELD: 8 (½-CUP) SERVINGS

Nutrition Information Per Serving
Serving Size: ½ Cup

Calories	60	Calories from Fat	0
		% Daily Value	
Total Fat	0g		0%
Saturated	0g		0%
Cholesterol	0mg		0%
Sodium	25mg		1%
Total Carbohydrate	14g		5%
Dietary Fiber	2g		8%
Sugars	11g		
Protein	1g		
Vitamin A	240%	Vitamin C	25%
Calcium	4%	Iron	0%

Dietary Exchanges: ½ Fruit, 1 Vegetable OR ½ Carbohydrate, 1 Vegetable

storing **Greens**

Refrigerate greens, unwashed, in a plastic bag. Tuck a paper towel into the bag to absorb excess moisture and prevent rot.

Spring Salad with Honey-Mustard Dressing

PREP TIME: 20 MINUTES

Salad

4 cups torn Bibb or leaf lettuce

2 cups torn curly endive

⅓ cup thinly sliced radishes

3 tablespoons thinly sliced green onions

Dressing

1 tablespoon apple juice

2 teaspoons honey

1 teaspoon olive oil

1 teaspoon white wine vinegar

1 teaspoon Dijon mustard

1. In large bowl, combine all salad ingredients; toss gently.

2. In small jar with tight-fitting lid, combine all dressing ingredients; shake until well blended. Pour dressing over salad; toss gently to mix.

YIELD: 6 (1⅓-CUP) SERVINGS

Nutrition Information Per Serving
Serving Size: 1⅓ Cups

Calories	45	Calories from Fat	20
		% Daily Value	
Total Fat	2g		3%
Saturated	0g		0%
Cholesterol	0mg		0%
Sodium	10mg		0%
Total Carbohydrate	6g		2%
Dietary Fiber	2g		8%
Sugars	5g		
Protein	1g		
Vitamin A	20%	Vitamin C	15%
Calcium	4%	Iron	4%

Dietary Exchanges: 1 Vegetable, ½ Fat

make-ahead Salads

Zucchini Salad with Hot Bacon Dressing

PREP TIME: 25 MINUTES

Dressing

2 slices bacon

¼ cup finely chopped onion

2 tablespoons sugar

2 teaspoons cornstarch

⅓ cup cider vinegar or lemon juice

⅓ cup water

1 teaspoon soy sauce or Worcestershire sauce

¼ teaspoon pepper

Salad

4 medium zucchini, shredded, drained (4 cups)

1 medium carrot, shredded

1. In small nonstick skillet or saucepan, cook bacon until crisp. Drain on paper towels.

2. Reserve 1 tablespoon bacon drippings in skillet. Add onion; cook over medium heat for 1 to 2 minutes or until tender. Stir in sugar and cornstarch. Blend in remaining dressing ingredients. Cook until mixture boils and thickens, stirring constantly. Cool slightly.

3. In large bowl, combine zucchini and carrot; toss to mix. Pour hot dressing over salad mixture; toss to coat. Crumble cooked bacon; sprinkle over salad.

YIELD: 6 (½-CUP) SERVINGS

Nutrition Information Per Serving
Serving Size: ½ Cup

Calories	60	Calories from Fat	10
		% Daily Value	
Total Fat	1g		2%
Saturated	0g		0%
Cholesterol	0mg		0%
Sodium	100mg		4%
Total Carbohydrate	11g		4%
Dietary Fiber	2g		8%
Sugars	8g		
Protein	2g		
Vitamin A	80%	Vitamin C	25%
Calcium	2%	Iron	4%

Dietary Exchanges: 2 Vegetable

Soups, Stews and Chilies

Ratatouille Stew (page 94)

Black Bean and Corn Soup

· ·

PREP TIME: 30 MINUTES

¾ lb. lean ground beef round

2 cups frozen whole kernel corn

2 (15-oz.) cans black beans, drained, rinsed

1 (14.5-oz.) can diced tomatoes, undrained

1 (14½-oz.) can ready-to-serve beef broth

1 teaspoon cumin

3 teaspoons chili powder

1. Spray nonstick Dutch oven or large saucepan with nonstick cooking spray. Add ground beef; cook over medium-high heat until browned. Drain beef on paper towels.

2. Return beef to Dutch oven. Add all remaining ingredients; mix well. Bring to a boil. Reduce heat; cover and simmer 15 minutes to blend flavors.

YIELD: 5 (1⅓-CUP) SERVINGS

Nutrition Information Per Serving
Serving Size: 1⅓ Cups

Calories	350	Calories from Fat	100
		% Daily Value	
Total Fat	11g		17%
Saturated	4g		20%
Cholesterol	40mg		13%
Sodium	800mg		33%
Total Carbohydrate	38g		13%
Dietary Fiber	10g		40%
Sugars	5g		
Protein	24g		
Vitamin A	20%	Vitamin C	20%
Calcium	8%	Iron	20%

Dietary Exchanges: 2 Starch, 1 Vegetable, 2 Medium-Fat Meat OR 2 Carbohydrate, 1 Vegetable, 2 Medium-Fat Meat

▼ Black Bean and Corn Soup

If you open a can of this corn product (which is whole corn kernels that have been processed to remove the hull and the germ), you'll have a favorite ingredient of Latin American cooking that makes a hearty soup thickener. The beloved "grits" of the American South is simply ground dried hominy.

Hominy Soup à la Mexicana

■ ■ ■ ■ ■ ■ ■ ■ ■ ■ ■ ■ ■ ■ ■ ■ ■ ■ ■

PREP TIME: 25 MINUTES
(READY IN 45 MINUTES)

¾ lb. extra-lean ground beef

⅓ cup finely chopped red bell pepper

2 (15.5-oz.) cans hominy, drained, rinsed

1 (14½-oz.) can ready-to-serve vegetable or beef broth

1 (12-oz.) bottle mild tomatillo or green taco sauce

2 cups water

2 teaspoons dried basil or marjoram leaves

Chopped fresh cilantro, if desired

1. In large nonstick saucepan or Dutch oven, cook ground beef and bell pepper over medium-high heat for 4 to 6 minutes or until beef is lightly browned, stirring occasionally. Remove beef mixture from saucepan; drain on paper towels. Return beef mixture to saucepan.

2. Stir in all remaining ingredients except cilantro. Bring to a boil. Reduce heat to medium; cover and cook 15 minutes to blend flavors.

3. To serve, ladle soup into 6 individual soup bowls. Sprinkle each with cilantro.

YIELD: 6 (1¼-CUP) SERVINGS

Nutrition Information Per Serving
Serving Size: 1¼ Cups

Calories	240	Calories from Fat	80
			% Daily Value
Total Fat	9g		14%
Saturated	3g		15%
Cholesterol	35mg		12%
Sodium	850mg		35%
Total Carbohydrate	26g		9%
Dietary Fiber	4g		16%
Sugars	3g		
Protein	13g		
Vitamin A	8%	Vitamin C	15%
Calcium	2%	Iron	10%

Dietary Exchanges: 1½ Starch, 1½ Medium-Fat Meat OR
1½ Carbohydrate, 1½ Medium-Fat Meat

Tomatillos are an important ingredient in Latin American cooking, especially when combined with green chile peppers to make a spicy condiment. They look like overgrown green cherry tomatoes in papery skins and have a flavor that is somewhat reminiscent of a tart apple. Look for fresh tomatillos in the produce section or canned tomatillos or jars of tomatillo salsa in the Latin American aisle of the grocery store.

Curried Sweet Potato Soup

PREP TIME: 15 MINUTES
(READY IN 35 MINUTES)

2 (14½-oz.) cans ready-to-serve fat-free chicken broth with ⅓ less sodium

2 cups coarsely chopped onions

2 to 3 garlic cloves, minced

3 teaspoons curry powder

2 teaspoons paprika

1 (18-oz.) can vacuum-packed sweet potatoes, chopped

1 (15-oz.) can garbanzo beans, drained

1 (14.5- or 16-oz.) can whole tomatoes, undrained, cut up

2 tablespoons frozen orange juice concentrate, thawed

⅓ cup chopped fresh parsley

1. Spray nonstick Dutch oven with nonstick cooking spray. Add ¼ cup of the broth; bring to a boil over medium-high heat. Add onions and garlic; cook 2 to 3 minutes or until liquid has almost evaporated, stirring frequently.

2. Stir in curry powder and paprika. Add remaining broth and all remaining ingredients except parsley. Bring to a boil. Reduce heat; cover and simmer 20 minutes or until sweet potatoes begin to fall apart. Mash any remaining chunks of sweet potato with back of spoon. Stir in parsley.

YIELD: 8 (1-CUP) SERVINGS

Nutrition Information Per Serving
Serving Size: 1 Cup

Calories	150	Calories from Fat 10
		% Daily Value
Total Fat 1g		2%
Saturated 0g		0%
Cholesterol 0mg		0%
Sodium 440mg		18%
Total Carbohydrate 30g		10%
Dietary Fiber 6g		24%
Sugars 15g		
Protein 6g		
Vitamin A 120%	Vitamin C 45%	
Calcium 6%	Iron 10%	

Dietary Exchanges: 2 Starch OR 2 Carbohydrate

Easy Vegetable Minestrone

PREP TIME: 25 MINUTES

3 (14½-oz.) cans ready-to-serve fat-free chicken broth with ⅓ less sodium

1 (14.5- or 16-oz.) can whole tomatoes, undrained, cut up

1 (6-oz.) can no-salt-added tomato paste

1 teaspoon dried basil leaves

½ teaspoon dried thyme leaves

¼ to ½ teaspoon pepper

3 oz. (1 cup) uncooked rotini (spiral pasta)

2 cups frozen mixed vegetables

1 (19-oz.) can cannellini or great northern beans, drained

1. In large nonstick saucepan, combine broth, tomatoes, tomato paste, basil, thyme and pepper; mix well. Bring to a boil.

2. Stir in all remaining ingredients. Simmer 10 to 15 minutes or until rotini and vegetables are tender. If desired, sprinkle with Parmesan cheese.

YIELD: 6 (1½-CUP) SERVINGS

about **Curry Powder**

Curry, a linchpin of the cuisine of India, is not a single spice but a complex blend with many variations. While you can certainly roast and grind spices for curry yourself (as traditional Indian cooks do daily), commercially available blends are convenient. The blends typically contain sharp spices such as black and red pepper and ginger in combination with sweet spices such as cinnamon, mace, dried coriander and cardamom, rounded out by "warm" flavors such as cumin, turmeric and fenugreek.

Nutrition Information Per Serving
Serving Size: 1½ Cups

Calories................................210	Calories from Fat 10	
	% Daily Value	
Total Fat 1g	...............................2%	
Saturated 0g	...............................0%	
Cholesterol 0mg	...............................0%	
Sodium 790mg	.............................33%	
Total Carbohydrate.............37g	.............................12%	
Dietary Fiber....................7g	.............................28%	
Sugars 6g		
Protein.............................12g		
Vitamin A............................40%	Vitamin C 30%	
Calcium 8%	Iron 20%	

Dietary Exchanges: 2 Starch, 1 Vegetable, 1 Very Lean Meat OR
2 Carbohydrate, 1 Vegetable, 1 Very Lean Meat

Hearty Tomato-Bean Soup

P REP T IME: 30 MINUTES

½ **cup chopped onion**

½ **cup chopped celery**

1 **(28-oz.) can whole tomatoes, undrained, cut up**

1 **(15.5-oz.) can light or dark red kidney beans, drained**

▼ Hearty Tomato-Bean Soup

1 **(11-oz.) can vacuum-packed whole kernel corn, undrained**

1 **(10¾-oz.) can condensed tomato soup**

½ **cup water**

1 **teaspoon sugar**

¼ **teaspoon dried thyme leaves, crushed**

⅛ **teaspoon pepper**

1. Spray 4-quart nonstick saucepan or Dutch oven with nonstick cooking spray. Add onion and celery; cook and stir until tender.

2. Stir in all remaining ingredients. Bring to a boil. Reduce heat to low; cover and simmer 10 to 15 minutes or until thoroughly heated.

Y IELD: 6 (1⅓-CUP) SERVINGS

Nutrition Information Per Serving
Serving Size: 1⅓ Cups

Calories................................190	Calories from Fat 20	
	% Daily Value	
Total Fat 2g	...............................3%	
Saturated 0g	...............................0%	
Cholesterol 0mg	...............................0%	
Sodium 720mg	.............................30%	
Total Carbohydrate.............35g	.............................12%	
Dietary Fiber....................8g	.............................32%	
Sugars 9g		
Protein.............................7g		
Vitamin A............................25%	Vitamin C 60%	
Calcium 6%	Iron 20%	

Dietary Exchanges: 2½ Starch OR 2½ Carbohydrate

Chicken and Root Vegetable Soup

PREP TIME: 25 MINUTES
(READY IN 45 MINUTES)

2 teaspoons oil

3 boneless, skinless chicken breast halves, cut into 1-inch pieces

1 medium onion, chopped

1 (10½-oz.) can condensed chicken broth

1⅔ cups water

3 medium carrots, cut into ¼-inch-thick slices (2 cups)

3 medium parsnips, peeled, cut into ¼-inch-thick slices (2 cups)

2 small turnips, peeled, cut into ¼-inch-thick slices and quartered (1 cup)

1 tablespoon chopped fresh thyme or 1 teaspoon dried thyme leaves

¼ cup chopped fresh parsley

1. Heat oil in large nonstick saucepan or Dutch oven until hot. Add chicken and onion; cook about 5 minutes or until chicken is no longer pink.

2. Add broth, water, carrots, parsnips, turnips and thyme; mix well. Bring to a boil. Reduce heat; cover and simmer 15 to 20 minutes or until vegetables are tender. Stir in parsley.

YIELD: 4 (1⅔-CUP) SERVINGS

Nutrition Information Per Serving
Serving Size: 1⅔ Cups

Calories................................260	Calories from Fat 50
	% Daily Value
Total Fat 6g	.........9%
Saturated 1g	.........5%
Cholesterol 55mg	.......18%
Sodium 580mg	.......24%
Total Carbohydrate 25g	.........8%
Dietary Fiber 7g	.......28%
Sugars 9g	
Protein 26g	
Vitamin A 310%	Vitamin C 35%
Calcium 10%	Iron 15%

Dietary Exchanges: 1½ Starch, 1 Vegetable, 3 Very Lean Meat OR
1½ Carbohydrate, 1 Vegetable, 3 Very Lean Meat

◀ Chicken and Root Vegetable Soup

Root *Vegetables*

Two underappreciated root vegetables add flavor and body to soups:

Parsnips Sweet nutty parsnips look like white carrots, but with fatter tops and skinnier ends. They get high nutritional ratings for fiber, vitamin C and folacin, a B vitamin especially important for women. Parsnips are best during the winter months. Peel them, then add to soup; steam them solo or with carrots; mash them with potatoes or turnips.

Turnips Firm, smooth and round, turnips have white flesh with a white skin tinged with purple. Small, young turnips are sweeter than older turnips, which develop a stronger flavor and woody texture. They provide vitamin C and fiber. Peel them and use them raw in salads; toss them into stir-fries; boil or steam them, then mash or puree, with or without potatoes.

tips for Freezing Soup

Many soups freeze well, giving you a ready arsenal of homemade last-minute suppers or lunches.

- Freeze soup in individual portions for flexibility, unless you're sure you'll be feeding a crowd.

- When using glass containers, select only those that are recommended for the freezer, such as canning jars. Other glass containers could shatter when food freezes and expands.

- Label containers with waterproof marker on freezer tape, adhesive labels or tie-on labels. Include the name of the soup and the date it was prepared.

- Most soups will retain best color, flavor and texture if frozen for no more than four to six weeks.

- Seal loose-fitting lids with freezer tape, which sticks better in cold temperatures than masking tape.

- Use a freezer thermometer to make sure the temperature stays at 0°F.

- Liquids expand as they freeze, so leave 1/2 inch empty at the top of the container.

- For a single portion, microwave reheating is convenient. Since multiple servings take proportionately longer in the microwave, heat larger batches on the stovetop.

Creamy Chicken and Pasta Soup

PREP TIME: 20 MINUTES

2 (14½-oz.) cans ready-to-serve fat-free chicken broth with ⅓ less sodium

5¼ oz. (2 cups) uncooked medium shell pasta

3 boneless, skinless chicken breast halves, cut into ½-inch cubes

4 cups skim milk

½ cup all-purpose flour

1 cup frozen sweet peas

1 (2-oz.) jar chopped pimientos, drained

½ to ¾ teaspoon dried basil leaves

Dash white pepper

1. In nonstick Dutch oven, bring broth to a boil. Add pasta and chicken. Reduce heat; cover and simmer 9 to 11 minutes or until pasta is of desired doneness.

2. In small bowl or jar with tight-fitting lid, combine 1 cup of the milk and flour. Beat with wire whisk or shake until well blended.

3. Add flour mixture, remaining 3 cups milk, peas, pimientos, basil and pepper to broth mixture; cook and stir over medium heat until soup is bubbly and thickened and chicken is no longer pink. If desired, add salt to taste.

YIELD: 6 (1½-CUP) SERVINGS

Nutrition Information Per Serving
Serving Size: 1½ Cups

Calories	280	Calories from Fat	20
		% Daily Value	
Total Fat	2g		3%
Saturated	1g		5%
Cholesterol	40mg		13%
Sodium	470mg		20%
Total Carbohydrate	39g		13%
Dietary Fiber	2g		8%
Sugars	9g		
Protein	26g		
Vitamin A	15%	Vitamin C	20%
Calcium	20%	Iron	15%

Dietary Exchanges: 2½ Starch, 2 Very Lean Meat OR 2½ Carbohydrate, 2 Very Lean Meat

Creole Chicken Gumbo Soup

■ ■ ■ ■ ■ ■ ■ ■ ■ ■ ■ ■ ■ ■ ■ ■ ■ ■ ■ ■

PREP TIME: 30 MINUTES

1 tablespoon margarine or butter

½ cup chopped green bell pepper

½ cup chopped onion

1 garlic clove, minced

1 tablespoon all-purpose flour

1 cup water

1 (14½-oz.) can ready-to-serve chicken broth

1 (14.5-oz.) can no-salt-added whole tomatoes, undrained, cut up

1 (10-oz.) pkg. frozen cut okra

1½ cups cubed cooked chicken

¼ cup uncooked regular long-grain white rice

¼ teaspoon dried thyme leaves

1 bay leaf

4 to 8 drops hot pepper sauce

1. Melt margarine in large nonstick saucepan over medium heat. Add bell pepper, onion, garlic and flour; cook and stir until flour is light golden brown.

2. Add all remaining ingredients. Bring to a boil. Reduce heat to medium-low; cover and cook 10 minutes. Uncover; cook an additional 10 to 15 minutes or until okra is tender, stirring occasionally. Remove and discard bay leaf.

YIELD: 6 (1-CUP) SERVINGS

Nutrition Information Per Serving
Serving Size: 1 Cup

Calories	180	Calories from Fat	60
		% Daily Value	
Total Fat	7g		11%
Saturated	2g		10%
Cholesterol	30mg		10%
Sodium	280mg		12%
Total Carbohydrate	16g		5%
Dietary Fiber	2g		8%
Sugars	3g		
Protein	14g		
Vitamin A	10%	Vitamin C	30%
Calcium	8%	Iron	10%

Dietary Exchanges: ½ Starch, 2 Vegetable, 1 Lean Meat, 1 Fat OR ½ Carbohydrate, 2 Vegetable, 1 Lean Meat, 1 Fat

Lima Bean, Corn and Chicken Soup

■ ■ ■ ■ ■ ■ ■ ■ ■ ■ ■ ■ ■ ■ ■ ■ ■ ■ ■ ■

PREP TIME: 30 MINUTES

2 boneless skinless chicken breast halves, cut into thin strips

2 (14½-oz.) cans ready-to-serve chicken broth

1 (10 oz.) pkg. frozen lima beans

2 cups frozen whole kernel corn

¼ cup uncooked quick-cooking barley

½ teaspoon dried summer savory leaves

½ teaspoon dried sage leaves

1. Spray large nonstick saucepan or Dutch oven with nonstick cooking spray. Heat over medium-high heat until hot. Add chicken; cook and stir 4 to 5 minutes or until no longer pink.

2. Add all remaining ingredients. Bring to a boil. Reduce heat; cover and simmer 10 to 15 minutes or until barley is tender, stirring occasionally.

YIELD: 4 (1½-CUP) SERVINGS

Nutrition Information Per Serving
Serving Size: 1½ Cup

Calories	290	Calories from Fat	35
		% Daily Value	
Total Fat	4g		6%
Saturated	1g		5%
Cholesterol	35mg		11%
Sodium	810mg		34%
Total Carbohydrate	39g		13%
Dietary Fiber	7g		28%
Sugars	3g		
Protein	25g		
Vitamin A	2%	Vitamin C	0%
Calcium	4%	Iron	15%

Dietary Exchanges: 2 Starch, 2 Vegetable, 2 Very Lean Meat, OR 2 Carbohydrate, 2 Vegetable, 2 Very Lean Meat

Light Chicken–Wild Rice Soup

PREP TIME: 30 MINUTES

2 (14½-oz.) cans ready-to-serve fat-free chicken broth with ⅓ less sodium

3 boneless, skinless chicken breast halves, cut into ¾-inch pieces

1 (6.2-oz.) pkg. quick-cooking long-grain and wild rice mix (with seasoning packet)

4 cups skim milk

¾ cup all-purpose flour

4 slices bacon, crisply cooked, crumbled

1½ teaspoons diced pimientos

1 tablespoon dry sherry, if desired

1. In nonstick Dutch oven or large saucepan, combine broth, chicken, rice and seasoning packet; mix well. Bring to a boil. Reduce heat; cover and simmer 5 to 10 minutes or until rice is tender.

2. In small jar with tight-fitting lid, combine 1 cup of the milk and flour; shake until well blended.

3. Add flour mixture, remaining 3 cups milk, bacon, pimientos and sherry to rice mixture; cook and stir over medium heat until soup is bubbly and thickened and chicken is no longer pink. If desired, add salt and pepper to taste.

YIELD: 6 (1½-CUP) SERVINGS

Nutrition Information Per Serving
Serving Size: 1½ Cups

Calories	310	Calories from Fat	35
		% Daily Value	
Total Fat	4g		6%
Saturated	1g		5%
Cholesterol	45mg		15%
Sodium	850mg		35%
Total Carbohydrate	42g		14%
Dietary Fiber	1g		4%
Sugars	9g		
Protein	27g		
Vitamin A	8%	Vitamin C	6%
Calcium	20%	Iron	15%

Dietary Exchanges: 3 Starch, 2 Very Lean Meat OR 3 Carbohydrate, 2 Very Lean Meat

Super Soup Noodles

Long flat noodles are traditional in canned chicken soup, though smaller noodles are easier to spoon up with broth. Whichever noodle you choose, plan to add it close enough to serving time so it's in the pot just long enough to cook it (or heat it) through; oversimmering will make the noodles mushy. Don't add too much pasta (or rice) if you anticipate leftovers; the noodles will continue to absorb liquid as they sit, resulting in soggy noodles and soup that's sludgy rather than "soupy."

Some good soup noodles:

Acini di pepe ("peppercorns") Tiny dot-shaped pasta

Alphabet noodles Fun for kids

Ditalini and tubettini Tiny short tubes

Egg pastina Very tiny, quick-cooking particles

Elbow macaroni Hollow C-shaped tubes

Fine egg noodles Visually reminiscent of bits of straw

Lasagna bits Ruffled miniatures of the full-sized favorites

Orzo, also called rosamarina Rice-shaped pasta

Pasta mista An assortment of small noodles in various lengths and widths

Rotini Little corkscrew shapes; tricolor blends are available

Shell pasta Look for small or medium varieties

Stelline ("little stars") A whimsical change of pace for dreamers

▲ Italian Turkey Soup

Italian Turkey Soup

PREP TIME: 25 MINUTES

½ lb. lean ground turkey

½ teaspoon fennel seed, crushed

½ teaspoon anise seed, crushed

2 garlic cloves, minced

2 (14.5-oz.) cans no-salt-added stewed
   tomatoes, undrained

1 (8-oz.) can no-salt-added tomato sauce

2 cups water

1 teaspoon dried basil leaves

1 teaspoon dried oregano leaves

½ teaspoon salt

½ cup uncooked orzo or rosamarina
   (rice-shaped pasta)

1. Spray nonstick Dutch oven or large saucepan with nonstick cooking spray. Add turkey, fennel seed, anise seed and garlic; cook over medium-high heat until turkey is no longer pink.

2. Add all remaining ingredients except orzo; mix well. Bring to a boil. Add orzo; return to a boil. Reduce heat to medium-low; cover and cook 12 minutes or until orzo is tender.

YIELD: 6 (1¼-CUP) SERVINGS

Nutrition Information Per Serving
Serving Size: 1¼ Cups

Calories 150	Calories from Fat 35	
	% Daily Value	
Total Fat 4g	.................6%	
Saturated 1g	.................5%	
Cholesterol 30mg	...............10%	
Sodium 240mg	...............10%	
Total Carbohydrate 19g	.................6%	
Dietary Fiber 2g	.................8%	
Sugars 5g		
Protein 10g		
Vitamin A 6%	Vitamin C 35%	
Calcium 6%	Iron 10%	

Dietary Exchanges: 1 Starch, 1 Vegetable, 1 Lean Meat OR
1 Carbohydrate, 1 Vegetable, 1 Lean Meat

Bean and Smoked Sausage Soup

■ ■

PREP TIME: 30 MINUTES

1 small onion, chopped

1 cup thinly sliced celery

1 cup chopped carrots

2 (14½-oz.) cans ready-to-serve fat-free chicken broth with ⅓ less sodium

2 (15.5-oz.) cans great northern beans, drained, rinsed

4 oz. smoked 95% fat-free turkey sausage, coarsely chopped

½ teaspoon dried thyme leaves, crushed

1 tablespoon chopped fresh parsley

¼ teaspoon pepper

1. In large nonstick saucepan, combine onion, celery, carrots and ¼ cup of the broth; cook over medium heat for 3 minutes or until onion is tender.

2. Stir in remaining broth and all remaining ingredients. Bring to a boil. Reduce heat; simmer 10 to 15 minutes or until celery and carrots are tender.

YIELD: 4 (1¾-CUP) SERVINGS

Nutrition Information Per Serving
Serving Size: 1¾ Cups

Calories...............................240	Calories from Fat 25
	% Daily Value
Total Fat ....3g...................................5%	
Saturated ....0g.................................0%	
Cholesterol ....20mg...............................7%	
Sodium..........................1,150mg.........................48%	
Total Carbohydrate............35g...........................12%	
Dietary Fiber ....11g.............................44%	
Sugars 4g	
Protein 17g	
Vitamin A..........................170%	Vitamin C 15%
Calcium 20%	Iron 20%

Dietary Exchanges: 2 Starch, 1 Vegetable, 1 Lean Meat OR
2 Carbohydrate, 1 Vegetable, 1 Lean Meat

One Bean *for another*

■ ■ ■ ■ ■ ■ ■ ■ ■ ■ ■ ■ ■ ■ ■

Bean choices in classic recipes are often based on ethnic traditions, but that doesn't mean you can't use a different bean. Beans are fairly interchangeable, so follow your own tastes or bean availability when choosing which bean to cook with.

Southwestern Turkey Chili Soup

■ ■ ■ ■ ■ ■ ■ ■ ■ ■ ■ ■ ■ ■ ■ ■ ■ ■ ■ ■

PREP TIME: 30 MINUTES

½ lb. lean ground turkey breast

1 (15.5-oz.) can light or dark red kidney beans, drained, rinsed

1 (14.5-oz.) can salsa tomatoes diced with green chiles, undrained*

1 (8-oz.) can tomato sauce

4 cups water

3 teaspoons beef-flavor instant bouillon

½ teaspoon chili powder

¼ teaspoon cumin

1. In large nonstick saucepan, brown ground turkey. Add all remaining ingredients; mix well. Bring to a boil.

2. Reduce heat to low; simmer 15 to 20 minutes to blend flavors, stirring occasionally.

YIELD: 6 (1⅓-CUP) SERVINGS

Tip: * If desired, Mexican-style stewed tomatoes or any spicy tomatoes can be substituted for the salsa tomatoes.

Nutrition Information Per Serving
Serving Size: 1⅓ Cups

Calories	140	Calories from Fat	10
		% Daily Value	
Total Fat	1g		2%
Saturated	0g		0%
Cholesterol	25mg		8%
Sodium	910mg		38%
Total Carbohydrate	18g		6%
Dietary Fiber	4g		16%
Sugars	5g		
Protein	14g		
Vitamin A	10%	Vitamin C	8%
Calcium	6%	Iron	10%

Dietary Exchanges: 1 Starch, 1 Vegetable, 1 Very Lean Meat OR
1 Carbohydrate, 1 Vegetable, 1 Very Lean Meat

Bean-*efits*

Name your bean, and you'll find it's high in dietary fiber and complex carbohydrates. A one-cup serving of beans has about 200 calories and is an excellent source of protein in a low-fat, low-sodium, cholesterol-free package. Beans provide B vitamins, iron and calcium, too.

Beans are a proven boon to diets tailored for diabetes, heart disease, weight control and hypertension. And a diet rich in beans is rich in fiber, which may help prevent colon cancer.

While vegetarians in years past fretted about making sure the ingredients at each meal complemented each other to form "complete" proteins, current wisdom takes a broader view and holds that there's no need to worry about carefully balancing beans at every meal with meat, dairy products or grains. As long as you eat a good variety of healthy foods over the course of each day, your body can use the protein in beans effectively.

Tuscan Bean Soup with Turkey

PREP TIME: 30 MINUTES

1 (14½-oz.) can ready-to-serve fat-free chicken broth with ⅓ less sodium

1 cup thinly sliced carrots

1 cup thinly sliced celery

½ cup chopped onion

½ teaspoon dried marjoram leaves

¼ teaspoon ground thyme

¼ teaspoon dried basil leaves

⅛ teaspoon pepper

2 garlic cloves, minced

1 bay leaf

1½ cups cubed cooked turkey

1½ cups tomato juice

1 (15-oz.) can cannellini beans, drained, rinsed

1. In large nonstick saucepan, combine broth, carrots, celery, onion, marjoram, thyme, basil, pepper, garlic and bay leaf. Bring to a boil. Reduce heat; simmer 15 minutes or until vegetables are tender.

2. Add all remaining ingredients; simmer until thoroughly heated. Remove and discard bay leaf.

YIELD: 4 (1⅓-CUP) SERVINGS

Nutrition Information Per Serving
Serving Size: 1⅓ Cups

Calories	220	Calories from Fat	25
		% Daily Value	
Total Fat	3g		5%
Saturated	1g		5%
Cholesterol	40mg		13%
Sodium	770mg		32%
Total Carbohydrate	25g		8%
Dietary Fiber	6g		24%
Sugars	7g		
Protein	23g		
Vitamin A	180%	Vitamin C	25%
Calcium	10%	Iron	20%

Dietary Exchanges: 1½ Starch, 1 Vegetable, 2 Very Lean Meat OR
1½ Carbohydrate, 1 Vegetable, 2 Very Lean Meat

Turkey–Wild Rice Tomato Soup

PREP TIME: 35 MINUTES

½ lb. bulk turkey breakfast sausage

¾ cup uncooked instant white rice

¾ cup uncooked instant wild rice*

1 (2.4-oz.) pkg. tomato with basil soup mix

1 (14.5-oz.) can no-salt-added stewed tomatoes, undrained

4 cups water

1 cup beef broth

1 tablespoon all-purpose flour

1 (12-oz.) can evaporated skimmed milk

1. Heat nonstick Dutch oven or large saucepan over medium-high heat until hot. Add sausage; cook 4 to 5 minutes or until no longer pink. With slotted spoon, remove sausage from Dutch oven; drain on paper towels.

◄ Quick Bulgur Minestrone (page 89)/Hominy Soup à la Mexicana (page 75)/Turkey–Wild Rice Tomato Soup

2. Wipe Dutch oven clean with paper towels. Return sausage to Dutch oven. Stir in all remaining ingredients except flour and milk. Bring to a boil. Reduce heat to medium-low; cover and cook 8 to 10 minutes or until rice is tender.

3. Meanwhile, in small bowl, combine flour and milk; blend well. Gradually stir into soup. Increase heat to medium-high; cook, stirring constantly, until bubbly.

YIELD: 6 (1½-CUP) SERVINGS

Tip: * If desired, an additional ¾ cup uncooked instant white rice can be substituted for the wild rice.

Nutrition Information Per Serving
Serving Size: 1½ Cups

Calories	270	Calories from Fat	50
		% Daily Value	
Total Fat	6g		9%
Saturated	2g		10%
Cholesterol	30mg		10%
Sodium	930mg		39%
Total Carbohydrate	39g		13%
Dietary Fiber	1g		4%
Sugars	11g		
Protein	16g		
Vitamin A	20%	Vitamin C	45%
Calcium	25%	Iron	15%

Dietary Exchanges: 2½ Starch, 1½ Lean Meat OR
2½ Carbohydrate, 1½ Lean Meat

stretching the Soup

Soup is the thrifty cook's dream, as you can almost always "throw something in" to use up leftovers or stretch the meal for an unexpected guest or two. Check your freezer, refrigerator and pantry for last-minute add-ins:

Frozen corn, peas, beans or odds and ends of leftover cooked vegetables

Rice left over from Chinese takeout

Chopped tomatoes or fresh salsa

Coleslaw mix (shredded cabbage and carrots)

Shredded spinach, bok choy or another green

Chopped leftover chicken, turkey, beef or ham

Chopped-up carrots, celery, bell pepper slices and green onions left on a relish tray

Extra noodles

A cup or so of spaghetti sauce

Parmesan cheese

Hearty Spinach and Mushroom Soup

■ ■

PREP TIME: 25 MINUTES

2 teaspoons margarine or butter

1 (8-oz.) pkg. (3 cups) sliced fresh mushrooms

½ cup finely shredded carrot

½ cup finely chopped onion

1 (14½-oz.) can ready-to-serve fat-free chicken broth with ⅓ less sodium

1½ cups frozen cut leaf spinach, thawed, squeezed to drain*

⅛ teaspoon nutmeg

Dash pepper

2 cups skim milk

¼ cup all-purpose flour

4 oz. fat-free cream cheese (from 8-oz. pkg.), cut into pieces

4 oz. (1 cup) shredded reduced-fat Swiss cheese

1. Melt margarine in large nonstick saucepan over medium heat. Add mushrooms, carrot and onion; cook and stir 3 minutes. Add broth, spinach, nutmeg and pepper; mix well.

2. In small bowl, combine milk and flour; blend until smooth. Add to spinach mixture; cook until bubbly and thickened, stirring constantly. Reduce heat to low. Add cream cheese and Swiss cheese; cook and stir until melted.

YIELD: 4 (1¼-CUP) SERVINGS

Tip: * To quickly thaw spinach, place on microwave-safe plate; microwave on HIGH for 1½ to 2½ minutes or until thawed. Squeeze dry with paper towels.

Nutrition Information Per Serving
Serving Size: 1¼ Cups

Calories.................................250	Calories from Fat 70	
	% Daily Value	
Total Fat 8g	....12%	
Saturated 4g	....20%	
Cholesterol 35mg	....12%	
Sodium 580mg	....24%	
Total Carbohydrate 23g	....8%	
Dietary Fiber 3g	....12%	
Sugars............................10g		
Protein 21g		
Vitamin A 140%	Vitamin C 15%	
Calcium 60%	Iron 10%	

Dietary Exchanges: 1 Starch, 2 Vegetable, 2 Lean Meat OR
1 Carbohydrate, 2 Vegetable, 2 Lean Meat

▼ Hearty Spinach and Mushroom Soup

Quick Bulgur Minestrone

PREP TIME: 35 MINUTES

2 (14½-oz.) cans ready-to-serve vegetable broth

2 cups water

¾ cup uncooked bulgur

1 (14.5-oz.) can Italian-style stewed tomatoes, undrained

2 medium zucchini, halved lengthwise, thinly sliced (1⅔ cups)

1 (1-lb.) pkg. frozen whole kernel corn

1 (15½-oz.) can navy beans, drained, rinsed

2 teaspoons dried oregano leaves

1. In nonstick Dutch oven over medium-high heat, bring broth and water to a boil. Stir in bulgur and tomatoes. Return to a boil. Reduce heat to medium-low; cover and cook 10 minutes.

2. Add zucchini, corn, beans and oregano; mix well. Cover; cook over medium-low heat for 8 to 10 minutes or until bulgur and zucchini are tender. If desired, add salt and pepper to taste.

YIELD: 6 (1⅔-CUP) SERVINGS

Nutrition Information Per Serving
Serving Size: 1⅔ Cups

Calories	270	Calories from Fat	20
		% Daily Value	
Total Fat	2g		3%
Saturated	0g		0%
Cholesterol	0mg		0%
Sodium	1,090mg		45%
Total Carbohydrate	52g		17%
Dietary Fiber	11g		44%
Sugars	13g		
Protein	11g		
Vitamin A	15%	Vitamin C	20%
Calcium	6%	Iron	15%

Dietary Exchanges: 3 Starch, 1 Vegetable OR 3 Carbohydrate, 1 Vegetable

Winter Squash Soup

PREP TIME: 25 MINUTES

1 tablespoon margarine or butter

½ cup finely chopped onion

2 tablespoons all-purpose flour

1 (10½-oz.) can condensed chicken broth

1 cup unsweetened apple juice

2 (12-oz.) pkg. frozen cooked winter squash

¼ teaspoon curry powder

¼ teaspoon dried rosemary leaves, crushed

¼ cup low-fat plain yogurt

1. Melt margarine in large nonstick saucepan over medium heat. Add onion; cook and stir until tender. Stir in flour; cook 1 to 2 minutes, stirring constantly. Gradually stir in broth and apple juice.

2. Add squash, curry powder and rosemary; mix well. Cook over medium-high heat until mixture begins to boil, stirring occasionally. Reduce heat; simmer 10 minutes to blend flavors.

3. To serve, ladle soup into 6 individual soup bowls; top with yogurt. If desired, garnish with fresh rosemary sprigs.

YIELD: 6 (¾-CUP) SERVINGS

Nutrition Information Per Serving
Serving Size: ¾ Cup

Calories	120	Calories from Fat	25
		% Daily Value	
Total Fat	3g		5%
Saturated	1g		5%
Cholesterol	0mg		0%
Sodium	340mg		14%
Total Carbohydrate	19g		6%
Dietary Fiber	4g		16%
Sugars	9g		
Protein	4g		
Vitamin A	80%	Vitamin C	15%
Calcium	4%	Iron	4%

Dietary Exchanges: 1 Starch, 1 Fat OR 1 Carbohydrate, 1 Fat

sweet Onions

If you've never tasted a sweet onion before, you're in for a revelation. The sweet onion season starts mid-March with big onions from Texas and winds up in August with onions from Washington state and Hawaii.

What makes a sweet onion unique? Its high water content and low sulfur levels. A higher level of water means sweet onions are juicy, but also extremely perishable. Store them in a dry, well-ventilated area in a single layer or in netting or hosiery with a knot separating each onion. When properly stored, sweet onions last two to three weeks at a time. Sulfur gives the common onion its sharp, pungent flavor and causes many a cook to cry. The sweet onion's low sulfur content makes it mild enough to enjoy raw in a salad or sandwich. When cooked, it becomes even sweeter.

Although each variety has its own unique flavor, sweet onions can be used interchangeably in recipes.

Speedy Onion Soup

PREP TIME: 30 MINUTES

2 teaspoons olive oil

2 large sweet onions, halved, thinly sliced

3 (14½-oz.) cans ready-to-serve fat-free chicken broth with ⅓ less sodium

⅛ teaspoon coarse ground black pepper

4 slices baguette or French bread (¾ inch thick)

1 (1-oz.) slice reduced-fat Swiss cheese, cut into quarters

2 teaspoons grated Parmesan cheese

1. Heat oil in nonstick Dutch oven or large saucepan over medium heat until hot. Add onions; cook 15 to 20 minutes or until tender and brown, stirring occasionally.

2. Stir in broth and pepper. Bring to a boil. Reduce heat to low; simmer 10 minutes.

3. Meanwhile, place bread slices on ungreased cookie sheet. Broil 4 to 6 inches from heat for 45 to 60 seconds or until lightly toasted. Turn slices over; top untoasted sides with Swiss cheese. Sprinkle with Parmesan cheese. Broil 30 to 45 seconds or until cheese is melted.

4. To serve, ladle soup into 4 individual soup bowls; top with cheese toast. Spoon small amount of broth over top.

YIELD: 4 (1½-CUP) SERVINGS

Nutrition Information Per Serving
Serving Size: 1½ Cups

Calories.............................150	Calories from Fat 25	
	% Daily Value	
Total Fat 3g	.............5%	
Saturated 1g	.............5%	
Cholesterol 3mg	.............1%	
Sodium 820mg	.............34%	
Total Carbohydrate 22g	.............7%	
Dietary Fiber 3g	.............12%	
Sugars.............................10g		
Protein.................................9g		
Vitamin A 0%	Vitamin C 15%	
Calcium 10%	Iron................................4%	

Dietary Exchanges: 1 Starch, 1 Vegetable, ½ Lean Meat OR
1 Carbohydrate, 1 Vegetable, ½ Lean Meat

Creamy Potato Cabbage Chowder

■ ■ ■ ■ ■ ■ ■ ■ ■ ■ ■ ■ ■ ■ ■ ■ ■ ■ ■

PREP TIME: 30 MINUTES

1 (14½-oz.) can ready-to-serve chicken broth

3 medium potatoes, peeled, cubed (about 3 cups)

½ cup skim milk

2 cups chopped cabbage

½ cup shredded carrot

2 teaspoons chopped fresh dill or ½ teaspoon dried dill weed

⅛ to ¼ teaspoon pepper

1. In medium nonstick saucepan, combine broth and potatoes. Bring to a boil. Reduce heat; cover and simmer 8 minutes or until potatoes are tender. Cool slightly.

2. Place 1 cup hot potato mixture in blender container or food processor bowl with metal blade. Add milk; cover and blend 30 seconds or until mixture is smooth. Add to saucepan.

3. Stir in all remaining ingredients; cook over medium heat for 5 minutes or until cabbage is crisp-tender.

YIELD: 5 (1-CUP) SERVINGS

Nutrition Information Per Serving
Serving Size: 1 Cup

Calories.................................100	Calories from Fat 10	
	% Daily Value	
Total Fat 1g	.................2%	
Saturated...........................0g	.................0%	
Cholesterol 0mg	.................0%	
Sodium 290mg	.................12%	
Total Carbohydrate..............19g	.................6%	
Dietary Fiber......................2g	.................8%	
Sugars 3g		
Protein 4g		
Vitamin A.............................60%	Vitamin C 25%	
Calcium 6%	Iron.............................4%	

Dietary Exchanges: 1 Starch, 1 Vegetable OR 1 Carbohydrate, 1 Vegetable

Creamy Crab and Corn Chowder

■ ■ ■ ■ ■ ■ ■ ■ ■ ■ ■ ■ ■ ■ ■ ■ ■ ■ ■ ■

PREP TIME: 15 MINUTES

1 to 2 garlic cloves, minced

8 oz. (2 cups) flaked imitation crabmeat (surimi)

2 (12-oz.) cans evaporated skimmed milk

1 (15-oz.) can cream-style corn

1 (11-oz.) can vacuum-packed whole kernel corn with red and green peppers

2 teaspoons dried dill weed

½ teaspoon salt

¼ teaspoon pepper

¼ teaspoon dried thyme leaves

½ cup mashed potato flakes

1. Spray nonstick Dutch oven with nonstick cooking spray. Heat over medium heat until hot. Add garlic; cook and stir 1 to 2 minutes or until golden brown. Add imitation crabmeat; cook 1 minute.

2. Stir in milk, cream-style and whole kernel corn, dill, salt, pepper and thyme. Bring just to a boil, stirring frequently. Add potato flakes; cook and stir until thickened.

YIELD: 6 (1-CUP) SERVINGS

Nutrition Information Per Serving
Serving Size: 1 Cup

Calories...................................250	Calories from Fat 10	
	% Daily Value	
Total Fat 1g	.................2%	
Saturated...........................0g	.................0%	
Cholesterol 15mg	.................5%	
Sodium 900mg	.................38%	
Total Carbohydrate..............43g	.................14%	
Dietary Fiber......................2g	.................8%	
Sugars..............................22g		
Protein 17g		
Vitamin A.............................10%	Vitamin C 6%	
Calcium 35%	Iron.............................6%	

Dietary Exchanges: 3 Starch, ½ Very Lean Meat OR 3 Carbohydrate, ½ Very Lean Meat

Steak and Bean Chowder

PREP TIME: 20 MINUTES
(READY IN 45 MINUTES)

¾ lb. boneless beef sirloin steak, cut into ½-inch pieces

1 medium onion, chopped

2 (14.5-oz.) cans whole tomatoes, undrained, cut up

1 (15-oz.) can spicy chili beans, undrained

2 baking potatoes, unpeeled, cut into ½-inch cubes (2 cups)

½ teaspoon cumin

1. Spray nonstick Dutch oven or large saucepan with nonstick cooking spray. Heat over medium-high heat until hot. Add beef; cook and stir until no longer pink.

2. Add onion; cook 1 minute, stirring constantly. Add all remaining ingredients. Bring to a boil. Reduce heat to medium-low; partially cover and simmer 20 to 25 minutes or until potatoes are tender.

YIELD: 4 (1½-CUP) SERVINGS

about Cumin

Cumin, an earthy-flavored spice, is a key ingredient in many blends of curry and chili powder and is an important seasoning in Latin American and Indian cooking. Cumin is sold in convenient ground form or as whole seeds, which somewhat resemble caraway seeds. Cumin has a fairly penetrating flavor, so add just a little at a time if you're improvising. Try a sprinkle in bean soups, chili or your favorite recipe for meat loaf or meatballs.

Nutrition Information Per Serving
Serving Size: 1½ Cups

Calories	320	Calories from Fat	45
		% Daily Value	
Total Fat	5g		8%
Saturated	2g		10%
Cholesterol	45mg		15%
Sodium	780mg		33%
Total Carbohydrate	44g		15%
Dietary Fiber	9g		36%
Sugars	7g		
Protein	24g		
Vitamin A	30%	Vitamin C	50%
Calcium	10%	Iron	30%

Dietary Exchanges: 3 Starch, 1½ Lean Meat OR 3 Carbohydrate, 1½ Lean Meat

Hunter's Stew with Chicken

PREP TIME: 15 MINUTES
(READY IN 6 HOURS 15 MINUTES)

1 medium onion, thinly sliced

1 medium green bell pepper, cut into 1-inch pieces

3 boneless, skinless chicken breast halves, cut into 2 × 1-inch pieces

1 (15-oz.) can garbanzo beans, drained

1 (14-oz.) jar spaghetti sauce

1 (8-oz.) can mushroom pieces and stems, drained

1. In 3½- to 4-quart slow cooker, combine all ingredients; mix well.

2. Cover; cook on low setting for at least 6 hours.

YIELD: 4 (1½-CUP) SERVINGS

Nutrition Information Per Serving
Serving Size: 1½ Cups

Calories	350	Calories from Fat	80
		% Daily Value	
Total Fat	9g		14%
Saturated	2g		10%
Cholesterol	55mg		18%
Sodium	870mg		36%
Total Carbohydrate	38g		13%
Dietary Fiber	10g		40%
Sugars	6g		
Protein	29g		
Vitamin A	25%	Vitamin C	35%
Calcium	8%	Iron	15%

Dietary Exchanges: 2 Starch, 1 Vegetable, 3 Very Lean Meat, 1 Fat OR 2 Carbohydrate, 1 Vegetable, 3 Very Lean Meat, 1 Fat

▲ Beef Stew

Beef Stew

PREP TIME: 30 MINUTES

¾ lb. boneless beef top sirloin steak, cut into ½-inch cubes

1 small onion, chopped

3 cups frozen southern-style hash-brown potatoes (from 32-oz. pkg.)

1½ cups thinly sliced carrots

1 cup thinly sliced celery

1 (4.5-oz.) jar sliced mushrooms, drained

1 envelope dry beef-mushroom soup mix

¼ teaspoon dried thyme leaves, crushed

¼ teaspoon pepper

3½ cups water

1. Heat nonstick Dutch oven or large saucepan over medium-high heat until hot. Add beef and onion; cook 5 minutes or until beef is browned.

2. Stir in potatoes, carrots, celery and mushrooms; cook and stir 2 minutes. Add soup mix, thyme, pepper and water; mix well. Bring to a boil. Reduce heat; simmer 15 minutes or until vegetables are tender. If desired, serve sprinkled with chopped fresh parsley.

YIELD: 5 (1⅓-CUP) SERVINGS

Nutrition Information Per Serving
Serving Size: 1⅓ Cups

Calories	240	Calories from Fat	35
		% Daily Value	
Total Fat	4g		6%
Saturated	1g		5%
Cholesterol	35mg		12%
Sodium	550mg		23%
Total Carbohydrate	34g		11%
Dietary Fiber	4g		16%
Sugars	4g		
Protein	17g		
Vitamin A	210%	Vitamin C	20%
Calcium	4%	Iron	15%

Dietary Exchanges: 2 Starch, 1 Vegetable, 1 Lean Meat OR
2 Carbohydrate, 1 Vegetable, 1 Lean Meat

Soups, Stews and Chilies **93**

Ratatouille Stew

PREP TIME: 15 MINUTES
(READY IN 45 MINUTES)

1 red or green bell pepper, chopped

1 medium zucchini, chopped

½ medium eggplant, peeled, cut into ½- to ¾-inch cubes (about 2½ cups)

1 (28-oz.) can whole tomatoes, undrained, cut up

1 cup water

3 garlic cloves, minced

1 teaspoon dried Italian seasoning

¼ teaspoon pepper

3 oz. (½ cup) orzo or rosamarina (rice-shaped pasta)

1. In large nonstick saucepan or Dutch oven, combine all ingredients except orzo. Bring to a boil over medium-high heat. Reduce heat to medium-low; cover and cook 15 minutes.

2. Add orzo; cover and cook 10 to 15 minutes or until orzo and vegetables are tender, stirring frequently.

YIELD: 4 (1¼-CUP) SERVINGS

Nutrition Information Per Serving
Serving Size: 1¼ Cups

Calories................................160	Calories from Fat 10
	% Daily Value
Total Fat ....1g 2%	
Saturated ....0g 0%	
Cholesterol ....0mg 0%	
Sodium ....330mg 14%	
Total Carbohydrate............31g 10%	
Dietary Fiber ....5g 20%	
Sugars 9g	
Protein..................................6g	
Vitamin A.............................50%	Vitamin C 80%
Calcium 8%	Iron 15%

Dietary Exchanges: 2 Starch OR 2 Carbohydrate

Sicilian Garbanzo Stew

∎ ∎ ∎ ∎ ∎ ∎ ∎ ∎ ∎ ∎ ∎ ∎ ∎ ∎ ∎ ∎ ∎ ∎ ∎

PREP TIME: 20 MINUTES
(READY IN 45 MINUTES)

4 cups water

1 tablespoon lemon juice

4 teaspoons vegetable or chicken-flavor instant bouillon

1 teaspoon fennel seed, crushed

½ teaspoon dried thyme leaves

1 bay leaf

1 medium onion, finely chopped*

1 stalk celery, chopped (½ cup)*

2 garlic cloves, minced*

4 medium baking potatoes, peeled, sliced*

3 large carrots, thinly sliced (2 cups)*

2 (15-oz.) cans garbanzo beans, drained, rinsed

1 cup packed fresh parsley including tender stems, chopped (about ½ cup)*

⅛ to ¼ teaspoon coarse ground black pepper

1. In nonstick Dutch oven, combine all ingredients except parsley and pepper; mix well. Bring to a boil. Reduce heat to medium-low; cover and simmer 15 to 20 minutes or until vegetables are very tender.

2. Remove and discard bay leaf. With potato masher, mash vegetables into broth to make a thick chunky mixture. (Garbanzo beans will not mash as thoroughly as other vegetables; leave as is for extra texture.) Stir in parsley and pepper.

YIELD: 6 (1½-CUP) SERVINGS

Tip: * To speed preparation, use food processor with metal blade to chop onion, celery and garlic. Replace metal blade with thin slicing disk; slice potatoes and carrots on top of chopped vegetables. Remove all vegetables from bowl. Clean and dry bowl before chopping parsley with metal blade.

Nutrition Information Per Serving
Serving Size: 1½ Cups

Calories 270		Calories from Fat 25
		% Daily Value
Total Fat 3g	....	5%
Saturated 0g	....	0%
Cholesterol 0mg	....	0%
Sodium 820mg	....	34%
Total Carbohydrate 50g	....	17%
Dietary Fiber 10g	....	40%
Sugars 6g		
Protein 11g		
Vitamin A 320%		Vitamin C 50%
Calcium 10%		Iron 15%

Dietary Exchanges: 3 Starch, 1 Very Lean Meat OR 3 Carbohydrate, 1 Very Lean Meat

in the **Thick** of things

∎ ∎ ∎ ∎ ∎ ∎ ∎ ∎ ∎ ∎ ∎ ∎ ∎ ∎ ∎ ∎ ∎

Even if you've sworn off high-fat dishes made with heavy cream, there are plenty of ways to achieve a satisfyingly rich-textured soup.

- Stir in unsweetened pureed canned pumpkin. Or cut a smooth-fleshed winter squash, such as butternut, in half lengthwise and remove the seeds. Mound a few unpeeled garlic cloves on a plate, invert the squash over the garlic so the cavity covers the garlic and microwave on HIGH until the squash is tender, 8 to 10 minutes. Scoop out the squash, squeeze the softened garlic out of the skin and stir it into soup.

- Thicken vegetable soups by removing a cup or two of vegetables with a little broth. Puree the mixture in the blender, then stir it back into the soup. Or puree all the soup with some skim milk for a delicious, rich-tasting cream-style soup.

- Crushed tomatoes or even a cup or so of leftover spaghetti sauce add flavor and thickness to soups made with beef, vegetables or chicken.

- Pureed potatoes offer one more way to thicken things up.

- Substitute nonfat half-and-half or evaporated skimmed milk for cream.

Chili Mac

- -

PREP TIME: 25 MINUTES

4 oz. (1 cup) uncooked elbow macaroni

½ lb. extra-lean ground beef

1 cup chopped green bell pepper or celery

1 medium onion, chopped

4 (8-oz.) cans no-salt-added tomato sauce

1 (15-oz.) can spicy chili beans, undrained

½ teaspoon salt

1. Cook macaroni to desired doneness as directed on package.

2. Meanwhile, spray large nonstick saucepan or skillet with nonstick cooking spray. Add ground beef, bell pepper and onion; cook over medium-high heat until beef is browned.

3. Drain macaroni. Add to ground beef mixture with all remaining ingredients. Cook until thoroughly heated.

YIELD: 6 (1¼-CUP) SERVINGS

Nutrition Information Per Serving
Serving Size: 1¼ Cups

Calories	250	Calories from Fat	50
		% Daily Value	
Total Fat	6g		9%
Saturated	2g		10%
Cholesterol	25mg		8%
Sodium	500mg		21%
Total Carbohydrate	34g		11%
Dietary Fiber	4g		16%
Sugars	7g		
Protein	15g		
Vitamin A	6%	Vitamin C	50%
Calcium	4%	Iron	20%

Dietary Exchanges: 2 Starch, 1 Vegetable, 1 Medium-Fat Meat OR
2 Carbohydrate, 1 Vegetable, 1 Medium-Fat Meat

▼ Chili Mac

leftover magic with **Chili**

Looking for imaginative ways to serve your leftover chili? Here are ten easy ideas for recycling America's favorite stew.

1. **Chili Burgers or Dogs** Serve reheated chili over hamburgers or hot dogs in a bun.

2. **Potato Topper** Use leftover chili as a delicious and nutritious topping for baked potatoes.

3. **Burrito** Wrap chili in a flour or corn tortilla with a sprinkle of cheese and heat it in the microwave.

4. **Shepherd's Pie** Layer chili in a casserole dish with a topping of mashed potatoes and bake until heated through and the top is golden.

5. **Party Dip** Combine leftover chili with shredded cheese and heat it in a small electric cooking pot. Serve with tortilla chips.

6. **Casserole** Mix chili with cooked pasta or rice and heat through.

7. **Nachos** Place a layer of tortilla chips in a baking dish and add chili, cheese and sliced scallions. Heat until cheese melts.

8. **Stuffed Peppers** Halve, seed and steam bell peppers and fill them with leftover chili.

9. **Huevos Rancheros** For a real eye-opener, spoon chili over your breakfast eggs.

10. **Tamale Pie** Drop spoonfuls of cornbread batter on top of chili in a casserole dish and bake it until the cornbread is golden brown.

Spicy Southwest Beef and Bean Chili

PREP TIME: 15 MINUTES
(READY IN 8 HOURS 15 MINUTES)

1 medium onion, chopped

1½ lb. boneless beef round steak (½ inch thick), cut into ¾ × ¾-inch pieces

4 (8-oz.) cans no-salt-added tomato sauce

1 (15.25-oz.) can whole kernel corn, drained

1 (15-oz.) can black beans, drained, rinsed

1 (4.5-oz.) can chopped green chiles

2 tablespoons chili powder

1. In 3½- to 4-quart slow cooker, combine all ingredients; mix well.
2. Cover; cook on low setting for at least 8 hours.

YIELD: 6 (1½-CUP) SERVINGS

Nutrition Information Per Serving
Serving Size: 1½ Cups

Calories	300	Calories from Fat	60
		% Daily Value	
Total Fat	7g		11%
Saturated	2g		10%
Cholesterol	55mg		18%
Sodium	660mg		28%
Total Carbohydrate	31g		10%
Dietary Fiber	6g		24%
Sugars	10g		
Protein	29g		
Vitamin A	25%	Vitamin C	40%
Calcium	4%	Iron	25%

Dietary Exchanges: 1½ Starch, 1 Vegetable, 3 Lean Meat OR
1½ Carbohydrate, 1 Vegetable, 3 Lean Meat

▲ White Chili

White Chili

∎ ∎

PREP TIME: 30 MINUTES

6 boneless, skinless chicken breast halves, cut into ½-inch pieces

2 cups chopped onions

2 medium green bell peppers, chopped

2 garlic cloves, minced

2 (15.5-oz.) cans great northern beans, drained, rinsed

1 (14½-oz.) can ready-to-serve chicken broth

2 (4.5-oz.) cans chopped green chiles, drained

¼ teaspoon cumin

1. Spray nonstick Dutch oven or large skillet with nonstick cooking spray. Heat over medium-high heat until hot. Add chicken, onions, bell peppers and garlic; cook until chicken is no longer pink.

2. Add all remaining ingredients. Bring to a boil. Reduce heat; simmer 10 to 15 minutes or until sauce thickens slightly.

YIELD: 6 (1½-CUP) SERVINGS

Nutrition Information Per Serving
Serving Size: 1½ Cups

Calories	290	Calories from Fat	35
		% Daily Value	
Total Fat	4g		6%
Saturated	1g		5%
Cholesterol	75mg		25%
Sodium	490mg		20%
Total Carbohydrate	28g		9%
Dietary Fiber	8g		32%
Sugars	5g		
Protein	36g		
Vitamin A	8%	Vitamin C	120%
Calcium	15%	Iron	20%

Dietary Exchanges: 1 Starch, 2 Vegetable, 4 Very Lean Meat OR
1 Carbohydrate, 2 Vegetable, 4 Very Lean Meat

turning up the *Heat*

Pepper is a highly personal matter. While a few people find even ordinary black pepper overpowering, there's a growing legion of firebreathers who relish products bearing labels such as "Shake well and good luck." In between, there's a continuum of pepper products, ranging from flavorful but mild to incendiary. Some of the hot ways you can add zing to dips and other appetizers:

Fresh hot peppers Add these to foods in very small quantities until you have determined the particular pepper's potency and your tolerance. Wear rubber gloves when preparing hot peppers, as they contain oils that can irritate eyes and skin. The ribs and seeds contain most of the heat, so to reduce the firery flavor remove them and use only the flesh.

Dried whole hot peppers Used extensively in Chinese cooking, dried red pepper pods take on an almost nutty flavor when cooked. Most people, however, won't notice the nutty flavor—they'll be too overwhelmed by the heat. Do timid guests a favor and remove the pods from the dish before serving.

Crushed pepper flakes Often found in shakers on the table at pizza parlors, these contain seeds and tiny bits of the flesh. They work equally well as a cooking ingredient or as a condiment.

Ground red pepper Follow recipe measurements carefully for this pure ground hot pepper (also called cayenne pepper). You can always add more, but it's hard to counteract an overgenerous measure.

Paprika Made from ground chile peppers, paprika may be either mild ("sweet") or hot." A sprinkle of the sweet variety makes a colorful garnish. Check for paprika's freshness by observing the color—if it's bright red it's fresh.

Pure ground chile As opposed to "chili powder," which is a blend of spices, pure ground chile contains nothing but chile peppers. Varieties range from mild to hot.

Hot pepper sauce Some of these contain mostly ground peppers in a vinegar base, perhaps with a little salt or pepper added; others may have a tomato base and include sugar or other flavorings. Use sparingly! Some of these are so strong that only a drop or two will have near-atomic effect.

Canned chiles These are usually marked with descriptors such as "mild," "medium" or "hot," so it's easy to achieve flavor and heat in the proportions you prefer.

Jarred peppers Jalapeños (hot) and chopped or whole cherry peppers (either hot or sweet) in a vinegary brine are among the most popular of jarred peppers. Use chopped peppers as a garnish or sandwich topper; mince and stir into dips and spreads; use them whole. on a relish tray.

Spicy Texas Chili

PREP TIME: 30 MINUTES

1 lb. boneless beef top round steak, cut into ½-inch pieces

1 medium onion, chopped

1 jalapeño chile, seeded, minced

3 garlic cloves, minced

3 (14.5-oz.) cans whole tomatoes, undrained, cut up

4 teaspoons chili powder

¼ teaspoon ground red pepper (cayenne)

1. Spray nonstick Dutch oven or large skillet with nonstick cooking spray. Heat over medium-high heat until hot. Add beef, onion, chile and garlic; cook until beef is no longer pink.

2. Stir in all remaining ingredients. Bring to a boil. Reduce heat; simmer 15 to 20 minutes or until chili is slightly thickened and flavors are blended, stirring occasionally. If desired, add salt to taste.

YIELD: 4 (1½-CUP) SERVINGS

Nutrition Information Per Serving
Serving Size: 1½ Cups

Calories	230	Calories from Fat	45
		% Daily Value	
Total Fat	5g		8%
Saturated	1g		5%
Cholesterol	65mg		22%
Sodium	580mg		24%
Total Carbohydrate	18g		6%
Dietary Fiber	5g		20%
Sugars	8g		
Protein	29g		
Vitamin A	60%	Vitamin C	70%
Calcium	10%	Iron	25%

Dietary Exchanges: 3 Vegetable, 3 Lean Meat

Cincinnati Chili

PREP TIME: 30 MINUTES

8 oz. uncooked spaghetti

1 teaspoon oil

1 medium onion, chopped

1 lb. lean ground turkey breast

1 tablespoon sugar

3 teaspoons chili powder

1 teaspoon cinnamon

½ teaspoon salt

¼ teaspoon ground red pepper (cayenne)

1 (28-oz.) can crushed tomatoes, undrained

1 (15.5-oz.) can dark red kidney beans, drained, rinsed

1. Cook spaghetti to desired doneness as directed on package.

2. Meanwhile, heat oil in large nonstick saucepan or Dutch oven over medium-high heat until hot. Add onion; cook 3 to 5 minutes or until tender, stirring frequently.

3. Stir in ground turkey; cook and stir until no longer pink. Add all remaining ingredients except kidney beans. Bring to a boil. Reduce heat; simmer 10 minutes. Add kidney beans; simmer until thoroughly heated.

4. Drain spaghetti. To serve, spoon spaghetti into 4 individual soup bowls. Ladle turkey mixture over spaghetti.

YIELD: 4 SERVINGS

Nutrition Information Per Serving
Serving Size: ¼ of Recipe

Calories	510	Calories from Fat	35
		% Daily Value	
Total Fat	4g		6%
Saturated	1g		5%
Cholesterol	70mg		23%
Sodium	780mg		33%
Total Carbohydrate	77g		26%
Dietary Fiber	10g		40%
Sugars	14g		
Protein	42g		
Vitamin A	35%	Vitamin C	25%
Calcium	15%	Iron	40%

Dietary Exchanges: 5 Starch, 3 Very Lean Meat OR 5 Carbohydrate, 3 Very Lean Meat

Poultry

5

Citrus-Ginger Marinated Chicken (page 132)

Light and Lemony Chicken

■ ■ ■ ■ ■ ■ ■ ■ ■ ■ ■ ■ ■ ■ ■ ■ ■ ■

PREP TIME: 25 MINUTES

Rice

3 cups hot cooked instant rice (cooked as directed on package, omitting margarine and salt)

Sauce

⅔ cup ready-to-serve fat-free chicken broth with ⅓ less sodium

1 teaspoon lite soy sauce

1 teaspoon grated lemon peel

¼ cup lemon juice

1 tablespoon sugar

1 tablespoon cornstarch

Dash pepper

Stir-fry

4 boneless, skinless chicken breast halves, cut into bite-sized strips

8 green onions, cut into 1-inch pieces

1 lb. fresh asparagus spears, trimmed, cut into 1-inch pieces (3 cups)

2 cups frozen baby cut carrots

1. While rice is cooking, in small bowl, combine all sauce ingredients; mix well. Set aside.

2. Spray large nonstick skillet or wok with nonstick cooking spray. Heat over high heat until hot. Add chicken and onions; cook and stir until chicken is lightly browned and no longer pink. Remove skillet from heat; place chicken and onions on plate.

3. Spray skillet again with cooking spray. Heat over high heat about 1 minute. Add asparagus and carrots; cook and stir 3 to 4 minutes or until vegetables are crisp-tender.

4. Return chicken and onions to skillet. Stir sauce well; pour over chicken and vegetables. Cook and stir just until sauce thickens. Serve over rice.

YIELD: 4 SERVINGS

Nutrition Information Per Serving
Serving Size: ¼ of Recipe

Calories	350	Calories from Fat	35
		% Daily Value	
Total Fat	4g		6%
Saturated	1g		5%
Cholesterol	75mg		25%
Sodium	260mg		11%
Total Carbohydrate	45g		15%
Dietary Fiber	6g		24%
Sugars	10g		
Protein	33g		
Vitamin A	290%	Vitamin C	30%
Calcium	8%	Iron	20%

Dietary Exchanges: 2½ Starch, 2 Vegetable, 3 Very Lean Meat OR 2½ Carbohydrate, 2 Vegetable, 3 Very Lean Meat

Chicken *nutrition*

No matter which chicken part you prefer, keep the profile as healthy as possible by trimming visible fat before cooking, choosing low-fat cooking techniques, removing skin before eating (cooking it with or without the skin makes no difference so long as you don't eat the skin) and controlling portion size.

3 oz. Cooked	Fat	Calories
White meat with skin	7 g	160
White meat without skin	3 g	130
Dark meat with skin	11 g	200
Dark meat without skin	7 g	160

about Cooking with Wine

Cooking with wine helps to tenderize meats and round out flavors. So-called cooking wine tends to be very salty, so you're probably better off using table wine. In fact, cooking is a good way to use leftover wine that's just past its prime; it's still fine for cooking. If you don't stock wine, try substituting white grape juice or apple juice in most recipes calling for wine.

Rosemary Chicken with Grapes

■ ■ ■ ■ ■ ■ ■ ■ ■ ■ ■ ■ ■ ■ ■

PREP TIME: 20 MINUTES

2 cups hot cooked instant brown rice (cooked as directed on package, omitting margarine and salt)

¾ cup chicken broth

¼ cup white wine or white grape juice

1 tablespoon cornstarch

1 tablespoon oil

4 boneless, skinless chicken breast halves, cut into thin strips

¼ to ½ teaspoon dried rosemary leaves, crushed

1 cup sliced fresh mushrooms

¼ cup sliced green onions

1 cup seedless red grapes

1. While rice is cooking, in small bowl, combine broth, wine and cornstarch; blend well. Set aside.
2. Heat oil in large nonstick skillet over medium-high heat until hot. Add chicken and rosemary; cook and stir 4 to 5 minutes or until chicken is no longer pink.
3. Add mushrooms and onions; cook and stir 2 minutes. Stir in grapes and broth mixture. Cook and stir until sauce is bubbly and thickened. Serve over rice.

YIELD: 4 SERVINGS

Nutrition Information Per Serving
Serving Size: ¼ of Recipe

Calories	340	Calories from Fat	70
		% Daily Value	
Total Fat	8g		12%
Saturated	2g		10%
Cholesterol	75mg		25%
Sodium	210mg		9%
Total Carbohydrate	33g		11%
Dietary Fiber	2g		8%
Sugars	8g		
Protein	31g		
Vitamin A	0%	Vitamin C	8%
Calcium	4%	Iron	10%

Dietary Exchanges: 1 Starch, 1 Fruit, 4 Very Lean Meat, 1 Fat OR 2 Carbohydrate, 4 Very Lean Meat, 1 Fat

Sesame Chicken Nuggets

■ ■ ■ ■ ■ ■ ■ ■ ■ ■ ■ ■ ■ ■ ■

PREP TIME: 20 MINUTES

2 tablespoons sesame seed

1 lb. precut chicken breast chunks, or 4 boneless, skinless chicken breast halves, cut into 1-inch chunks

1 tablespoon oil

¾ cup purchased sweet-and-sour or barbecue sauce or ½ cup honey

1. In large nonstick skillet over medium heat, toast sesame seed until golden brown, stirring frequently. Sprinkle toasted seed over chicken chunks.
2. Heat oil in same skillet over medium-high heat until hot. Add chicken; cook and stir 5 to 6 minutes or until chicken is no longer pink. Serve chicken nuggets with sauce.

YIELD: 4 SERVINGS

Nutrition Information Per Serving
Serving Size: ¼ of Recipe

Calories	230	Calories from Fat	70
		% Daily Value	
Total Fat	8g		12%
Saturated	1g		5%
Cholesterol	65mg		22%
Sodium	210mg		9%
Total Carbohydrate	14g		5%
Dietary Fiber	0g		0%
Sugars	11g		
Protein	25g		
Vitamin A	0%	Vitamin C	0%
Calcium	2%	Iron	8%

Dietary Exchanges: 1 Fruit, 3 Very Lean Meat, 1 Fat OR 1 Carbohydrate, 3 Very Lean Meat, 1 Fat

Chicken Marengo

1 tablespoon olive or vegetable oil

4 bone-in chicken breast halves, skin removed

1 tablespoon all-purpose flour

½ teaspoon dried basil leaves

¼ teaspoon garlic powder

⅛ teaspoon pepper

½ cup dry white wine or chicken broth

2 tablespoons tomato paste

2 (14.5- or 16-oz.) cans regular or Italian whole tomatoes, well drained, cut up

½ cup coarsely chopped green bell pepper

1 medium onion, cut into 8 thin wedges

¼ cup halved or sliced ripe olives

1. Heat oil in large nonstick skillet over medium-high heat until hot. Add chicken breast halves; cook until browned on all sides.

2. Meanwhile, in medium bowl, combine flour, basil, garlic powder, pepper, wine and tomato paste; blend until smooth. Stir in tomatoes.

3. Move chicken to side of skillet; add tomato mixture. Place chicken, meaty side up, in tomato mixture. Bring to a boil. Reduce heat to medium-low; cover and cook 10 minutes, stirring occasionally.

4. Turn chicken; stir in bell pepper and onion. Cover; cook an additional 8 to 10 minutes or until chicken is fork-tender and juices run clear, stirring occasionally. Stir in olives.

YIELD: 4 SERVINGS

Nutrition Information Per Serving
Serving Size: ¼ of Recipe

Calories	280	Calories from Fat	70
		% Daily Value	
Total Fat	8g		12%
Saturated	1g		5%
Cholesterol	75mg		25%
Sodium	230mg		10%
Total Carbohydrate	17g		6%
Dietary Fiber	3g		12%
Sugars	7g		
Protein	30g		
Vitamin A	15%	Vitamin C	60%
Calcium	10%	Iron	20%

Dietary Exchanges: ½ Starch, 2 Vegetable, 3½ Lean Meat OR
½ Carbohydrate, 2 Vegetable, 3½ Lean Meat

Chicken Vegetable Alfredo

6 oz. uncooked linguine

2 cups fresh broccoli florets

2 cups thinly sliced carrots

2 tablespoons margarine or butter

½ cup chopped onion

1 garlic clove, minced

3 tablespoons all-purpose flour

2 teaspoons very low-sodium chicken-flavor instant bouillon

½ teaspoon salt

¼ teaspoon pepper

2 cups skim milk

1½ cups cubed cooked chicken

1 (8-oz.) container light sour cream

⅓ cup grated Parmesan cheese

¼ cup sliced ripe olives, if desired

tips for cooking
Chicken Breasts

Boneless, skinless chicken breasts have the lowest fat on the chicken. To cook them:

- Trim any visible fat.

- Broil, grill, poach or sauté (in a nonstick skillet coated with nonstick cooking spray). Or cut chicken breasts into strips or chunks for stir-frying.

- Cook until meat is no longer pink.

- To avoid dry meat, be careful not to overcook.

1. Cook linguine to desired doneness as directed on package.

2. Meanwhile, in medium saucepan, bring 4 cups water to a boil. Add broccoli and carrots; return to a boil. Reduce heat; cook about 5 minutes or until crisp-tender. Drain well.

3. Melt margarine in large nonstick saucepan or Dutch oven over medium heat. Add onion and garlic; cook until onion is tender. Stir in flour, bouillon, salt and pepper. Gradually stir in milk. Cook until mixture boils and thickens, stirring constantly.

4. Stir in cooked broccoli and carrots, chicken, sour cream and ¼ cup of the Parmesan cheese. Cook until thoroughly heated. DO NOT BOIL.

5. Drain linguine. Add to vegetable mixture; toss to mix. Place on serving platter; sprinkle with remaining Parmesan cheese and olives.

YIELD: 6 (1¼-CUP) SERVINGS

Nutrition Information Per Serving
Serving Size: 1¼ Cups

Calories.................360	Calories from Fat..........110	
	% Daily Value	
Total Fat......................12g 18%		
Saturated ....5g 25%		
Cholesterol ....50mg 17%		
Sodium ....510mg 21%		
Total Carbohydrate ....41g 14%		
Dietary Fiber ....3g 12%		
Sugars 11g		
Protein 22g		
Vitamin A 260%	Vitamin C 35%	
Calcium 25%	Iron 15%	

Dietary Exchanges: 2½ Starch, 1 Vegetable, 2 Lean Meat, 1 Fat OR
2½ Carbohydrate, 1 Vegetable, 2 Lean Meat, 1 Fat

▼ Chicken Vegetable Alfredo

Chicken and Snow Pea Pasta

PREP TIME: 25 MINUTES

6 oz. vermicelli, broken into fourths

2 teaspoons oil

1 lb. boneless, skinless chicken breast halves, cut crosswise into ½-inch-wide strips

1 (6-oz.) pkg. frozen snow pea pods, partially thawed

1 cup skim milk

2 teaspoons cornstarch

1 teaspoon chicken-flavor instant bouillon

½ teaspoon garlic powder

¼ to ½ teaspoon dried basil leaves

1 cup cherry tomatoes, cut into quarters

¼ cup grated Parmesan cheese

1. Cook vermicelli to desired doneness as directed on package.

2. Meanwhile, in nonstick Dutch oven or large saucepan, heat oil over medium-high heat until hot. Add chicken and pea pods; cook until chicken is no longer pink and pea pods are completely thawed, stirring frequently.

3. In small bowl, combine milk, cornstarch, bouillon, garlic powder and basil; blend well. Add to chicken mixture; mix well. Bring to a boil, stirring constantly. Gently stir in tomatoes. Remove from heat.

about **Cherry Tomatoes**

To avoid a messy squirt, cut cherry tomatoes with a very sharp knife; a serrated blade may work best.

4. Drain vermicelli; stir into chicken mixture. Sprinkle with Parmesan cheese.

YIELD: 4 (1¾-CUP) SERVINGS

Nutrition Information Per Serving
Serving Size: 1¾ Cups

Calories	390	Calories from Fat	70
		% Daily Value	
Total Fat	8g		12%
Saturated	3g		15%
Cholesterol	75mg		25%
Sodium	220mg		9%
Total Carbohydrate	42g		14%
Dietary Fiber	2g		8%
Sugars	6g		
Protein	37g		
Vitamin A	8%	Vitamin C	20%
Calcium	20%	Iron	20%

Dietary Exchanges: 2½ Starch, 1 Vegetable, 4 Very Lean Meat, ½ Fat OR 2½ Carbohydrate, 1 Vegetable, 4 Very Lean Meat, ½ Fat

Five-Spice Chicken with Noodles

PREP TIME: 30 MINUTES

8 oz. uncooked soba noodles*

2 teaspoons oil

1¼ lb. boneless, skinless chicken breast halves, cut into bite-sized pieces

1 large carrot, thinly sliced

1 (14½-oz.) can ready-to-serve fat-free chicken broth with ⅓ less sodium

⅓ cup lite teriyaki sauce

2 tablespoons cornstarch

2 teaspoons Chinese five-spice powder

4 green onions, diagonally sliced

2 tablespoons chopped fresh cilantro

1. Cook noodles as directed on package.

2. Meanwhile, heat oil in large nonstick skillet or wok over medium-high heat until hot. Add chicken; cook and stir 3 to 4 minutes or until lightly browned. Add carrot; cook and stir 3 to 4 minutes or until crisp-tender.

3. In medium bowl, combine broth, teriyaki sauce, cornstarch and five-spice powder; blend well. Add to

about Five-Spice Powder

Five-spice powder, a popular seasoning for Chinese chicken, is a blend of sweet and savory spices. Blends may vary slightly, but often include ground anise, star anise, cinnamon, Szechuan peppercorns and dried orange peel or ground cardamom. It's very fragrant and imparts a pungent-sweet flavor. Delicious!

chicken and carrot; mix well. Reduce heat; cover and cook 5 minutes or until chicken is no longer pink and carrot is tender, stirring occasionally.

4. Drain noodles; add to chicken mixture. Cook 2 to 3 minutes or until thoroughly heated. Sprinkle with onions and cilantro.

YIELD: 6 (1-CUP) SERVINGS

Tip: * Uncooked soba noodles can be found in the Asian food section of the supermarket. If noodles come with seasoning packet, discard packet. If soba noodles are unavailable, uncooked linguine or spaghetti can be used.

Nutrition Information Per Serving
Serving Size: 1 Cup

Calories	240	Calories from Fat	35
		% Daily Value	
Total Fat	4g		6%
Saturated	1g		5%
Cholesterol	60mg		20%
Sodium	600mg		25%
Total Carbohydrate	23g		8%
Dietary Fiber	2g		8%
Sugars	6g		
Protein	27g		
Vitamin A	110%	Vitamin C	6%
Calcium	4%	Iron	10%

Dietary Exchanges: 1 1/2 Starch, 3 Very Lean Meat OR 1 1/2 Carbohydrate, 3 Very Lean Meat

Sweet-and-Sour Chicken with Vegetables

▪ ▪ ▪ ▪ ▪ ▪ ▪ ▪ ▪ ▪ ▪ ▪ ▪ ▪ ▪ ▪ ▪ ▪ ▪ ▪

PREP TIME: 25 MINUTES

3 cups hot cooked instant rice (cooked as directed on package, omitting margarine and salt)

1 teaspoon oil

¾ cup coarsely chopped onions

¾ cup thin diagonally sliced carrots

¾ cup sliced celery

1 small green bell pepper, cut into short thin strips

2 boneless, skinless chicken breast halves, cut into bite-sized pieces

1 (8-oz.) can pineapple tidbits in unsweetened juice, drained

1 (9-oz.) jar (about 1 cup) sweet-and-sour sauce

1. While rice is cooking, heat oil in large nonstick skillet over medium-high heat until hot. Add onions and carrots; cook 5 minutes, stirring occasionally. Add celery and bell pepper; cook and stir 3 minutes.

2. Stir in chicken, pineapple and sweet-and-sour sauce. Bring to a boil. Boil gently 5 minutes or until chicken is no longer pink, stirring occasionally. Serve over rice.

YIELD: 6 SERVINGS

Nutrition Information Per Serving
Serving Size: 1/6 of Recipe

Calories	200	Calories from Fat	20
		% Daily Value	
Total Fat	2g		3%
Saturated	0g		0%
Cholesterol	25mg		8%
Sodium	150mg		6%
Total Carbohydrate	35g		12%
Dietary Fiber	2g		8%
Sugars	13g		
Protein	11g		
Vitamin A	90%	Vitamin C	15%
Calcium	4%	Iron	8%

Dietary Exchanges: 1 Starch, 1 Fruit, 1 Vegetable, 1 Very Lean Meat OR 2 Carbohydrate, 1 Vegetable, 1 Very Lean Meat

Chicken Parmesan
Italiano

■ ■ ■ ■ ■ ■ ■ ■ ■ ■ ■ ■ ■ ■ ■ ■ ■ ■ ■ ■

PREP TIME: 30 MINUTES

2 tablespoons Italian-style bread crumbs

2 tablespoons shredded fresh Parmesan cheese

½ teaspoon dried oregano leaves

1 tablespoon lemon juice

1 small garlic clove, minced

2 boneless, skinless chicken breast halves

Nonstick cooking spray

1. Heat oven to 425°F. Line cookie sheet with foil; spray foil with nonstick cooking spray.

2. In shallow dish, combine bread crumbs, cheese and oregano; mix well. In small cup or bowl, combine lemon juice and garlic.

3. Brush both sides of chicken with lemon juice mixture; coat with bread crumb mixture. Place on sprayed foil-lined cookie sheet. Lightly spray chicken with cooking spray.

4. Bake at 425°F. for 15 to 20 minutes or until chicken is fork-tender and juices run clear.

YIELD: 2 SERVINGS

Nutrition Information Per Serving
Serving Size: ½ of Recipe

Calories	210	Calories from Fat	60
		% Daily Value	
Total Fat	7g		11%
Saturated	2g		10%
Cholesterol	80mg		27%
Sodium	280mg		12%
Total Carbohydrate	6g		2%
Dietary Fiber	0g		0%
Sugars	0g		
Protein	30g		
Vitamin A	0%	Vitamin C	2%
Calcium	10%	Iron	8%

Dietary Exchanges: ½ Starch, 4 Very Lean Meat, ½ Fat OR
½ Carbohydrate, 4 Very Lean Meat, ½ Fat

▼ Chicken Parmesan Italiano

Wilted Spinach Chicken Fettuccine

PREP TIME: 25 MINUTES

16 oz. uncooked fettuccine

3 tablespoons olive oil

1 lb. boneless, skinless chicken breast halves, cut into thin strips

1 (8-oz.) pkg. (3 cups) sliced fresh mushrooms

3 tablespoons finely chopped shallots or ½ cup chopped onion

1 to 2 teaspoons finely chopped fresh marjoram or basil

¼ teaspoon salt

⅛ teaspoon pepper

3 cups torn fresh spinach leaves

3 Italian plum tomatoes, chopped (¾ cup)

Tomato slices and fresh marjoram, if desired

1. In large saucepan or Dutch oven, cook fettuccine to desired doneness as directed on package.

2. Meanwhile, heat oil in large nonstick skillet over medium heat until hot. Add chicken; cook and stir until no longer pink. Add mushrooms, shallots and 1 to 2 teaspoons marjoram; cook until thoroughly heated. Stir in salt and pepper.

3. Drain fettuccine; return to saucepan. Stir in spinach and hot chicken mixture. Cook over low heat until thoroughly heated, stirring occasionally. Stir in chopped tomatoes. Spoon onto large serving platter. Garnish with tomato slices and fresh marjoram.

YIELD: 8 (1½-CUP) SERVINGS

Nutrition Information Per Serving
Serving Size: 1½ Cups

Calories	350	Calories from Fat	80
		% Daily Value	
Total Fat	9g		14%
Saturated	2g		10%
Cholesterol	85mg		28%
Sodium	130mg		5%
Total Carbohydrate	44g		15%
Dietary Fiber	3g		12%
Sugars	3g		
Protein	22g		
Vitamin A	40%	Vitamin C	15%
Calcium	4%	Iron	25%

Dietary Exchanges: 2½ Starch, 1 Vegetable, 2 Very Lean Meat, 1 Fat OR 2½ Carbohydrate, 1 Vegetable, 2 Very Lean Meat, 1 Fat

convenience Chicken

No time to roast a whole chicken? Look for these quick-prep or no-prep forms of chicken in the supermarket.

Meat department

Boneless, skinless chicken breast halves
Preseasoned chicken breast halves
Boneless chicken strips for stir-frying
Uncooked chicken patties

Frozen food section

Cubed cooked chicken

Canned food section

Water-packed canned chicken

Deli

Sliced cooked chicken

Creamy Basil Chicken-Pasta

PREP TIME: 25 MINUTES

6 oz. (2½ cups) uncooked rainbow rotini (spiral pasta)

2 cups frozen cut broccoli

1 cup nonfat sour cream

2 teaspoons all-purpose flour

½ cup skim milk

1½ cups diced cooked chicken breast

¾ teaspoon dried basil leaves

1 (4.5-oz.) jar sliced mushrooms, drained

4 tablespoons grated Parmesan cheese

1. In large saucepan or Dutch oven, cook rotini to desired doneness as directed on package, adding broccoli during last 5 minutes of cooking time.

2. Meanwhile, in medium saucepan, combine sour cream and flour; blend well. Stir in milk. Cook over medium heat, stirring constantly, until hot but not boiling. Stir in chicken, basil, mushrooms and 3 tablespoons of the cheese. Cook until thoroughly heated.

3. Drain rotini and broccoli; return to saucepan. Add chicken mixture; toss to coat. Place mixture in serving dish or on serving platter; sprinkle with remaining 1 tablespoon cheese.

YIELD: 4 (1½-CUP) SERVINGS

slicing **Chicken**

When a recipe calls for diagonally sliced chicken, put it in the freezer for 20 to 30 minutes first. The meat will firm up just enough to make diagonal slicing easier.

Nutrition Information Per Serving
Serving Size: 1½ Cups

Calories	360	Calories from Fat	45
		% Daily Value	
Total Fat	5g		8%
Saturated	2g		10%
Cholesterol	50mg		17%
Sodium	450mg		19%
Total Carbohydrate	45g		15%
Dietary Fiber	5g		20%
Sugars	9g		
Protein	33g		
Vitamin A	50%	Vitamin C	60%
Calcium	25%	Iron	20%

Dietary Exchanges: 2½ Starch, 1 Vegetable, 3½ Very Lean Meat OR 2½ Carbohydrate, 1 Vegetable, 3½ Very Lean Meat

Chicken and Spinach Calzones

PREP TIME: 35 MINUTES
(READY IN 50 MINUTES)

1 tablespoon cornmeal, if desired

2 boneless, skinless chicken breast halves, cut into ½-inch cubes

1 small onion, chopped

2 garlic cloves, minced

½ cup pizza sauce

2 tablespoons grated Romano cheese

2 cups frozen cut leaf spinach, thawed, squeezed to drain and coarsely chopped*

3 oz. mozzarella cheese, cut into ¼-inch cubes (⅔ cup)

1 (10-oz.) can refrigerated pizza crust

1. Heat oven to 425°F. Line cookie sheet with foil; spray foil with nonstick cooking spray. Sprinkle with cornmeal.

2. Spray medium nonstick skillet with cooking spray. Heat over medium-high heat until hot. Add chicken; cook and stir 5 to 6 minutes or until no longer pink. Add onion and garlic; cook 1 to 2 minutes or until onion is tender.

3. Stir in pizza sauce and Romano cheese. Remove from heat; stir in spinach and mozzarella cheese.

Chicken storage *and safety*

- At the supermarket, check the "sell by" date on the package and plan to use it within two days (one is better), regardless of the freshness date on the package.

- Bring chicken directly home from the market and store it in the coldest part of the refrigerator. Set the package on a plate to catch any drips.

- Refrigerate chicken in its original wrapper; if torn, overwrap it with plastic.

- Scrub your hands before and after handling raw chicken.

- Use hot, soapy water to wash knives, cutting boards and anything else that has come into contact with raw chicken.

- For best quality, use whole frozen chicken within one year, parts within nine months and giblets or ground meat within four months.

- Although freezer burn is unpleasant, it is not dangerous. Use a sharp knife to cut away any dried out, discolored areas.

- Cook chicken until the juices run clear and no trace of pink remains.

- Put food away as soon as possible after the meal, but definitely within two hours. Cooked leftover chicken can be refrigerated for three to four days.

- Frozen leftovers will be best if used within three to six months. Longer freezing will not affect safety, but the flavor, texture and color qualities may deteriorate.

4. Remove pizza dough from can; do not unroll. Cut roll of dough into 4 equal portions. Press or roll each portion into 6- to 7-inch round.

5. Spoon ¼ of spinach mixture onto half of each round. Fold untopped half of dough over filling; press edges together with fork to seal. Place calzones on cookie sheet; reshape into semicircles, if necessary. If desired, spray tops lightly with cooking spray.

6. Bake at 425°F. for 10 to 15 minutes or until crusts are golden brown.

YIELD: 4 CALZONES

Tip: * To quickly thaw spinach, place in colander or strainer; rinse with warm water until thawed. Squeeze dry with paper towels.

Nutrition Information Per Serving
Serving Size: 1 Calzone

Calories	370	Calories from Fat	80
		% Daily Value	
Total Fat	9g		14%
Saturated	4g		20%
Cholesterol	50mg		17%
Sodium	810mg		34%
Total Carbohydrate	41g		14%
Dietary Fiber	3g		12%
Sugars	5g		
Protein	29g		
Vitamin A	45%	Vitamin C	10%
Calcium	30%	Iron	20%

Dietary Exchanges: 2 Starch, 2 Vegetable, 3 Lean Meat OR
2 Carbohydrate, 2 Vegetable, 3 Lean Meat

a good **Pounding**

Flattening a chicken breast gives a uniform thickness for more even cooking and tenderizes the meat by breaking down some of the fibers. To flatten, place a boneless breast on a work surface between two pieces of plastic wrap and pound lightly with a kitchen mallet or the side of a 1- or 2-pound can.

Chicken Piccata

PREP TIME: 35 MINUTES

6 boneless, skinless chicken breast halves

⅓ cup all-purpose flour

½ teaspoon white pepper

Dash salt

2 teaspoons olive oil

½ cup chicken broth

1 cup sliced fresh mushrooms

1 medium onion, sliced, separated into rings

¼ cup chopped fresh parsley or 1 tablespoon dried parsley flakes

¼ cup drained capers

¼ cup fresh lemon juice

Lemon slices, if desired

1. Place 1 chicken breast half, boned side up, between 2 pieces of plastic wrap or waxed paper. Working from center, lightly pound chicken with flat side of mallet or rolling pin until about ½ inch larger in diameter; remove wrap. Repeat with remaining chicken breast halves.

2. In small bag, combine flour, pepper and salt; shake until well mixed. Place 1 chicken breast half in bag; shake to coat completely with flour mixture. Repeat with remaining chicken breast halves.

3. Heat 1 teaspoon of the oil in large nonstick skillet over medium-high heat until hot. Cook 3 chicken breast halves until browned on both sides and no longer pink in center. Remove from skillet; cover to keep warm. Repeat with remaining 1 teaspoon oil and 3 chicken breast halves. Remove from skillet; cover to keep warm.

4. Add broth to same skillet; bring to a boil. Add mushrooms and onion; cook 5 to 8 minutes or until liquid evaporates, stirring occasionally. Add parsley, capers, lemon juice and chicken breast halves; cook until thoroughly heated. Garnish with lemon slices.

YIELD: 6 SERVINGS

Nutrition Information Per Serving
Serving Size: ⅙ of Recipe

Calories	190	Calories from Fat	45
		% Daily Value	
Total Fat	5g		8%
Saturated	1g		5%
Cholesterol	75mg		25%
Sodium	270mg		11%
Total Carbohydrate	9g		3%
Dietary Fiber	1g		4%
Sugars	2g		
Protein	28g		
Vitamin A	4%	Vitamin C	15%
Calcium	2%	Iron	10%

Dietary Exchanges: ½ Starch, 4 Very Lean Meat OR ½ Carbohydrate, 4 Very Lean Meat

▼ Chicken Piccata

Oven Chicken Cordon Bleu

■ ■ ■ ■ ■ ■ ■ ■ ■ ■ ■ ■ ■ ■ ■ ■ ■ ■ ■

PREP TIME: 20 MINUTES
(READY IN 50 MINUTES)

4 boneless, skinless chicken breast halves

2 teaspoons Dijon mustard

4 teaspoons chopped fresh chives

4 very thin slices cooked lean ham (about ¾ oz. each)

4 very thin slices reduced-fat Swiss cheese (about ¾ oz. each)

1 egg white

1 tablespoon water

⅓ cup corn flake crumbs

¼ teaspoon paprika

1. Heat oven to 375°F. Spray 8-inch square (2-quart) baking dish with nonstick cooking spray. Place 1 chicken breast half between 2 pieces of plastic wrap or waxed paper. Working from center, gently pound chicken with flat side of mallet or rolling pin until about ¼ inch thick; remove wrap. Repeat with remaining chicken breast halves.

2. Spread each chicken breast half with ½ teaspoon mustard; sprinkle each with 1 teaspoon chives. Cut ham and cheese slices to fit chicken. Top each chicken breast half with ham and cheese slice. Roll up, tucking ends inside.

3. In shallow bowl, combine egg white and water; beat slightly. Place corn flake crumbs in shallow dish. Coat chicken rolls with egg white mixture; roll in crumbs. Place in sprayed baking dish; sprinkle with paprika.

4. Bake at 375°F. for 25 to 30 minutes or until chicken is fork-tender and juices run clear.

YIELD: 4 SERVINGS

Nutrition Information Per Serving
Serving Size: ¼ of Recipe

Calories	250	Calories from Fat	60
		% Daily Value	
Total Fat	7g		11%
Saturated	3g		15%
Cholesterol	95mg		32%
Sodium	550mg		23%
Total Carbohydrate	7g		2%
Dietary Fiber	0g		0%
Sugars	1g		
Protein	39g		
Vitamin A	15%	Vitamin C	10%
Calcium	25%	Iron	8%

Dietary Exchanges: ½ Starch, 4 Lean Meat OR ½ Carbohydrate, 4 Lean Meat

---

how much chicken Do You Need?

■ ■ ■ ■ ■ ■ ■ ■ ■ ■ ■ ■ ■ ■ ■ ■ ■ ■ ■

Plan on about ½ pound of chicken on the bone or ¼ pound boneless per serving. For recipes that call for cooked or cubed chicken:

• One 3- to 4-lb. fryer yields 3 to 4 cups.

• Two whole chicken breasts (1 ½ lb. with skin and bone) or ¾ lb. chicken breast (boned, skinned) yields about 2 cups.

• A 5-oz. can of chunk chicken (drained, flaked) yields 1 cup.

Curried Chicken and Rice

PREP TIME: 20 MINUTES
(READY IN 40 MINUTES)

¾ lb. boneless, skinless chicken breast halves, cut into bite-sized pieces

1⅓ cups water

1 (14.5-oz.) can stewed tomatoes, undrained

⅓ cup raisins

1 tablespoon brown sugar

1 tablespoon fresh lemon juice

1 teaspoon chicken-flavor instant bouillon

1 teaspoon curry powder

½ teaspoon cinnamon

¼ teaspoon salt

¼ teaspoon ginger

1 cup uncooked basmati rice, rinsed, or regular long-grain rice

1. In large saucepan, combine all ingredients except rice. Bring to a boil.

2. Stir in rice. Reduce heat; cover and simmer 20 minutes or until chicken is no longer pink, rice is tender and liquid is absorbed.

YIELD: 4 (1¼-CUP) SERVINGS

Nutrition Information Per Serving
Serving Size: 1¼ Cups

Calories.................................340	Calories from Fat...........25
	% Daily Value
Total Fat.........................3g.......................5%	
Saturated........................1g........................5%	
Cholesterol...................55mg.......................18%	
Sodium..........................490mg.......................20%	
Total Carbohydrate...........55g.......................18%	
Dietary Fiber....................2g.......................8%	
Sugars............................14g	
Protein...............................24g	
Vitamin A.......................15%	Vitamin C...................20%
Calcium............................6%	Iron.............................20%

Dietary Exchanges: 3 Starch, ½ Fruit, 2 Very Lean Meat OR 3½ Carbohydrate, 2 Very Lean Meat

White Burgundy Coq au Vin

PREP TIME: 20 MINUTES
(READY IN 40 MINUTES)

1 tablespoon oil

4 boneless, skinless chicken breast halves

3 tablespoons all-purpose flour

½ cup chicken broth

½ cup white or red burgundy wine or chicken broth

1 (8-oz.) pkg. fresh small whole mushrooms

¼ teaspoon garlic powder

¼ teaspoon dried marjoram leaves

Dash pepper

¼ cup sliced green onions

1. Heat oil in large nonstick skillet over medium-high heat until hot. Coat chicken with flour; add to skillet. Cook until browned on both sides.

2. Move chicken pieces to side of skillet. Add any remaining flour, broth, wine, mushrooms, garlic powder, marjoram and pepper; blend well. Arrange chicken pieces in wine mixture. Bring to a boil. Reduce heat to low; cover and simmer 10 to 15 minutes or until chicken is fork-tender and juices run clear, stirring occasionally. Add onions; cook an additional 5 minutes.

YIELD: 4 SERVINGS

Nutrition Information Per Serving
Serving Size: ¼ of Recipe

Calories.................................230	Calories from Fat...........60
	% Daily Value
Total Fat.........................7g.......................11%	
Saturated........................1g........................5%	
Cholesterol...................75mg.......................25%	
Sodium..........................170mg.......................7%	
Total Carbohydrate...........8g.......................3%	
Dietary Fiber....................1g.......................4%	
Sugars............................1g	
Protein...............................29g	
Vitamin A.........................0%	Vitamin C...................4%
Calcium............................2%	Iron.............................10%

Dietary Exchanges: ½ Starch, 4 Very Lean Meat, 1 Fat OR ½ Carbohydrate, 4 Very Lean Meat, 1 Fat

◄ Curried Chicken and Rice

Baking chicken in a seasoned crumb crust simulates some of the mouthwatering appeal of fried chicken (crisp, flavorful exterior, moist interior) but with significantly less fat than traditional stovetop frying. Baking also offers the advantage of unattended cooking time, whereas frying requires constant vigilance. To promote browning, spritz the chicken very lightly with nonstick cooking spray before baking.

Oven-Fried Herb Chicken

PREP TIME: 30 MINUTES

½ cup corn flake crumbs

¼ teaspoon salt

¼ teaspoon garlic powder

¼ teaspoon paprika

⅛ teaspoon ground red pepper (cayenne)

1 egg white

1 teaspoon water

8 boneless, skinless chicken breast halves

1. Heat oven to 450°F. Line 15×10×1-inch baking pan with foil; spray foil with nonstick cooking spray.
2. In small bowl, combine corn flake crumbs, salt, garlic powder, paprika and ground red pepper; mix well. In another small bowl, beat egg white and water until frothy. Place chicken in sprayed foil-lined pan. Brush with egg white mixture; sprinkle with crumb mixture.
3. Bake at 450°F. for 15 to 20 minutes or until chicken is fork-tender and juices run clear.

YIELD: 8 SERVINGS

Nutrition Information Per Serving
Serving Size: ⅛ of Recipe

Calories	160	Calories from Fat	25
		% Daily Value	
Total Fat	3g		5%
Saturated	1g		5%
Cholesterol	75mg		25%
Sodium	190mg		8%
Total Carbohydrate	5g		2%
Dietary Fiber	0g		0%
Sugars	0g		
Protein	28g		
Vitamin A	6%	Vitamin C	4%
Calcium	0%	Iron	6%

Dietary Exchanges: ½ Starch, 3½ Very Lean Meat OR ½ Carbohydrate, 3½ Very Lean Meat

Caramelized Garlic Chicken

PREP TIME: 25 MINUTES

2 teaspoons olive oil

4 garlic cloves, minced

4 teaspoons brown sugar

4 boneless, skinless chicken breast halves

1. Heat oven to 500°F. Line shallow roasting pan with foil; spray foil with nonstick cooking spray.
2. Heat oil in small nonstick skillet over medium-low heat until hot. Add garlic; cook 1 to 2 minutes or until garlic begins to soften. Remove from heat; stir in brown sugar until well mixed.
3. Place chicken breast halves in sprayed foil-lined pan; spread garlic mixture evenly over chicken.
4. Bake at 500°F. for 10 to 15 minutes or until chicken is fork-tender and juices run clear.

YIELD: 4 SERVINGS

Nutrition Information Per Serving
Serving Size: ¼ of Recipe

Calories	170	Calories from Fat	45
		% Daily Value	
Total Fat	5g		8%
Saturated	1g		5%
Cholesterol	75mg		25%
Sodium	65mg		3%
Total Carbohydrate	5g		2%
Dietary Fiber	0g		0%
Sugars	5g		
Protein	27g		
Vitamin A	0%	Vitamin C	0%
Calcium	2%	Iron	6%

Dietary Exchanges: ½ Fruit, 4 Very Lean Meat OR ½ Carbohydrate, 4 Very Lean Meat

▲ Honey-Mustard Chicken and Carrots

Honey-Mustard Chicken and Carrots

■ ■

PREP TIME: 30 MINUTES

2 teaspoons margarine or butter

4 boneless, skinless chicken breast halves

½ cup apple juice

2 cups frozen baby cut carrots

2 tablespoons sweet honey mustard

3 tablespoons coarsely chopped honey-roasted peanuts

1. Melt margarine in large nonstick skillet over medium-high heat. Add chicken; cook 5 to 8 minutes or until chicken is browned on both sides.

2. Add apple juice. Reduce heat to medium; cover and cook 5 minutes. Add carrots; cover and cook 5 to 10 minutes or until chicken is fork-tender, its juices run clear and carrots are crisp-tender.

3. With slotted spoon, remove chicken and carrots from skillet; cover to keep warm. Stir mustard into liquid in skillet. Spoon mustard sauce over chicken and carrots; sprinkle with peanuts.

YIELD: 4 SERVINGS

Nutrition Information Per Serving
Serving Size: ¼ of Recipe

Calories	250	Calories from Fat	80
		% Daily Value	
Total Fat	9g		14%
Saturated	2g		10%
Cholesterol	75mg		25%
Sodium	210mg		9%
Total Carbohydrate	13g		4%
Dietary Fiber	3g		12%
Sugars	9g		
Protein	29g		
Vitamin A	170%	Vitamin C	0%
Calcium	4%	Iron	8%

Dietary Exchanges: ½ Fruit, 1 Vegetable, 4 Very Lean Meat, 1 Fat OR ½ Carbohydrate, 1 Vegetable, 4 Very Lean Meat, 1 Fat

Presto Chicken Primavera Potatoes

4 medium baking potatoes (about 2 lb.)

1 teaspoon oil

¾ cup chopped zucchini

½ cup chopped red bell pepper

1 tablespoon all-purpose flour

¼ teaspoon garlic powder

⅛ teaspoon pepper

1½ cups skim milk

⅓ cup grated Parmesan cheese

2 cups cubed cooked chicken breast

Microwave Directions: 1. Pierce potatoes with fork; place on microwave-safe paper towel or roasting rack in microwave. Microwave on HIGH for 10 to 15 minutes or until tender, turning once halfway through cooking. Cover; let stand 5 minutes.

2. Meanwhile, heat oil in medium nonstick saucepan over medium-high heat until hot. Add zucchini and bell pepper; cook and stir until zucchini is crisp-tender. Stir in flour, garlic powder and pepper. Add milk; stir until well blended. Cook and stir until thickened and bubbly. Stir in cheese and chicken; cook until thoroughly heated.

3. To serve, cut potatoes in half lengthwise, cutting to but not through bottom of potatoes. Mash slightly with fork. Spoon chicken mixture over potatoes.

YIELD: 4 SERVINGS

Nutrition Information Per Serving
Serving Size: ¼ of Recipe

Calories	350	Calories from Fat	60
		% Daily Value	
Total Fat	7g		11%
Saturated	3g		15%
Cholesterol	70mg		23%
Sodium	260mg		11%
Total Carbohydrate	39g		13%
Dietary Fiber	4g		16%
Sugars	7g		
Protein	32g		
Vitamin A	20%	Vitamin C	50%
Calcium	25%	Iron	15%

Dietary Exchanges: 2½ Starch, 3 Lean Meat OR 2½ Carbohydrate, 3 Lean Meat

great recipes that use
Cooked Chicken or Turkey

When you have leftover chicken or turkey on hand, put it to use in one of these recipes:

Chicken Vegetable Alfredo (page 104)
Creamy-Basil Chicken Pasta (page 110)
Creamy Turkey Burritos (page 144)
Creamy Turkey Lasagna (page 139)
Presto Chicken Primavera Potatoes (above)
Swiss Turkey Broccoli Melts (page 144)
Turkey Pita Fajitas (page 142)
Turkey Veggie Omelet (page 141)

Presto Chicken Primavera Potatoes ▶

▲ Barbecued Chicken Pizza

Barbecued Chicken Pizza

■ ■ ■ ■ ■ ■ ■ ■ ■ ■ ■ ■ ■ ■ ■ ■ ■ ■ ■

PREP TIME: 30 MINUTES

2 cups shredded cooked chicken breast

⅓ cup barbecue sauce

1 (10-oz.) prebaked thin-crust Italian bread shell (12-inch)

3 Italian plum tomatoes, sliced

4 oz. (1 cup) shredded reduced-fat Monterey Jack cheese

Fresh cilantro leaves

1. Heat oven to 450°F. In small bowl, combine chicken and barbecue sauce; mix well. Place bread shell on ungreased cookie sheet; spread chicken mix-ture over shell. Arrange tomatoes over chicken; sprinkle with cheese.

2. Bake at 450°F. for 10 minutes or until cheese is melted and bread shell is browned. Sprinkle with cilantro.

YIELD: 6 SERVINGS

Nutrition Information Per Serving
Serving Size: ⅙ of Recipe

Calories	270	Calories from Fat	70
			% Daily Value
Total Fat	8g		12%
Saturated	3g		15%
Cholesterol	55mg		18%
Sodium	510mg		21%
Total Carbohydrate	24g		8%
Dietary Fiber	1g		3%
Sugars	2g		
Protein	26g		
Vitamin A	8%	Vitamin C	6%
Calcium	20%	Iron	10%

Dietary Exchanges: 1½ Starch, 3 Very Lean Meat, 1 Fat OR
1½ Carbohydrate, 3 Very Lean Meat, 1 Fat

boning a **Chicken Breast**

To bone a whole chicken breast:

1. Remove the skin and lay the breast, bone side up, on the work surface. Using a sharp knife, run the blade down the center to cut the thin membrane, exposing the keel bone (dark, spoon-shaped bone) and white cartilage.

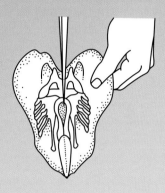

2. Remove the keel bone by placing your thumbs at the base and top of the keel bone. Bend the bone back until it breaks through the membrane. Run your finger under the edge of the keel bone and pull partially away from the breast. Pull down to remove the white cartilage.

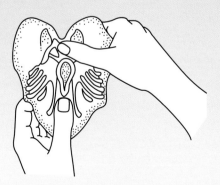

3. To remove the ribs, insert the point of a sharp knife under the ribs on one side of the breast and gradually scrape the meat away from the bones. Cut the ribs away. Cut through and under the shoulder joint and remove. Repeat with the other side of the breast. Locate the wishbone at the top of the center of the breast. Run the point of the knife close to the bone to remove the bone.

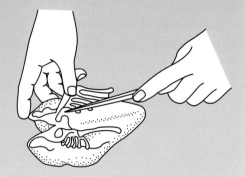

4. Lay the breast flat and cut it in half along the cleft that contained the keel bone. Remove the white tendon and trim away the fat.

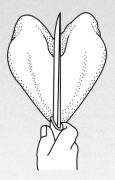

5. If desired, cut out the "tenderloin" section, a smaller, separate muscle that's easily removed from the main portion of the breast and can be cooked as a separate little morsel or incorporated into the main dish.

Glazed Chicken over Couscous Pilaf

PREP TIME: 25 MINUTES

Pilaf

½ **cup frozen sweet peas**

¾ **cup water**

⅛ **teaspoon salt**

⅛ **teaspoon ginger**

½ **cup uncooked couscous**

Chicken

2 **tablespoons orange juice**

1 **tablespoon apricot preserves or honey**

½ **teaspoon spicy brown mustard**

2 **boneless, skinless chicken breast halves**

▼ Glazed Chicken over Couscous Pilaf

1. In medium saucepan, combine peas, water, salt and ginger. Bring to a boil over high heat. Reduce heat to medium-low; cover and simmer 2 minutes. Remove from heat; stir in couscous. Cover; let stand 5 minutes.

2. Meanwhile, in small bowl, combine orange juice, preserves and mustard; blend well. Pour half of mixture (about 2 tablespoons) into another small dish; reserve for topping. Place chicken on broiler pan; brush with about half of remaining orange juice glaze.

3. Broil 4 to 6 inches from heat for 5 minutes. Turn chicken. Brush with glaze; discard any remaining glaze. Broil an additional 3 to 5 minutes or until chicken is fork-tender and juices run clear.

4. Stir couscous mixture lightly with fork; divide evenly onto 2 serving plates. Top each with chicken; drizzle with reserved orange juice mixture.

YIELD: 2 SERVINGS

Nutrition Information Per Serving
Serving Size: 1/2 of Recipe

Calories	370	Calories from Fat	35

		% Daily Value
Total Fat	4g	6%
Saturated	1g	5%
Cholesterol	75mg	25%
Sodium	280mg	12%
Total Carbohydrate	49g	16%
Dietary Fiber	4g	16%
Sugars	8g	
Protein	34g	

Vitamin A	4%	Vitamin C	15%
Calcium	4%	Iron	10%

Dietary Exchanges: 3 Starch, 3 1/2 Very Lean Meat OR 3 Carbohydrate, 3 1/2 Very Lean Meat

chicken without Stickin'

■ ■ ■ ■ ■ ■ ■ ■ ■ ■ ■ ■ ■ ■ ■ ■ ■ ■ ■

Two innovations of recent years make it possible to sauté chicken as well as other ingredients without all the oil: the nonstick skillet and nonstick cooking spray. This duo mimics the desirable effects of traditional sautéing in oil (appealing brown color, enhanced flavor) with far less fat.

Nonstick cooking spray is real oil, plus small amounts of propellants, packaged in an aerosol can, which makes it possible to disperse oil in a far thinner layer than would be possible with regular oil or butter. A 1-second spray contains about .6 grams of fat.

For best results, spray the frying pan cold, then heat the pan.

A nonstick pan can last years if it is properly maintained.

- Use only plastic or wooden utensils, not metal, which could mar the finish.

- Since the finish resists food sticking, washing with hot soapy water and a sponge or plastic scrubber should suffice; do not use steel wool or abrasive powders.

- Do not store other pans or dishes directly on the nonstick surface. If you must stack pans, protect each one with a kitchen or paper towel in between.

Skillet Arroz Con Pollo

■ ■ ■ ■ ■ ■ ■ ■ ■ ■ ■ ■ ■ ■ ■ ■ ■ ■ ■

PREP TIME: 40 MINUTES

2 teaspoons olive oil

4 chicken drumsticks, skin removed

4 chicken thighs, skin removed

1 (14 1/2-oz.) can ready-to-serve chicken broth

1 cup uncooked converted or regular long-grain white rice

1/2 cup sliced green onions

1/2 cup chopped red or green bell pepper

1/4 teaspoon turmeric or saffron

1/8 teaspoon garlic powder

1/8 to 1/4 teaspoon ground red pepper (cayenne)

1. Heat oil in large nonstick skillet over medium-high heat until hot. Add chicken; cook until browned on all sides.

2. Move chicken to side of skillet. Add all remaining ingredients; blend well. Place chicken on rice mixture. Bring to a boil. Reduce heat to low; cover and simmer 15 minutes, stirring occasionally.

3. Turn chicken; cover and simmer an additional 5 to 10 minutes or until chicken is fork-tender and juices run clear.

YIELD: 4 SERVINGS

Nutrition Information Per Serving
Serving Size: 1/4 of Recipe

Calories	390	Calories from Fat	100

		% Daily Value
Total Fat	11g	17%
Saturated	3g	15%
Cholesterol	90mg	30%
Sodium	420mg	18%
Total Carbohydrate	40g	13%
Dietary Fiber	1g	4%
Sugars	1g	
Protein	32g	

Vitamin A	15%	Vitamin C	30%
Calcium	6%	Iron	20%

Dietary Exchanges: 2 Starch, 2 Vegetable, 3 Lean Meat, 1/2 Fat OR 2 Carbohydrate, 2 Vegetable, 3 Lean Meat, 1/2 Fat

Mexican-Style Chicken-Filled Tortillas

PREP TIME: 20 MINUTES

4 boneless, skinless chicken breast halves, cut into thin bite-sized strips

1 cup frozen whole kernel corn

1 cup chunky-style salsa

1 (2¼-oz.) can sliced ripe olives, well drained

8 (8- to 10-inch) fat-free flour tortillas

1. Spray large nonstick skillet with nonstick cooking spray. Heat over medium-high heat until hot. Add

▼ Mexican-Style Chicken-Filled Tortillas

about Salsa

Literally "sauce" in Spanish, *salsa* also refers to a popular type of Latin American dance music but is most commonly known on U.S. menus as a zesty condiment that rivals ketchup for popularity. To make a fresh salsa for dipping chips or spreading on burgers, mince fresh tomato, onion and cucumber and season with chopped fresh cilantro and hot pepper sauce and salt to taste.

chicken; cook and stir 5 to 6 minutes or until no longer pink.

2. Stir in corn, salsa and olives. Reduce heat to medium; cook 4 to 6 minutes or until thoroughly heated.

3. Meanwhile, warm tortillas as directed on package. Spoon ¼ of chicken mixture onto half of each tortilla. Fold tortillas over. If desired, serve with light sour cream and additional salsa.

YIELD: 4 SERVINGS

Nutrition Information Per Serving
Serving Size: ¼ of Recipe

Calories................................420		Calories from Fat..........45	
		% Daily Value	
Total Fat 5g		..........8%	
Saturated 1g		..........5%	
Cholesterol 75mg		..........25%	
Sodium 1,170mg		..........49%	
Total Carbohydrate 59g		..........20%	
Dietary Fiber 3g		..........12%	
Sugars 5g			
Protein 34g			
Vitamin A 6%		Vitamin C 15%	
Calcium 2%		Iron 20%	

Dietary Exchanges: 4 Starch, 3 Very Lean Meat OR 4 Carbohydrate, 3 Very Lean Meat

Chicken Cacciatore Sandwiches

■ ■

PREP TIME: 30 MINUTES

4 boneless, skinless chicken breast halves

½ teaspoon dried Italian seasoning

2 cups purchased nonfat chunky vegetable pasta sauce

2 oz. (½ cup) shredded mozzarella cheese

4 (¾-inch-thick) diagonal slices French or Italian bread, lightly toasted*

1. Spray large nonstick skillet with nonstick cooking spray. Heat over medium-high heat until hot. Sprinkle both sides of chicken breast halves with Italian seasoning. Place chicken in skillet; cook about 5 minutes on each side or until lightly browned.

2. Add pasta sauce; bring to a boil. Reduce heat to medium; cover and cook 5 to 6 minutes or until chicken is no longer pink in center.

3. Sprinkle cheese over chicken; cover and cook 1 minute or until cheese is melted.

4. Place 1 slice of toasted bread on each of 4 plates. Top each with ¼ of sauce and 1 chicken breast half.

YIELD: 4 SANDWICHES

Tip: * To toast bread, place on cookie sheet; broil 2 to 4 inches from heat for about 30 seconds on each side or until lightly toasted.

Nutrition Information Per Serving
Serving Size: 1 Sandwich

Calories..............290		Calories from Fat..........50
		% Daily Value
Total Fat..............6g		..........9%
Saturated..............3g		..........15%
Cholesterol..............80mg		..........27%
Sodium..............690mg		..........29%
Total Carbohydrate..............25g		..........8%
Dietary Fiber..............2g		..........8%
Sugars..............10g		
Protein..............35g		
Vitamin A..............10%		Vitamin C..............0%
Calcium..............15%		Iron..............15%

Dietary Exchanges: 1½ Starch, 1 Vegetable, 4 Very Lean Meat OR 1½ Carbohydrate, 1 Vegetable, 4 Very Lean Meat

cutting the fat in Sandwiches

■ ■

- Spread bread with mustard (0.5 g fat/tablespoon) instead of butter (11.5 g fat/tablespoon).

- Replace mayonnaise (11 g fat/tablespoon) with light (5 g fat/tablespoon) or nonfat mayonnaise.

- Trade regular cream cheese (10 g fat/ 2 tablespoons) for light (5 g fat/2 tablespoons) or nonfat cream cheese.

- Choose reduced-fat (6 g fat/ounce) or nonfat Cheddar cheese instead of regular Cheddar (9 g fat/ounce).

- Bypass tuna packed in oil (4.5 g fat/ounce) for tuna packed in water (0.5 g fat/ounce).

- Use smaller portions of salad mixtures such as chicken or tuna salad, and bulk up the sandwich with lettuce, slices of tomato or pickles, fresh sprouts and cucumber slices.

Grilled Hawaiian Chicken Sandwiches

PREP TIME: 35 MINUTES

¼ **cup soy sauce**

1 **(8-oz.) can pineapple slices in unsweetened juice, drained, reserving 3 tablespoons liquid**

2 **tablespoons honey**

2 ¼ **teaspoons sesame oil**

½ **teaspoon garlic powder**

½ **teaspoon ginger**

4 **boneless, skinless chicken breast halves**

⅓ **cup sliced green onions**

¼ **cup fat-free mayonnaise or salad dressing**

3 **tablespoons purchased chutney**

4 **(¾-inch-thick) slices Hawaiian sweet bread or sourdough bread**

Grill Directions: 1. In medium bowl, combine soy sauce, reserved 3 tablespoons pineapple liquid, honey, 2 teaspoons of the sesame oil, garlic powder and ginger; mix well. Set aside.

2. Place 1 chicken breast half between 2 pieces of plastic wrap or waxed paper. Working from center, gently pound with flat side of mallet or rolling pin until about ¼ inch thick; remove wrap. Repeat with remaining chicken breast halves.

3. Add chicken to soy sauce mixture; turn to coat. Cover; let stand at room temperature for 15 minutes to marinate.

4. Heat grill. In small bowl, combine onions, mayonnaise, chutney and remaining ¼ teaspoon sesame oil. Set aside.

5. When ready to grill, remove chicken from marinade; place pineapple slices in marinade. Place chicken on gas grill over medium heat or on charcoal grill 4 to 6 inches from medium coals. Cook 6 to 8 minutes or until chicken is fork-tender and juices run clear, turning once.

6. Remove pineapple from marinade; discard marinade. Place pineapple on grill; cook about 2 minutes or until browned, turning once. Place bread slices on grill; cook about 1 minute or until toasted, turning once.

7. Spread each slice of toasted bread with about 2 tablespoons mayonnaise mixture; cut bread slices in half crosswise. Place chicken on halves of bread. Top with pineapple slices and other halves of bread.

Broiler Directions: 1. Prepare and marinate chicken breast halves as directed above. Prepare mayonnaise mixture as directed above.

2. Remove chicken from marinade; place on broiler pan. Place pineapple slices in marinade.

3. Broil 4 to 6 inches from heat for 6 to 8 minutes or until chicken is fork-tender and juices run clear, turning once.

4. Remove pineapple from marinade; discard marinade. Place pineapple on broiler pan; broil about 2 minutes or until browned, turning once. Place bread slices on broiler pan; broil about 1 minute or until toasted, turning once. Continue as directed above.

YIELD: 4 SANDWICHES

Nutrition Information Per Serving
Serving Size: 1 Sandwich

Calories	320	Calories from Fat	50
		% Daily Value	
Total Fat	6g		9%
Saturated	2g		10%
Cholesterol	90mg		30%
Sodium	750mg		31%
Total Carbohydrate	38g		13%
Dietary Fiber	1g		4%
Sugars	10g		
Protein	29g		
Vitamin A	0%	Vitamin C	8%
Calcium	8%	Iron	15%

Dietary Exchanges: 2 Starch, ½ Fruit, 3 Very Lean Meat, ½ Fat OR 2½ Carbohydrate, 3 Very Lean Meat, ½ Fat

Honey-Grilled Chicken Sandwiches

▪ ▪

PREP TIME: 35 MINUTES

Marinade

3 tablespoons orange juice

1 tablespoon white wine or orange juice

1 tablespoon honey

Sandwiches

2 boneless, skinless chicken breast halves

4 teaspoons fat-free mayonnaise or salad dressing

1 teaspoon honey

2 whole wheat sandwich buns, split

2 lettuce leaves

Grill Directions: 1. In small bowl, combine all marinade ingredients; beat with wire whisk until well blended.

2. Keeping strips connected at one end, cut chicken breast halves lengthwise into $^3/_4$-inch-wide strips, cutting to within $^1/_2$ inch of one end. Add chicken to marinade; turn to coat. Cover; let stand at room temperature for 15 minutes to marinate. Meanwhile, in small bowl, combine mayonnaise and 1 teaspoon honey.

3. Heat grill. When ready to grill, remove chicken from marinade; reserve marinade. Place chicken on gas grill over medium heat or on charcoal grill 4 to 6 inches from medium coals. Brush chicken with reserved marinade; discard remaining marinade. Cook 6 to 8 minutes or until chicken is fork-tender and juices run clear, turning once.

4. To serve, place chicken on bottom halves of buns. Top with lettuce, mayonnaise mixture and top halves of buns.

Broiler Directions: 1. Marinate chicken breast halves and prepare mayonnaise mixture as directed above. Place chicken on broiler pan. Brush chicken with reserved marinade; discard remaining marinade.

2. Broil 4 to 6 inches from heat for 6 to 8 minutes or until chicken is fork-tender and juices run clear, turning once. Continue as directed above.

YIELD: 2 SANDWICHES

Nutrition Information Per Serving
Serving Size: 1 Sandwich

Calories	280	Calories from Fat	45
		% Daily Value	
Total Fat	5g		8%
Saturated	1g		5%
Cholesterol	75mg		25%
Sodium	400mg		17%
Total Carbohydrate	27g		9%
Dietary Fiber	3g		12%
Sugars	8g		
Protein	31g		
Vitamin A	0%	Vitamin C	4%
Calcium	4%	Iron	15%

Dietary Exchanges: 2 Starch, 3 Very Lean Meat OR 2 Carbohydrate, 3 Very Lean Meat

thawing Chicken

▪ ▪

There are three safe ways to thaw frozen chicken:

1. Place frozen wrapped chicken on a tray and let it thaw gradually in the refrigerator. It takes about 12 hours to defrost 2 to 3 pounds of chicken.

2. A speedier method is to place the frozen wrapped chicken in cold water. Change the water often and allow about 30 minutes of thawing time for each pound of chicken.

3. Thaw chicken in the microwave following the manufacturer's instructions. Cook microwave-thawed chicken as soon as defrosting is completed.

Grilled Chicken Breasts with Georgia Peach Salsa

PREP TIME: 30 MINUTES

Salsa

1 cup chopped peeled ripe peaches

1 tablespoon fresh lime juice

2 teaspoons brown sugar

½ cup diced red bell pepper

2 tablespoons thinly sliced green onions

1 tablespoon minced jalapeño chile pepper

Dash salt

Chicken

4 boneless, skinless chicken breast halves

⅛ teaspoon salt

⅛ teaspoon pepper

Grill Directions: 1. Heat grill. In medium bowl, combine peaches, lime juice and brown sugar; mix well. Stir in bell pepper, onions, chile and dash of salt.

2. Place 1 chicken breast half between 2 pieces of plastic wrap or waxed paper. Working from center, gently pound with flat side of mallet or rolling pin until about ¼ inch thick; remove wrap. Repeat with remaining chicken breast halves.

3. When ready to grill, oil grill rack. Lightly sprinkle chicken with ⅛ teaspoon salt and pepper. Place chicken on gas grill over medium heat or on charcoal grill 4 to 6 inches from medium coals. Cook 6 to 10 minutes or until chicken is fork-tender and juices run clear, turning once. Serve chicken with salsa.

Broiler Directions: 1. Prepare salsa and flatten chicken breast halves as directed above. Lightly sprinkle chicken with ⅛ teaspoon salt and pepper; place on broiler pan.

2. Broil 4 to 6 inches from heat for 6 to 10 minutes or until chicken is fork-tender and juices run clear, turning once. Serve chicken with salsa.

YIELD: 4 SERVINGS

Cooked Chicken *in a flash*

Use your microwave to quickly cook four to five boneless chicken breasts.

- Place the chicken, skin side up, in a 12 × 8-inch (2-quart) microwave-safe baking dish, placing the thickest portions of the chicken toward the outside edges of the dish. Cover with microwave-safe waxed paper.

- Microwave the chicken on HIGH for 12 to 16 minutes or until it is fork-tender and juices run clear, turning the breasts over once halfway through cooking.

Nutrition Information Per Serving
Serving Size: ¼ of Recipe

Calories	160	Calories from Fat	25
		% Daily Value	
Total Fat	3g		5%
Saturated	1g		5%
Cholesterol	75mg		25%
Sodium	180mg		8%
Total Carbohydrate	6g		2%
Dietary Fiber	1g		3%
Sugars	5g		
Protein	27g		
Vitamin A	20%	Vitamin C	45%
Calcium	2%	Iron	8%

Dietary Exchanges: ½ Fruit, 4 Very Lean Meat OR ½ Carbohydrate, 4 Very Lean Meat

chicken on the Grill

Grilling chicken is very simple in theory, but involves art as well as science. The thickness of the meat, style of the grill and intensity of the heat will affect grilling time. Be sure to watch the chicken carefully so it cooks through but doesn't become dry or burn. Some general grilling guidelines:

Whole Chicken (about 3½ pounds)

Cooking can be speeded slightly by splitting the chicken entirely in half or splitting it along the backbone and flattening it open. Grill whole chickens, skin side up, about 1 hour over indirect heat, until juices run clear when skin between thigh and body is pierced. There's no need to turn the meat over when using the indirect grilling method. (To use the indirect cooking method, arrange hot coals around the sides of the grill and cook the meat in the middle, covering the grill.)

Boneless Chicken Breast Halves and Thighs (about ¼ pound each)

Grill over direct heat for 10 to 18 minutes, or until no pink remains and juices run clear when you cut into meat. Turn the pieces over halfway through the cooking time.

Chicken Breast Halves, Thighs and Drumsticks with Bone In (2½ to 3 pounds total)

Grill over direct heat for 35 to 45 minutes, or until no pink remains and juices run clear when you cut into the thickest part of the meat. (Smaller pieces may cook more quickly.) Turn pieces over halfway through the cooking time.

Chicken Wings

Grill over direct heat for 25 to 35 minutes, or until no pink remains and juices run clear. Turn pieces over halfway through the cooking time.

Saucy Barbecued Chicken

PREP TIME: 25 MINUTES
(READY IN 35 MINUTES)

⅓ cup ketchup

2 tablespoons water

1 tablespoon Worcestershire sauce

1½ teaspoons brown sugar

1 to 2 teaspoons chili powder

½ teaspoon paprika

4 boneless skinless chicken breast halves

Grill Directions: 1. Heat grill. In 12 × 8-inch (2-quart) baking dish, combine all ingredients except chicken; blend well. Place chicken in sauce mixture; turn to coat. Let stand at room temperature for 10 minutes to marinate.

2. When ready to grill, place chicken on gas grill over medium heat or on charcoal grill 4 to 6 inches from medium coals. Cook 15 to 20 minutes or until chicken is fork-tender and juices run clear, turning occasionally and brushing frequently with sauce. Discard any remaining sauce.

YIELD: 4 SERVINGS

Note: To broil, place chicken on broiler pan; broil 4 to 6 inches from heat using times above as a guide.

Nutrition Information Per Serving
Serving Size: ¼ of Recipe

Calories	140	Calories from Fat	25
		% Daily Value	
Total Fat	3g		5%
Saturated	1g		5%
Cholesterol	75mg		25%
Sodium	135mg		6%
Total Carbohydrate	2g		1%
Dietary Fiber	0g		0%
Sugars	1g		
Protein	27g		
Vitamin A	4%	Vitamin C	0%
Calcium	0%	Iron	6%

Dietary Exchanges: 4 Very Lean Meat

Teriyaki Chicken Burgers

PREP TIME: 25 MINUTES

1 lb. lean ground chicken

1 cup corn flakes cereal, crushed

2 teaspoons sugar

1 teaspoon grated gingerroot

1 teaspoon soy sauce

½ teaspoon sesame oil

2 green onions, chopped

1 garlic clove, minced

Grill Directions: 1. Heat grill. In large bowl, combine all ingredients; mix well. Shape mixture into 6 patties, ¹/₂ inch thick.

2. When ready to grill, lightly oil grill rack. Place patties on gas grill over medium heat or on charcoal grill 4 to 6 inches from medium coals. Cook 8 to 10 minutes or until burgers are no longer pink in center, turning once. If desired, serve on burger buns; garnish with pineapple slices and sliced green onions.

YIELD: 6 BURGERS

Nutrition Information Per Serving
Serving Size: 1 Burger

Calories	180	Calories from Fat	60
		% Daily Value	
Total Fat	7g		11%
Saturated	2g		10%
Cholesterol	55mg		18%
Sodium	260mg		11%
Total Carbohydrate	14g		5%
Dietary Fiber	1g		2%
Sugars	2g		
Protein	16g		
Vitamin A	15%	Vitamin C	10%
Calcium	0%	Iron	6%

Dietary Exchanges: 1 Starch, 2 Lean Meat OR 1 Carbohydrate, 2 Lean Meat

Mustard and Apricot-Glazed Chicken

PREP TIME: 25 MINUTES

½ cup apricot preserves

2 to 3 tablespoons coarse-ground or Dijon mustard

4 boneless skinless chicken breast halves

Grill Directions: 1. Heat grill. In small bowl, combine preserves and mustard; blend well.

2. When ready to grill, brush chicken with apricot mixture; place on gas grill over medium heat or on charcoal grill 4 to 6 inches from medium coals. Cook 15 to 20 minutes or until chicken is fork-tender and juices run clear, turning occasionally and brushing frequently with apricot mixture. Discard any remaining apricot mixture.

YIELD: 4 SERVINGS

Note: To broil, place chicken on broiler pan; broil 4 to 6 inches from heat using times above as a guide.

Nutrition Information Per Serving
Serving Size: ¹/₄ of Recipe

Calories	170	Calories from Fat	35
		% Daily Value	
Total Fat	4g		6%
Saturated	1g		5%
Cholesterol	75mg		25%
Sodium	330mg		14%
Total Carbohydrate	7g		2%
Dietary Fiber	0g		0%
Sugars	5g		
Protein	27g		
Vitamin A	0%	Vitamin C	0%
Calcium	2%	Iron	6%

Dietary Exchanges: ½ Fruit, 4 Very Lean Meat OR ½ Carbohydrate, 4 Very Lean Meat

◀ Teriyaki Chicken Burgers

Citrus-Ginger Marinated Chicken

■ ■ ■ ■ ■ ■ ■ ■ ■ ■ ■ ■ ■ ■ ■ ■ ■ ■

PREP TIME: 25 MINUTES
(READY IN 40 MINUTES)

⅔ cup frozen pineapple-orange juice concentrate, thawed

2 tablespoons hoisin sauce

1 tablespoon dark brown sugar

1 tablespoon grated gingerroot

¼ teaspoon crushed red pepper flakes

4 boneless skinless chicken breast halves

Grill Directions: 1. Heat grill. In 12 × 8-inch (2-quart) baking dish, combine all ingredients except chicken; blend well. Place chicken in sauce mixture; turn to coat. Let stand at room temperature for 15 minutes to marinate.

2. When ready to grill, place chicken on gas grill over medium heat or on charcoal grill 4 to 6 inches from medium coals. Cook 15 to 20 minutes or until chicken is fork-tender and juices run clear, turning occasionally and brushing frequently with sauce mixture. Discard any remaining marinade.

YIELD: 4 SERVINGS

Note: To broil, place chicken on broiler pan; broil 4 to 6 inches from heat using times above as a guide.

Nutrition Information Per Serving
Serving Size: ¼ of Recipe

Calories	190	Calories from Fat	25
		% Daily Value	
Total Fat	3g		5%
Saturated	1g		5%
Cholesterol	75mg		25%
Sodium	140mg		6%
Total Carbohydrate	14g		5%
Dietary Fiber	0g		0%
Sugars	13g		
Protein	27g		
Vitamin A	0%	Vitamin C	10%
Calcium	2%	Iron	6%

Dietary Exchanges: 1 Fruit, 4 Very Lean Meat OR 1 Carbohydrate, 4 Very Lean Meat

Turkey and Pepper Penne

■ ■ ■ ■ ■ ■ ■ ■ ■ ■ ■ ■ ■ ■ ■ ■ ■ ■

PREP TIME: 20 MINUTES

8 oz. (2½ cups) uncooked penne (tube-shaped pasta)

1 (16-oz.) pkg. frozen bell pepper stir-fry

1½ cups cubed cooked turkey

½ cup skim milk

1 (10¾-oz.) can condensed 98% fat-free cream of chicken soup with 30% less sodium

improvising with Leftover Chicken or Turkey

■ ■ ■ ■ ■ ■ ■ ■ ■ ■ ■ ■ ■ ■ ■ ■ ■ ■

1. Spike some nonfat mayonnaise with Dijon mustard and mix with cubed chicken, chopped celery, minced onion and cooked potatoes.

2. Toss leftover chicken with chopped scallions, water chestnuts, bean sprouts, mandarin orange slices and a vinaigrette made from peanut oil, rice wine vinegar, a drop of sesame oil and grated fresh ginger. Garnish with chopped peanuts or minced fresh cilantro.

3. Stir chicken into prepared broth along with frozen peas and chopped parsley and chives.

4. Reheat shredded cooked chicken in a flour tortilla with a dollop of salsa and a slice of low-fat cheese.

5. Heat diced chicken in a skillet with sautéed chopped onions, curry powder, raisins and a bit of broth; serve over rice.

1. Cook penne to desired doneness as directed on package.
2. Meanwhile, spray large nonstick skillet with nonstick cooking spray. Heat over medium-high heat until hot. Add bell pepper stir-fry; cook and stir 4 minutes or until crisp-tender.
3. Stir in turkey, milk and soup; mix well. Cook until bubbly, stirring occasionally. If desired, add salt and pepper to taste.
4. Drain penne. Add to turkey mixture; toss to combine.

YIELD: 4 SERVINGS

Nutrition Information Per Serving
Serving Size: 1/4 of Recipe

Calories	380	Calories from Fat	45
		% Daily Value	
Total Fat	5g		8%
Saturated	2g		10%
Cholesterol	45mg		15%
Sodium	380mg		16%
Total Carbohydrate	57g		19%
Dietary Fiber	4g		16%
Sugars	10g		
Protein	26g		
Vitamin A	15%	Vitamin C	25%
Calcium	6%	Iron	20%

Dietary Exchanges: 3 Starch, 2 Vegetable, 2 Very Lean Meat, 1/2 Fat OR
3 Carbohydrate, 2 Vegetable, 2 Very Lean Meat, 1/2 Fat

Cacciatore with a Twist

■ ■ ■ ■ ■ ■ ■ ■ ■ ■ ■ ■ ■ ■ ■

PREP TIME: 30 MINUTES

2 teaspoons olive or vegetable oil

1 medium onion, sliced

1 small green bell pepper, cut into strips

2 garlic cloves, minced

4 fresh turkey breast slices (about 1/2 lb.), cut into strips

3 oz. (1 cup) uncooked rotini (spiral pasta)

1 (15-oz.) can tomato sauce

1 (15-oz.) can garbanzo beans, drained, rinsed

3/4 teaspoon dried oregano leaves

about Garbanzo Beans

These roundish tan legumes, also known as chickpeas or ceci peas, are a key ingredient in Middle Eastern hummus dip and in Spain's beloved *cocido madrileño,* a hearty soup made with sausage.

1. Heat oil in large nonstick skillet over medium heat until hot. Add onion, bell pepper, garlic and turkey; cook and stir 5 to 10 minutes or until turkey is no longer pink.
2. Meanwhile, cook rotini to desired doneness as directed on package.
3. Add tomato sauce, beans and oregano to turkey mixture; mix well. Bring to a boil. Reduce heat; cover and simmer 10 minutes or until thoroughly heated.
4. Drain rotini. Serve turkey mixture over rotini.

YIELD: 4 SERVINGS

Nutrition Information Per Serving
Serving Size: 1/4 of Recipe

Calories	290	Calories from Fat	35
		% Daily Value	
Total Fat	4g		6%
Saturated	1g		5%
Cholesterol	35mg		12%
Sodium	870mg		36%
Total Carbohydrate	42g		14%
Dietary Fiber	6g		24%
Sugars	7g		
Protein	21g		
Vitamin A	25%	Vitamin C	35%
Calcium	6%	Iron	20%

Dietary Exchanges: 2 1/2 Starch, 1 Vegetable, 2 Very Lean Meat OR
2 1/2 Carbohydrate, 1 Vegetable, 2 Very Lean Meat

Springtime Pasta and Sausage

■ ■ ■ ■ ■ ■ ■ ■ ■ ■ ■ ■ ■ ■ ■ ■ ■ ■ ■ ■

PREP TIME: 30 MINUTES

8 oz. uncooked regular or whole wheat spaghetti

12 oz. Italian turkey sausage, thinly sliced

½ teaspoon fennel seed

2 garlic cloves, minced

8 oz. (2 cups) fresh sugar snap peas, trimmed, or 1 (9-oz.) pkg. frozen sugar snap peas in a pouch, thawed*

2 cups sliced fresh mushrooms

⅓ cup chicken broth

4 Italian plum tomatoes, chopped

4 green onions, cut into 1-inch pieces

⅓ cup chopped fresh parsley

1. In Dutch oven or large saucepan, cook spaghetti to desired doneness as directed on package.

2. Meanwhile, in large nonstick skillet over medium heat, cook sausage, fennel and garlic until sausage is no longer pink. Drain; remove from skillet.

3. Add sugar snap peas, mushrooms and broth to skillet; heat until bubbly. Simmer 3 to 4 minutes, stirring frequently. Stir in tomatoes and onions; cook and stir over medium heat for 2 minutes. Add sausage mixture and parsley; cook an additional 1 minute or until hot.

4. Drain spaghetti; return to Dutch oven. Add sausage mixture; toss gently until well mixed.

YIELD: 6 (1⅓-CUP) SERVINGS

Tip: * To quickly thaw sugar snap peas, place in colander or strainer; rinse with warm water until thawed. Drain well.

Nutrition Information Per Serving
Serving Size: 1⅓ Cups

Calories	280	Calories from Fat	60
		% Daily Value	
Total Fat	7g		11%
Saturated	2g		10%
Cholesterol	30mg		10%
Sodium	430mg		18%
Total Carbohydrate	36g		12%
Dietary Fiber	6g		24%
Sugars	4g		
Protein	17g		
Vitamin A	10%	Vitamin C	40%
Calcium	6%	Iron	25%

Dietary Exchanges: 2 Starch, 1 Vegetable, 2 Lean Meat OR
2 Carbohydrate, 1 Vegetable, 2 Lean Meat

Turkey Sausage and Zucchini Frittata

■ ■ ■ ■ ■ ■ ■ ■ ■ ■ ■ ■ ■ ■ ■ ■ ■ ■ ■ ■

PREP TIME: 30 MINUTES

1½ cups refrigerated or frozen fat-free egg product, thawed, or 6 eggs

2 tablespoons skim milk

¼ teaspoon salt, if desired

¼ teaspoon dried Italian seasoning

¼ lb. turkey sausage links, cut into ¼-inch pieces, or bulk turkey sausage

¼ cup finely chopped carrot

¼ cup finely chopped green onions

1 medium zucchini, chopped

1 oz. (¼ cup) shredded mozzarella cheese

1. In medium bowl, combine egg product, milk, salt and Italian seasoning; beat well. Set aside.

2. Spray 10- or 12-inch nonstick skillet with nonstick cooking spray. Add sausage; cook and stir over medium heat for 8 to 10 minutes or until no longer pink. Drain well.

3. Add carrot and onions; cook and stir over medium heat for 2 to 3 minutes or until softened. Add zucchini; cook and stir an additional 2 minutes.

4. Add egg mixture to skillet; cover and cook over low heat for 8 to 10 minutes or until set, lifting edges occasionally to allow uncooked egg mixture to flow to bottom of skillet.

5. Sprinkle with cheese. Cover; cook an additional 1 minute or until cheese is melted. To serve, cut into wedges.

Y I E L D : 4 SERVINGS

Nutrition Information Per Serving
Serving Size: ¼ of Recipe

Calories................................140	Calories from Fat 45
	% Daily Value
Total Fat ....5g 8%	
Saturated ....2g 10%	
Cholesterol ....25mg 8%	
Sodium ....490mg 20%	
Total Carbohydrate..............6g 2%	
Dietary Fiber..................2g 8%	
Sugars 4g	
Protein 17g	
Vitamin A..........................60%	Vitamin C 10%
Calcium 15%	Iron 15%

Dietary Exchanges: 1 Vegetable, 2 Lean Meat

Turkey Scaloppine with Vegetables

■ ■ ■ ■ ■ ■ ■ ■ ■ ■ ■ ■ ■ ■ ■ ■ ■ ■

P R E P T I M E : 30 MINUTES

Pasta
12 oz. uncooked angel hair pasta

2 tablespoons grated Parmesan cheese

1 tablespoon dried parsley flakes

Scaloppine
2 teaspoons olive oil

**2 teaspoons chopped fresh rosemary or
½ teaspoon dried rosemary leaves, crushed**

**2 teaspoons chopped fresh lemon thyme or thyme
or ½ teaspoon dried thyme leaves**

2 garlic cloves, crushed

**1½ lb. turkey tenderloins, cut diagonally into
½-inch-thick slices**

1½ cups fresh baby carrots

1 small onion, cut into eighths, separated

½ teaspoon salt

¼ teaspoon pepper

¼ cup dry white wine or chicken broth

1½ cups fresh or frozen sugar snap peas

1. Cook pasta to desired doneness as directed on package.

2. Meanwhile, heat oil in large nonstick skillet over medium-high heat until hot. Stir in rosemary, thyme and garlic. Cook 2 minutes, stirring constantly. Add turkey slices; cook 2 minutes. Turn slices; cook an additional 2 minutes.

3. Stir in carrots, onion, salt, pepper and wine. Reduce heat to medium-low; cover and cook 10 to 15 minutes or until turkey is no longer pink and carrots are crisp-tender.

4. Drain pasta; place in serving bowl. Add cheese and parsley; toss gently. Cover to keep warm.

5. Add sugar snap peas to turkey mixture; mix well. Cover; cook an additional 5 minutes or until peas are crisp-tender, stirring occasionally. Serve turkey mixture with pasta.

Y I E L D : 6 SERVINGS

Nutrition Information Per Serving
Serving Size: ⅙ of Recipe

Calories................................380	Calories from Fat 35
	% Daily Value
Total Fat ....4g 6%	
Saturated ....1g 5%	
Cholesterol ....75mg 25%	
Sodium ....280mg 12%	
Total Carbohydrate..............49g 16%	
Dietary Fiber..................3g 12%	
Sugars 5g	
Protein 36g	
Vitamin A..........................160%	Vitamin C 15%
Calcium 8%	Iron 25%

Dietary Exchanges: 3 Starch, 1 Vegetable, 3 Very Lean Meat OR
3 Carbohydrate, 1 Vegetable, 3 Very Lean Meat

Turkey *nutrition*

Per 3-oz. Serving	Fat	Calories
White meat with skin	4 g	140
White meat without skin	0.5 g	90
Dark meat with skin	6 g	155
Dark meat without skin	4 g	140

Turkey Meatballs in Light Tomato Sauce

PREP TIME: 35 MINUTES

8 cups hot cooked instant rice (cooked as directed on package, omitting margarine and salt)

1 (14.5-oz.) can diced tomatoes, undrained

4 medium carrots, cut into ½-inch chunks

1 leek, cut into ½-inch slices (white portion only)

1½ lb. lean ground turkey

1 cup rolled oats

4 oz. fresh mushrooms, finely chopped

½ teaspoon dried oregano leaves

½ teaspoon dried basil leaves

½ teaspoon dried thyme leaves

1 teaspoon salt

½ teaspoon pepper

1 tablespoon lemon juice

2 medium zucchini, cut into ½-inch chunks

1. While rice is cooking, in Dutch oven, combine tomatoes, carrots and leek; mix well. Bring to a boil. Reduce heat; cover and simmer while preparing meatballs.

2. In large bowl, combine all remaining ingredients except zucchini; mix thoroughly. Shape mixture into 1-inch balls. Place in simmering sauce; cook 5 minutes.

3. Add zucchini; simmer an additional 5 to 7 minutes or until meatballs are no longer pink in center. Serve over rice.

YIELD: 8 SERVINGS

Nutrition Information Per Serving
Serving Size: ⅛ of Recipe

Calories	400	Calories from Fat	60
		% Daily Value	
Total Fat	7g		11%
Saturated	2g		10%
Cholesterol	55mg		18%
Sodium	450mg		19%
Total Carbohydrate	61g		20%
Dietary Fiber	4g		16%
Sugars	5g		
Protein	24g		
Vitamin A	210%	Vitamin C	20%
Calcium	8%	Iron	25%

Dietary Exchanges: 3½ Starch, 1 Vegetable, 2 Lean Meat OR 3½ Carbohydrate, 1 Vegetable, 2 Lean Meat

Tomatoes *and your health*

Lycopene, found in tomatoes and processed tomato products, is an antioxidant that preliminary data suggest may reduce the risk of certain types of cancer, including prostate cancer. Lycopene may owe its possible protective effects to its antioxidant properties, which are thought to help thwart tissue damage. Cooked tomatoes may be particularly beneficial because heat appears to increase the amount of lycopene available to the body.

◀ Turkey Meatballs in Light Tomato Sauce

Barbecued Turkey Tenderloin

■ ■

PREP TIME: 30 MINUTES

1 (1½-lb.) turkey tenderloin, cut into 16 slices

½ cup barbecue sauce

⅓ cup finely chopped green bell pepper

3 tablespoons finely chopped red onion

1. Place turkey slices in shallow dish or resealable plastic bag. In small bowl, combine barbecue sauce, bell pepper and onion; mix well. Pour over turkey slices; turn to coat well. Cover dish or seal bag; let stand at room temperature for 15 minutes to marinate.
2. Line 15 × 10 × 1-inch baking pan with foil; spray foil with nonstick cooking spray. Place turkey slices in sprayed foil-lined pan; reserve marinade.
3. Broil 4 to 6 inches from heat for 4 minutes. Turn slices; baste with remaining marinade. Broil an additional 2 to 4 minutes or until turkey is no longer pink.

YIELD: 4 SERVINGS

turkey Tenderloin

■ ■ ■ ■ ■ ■ ■ ■ ■ ■ ■ ■ ■ ■ ■ ■ ■ ■ ■

Turkey tenderloin, a boneless whole muscle from the center of the breast half, is the leanest turkey cut. Each 3-ounce serving contains about 115 calories and less than 1 gram of fat.

- Cook tenderloin whole or cut it into slices.

- Broil, grill, stir-fry or sauté (using a nonstick skillet coated with nonstick cooking spray).

- Cook until the meat is no longer pink.

- Be careful not to overcook, or the meat will be dry.

Nutrition Information Per Serving
Serving Size: ¼ of Recipe

Calories	190	Calories from Fat	20
		% Daily Value	
Total Fat	2g		3%
Saturated	0g		0%
Cholesterol	105mg		35%
Sodium	320mg		13%
Total Carbohydrate	5g		2%
Dietary Fiber	1g		3%
Sugars	1g		
Protein	39g		
Vitamin A	6%	Vitamin C	10%
Calcium	2%	Iron	15%

Dietary Exchanges: ½ Fruit, 5 Very Lean Meat OR ½ Carbohydrate, 5 Very Lean Meat

Potato-Topped Turkey and Green Bean Bake

■ ■

PREP TIME: 20 MINUTES
(READY IN 50 MINUTES)

1 lb. lean ground turkey

½ cup chopped onion

½ teaspoon garlic powder

¾ to 1 teaspoon dried thyme leaves

⅔ cup skim milk

2 (9-oz.) pkg. frozen French-style green beans, thawed, drained*

1 (10¾-oz.) can condensed 98% fat-free cream of mushroom soup

1 (8-oz.) can sliced water chestnuts, drained

1 (4.5-oz.) jar sliced mushrooms, drained

1 (16-oz.) pkg. frozen seasoned potato nuggets

1. Heat oven to 450°F. Spray 13 × 9-inch (3-quart) baking dish with nonstick cooking spray.
2. Spray large nonstick skillet with nonstick cooking spray. Add turkey, onion, garlic powder and thyme; cook over medium-high heat until turkey is browned. Stir in milk, green beans, soup, water chestnuts and mushrooms. Bring to a boil. Pour turkey mixture into sprayed baking dish. Top with potato nuggets.
3. Bake at 450°F. for 20 to 25 minutes or until hot and bubbly. Let stand 5 minutes before serving.

YIELD: 8 (1⅓-CUP) SERVINGS

Tip: * To quickly thaw green beans, place in colander or strainer; rinse with warm water until thawed. Drain well.

Nutrition Information Per Serving
Serving Size: 1 1/3 Cups

Calories 310		Calories from Fat 120
		% Daily Value
Total Fat 13g	....	20%
Saturated 5g	....	25%
Cholesterol 45mg	....	15%
Sodium 680mg	....	28%
Total Carbohydrate 32g	....	11%
Dietary Fiber 5g	....	20%
Sugars 6g		
Protein 17g		
Vitamin A 8%		Vitamin C 10%
Calcium 15%		Iron 15%

Dietary Exchanges: 2 Starch, 1 Vegetable, 1 Lean Meat, 1 1/2 Fat OR
2 Carbohydrate, 1 Vegetable, 1 Lean Meat, 1 1/2 Fat

Creamy Turkey Lasagna

■ ■

PREP TIME: 25 MINUTES
(READY IN 45 MINUTES)

6 oz. (3 cups) uncooked mini lasagna noodles (mafalda)

1 cup frozen cut leaf spinach, thawed, squeezed to drain*

2 cups cubed cooked turkey

1 (10¾-oz.) can condensed 98% fat-free cream of chicken soup with 30% less sodium

1 (4-oz.) can mushroom pieces and stems, drained

1 tablespoon instant minced onion

½ teaspoon dried sage leaves**

¼ teaspoon ground thyme**

¼ teaspoon pepper

⅛ teaspoon garlic powder

1 cup nonfat cottage cheese

4 oz. mozzarella cheese slices

1. Cook noodles to desired doneness as directed on package.

2. Meanwhile, heat oven to 350°F. Spray 10 × 6-inch (1½-quart) baking dish with nonstick cooking spray. In medium saucepan, combine all remaining ingredients except cottage cheese and mozzarella cheese; mix well. Bring to a boil over medium heat, stirring constantly. Cook and stir 1 minute; remove from heat. Stir in cottage cheese.

3. Drain noodles; place in sprayed baking dish. Spoon turkey mixture evenly over noodles. Arrange cheese slices over top.

4. Bake at 350°F. for 15 to 18 minutes or until bubbly around edges.

YIELD: 6 SERVINGS

Tips: * To quickly thaw spinach, place in colander or strainer; rinse with warm water until thawed. Squeeze dry with paper towels.

** One-half teaspoon dried rosemary leaves, finely crushed, can be substituted for the sage and thyme.

Nutrition Information Per Serving
Serving Size: 1/6 of Recipe

Calories 270		Calories from Fat 50
		% Daily Value
Total Fat 6g	....	9%
Saturated 3g	....	15%
Cholesterol 35mg	....	12%
Sodium 560mg	....	23%
Total Carbohydrate 30g	....	10%
Dietary Fiber 2g	....	8%
Sugars 4g		
Protein 23g		
Vitamin A 45%		Vitamin C 8%
Calcium 25%		Iron 15%

Dietary Exchanges: 2 Starch, 2 Lean Meat OR 2 Carbohydrate, 2 Lean Meat

Turkey-Veggie Omelet

■ ■

PREP TIME: 30 MINUTES

1 teaspoon olive oil

⅓ cup sliced fresh mushrooms

¼ cup chopped onion

¼ cup chopped red bell pepper

1 garlic clove, minced

½ cup diced cooked turkey

¼ teaspoon dried basil leaves, if desired

1 (8-oz.) carton (1 cup) refrigerated or frozen fat-free egg product, thawed, or 4 eggs

⅛ teaspoon salt

⅛ teaspoon pepper

1. Heat ½ teaspoon of the oil in large nonstick skillet over medium heat until hot. Add mushrooms, onion, bell pepper and garlic; cook and stir 2 to 3 minutes or until onion and bell pepper are crisp-tender. Add turkey and basil; cook 1 to 2 minutes or until hot. Remove from skillet; set aside.

2. In small bowl, combine egg product, salt and pepper; blend well. Heat remaining ½ teaspoon oil in same skillet over medium heat until hot. Pour egg mixture into skillet. Cook until egg mixture is set, lifting edges occasionally to allow uncooked egg mixture to flow to bottom of skillet.

3. Spoon turkey-vegetable mixture over half of omelet; loosen edge of omelet and fold other half over filling.

YIELD: 2 SERVINGS

Tip: If desired, omelet can be topped with 4 fresh tomato slices and 1 oz. (¼ cup) shredded Cheddar cheese. Cover; cook over low heat for 1 to 2 minutes or until cheese begins to melt.

Nutrition Information Per Serving
Serving Size: ½ of Recipe

Calories	150	Calories from Fat	35
		% Daily Value	
Total Fat	4g		6%
Saturated	1g		5%
Cholesterol	25mg		8%
Sodium	340mg		14%
Total Carbohydrate	6g		2%
Dietary Fiber	1g		3%
Sugars	4g		
Protein	22g		
Vitamin A	25%	Vitamin C	30%
Calcium	6%	Iron	15%

Dietary Exchanges: 1 Vegetable, 2 Lean Meat

turkey: Smart Parts

■ ■

Packaged turkey parts are a convenient alternative to cooking a whole bird. Available in most stores are:

Turkey cutlets Slices of breast meat that cook quickly; good substitute for veal cutlets.

Turkey tenderloin The boneless whole muscle from the center of the breast half. It's the leanest part of the turkey.

Legs Perfect for soup, or roast a bunch of them for a drumstick-loving family.

Wings Rich flavor for soup.

Thighs Good for roasting or braising, though higher in fat than breast meat.

Whole turkey breast Roast and serve with a spicy barbecue sauce, cook and slice for a lower-cost alternative to deli meat or cut up to use in casseroles.

Ground turkey A mild-flavored, lower-fat substitution for ground beef.

◀ Turkey-Veggie Omelet

Turkey Pita Fajitas

Sauce

1½ cups nonfat sour cream

¼ cup salsa

Fajitas

1½ cups chopped red, yellow or green bell peppers

1 medium onion, thinly sliced, separated into rings

½ teaspoon garlic powder

6 oz. cooked turkey, cut into 2 × ¼ × ¼-inch strips (1 cup)

1 cup frozen whole kernel corn, thawed

1 (15-oz.) can black beans, drained, rinsed

6 (7- or 8-inch) Greek-style pitas, heated

1. In small bowl, combine sauce ingredients; blend well. Refrigerate until serving time.

2. Spray large nonstick skillet with nonstick cooking spray. Add bell peppers, onion and garlic powder; cook over medium-high heat for 2 to 3 minutes or until vegetables are crisp-tender.

3. Stir in turkey, corn and beans. Reduce heat to medium-low; cover and cook 4 to 6 minutes or until thoroughly heated. Spoon turkey mixture onto center of heated pitas; top with sauce. Fold pitas over filling.

YIELD: 6 FAJITAS

Nutrition Information Per Serving
Serving Size: 1 Fajita

Calories	400	Calories from Fat	20
		% Daily Value	
Total Fat	2g		3%
Saturated	0g		0%
Cholesterol	30mg		10%
Sodium	760mg		32%
Total Carbohydrate	72g		24%
Dietary Fiber	6g		24%
Sugars	8g		
Protein	23g		
Vitamin A	35%	Vitamin C	70%
Calcium	15%	Iron	20%

Dietary Exchanges: 4½ Starch, 1 Very Lean Meat OR 4½ Carbohydrate, 1 Very Lean Meat

Turkey Ham Veggie Pizza

1 (10-oz.) can refrigerated pizza crust

2 large or 3 medium tomatoes, thinly sliced

1 teaspoon dried oregano leaves

½ medium green bell pepper, thinly sliced

1 small onion, thinly sliced, separated into rings

3 oz. thinly sliced cooked turkey ham, cut into ¼-inch strips

4 oz. (1 cup) shredded reduced-fat mozzarella cheese

1. Heat oven to 425°F. Grease 15 × 10 × 1-inch baking pan. Unroll pizza crust; place in greased pan. Starting at center, press out with hands, forming ½-inch rim. Bake at 425°F. for 7 to 9 minutes or until crust begins to brown.

2. Top partially baked crust with tomato slices; sprinkle evenly with oregano. Top with bell pepper, onion, turkey ham and cheese. Return to oven; bake an additional 5 to 8 minutes or until crust is deep golden brown.

YIELD: 6 SERVINGS

Nutrition Information Per Serving
Serving Size: ⅙ of Recipe

Calories	220	Calories from Fat	50
		% Daily Value	
Total Fat	6g		9%
Saturated	3g		15%
Cholesterol	20mg		7%
Sodium	510mg		21%
Total Carbohydrate	27g		9%
Dietary Fiber	2g		8%
Sugars	4g		
Protein	13g		
Vitamin A	10%	Vitamin C	20%
Calcium	15%	Iron	10%

Dietary Exchanges: 1½ Starch, 1 Vegetable, 1 Medium-Fat Meat OR 1½ Carbohydrate, 1 Vegetable, 1 Medium-Fat Meat

Turkey and Pepper Hoagies ▶

Turkey and Pepper Hoagies

■ ■ ■ ■ ■ ■ ■ ■ ■ ■ ■ ■ ■ ■ ■ ■ ■ ■ ■ ■

PREP TIME: 15 MINUTES

½ cup fat-free mayonnaise or salad dressing

1 teaspoon dried Italian seasoning

8 oz. smoked turkey breast slices, cut into strips

2 cups frozen bell pepper stir-fry

4 (6- or 7-inch) hoagie buns, split

1. In small bowl, combine mayonnaise and Italian seasoning; mix well. Set aside.

2. Spray large nonstick skillet with nonstick cooking spray. Heat over medium-high heat until hot. Add turkey strips and bell pepper stir-fry; cook and stir 1 minute. Cover; cook 2 minutes. Uncover; cook and stir an additional 1 to 3 minutes or until liquid evaporates and bell peppers are tender.

3. Meanwhile, spread about 1 tablespoon mayonnaise mixture on each cut side of buns. Spoon ¼ of turkey mixture onto bottom half of each bun. Cover with top halves of buns.

YIELD: 4 SANDWICHES

Nutrition Information Per Serving
Serving Size: 1 Sandwich

Calories	350	Calories from Fat	50
		% Daily Value	
Total Fat	6g		9%
Saturated	1g		5%
Cholesterol	15mg		5%
Sodium	1,390mg		58%
Total Carbohydrate	57g		19%
Dietary Fiber	4g		16%
Sugars	5g		
Protein	17g		
Vitamin A	4%	Vitamin C	8%
Calcium	10%	Iron	15%

Dietary Exchanges: 3½ Starch, 1 Vegetable, 1 Very Lean Meat OR
3½ Carbohydrate, 1 Vegetable, 1 Very Lean Meat

▼ Turkey and Pepper Hoagies

Swiss Turkey Broccoli Melts

■ ■ ■ ■ ■ ■ ■ ■ ■ ■ ■ ■ ■ ■ ■ ■ ■ ■ ■

PREP TIME: 25 MINUTES

16 fresh medium broccoli spears (1 lb.)

4 slices sourdough bread (6 to 7 inches in diameter), lightly toasted

3 tablespoons nonfat sour cream

2 to 3 teaspoons prepared horseradish

2 teaspoons Dijon mustard

4 oz. thinly sliced cooked turkey breast

½ cup roasted red bell peppers (from 7.25-oz. jar), drained, cut into strips

3 (1-oz.) slices reduced-fat Swiss cheese, cut into 12 strips

1. In large nonstick skillet, bring ³/₄ cup water and broccoli to a boil. Reduce heat; cover and simmer 4 to 7 minutes or until broccoli is crisp-tender.*

2. Meanwhile, place bread slices on ungreased cookie sheet. In small bowl, combine sour cream, horseradish and mustard; mix well. Spread over bread. Place turkey slices on bread.

3. Drain broccoli. Top each sandwich with 4 cooked broccoli spears, bell pepper strips and 3 strips of cheese.

4. Broil 3 to 4 inches from heat for 2 to 3 minutes or until cheese is melted.

YIELD: 4 SANDWICHES

Tip: * To cook broccoli in microwave, combine broccoli and ¹/₄ cup water in 12 × 8-inch (2-quart) microwave-safe dish. Cover with microwave-safe plastic wrap. Microwave on HIGH for 3 to 5 minutes or just until broccoli is bright green and crisp-tender. Drain.

Nutrition Information Per Serving

Serving Size: 1 Sandwich

Calories	220	Calories from Fat	35
		% Daily Value	
Total Fat	4g		6%
Saturated	2g		10%
Cholesterol	35mg		12%
Sodium	560mg		23%
Total Carbohydrate	27g		9%
Dietary Fiber	5g		20%
Sugars	6g		
Protein	20g		
Vitamin A	70%	Vitamin C	200%
Calcium	25%	Iron	15%

Dietary Exchanges: 1½ Starch, 1 Vegetable, 2 Very Lean Meat OR
1½ Carbohydrate, 1 Vegetable, 2 Very Lean Meat

Creamy Turkey Burritos

■ ■ ■ ■ ■ ■ ■ ■ ■ ■ ■ ■ ■ ■ ■ ■ ■ ■ ■

PREP TIME: 20 MINUTES

1½ cups chopped cooked turkey

1 cup nonfat sour cream

2 tablespoons 40% less sodium taco seasoning mix

2 oz. (½ cup) shredded reduced-fat sharp Cheddar cheese

4 (8-inch) fat-free flour tortillas

Microwave Directions: 1. In medium bowl, combine turkey, sour cream, taco seasoning mix and ¹/₄ cup of the cheese; mix well.

2. Spread ¹/₄ of turkey mixture down center of each tortilla; roll up. Place 1 burrito on each of 4 microwave-safe plates. Sprinkle each with 1 table-

about **Tortillas**

Mexico's famous flatbread, the tortilla, comes in two basic versions: corn and flour. Corn tortillas have a more crumbly texture and typically have almost no fat. Flour tortillas, available in white and whole wheat styles, are softer and may contain a small amount of fat—read the package label. And if you go to Spain and order a tortilla, you'll get something completely different: an omelet.

spoon of the remaining cheese. Cover with microwave-safe plastic wrap.

3. Microwave each burrito on HIGH for 1 to 2 minutes or until thoroughly heated. If desired, serve with salsa and shredded lettuce.

YIELD: 4 BURRITOS

Nutrition Information Per Serving
Serving Size: 1 Burrito

Calories	300	Calories from Fat	70
		% Daily Value	
Total Fat	8g		12%
Saturated	3g		15%
Cholesterol	50mg		17%
Sodium	680mg		28%
Total Carbohydrate	29g		10%
Dietary Fiber	1g		4%
Sugars	6g		
Protein	27g		
Vitamin A	15%	Vitamin C	0%
Calcium	25%	Iron	10%

Dietary Exchanges: 2 Starch, 2½ Lean Meat OR 2 Carbohydrate, 2½ Lean Meat

Chile Burgers with Rajas

■ ■ ■ ■ ■ ■ ■ ■ ■ ■ ■ ■ ■ ■ ■ ■

PREP TIME: 30 MINUTES

1 lb. lean ground turkey

2 teaspoons Worcestershire sauce

½ teaspoon onion powder

¼ cup light cream cheese (from 8-oz. tub)

¼ teaspoon ground red pepper (cayenne)

1 teaspoon chili powder

4 large Anaheim chiles

4 whole-grain or onion burger buns, split*

¼ cup salsa

Grill Directions: 1. Heat grill. In medium bowl, combine turkey, Worcestershire sauce and onion powder; mix well. Shape into 4 patties.
2. In small bowl, combine cream cheese and ground red pepper; mix well. Spoon about 1 tablespoon cheese mixture onto center of each patty. Wrap turkey mixture around cheese to enclose completely; seal well. Flatten each into ½-inch-thick patty. Sprin-

kle both sides of each patty with about ⅛ teaspoon chili powder.
3. When ready to grill, oil grill rack. Place turkey patties on gas grill over medium heat or on charcoal grill 4 to 6 inches from medium-high coals. Cook patties 6 to 8 minutes. Turn patties; cook an additional 6 to 8 minutes or until no longer pink in center.
4. Meanwhile, place chiles on grill; cook 5 minutes. Turn chiles; cook an additional 5 minutes or until tender and slightly charred. Remove chiles from grill; peel any blistered skin that comes off easily. Slice chiles lengthwise into ½-inch-wide strips, removing seeds if desired. Serve burgers in buns, topped with chile strips and salsa.

Broiler Directions: 1. Prepare patties as directed above. Place patties and chiles on broiler pan.
2. Broil 4 to 6 inches from heat. Broil chiles about 3 minutes on each side or until tender and slightly charred; broil turkey patties for 6 to 8 minutes on each side or until no longer pink in center. Continue as directed above.

YIELD: 4 BURGERS

Tip: * If desired, flour tortillas can be used. Shape filled patties into oval shape. Grill or broil; wrap burgers topped with chile strips and salsa in warm flour tortillas.

Nutrition Information Per Serving
Serving Size: 1 Burger

Calories	350	Calories from Fat	110
		% Daily Value	
Total Fat	12g		18%
Saturated	4g		20%
Cholesterol	85mg		28%
Sodium	610mg		25%
Total Carbohydrate	30g		10%
Dietary Fiber	5g		20%
Sugars	6g		
Protein	30g		
Vitamin A	20%	Vitamin C	225%
Calcium	10%	Iron	20%

Dietary Exchanges: 2 Starch, 3 Lean Meat, ½ Fat OR 2 Carbohydrate, 3 Lean Meat, ½ Fat

cooking **Kabobs**

In Turkey, many a marching army made shish-kabobs in the field by roasting meats on swords (*shish* means skewer; *kabob* means small piece of roasted meat); you can use ordinary skewers.

Metal Skewers Choose skewers with flat, square or twisted shafts to prevent the food from spinning around when the kabobs are turned.

Wooden or Bamboo Skewers Soak skewers in water for 15 to 30 minutes prior to grilling to prevent burning.

Greek-Style Turkey Kabobs with Couscous

PREP TIME: 30 MINUTES

Marinade
2 tablespoons white wine vinegar

1 tablespoon chopped fresh oregano or 1 teaspoon dried oregano leaves

1 tablespoon olive oil

⅛ teaspoon salt

Dash pepper

1 garlic clove, minced

Kabobs
6 oz. turkey tenderloin, cut into 6 (1-inch) cubes

1 small onion

½ large green bell pepper

6 fresh whole mushrooms

6 cherry tomatoes

Couscous
1 cup water

1 tablespoon margarine or butter

¼ teaspoon salt

1 cup uncooked couscous

Grill Directions: 1. In small bowl, combine all marinade ingredients; beat with wire whisk until well blended. Add turkey cubes; toss to coat. Let stand at room temperature to marinate while preparing vegetables.

2. Heat grill. Cut onion into 6 wedges; cut bell pepper into 6 pieces. To prepare kabobs, drain turkey, reserving marinade. Alternately thread 3 pieces turkey, 3 mushrooms, 3 tomatoes, 3 onion wedges and 3 bell pepper pieces on each of two 12- to 14-inch metal skewers.

3. When ready to grill, place kabobs on gas grill over medium heat or on charcoal grill 4 to 6 inches from medium coals. Brush kabobs with reserved marinade; discard remaining marinade. Cook 10 to 15 minutes or until turkey is no longer pink and vegetables are crisp-tender, turning occasionally.

4. Meanwhile, in medium saucepan, combine water, margarine and ¼ teaspoon salt. Bring to a boil. Stir in couscous. Remove from heat. Cover; let stand 5 minutes. Fluff couscous with fork before serving. Serve kabobs over couscous.

Broiler Directions: 1. Prepare kabobs as directed above. Place on broiler pan. Brush kabobs with reserved marinade; discard remaining marinade.

2. Broil 4 to 6 inches from heat for 14 to 18 minutes or until turkey is no longer pink and vegetables are crisp-tender, turning once.

3. Meanwhile, prepare couscous. Serve as directed above.

YIELD: 2 SERVINGS

Nutrition Information Per Serving
Serving Size: ½ of Recipe

Calories	540	Calories from Fat	80
			% Daily Value
Total Fat	9g		14%
Saturated	2g		10%
Cholesterol	55mg		18%
Sodium	115mg		5%
Total Carbohydrate	81g		27%
Dietary Fiber	7g		28%
Sugars	6g		
Protein	33g		
Vitamin A	15%	Vitamin C	40%
Calcium	4%	Iron	15%

Dietary Exchanges: 5 Starch, 1 Vegetable, 2 Very Lean Meat, 1 Fat OR
5 Carbohydrate, 1 Vegetable, 2 Very Lean Meat, 1 Fat

▼ Greek-Style Turkey Kabobs with Couscous

Cornish Game Hen with Mustard-Orange Glaze

. . . .

PREP TIME: 25 MINUTES
(READY IN 1 HOUR 5 MINUTES)

3 (24-oz.) Cornish game hens

2 tablespoons soy sauce

⅛ teaspoon salt

⅛ teaspoon pepper

Glaze

¾ cup orange juice

⅓ cup brown sugar

⅓ cup honey mustard

¼ cup dark corn syrup

¾ teaspoon ginger

1. Heat oven to 425°F. Line $15 \times 10 \times 1$-inch baking pan with foil. Remove and discard giblets from Cornish game hens. Using kitchen scissors, cut game hens in half, cutting through center of breast and along backbone. Remove and discard skin.

2. Place hen halves cut side down in foil-lined pan. Brush with soy sauce; sprinkle lightly with salt and pepper.

3. In small bowl, combine all glaze ingredients; mix well. Generously brush hen halves with glaze.

4. Bake at 425°F. for 30 to 40 minutes or until hens are fork-tender and juices run clear, brushing frequently with glaze.

5. In small saucepan, bring remaining glaze to a boil over medium heat. Boil 1 minute or until hot and slightly thickened. Spoon over hen halves.

YIELD: 6 SERVINGS

timetable for Roasting Poultry

Oven temperature: 325°F. Thermometer reading: 180 to 180°F.

Poultry	Weight (lbs.)	Time (hours)
Chicken (stuffed)	2½ to 4½	2 to 3½
Capon (stuffed)	4 to 8	2½ to 4½
Turkey (stuffed)	4 to 6	2 to 3
	6 to 8	3 to 3½
	8 to 12	3½ to 4½
	12 to 16	4½ to 5½
	16 to 20	5½ to 6½
	20 to 24	6½ to 7
	24 to 28	7 to 8½
Cornish Game Hen (stuffed or unstuffed)*	1 to 1½	1 to 2

*Roast at 350°F.

Beef, Pork and Lamb

6

Pepper Steaks with Blackberry Glaze (page 174)

Asian Beef in Ginger Sauce

■ ■ ■ ■ ■ ■ ■ ■ ■ ■ ■ ■ ■ ■ ■ ■ ■ ■ ■ ■

PREP TIME: 20 MINUTES

4 cups hot cooked instant rice, if desired (cooked as directed on package, omitting margarine and salt)

1 teaspoon light sesame or vegetable oil

½ lb. stir-fry beef flank or sirloin steak strips*

1 medium onion, thinly sliced

3 cups fresh broccoli florets

¼ cup purchased stir-fry sauce with ginger and garlic

¼ cup water

2 teaspoons water

2 teaspoons cornstarch

1. While rice is cooking, heat oil in large nonstick skillet or wok over high heat until hot. Add beef and onion; cook 3 to 5 minutes or until beef is lightly browned, stirring occasionally.

2. Stir in broccoli, stir-fry sauce and ¼ cup water. Reduce heat to medium; cover and cook 4 minutes or until broccoli is crisp-tender, stirring occasionally.

3. In measuring cup or small bowl, combine 2 teaspoons water and cornstarch; blend well. Add to skillet; cook and stir about 1 minute or until thickened. Serve over rice.

YIELD: 4 SERVINGS

Tip: * If precut stir-fry beef strips are unavailable, ½ lb. beef flank or sirloin steak can be used. Place in freezer until partially frozen; slice into thin strips.

Nutrition Information Per Serving
Serving Size: ¼ of Recipe

Calories	300	Calories from Fat	60
		% Daily Value	
Total Fat	7g		11%
Saturated	2g		10%
Cholesterol	20mg		7%
Sodium	360mg		15%
Total Carbohydrate	45g		15%
Dietary Fiber	3g		12%
Sugars	5g		
Protein	14g		
Vitamin A	40%	Vitamin C	70%
Calcium	6%	Iron	15%

Dietary Exchanges: 2½ Starch, 1 Vegetable, 1 Medium-Fat Meat OR 2½ Carbohydrate, 1 Vegetable, 1 Medium-Fat Meat

soy and other Asian Flavorings

■ ■

Salty, savory soy sauce is a building block of much Chinese cooking, as well as a foundation for many sauces and pastes. Basic soy keeps at room temperature, tightly sealed, but most other sauces require refrigeration. Check the label.

Stir-fry sauce with ginger and garlic This combines soy sauce with ginger, garlic and cornstarch for a thick sauce that makes a stir-fry supper very easy to prepare.

Soy sauce This familiar condiment is mild and salty with a thin consistency. The Japanese version is called *shoyu* (SHOI-you). Tamari is a slightly richer and thicker version.

Fish sauce A popular flavoring in the cuisines of Thailand, Vietnam and Myanmar, fish sauce is a salty brown liquid with a thin consistency.

Oyster sauce A Chinese classic, oyster sauce mixes soy with oyster extract. The oyster flavor enhances but doesn't dominate. It's a very thick sauce, good with beef and green vegetables.

Canton Beef and Asparagus

PREP TIME: 20 MINUTES

4 cups hot cooked instant rice (cooked as directed on package, omitting margarine and salt)

⅓ cup oyster sauce*

¼ cup water*

1 teaspoon cornstarch

½ lb. beef flank steak, cut into thin strips

2 garlic cloves, minced

1 (9-oz.) pkg. frozen asparagus cuts in a pouch, thawed**

1 (8-oz.) can sliced water chestnuts, drained

1 small red bell pepper, cut into 2 × ¼ × ¼-inch strips

1. While rice is cooking, in small bowl, combine oyster sauce, water and cornstarch; blend well. Set aside.

2. Spray large nonstick wok or skillet with nonstick cooking spray. Heat over medium-high heat until hot. Add beef and garlic; cook and stir 2 to 3 minutes or until beef is browned.

3. Stir in asparagus, water chestnuts, bell pepper and oyster sauce mixture. Reduce heat to medium-low; cover and cook 3 to 5 minutes or until vegetables are crisp-tender. Serve over rice.

YIELD: 4 SERVINGS

Tips: * Oyster sauce can be found in the Asian foods section of large supermarkets or in Asian markets. If unavailable, omit water and use ⅓ cup purchased stir-fry sauce.

**** To quickly thaw asparagus, place in colander or strainer; rinse with warm water until thawed. Drain well.

Nutrition Information Per Serving
Serving Size: ¼ of Recipe

Calories	360	Calories from Fat	45
		% Daily Value	
Total Fat	5g		8%
Saturated	2g		10%
Cholesterol	20mg		7%
Sodium	1,080mg		45%
Total Carbohydrate	64g		21%
Dietary Fiber	3g		12%
Sugars	9g		
Protein	15g		
Vitamin A	20%	Vitamin C	40%
Calcium	4%	Iron	25%

Dietary Exchanges: 3½ Starch, 1 Vegetable, 1 Lean Meat OR 3½ Carbohydrate, 1 Vegetable, 1 Lean Meat

Freezer *smarts*

- Rewrap or overwrap meat and poultry packages before freezing them—the original wrapping is too thin to protect the meat from freezer burn. Use heavy plastic wrap or freezer bags (squeeze out the air).

- Use foil to wrap foods if you're sure you won't want to microwave-defrost. Don't reuse foil to wrap foods for freezing, however; tiny holes created when the foil was first crinkled can let in air.

- Freeze meat in small quantities for quick defrosting. Shape ground beef into patties; wrap chops and chicken parts individually. Pop the individually wrapped items into a heavy-duty, self-sealing freezer bag labeled with the contents and date.

- Likewise, freeze leftover soup, lasagna and other large dishes in single portions for quick lunches or solo dinners.

- If you need to cut up meat for a recipe, do it while it's still slightly frozen—it's easier.

- Go ahead and use that frozen casserole for dinner tonight. If you wait for too many "rainy days," the dinner may have passed its prime.

Spicy Broccoli Beef Stir-Fry

■ ■

PREP TIME: 25 MINUTES

8 oz. uncooked vermicelli

Sauce

½ cup orange juice

1 tablespoon cornstarch

2 tablespoons soy sauce

2 teaspoons sugar

¾ teaspoon Chinese five-spice powder

⅛ to ¼ teaspoon crushed red pepper flakes

Stir-Fry

¾ lb. boneless beef sirloin steak, thinly sliced

1 medium onion, cut into 16 wedges

1 garlic clove, minced

3 cups fresh broccoli florets (about 6 oz.)

1 small red bell pepper, cut into thin strips (about 1 cup)

1. Cook vermicelli to desired doneness as directed on package.

2. Meanwhile, in small bowl, combine all sauce ingredients; mix until well blended. Set aside.

3. Spray large nonstick skillet or wok with nonstick cooking spray. Heat over medium-high heat until hot. Add beef, onion and garlic; cook and stir 3 to 5 minutes or until beef is no longer pink and onion is crisp-tender.

4. Add broccoli and bell pepper. Cover; cook 2 to 4 minutes or until vegetables are crisp-tender, stirring occasionally. Add sauce; cook and stir 2 to 3 minutes or until bubbly and thickened.

5. Drain vermicelli. Serve beef mixture over vermicelli.

YIELD: 4 SERVINGS

Nutrition Information Per Serving
Serving Size: ¼ of Recipe

Calories	380	Calories from Fat	45
		% Daily Value	
Total Fat	5g		8%
Saturated	2g		10%
Cholesterol	45mg		15%
Sodium	570mg		24%
Total Carbohydrate	57g		19%
Dietary Fiber	4g		16%
Sugars	10g		
Protein	26g		
Vitamin A	50%	Vitamin C	110%
Calcium	6%	Iron	25%

Dietary Exchanges: 3 Starch, 1 Vegetable, 2 Lean Meat OR
3 Carbohydrate, 1 Vegetable, 2 Lean Meat

don't **Chop 'Til You Drop**

▪ ▪ ▪ ▪ ▪ ▪ ▪ ▪ ▪ ▪ ▪ ▪ ▪ ▪ ▪ ▪ ▪ ▪ ▪

Precut vegetables in the refrigerated produce section let you skip the most time-consuming step of stir-frying: chopping. Other convenient ingredients to round out a stir-fry include canned baby corn, water chestnuts, straw mushrooms or bamboo shoots; fresh bean sprouts; tofu; frozen vegetables.

Spicy Broccoli Beef Stir-Fry ▶

Stir-Fry Techniques:

it matters how you cut it

Each ingredient for a stir-fry dish should be cut uniformly to cook evenly. Many recipes specify cutting all ingredients in the same shape: all in cubes, for instance, or all in strips. This is not really necessary as long as all the carrots, say, are cut into strips and all the celery into diagonal slices. In fact, a contrast of shapes can look more appealing. Some of the most common techniques include:

Diagonal slicing Cutting ingredients into thin bias-cut slices serves two purposes. It exposes more surface area to the heat and thus speeds cooking, and since it shortens fibers in meat and in stringy vegetables like celery, it has a tenderizing effect, too.

Julienne cutting All this means is cutting food into matchstick-like strips. Cut the vegetable into slices, then stack the slices and cut into strips about 1/4 inch wide.

Chopping, cubing or dicing Prepare a stack of slices as for julienne, but cut the strips a little wider; then cut across the strips to make cubes.

Meat Meat will be most tender when cut into thin slices across the grain. For easier slicing, place the raw meat in the freezer for 30 to 60 minutes before cutting.

Orange Beef and Spinach Stir-Fry

■ ■ ■ ■ ■ ■ ■ ■ ■ ■ ■ ■ ■ ■ ■ ■ ■ ■ ■ ■

PREP TIME: 15 MINUTES

1 (3-oz.) pkg. reduced-fat oriental-flavor ramen noodle soup mix

¾ lb. boneless beef sirloin steak, cut into thin strips

2 garlic cloves, minced

1 (8-oz.) pkg. (3 cups) sliced fresh mushrooms

6 green onions, cut into 1-inch pieces

1 (10-oz.) pkg. prewashed fresh spinach, stems removed (4½ cups tightly packed)

2 tablespoons frozen orange juice concentrate

2 tablespoons water

¼ teaspoon ginger

1. Remove noodles from package; reserve seasoning packet. Break block of noodles in half. In medium saucepan, bring 2 cups water to a boil. Add noodles; reduce heat and simmer uncovered 3 minutes, stirring occasionally. Remove from heat; drain.

2. Heat 5-quart nonstick Dutch oven or wok over medium-high heat until hot. Add beef strips and garlic; cook and stir 3 minutes. Add mushrooms; cook and stir 3 minutes or until mushrooms are tender and beef is no longer pink.

3. Stir in onions. Add spinach in batches, stirring 30 seconds per batch until spinach wilts. Remove from heat; stir in seasoning packet, juice concentrate, 2 tablespoons water and ginger. Add cooked noodles; toss to combine.

YIELD: 4 (1-CUP) SERVINGS

Nutrition Information Per Serving
Serving Size: 1 Cup

Calories................................230	Calories from Fat 45
	% Daily Value
Total Fat 5g	.................................8%
Saturated 1g	..................................5%
Cholesterol 45mg	.............................15%
Sodium 480mg	...............................20%
Total Carbohydrate 26g	.................................9%
Dietary Fiber 4g	..............................16%
Sugars 5g	
Protein 21g	
Vitamin A.............................90%	Vitamin C 40%
Calcium 10%	Iron 30%

Dietary Exchanges: 1 Starch, 2 Vegetable, 2 Lean Meat OR
1 Carbohydrate, 2 Vegetable, 2 Lean Meat

Beef and Vegetable Curry

∎ ∎ ∎ ∎ ∎ ∎ ∎ ∎ ∎ ∎ ∎ ∎ ∎ ∎ ∎ ∎

PREP TIME: 25 MINUTES

**4 cups hot cooked instant rice (cooked as
directed on package, omitting margarine and
salt)**

½ lb. boneless beef top round steak, thinly sliced

1 medium onion, sliced

3 garlic cloves, minced

1 medium carrot, sliced (⅔ cup)

1 medium red bell pepper, cut into 1-inch pieces

1 (8-oz.) pkg. fresh whole mushrooms, quartered

⅔ cup light coconut milk*

1 tablespoon curry powder

1 tablespoon fish sauce or soy sauce

1. While rice is cooking, spray large nonstick
saucepan or Dutch oven with nonstick cooking
spray. Heat over medium-high heat until hot. Add
beef; cook until no longer pink, stirring occasionally.
Add onion and garlic; cook about 30 seconds.

2. Add all remaining ingredients except rice.
Reduce heat to medium-low; cover and cook 10 to
15 minutes or until beef is tender, stirring occasionally. Serve over rice.

YIELD: 4 SERVINGS

Tip: * To substitute for coconut milk, combine
³/₄ cup skim milk, 2 teaspoons cornstarch and 1 teaspoon coconut extract; mix well.

Nutrition Information Per Serving
Serving Size: ¹/₄ of Recipe

Calories................................310	Calories from Fat 45
	% Daily Value
Total Fat 5g	.................................8%
Saturated 3g	..............................15%
Cholesterol 35mg	.............................12%
Sodium 340mg	...............................14%
Total Carbohydrate 46g	...............................15%
Dietary Fiber 4g	..............................16%
Sugars 6g	
Protein 19g	
Vitamin A...........................120%	Vitamin C 50%
Calcium 4%	Iron 25%

Dietary Exchanges: 3 Starch, 1 ½ Lean Meat OR 3 Carbohydrate,
1 ½ Lean Meat

▼ Beef and Vegetable Cury

Beef Stroganoff

PREP TIME: 30 MINUTES

8 cups hot cooked noodles or instant rice (cooked as directed on package, omitting margarine and salt)

⅓ cup all-purpose flour

½ teaspoon salt

⅛ teaspoon pepper

2½ lb. boneless beef sirloin steak, cut into 3 × ½ × ¼-inch strips

1 tablespoon oil

1 (8-oz.) pkg. (3 cups) sliced fresh mushrooms

1 (10½-oz.) can condensed beef broth

½ cup water

3 tablespoons tomato paste

1 tablespoon Worcestershire sauce

1½ cups nonfat sour cream

1. While noodles are cooking, in plastic bag, combine flour, salt and pepper. Add beef strips; shake to coat.

2. Heat oil in large nonstick skillet or Dutch oven over medium-high heat until hot. Add beef; cook until browned. Add mushrooms; cook and stir 1 minute. Add broth, water, tomato paste and Worcestershire sauce; mix well. Reduce heat; simmer 15 to 20 minutes or until beef is tender.

3. Stir in sour cream; cook until thoroughly heated. DO NOT BOIL. Serve over noodles.

YIELD: 8 SERVINGS

Nutrition Information Per Serving
Serving Size: ⅛ of Recipe

Calories	460	Calories from Fat	80
		% Daily Value	
Total Fat	9g		14%
Saturated	3g		15%
Cholesterol	75mg		25%
Sodium	470mg		20%
Total Carbohydrate	57g		19%
Dietary Fiber	3g		12%
Sugars	6g		
Protein	38g		
Vitamin A	10%	Vitamin C	4%
Calcium	8%	Iron	35%

Dietary Exchanges: 4 Starch, 3 Lean Meat OR 4 Carbohydrate, 3 Lean Meat

Herbed Spaghetti

PREP TIME: 25 MINUTES

½ lb. extra-lean ground beef

1 small onion, chopped

1 garlic clove, minced

2 (8-oz.) cans no-salt-added tomato sauce

1 (14.5-oz.) can no-salt-added whole tomatoes, undrained, cut up

2 tablespoons grated Parmesan cheese

1 teaspoon sugar

1 teaspoon salt-free seasoning

1 teaspoon dried basil leaves

½ teaspoon dried oregano leaves

8 oz. uncooked spaghetti

1. In large nonstick skillet over medium heat, cook ground beef, onion and garlic until beef is browned and onion is tender; drain. Stir in all remaining ingredients except spaghetti. Bring to a boil. Reduce heat; simmer 25 minutes.

2. Meanwhile, cook spaghetti to desired doneness as directed on package. Drain spaghetti. Serve sauce over spaghetti.

YIELD: 4 SERVINGS

about Nonfat Sour Cream

The availability of good-quality nonfat sour cream is a boon to the low-fat cook. Today's nonfat sour creams perform well in uncooked dishes such as dips or dessert toppings and in cooked dishes with creamy textured sauces. As with regular sour cream, however, avoid curdling by making sure the sauce does not come to a boil.

Nutrition Information Per Serving
Serving Size: ¼ of Recipe

Calories	390	Calories from Fat	80
		% Daily Value	
Total Fat	9g		14%
Saturated	3g		15%
Cholesterol	40mg		13%
Sodium	125mg		5%
Total Carbohydrate	55g		18%
Dietary Fiber	3g		12%
Sugars	9g		
Protein	22g		
Vitamin A	6%	Vitamin C	45%
Calcium	10%	Iron	25%

Dietary Exchanges: 3½ Starch, 1½ Medium-Fat Meat OR
3½ Carbohydrate, 1½ Medium-Fat Meat

rinse away Fat

A simple rinsing technique can reduce the overall content of cooked ground meat by up to 50 percent. Here's how:

1. Break the meat up into small crumbles and brown thoroughly in a frying pan.

2. Using a slotted spoon, scoop the meat out of the pan and let it drain on several layers of white paper toweling.

3. Transfer the meat to a colander and rinse with four cups of hot water. Drain for five minutes.

4. Proceed with the recipe.

Rinsing reduces the flavor of the meat slightly, but usually not significantly if the meat will be combined with other ingredients. Be sure to add salt, pepper, herbs and other flavorings after rinsing. (Garlic and onions should still brown along with the meat.)

Mexican Beef and Tomato Tortillas

PREP TIME: 25 MINUTES

½ lb. ground beef top round

1 (15.5-oz.) can pinto beans, drained, rinsed

1 (10-oz.) can tomatoes with green chiles, undrained

4 teaspoons chili powder

½ teaspoon cumin

8 (6-inch) soft corn tortillas

3 oz. (¾ cup) shredded reduced-fat sharp Cheddar cheese

½ cup nonfat sour cream, if desired

1. Heat medium nonstick skillet over medium-high heat until hot. Add ground beef; cook 2 to 4 minutes or until browned. Remove beef from skillet; drain on paper towels.

2. Wipe skillet dry with paper towels. Return beef to skillet; stir in beans, tomatoes, chili powder and cumin. Bring to a boil. Reduce heat; cover and simmer 10 minutes.

3. Meanwhile, heat tortillas as directed on package.

4. To serve, sprinkle cheese evenly over tortillas. Top with beef mixture and sour cream; fold in half.

YIELD: 4 SERVINGS

Nutrition Information Per Serving
Serving Size: ¼ of Recipe

Calories	350	Calories from Fat	70
		% Daily Value	
Total Fat	8g		12%
Saturated	3g		15%
Cholesterol	45mg		15%
Sodium	760mg		32%
Total Carbohydrate	41g		14%
Dietary Fiber	7g		28%
Sugars	5g		
Protein	28g		
Vitamin A	35%	Vitamin C	8%
Calcium	35%	Iron	15%

Dietary Exchanges: 2½ Starch, 1 Vegetable, 2½ Lean Meat OR
2½ Carbohydrate, 1 Vegetable, 2½ Lean Meat

Beef with Garbanzo Beans, Peppers and Couscous

■ ■ ■ ■ ■ ■ ■ ■ ■ ■ ■ ■ ■ ■ ■ ■ ■ ■ ■

PREP TIME: 15 MINUTES

1½ cups water

1 teaspoon beef-flavor instant bouillon

1 cup uncooked couscous

1 teaspoon olive oil

2 medium green bell peppers, cut into
    2 × ¼ × ¼-inch strips

1 tablespoon water

⅓ cup red wine vinegar

2 teaspoons cumin

¼ teaspoon ground red pepper (cayenne)

½ lb. thinly sliced deli cooked roast beef, as rare
    as possible, cut into 1 × ¼-inch strips

12 pitted ripe olives, cut into wedges

1 (15-oz.) can garbanzo beans, drained, rinsed

1. Bring 1½ cups water to a boil in medium saucepan. Add bouillon; stir until dissolved. Stir in couscous. Remove from heat; cover and let stand 5 minutes.

2. Meanwhile, heat oil in large nonstick skillet over medium-high heat until hot. Add bell peppers and 1 tablespoon water; stir to coat peppers with oil. Cover; cook 2 minutes.

about Couscous

Couscous resembles a grain but is actually a tiny pasta that's very popular in Middle Eastern cooking. Its mild flavor makes it a good complement to a variety of savory dishes, and the quick-cooking version found in most supermarkets takes only 5 minutes to prepare.

3. Stir in remaining ingredients and cooked couscous. Reduce heat to medium-low; cover and cook 2 to 3 minutes or until thoroughly heated. Fluff with fork before serving. If desired, sprinkle with freshly ground black pepper.

YIELD: 6 (1¼-CUP) SERVINGS

Nutrition Information Per Serving
Serving Size: 1¼ Cups

Calories	280	Calories from Fat	50
		% Daily Value	
Total Fat	6g		9%
Saturated	1g		5%
Cholesterol	35mg		12%
Sodium	630mg		26%
Total Carbohydrate	37g		12%
Dietary Fiber	5g		20%
Sugars	2g		
Protein	20g		
Vitamin A	4%	Vitamin C	25%
Calcium	4%	Iron	15%

Dietary Exchanges: 2 Starch, 1 Vegetable, 2 Lean Meat OR
2 Carbohydrate, 1 Vegetable, 2 Lean Meat

Sirloin and Mushrooms in Rich Beef Dijon Sauce

■ ■ ■ ■ ■ ■ ■ ■ ■ ■ ■ ■ ■ ■ ■ ■ ■ ■ ■

PREP TIME: 25 MINUTES

8 oz. uncooked angel hair pasta

1 lb. boneless beef top sirloin steak, cut into
    1-inch pieces

2 garlic cloves, minced

1 (8-oz.) pkg. (3 cups) sliced fresh mushrooms

1 cup beef broth

¼ cup diagonally sliced green onions

2 tablespoons all-purpose flour

3 tablespoons skim milk

2 tablespoons Dijon mustard

Coarse ground black pepper

the leanest Cuts of Meat

Beef cuts with "loin" or "round" in the name tend to be the leanest; for pork, veal and lamb, look for the words "loin" or "leg." Here are some of the best meat choices for fat-conscious cooking, along with some poultry numbers for comparison:

Beef	Calories*	Fat (g)*
Tenderloin	180	8.5
Top loin	180	8
Sirloin	170	6
Bottom round steak	180	7
Round tip	160	6
Top round	150	4
Eye of round	140	4
Pork		
Loin rib chop	190	8
Center loin chop	170	7
Top loin chop	170	7
Top loin roast	140	6
Tenderloin roast	140	4

Lamb	Calories*	Fat (g)*
Shoulder arm chop	170	8
Loin chop	180	8
Whole leg	160	7
Shank	160	5
Poultry		
Chicken, white meat without skin	130	3
Chicken, dark meat with skin	200	11
Turkey, white meat without skin	90	0.5
Turkey, dark meat with skin	155	6

*Calories and grams of fat per 3-ounce serving, trimmed and cooked without added fat.
Sources: USDA, Food Marketing Institute, Beef Industry Council and National Cattlemen's Beef Association

1. Cook pasta to desired doneness as directed on package.

2. Meanwhile, spray 12-inch nonstick skillet with nonstick cooking spray. Heat over medium-high heat until hot. Add beef and garlic; cook about 4 minutes, stirring frequently. Add mushrooms, broth and onions. Reduce heat; cover and cook 3 minutes. Uncover; cook an additional 2 to 3 minutes.

3. In small bowl, combine flour and milk; blend until smooth. Add to skillet; cook and stir 2 minutes or until slightly thickened. Stir in mustard until smooth.

4. Drain pasta; arrange on serving platter. Spoon beef-mushroom mixture and sauce over pasta. Sprinkle with pepper.

YIELD: 4 SERVINGS

Nutrition Information Per Serving
Serving Size: ¼ of Recipe

Calories	390	Calories from Fat	70

		% Daily Value
Total Fat	8g	12%
Saturated	3g	15%
Cholesterol	50mg	17%
Sodium	340mg	14%
Total Carbohydrate	50g	17%
Dietary Fiber	2g	8%
Sugars	3g	
Protein	29g	

Vitamin A	0%	Vitamin C	4%
Calcium	4%	Iron	25%

Dietary Exchanges: 3 Starch, 1 Vegetable, 2½ Lean Meat OR
3 Carbohydrate, 1 Vegetable, 2½ Lean Meat

Favorite Salisbury Steak

Patties

1 lb. extra-lean ground beef

½ cup unseasoned bread crumbs

½ cup skim milk

1 egg white

¼ cup finely chopped onion

1 teaspoon Worcestershire sauce

¼ teaspoon salt

¼ teaspoon pepper

Gravy

¾ cup beef broth

¼ cup dry red wine or beef broth*

1 tablespoon cornstarch

¼ teaspoon dried thyme leaves

1 (2.5-oz.) jar sliced mushrooms, drained

1. In medium bowl, combine all pattie ingredients; mix gently. (Mixture will be moist.) Shape into 6 oval patties, about ¾ inch thick.

2. Spray large nonstick skillet with nonstick cooking spray. Heat over medium heat until hot. Add patties; cook 3 minutes on each side or until browned. Remove patties from skillet; drain, if necessary.

3. In small bowl, combine broth, wine, cornstarch and thyme; blend well. Pour into same skillet. Cook over low heat until mixture boils and thickens, stirring constantly. Stir in mushrooms. Return patties to skillet. Cover; simmer about 15 minutes or until patties are no longer pink in center.

YIELD: 6 SERVINGS

Tip: * One-fourth cup water plus 1 teaspoon Worcestershire sauce can be substituted for red wine.

Nutrition Information Per Serving
Serving Size: ⅙ of Recipe

Calories	200	Calories from Fat	90
		% Daily Value	
Total Fat	10g		15%
Saturated	4g		20%
Cholesterol	45mg		15%
Sodium	380mg		16%
Total Carbohydrate	10g		3%
Dietary Fiber	1g		3%
Sugars	2g		
Protein	17g		
Vitamin A	0%	Vitamin C	0%
Calcium	6%	Iron	10%

Dietary Exchanges: ½ Starch, 2 Medium-Fat Meat OR ½ Carbohydrate, 2 Medium-Fat Meat

tips for reducing fat in Ground Meat Dishes

- Substitute ground turkey for part or all of the ground beef in the recipe.

- Purchase the leanest ground beef available.

- Broil on a rack or grill, which allows fat to drain away, rather than frying, which may require added fat and which soaks the meat in its own fat as it cooks.

- Blot cooked ground meat with white paper towels to soak up some of the surface fat.

meat: Safe Handling Tips

- Check "sell by" dates on the package.

- Store meat in the coldest part of the refrigerator. Cook or freeze it within a day.

- For freezing, repackage meats with heavy-duty, moisture-proof wrap. Label and date the packages.

- Avoid cross-contamination. Wash knives, work surfaces and any other cooking tools that come in contact with raw meat in hot soapy water before using for anything else.

- Wash your hands thoroughly after handling raw meat.

- Cook ground beef until no trace of pink remains.

- Refrigerate leftovers promptly and use within three to four days.

Peppered Cube Steaks with Mashed Potatoes and Gravy

PREP TIME: 15 MINUTES

2 cups hot instant mashed potatoes (prepared as directed on package)*

4 beef cube steaks (about 1 lb.)

1 teaspoon garlic-pepper seasoning

1 cup beef broth

¼ cup water

1 tablespoon cornstarch

1. Prepare mashed potatoes.

2. Sprinkle both sides of each cube steak with garlic-pepper seasoning. Spray 12-inch nonstick skillet with nonstick cooking spray. Heat skillet over medium-high heat until hot. Add steaks; cook 3 to 4 minutes on each side or to desired doneness. Remove steaks from skillet; cover to keep warm.

3. In same skillet, combine broth, water and cornstarch; cook until bubbly and thickened, stirring constantly. Serve gravy over cube steaks and hot mashed potatoes.

YIELD: 4 SERVINGS

Tip: * Microwave-baked potatoes can be substituted for mashed potatoes.

Nutrition Information Per Serving
Serving Size: ¼ of Recipe

Calories	260	Calories from Fat	70
			% Daily Value
Total Fat	8g		12%
Saturated	2g		10%
Cholesterol	65mg		22%
Sodium	710mg		30%
Total Carbohydrate	20g		7%
Dietary Fiber	2g		8%
Sugars	2g		
Protein	27g		
Vitamin A	4%	Vitamin C	8%
Calcium	4%	Iron	15%

Dietary Exchanges: 1½ Starch, 2½ Lean Meat OR 1½ Carbohydrate, 2½ Lean Meat

Teriyaki Beef with Rice Noodles

PREP TIME: 30 MINUTES

6 oz. uncooked rice sticks*

¼ cup soy sauce

2 tablespoons brown sugar

2 tablespoons rice or cider vinegar

¼ teaspoon dry mustard

2 garlic cloves, minced

¾ lb. lean boneless beef sirloin or eye of round steak

2 green onions, cut lengthwise into thin strips and crosswise into 1-inch pieces

1. In large saucepan, bring 8 cups water to a boil over high heat. Break rice sticks into water; return to a boil. Reduce heat to medium-low; cook 3 minutes. Drain rice sticks; return to saucepan.

2. In small bowl, combine soy sauce, brown sugar, vinegar, dry mustard and garlic; mix well. Place beef in resealable plastic bag or shallow dish; pour sauce over beef. Seal bag or cover dish. Let stand at room temperature for 10 minutes to marinate, turning beef once to coat both sides.

3. Place beef on broiler pan; pour marinade into small saucepan. Broil beef 2 to 3 inches from heat for 3 minutes. Turn; broil an additional 3 to 6 minutes for medium-rare or to desired doneness. Let stand 3 minutes; cut into ⅛-inch-thick strips.

4. Bring marinade to a boil. Reserve 2 tablespoons; pour remaining marinade over noodles and toss gently. Place noodles on serving platter. Top with beef; drizzle with reserved marinade. Garnish with green onion strips.

YIELD: 4 SERVINGS

Tip: * Rice sticks (noodles) can be found in the Asian foods section of large supermarkets or in Asian markets. If unavailable, use vermicelli; cook as directed on package.

Nutrition Information Per Serving
Serving Size: ¼ of Recipe

Calories	300	Calories from Fat	35
		% Daily Value	
Total Fat	4g		6%
Saturated	1g		5%
Cholesterol	45mg		15%
Sodium	1,090mg		45%
Total Carbohydrate	46g		15%
Dietary Fiber	1g		4%
Sugars	7g		
Protein	19g		
Vitamin A	0%	Vitamin C	2%
Calcium	2%	Iron	20%

Dietary Exchanges: 3 Starch, 1 Lean Meat OR 3 Carbohydrate, 1 Lean Meat

▪ PRODUCE POINTERS

Garlic *from mild to potent*

Garlic has multiple personalities that you can tame through preparation. Hottest and most potent when raw, garlic mellows with cooking.

- For the strongest flavor, add raw garlic to a finished dish or sauce. The more you chop and mince garlic, the more robust it becomes, so if you appreciate the bite but don't want the burn, use whole or halved cloves; remove them before serving.

- Cooking tames garlic's zest and odor. A quick sauté tempers garlic's punch; a long, slow simmer or bake delivers a sweet and nutty essence. As with raw garlic, the smaller the pieces, the fuller the flavor. Watch your garlic sauté carefully; those little pieces burn easily, turning bitter.

- For the most delicate flavor, cook with whole cloves—unpeeled—and remove them before serving.

◀ Teriyaki Beef with Rice Noodles

Keep-It-Simple Lasagna

■ ■

PREP TIME: 15 MINUTES
(READY IN 50 MINUTES)

6 oz. (3 cups) mini lasagna noodles (mafalda)

1 medium zucchini, sliced

1 cup low-fat cottage cheese

1 egg white

2 oz. (½ cup) shredded mozzarella cheese

¼ lb. extra-lean ground beef

1 (25.5-oz.) jar reduced-fat, reduced-sodium chunky vegetable spaghetti sauce

1 teaspoon fennel seed, crushed

¼ cup grated Parmesan cheese

▼ Keep-It-Simple Lasagna

1. Cook noodles to desired doneness as directed on package, adding zucchini during last 2 minutes of cooking time.

2. Meanwhile, heat oven to 400°F. Spray 9-inch square pan with nonstick cooking spray. In small bowl, combine cottage cheese, egg white and ¼ cup of the mozzarella cheese; mix well. Set aside.

3. In large nonstick skillet over medium-high heat, brown ground beef; drain. Stir in spaghetti sauce and fennel; simmer 5 minutes.

4. Drain noodles and zucchini. Spread small amount of sauce in bottom of sprayed pan. Layer half each of noodles, zucchini, cottage cheese mixture and sauce; repeat layers. Top with remaining ¼ cup mozzarella cheese and Parmesan cheese.

5. Bake at 400°F. for 25 to 35 minutes or until lasagna is bubbly and top is golden brown.

YIELD: 6 SERVINGS

Nutrition Information Per Serving
Serving Size: ⅙ of Recipe

Calories	280	Calories from Fat	60
		% Daily Value	
Total Fat	7g		11%
Saturated	3g		15%
Cholesterol	20mg		7%
Sodium	680mg		28%
Total Carbohydrate	35g		12%
Dietary Fiber	3g		12%
Sugars	12g		
Protein	19g		
Vitamin A	45%	Vitamin C	10%
Calcium	20%	Iron	15%

Dietary Exchanges: 2 Starch, 1 Vegetable, 2 Lean Meat OR
2 Carbohydrate, 1 Vegetable, 2 Lean Meat

Baked Beef Tenderloin with Diane Sauce

■ ■ ■ ■ ■ ■ ■ ■ ■ ■ ■ ■ ■ ■ ■ ■ ■ ■ ■

PREP TIME: 10 MINUTES
(READY IN 50 MINUTES)

1½ lb. beef tenderloin

1 cup beef broth

2 teaspoons cornstarch

1 teaspoon oil

¼ cup chopped green onions

¼ cup chopped fresh parsley

1 teaspoon coarse ground black pepper

2 teaspoons Dijon mustard

1 tablespoon lemon juice

1. Heat oven to 400°F. Place sheet of foil on 15 × 10 × 1-inch baking pan or cookie sheet. Place beef tenderloin on foil; tuck narrow end under. Turn edges of foil up around tenderloin to contain juices. Bake at 400°F. for 30 to 40 minutes for medium doneness.*

2. Meanwhile, in small bowl, combine broth and cornstarch; blend well. Set aside.

3. Heat oil in small nonstick skillet until hot. Add onions; cook about 1 minute. Stir in parsley, pepper, mustard and lemon juice. Add cornstarch mixture; cook and stir over medium heat for 4 to 6 minutes or until sauce is bubbly and slightly thickened.

4. To serve, cut tenderloin into ½-inch slices. Serve sauce over slices.

YIELD: 6 SERVINGS

Tip: * To assure optimum doneness, check internal temperature with meat thermometer. For medium doneness, thermometer should reach 160°F.; for well done, thermometer should reach 170°F.

Nutrition Information Per Serving
Serving Size: ⅙ of Recipe

Calories	130	Calories from Fat	50
		% Daily Value	
Total Fat	6g		9%
Saturated	2g		10%
Cholesterol	45mg		15%
Sodium	210mg		9%
Total Carbohydrate	2g		1%
Dietary Fiber	0g		0%
Sugars	0g		
Protein	16g		
Vitamin A	2%	Vitamin C	6%
Calcium	0%	Iron	15%

Dietary Exchanges: 2 Lean Meat

Meat:
nutrition facts

■ ■ ■ ■ ■ ■ ■ ■ ■ ■ ■ ■ ■ ■ ■

Beef, pork and lamb are excellent sources of protein and iron as well as zinc, phosphorus, thiamine, riboflavin, niacin and vitamins B_6 and B_{12}. When eaten in moderation, meat makes a substantial contribution to the well-balanced diet. Some tips:

- Figure 3 to 4 ounces of meat per person rather than mammoth plate-covering servings.

- Trim visible fat before cooking.

- Choose cooking methods that do not require added fat, such as broiling, roasting, grilling, braising and stewing.

- Stretch a small amount of meat in a main dish with lots of vegetables and/or pasta or other grains.

Beef Tenderloin with Mushroom Shallot Sauce

■ ■ ■ ■ ■ ■ ■ ■ ■ ■ ■ ■ ■ ■ ■ ■ ■ ■ ■ ■

PREP TIME: 20 MINUTES

2 (4-oz.) beef tenderloin steaks (filet mignon)

1 large garlic clove, peeled, halved

¼ teaspoon coarse ground black pepper

1 teaspoon margarine or butter

1 cup fresh whole mushrooms, halved

2 shallots, thinly sliced

¼ cup Cabernet Sauvignon or other dry red wine

¼ cup beef broth

1 teaspoon cornstarch

1. Line 15 × 10 × 1-inch baking pan with foil. Rub both sides of each steak with cut side of garlic. Sprinkle each side with pepper. Place steaks on foil-lined pan. Broil 4 to 6 inches from heat for 6 to 8 minutes on each side or until of desired doneness.

2. Meanwhile, melt margarine in small nonstick skillet over medium heat. Add mushrooms and shallots; cook and stir 4 to 6 minutes or until shallots are tender and mushrooms begin to brown. Add wine; cook 1 minute, stirring occasionally.

3. In small bowl, combine broth and cornstarch; blend well. Stir into wine mixture; cook and stir until bubbly and thickened. Serve sauce over steaks.

YIELD: 2 SERVINGS

Nutrition Information Per Serving
Serving Size: ¹/₂ of Recipe

Calories	220	Calories from Fat	80
		% Daily Value	
Total Fat	9g		14%
Saturated	3g		15%
Cholesterol	50mg		17%
Sodium	170mg		7%
Total Carbohydrate	7g		2%
Dietary Fiber	1g		4%
Sugars	1g		
Protein	19g		
Vitamin A	40%	Vitamin C	4%
Calcium	2%	Iron	20%

Dietary Exchanges: 1 Vegetable, 2 Lean Meat, 2 Fat

▼ Beef Tenderloin with Mushroom Shallot Sauce

about **Shallots**

Shallots, with their papery brown skin, have a flavor somewhere between onion and garlic. They tend to be a little pricier than either onions or garlic, but a little goes a long way, and most recipes require only one or two shallots.

ter of pouch; microwave on **HIGH** for 2 to 3 minutes or until thawed. Remove spinach from pouch; squeeze dry with paper towels.

Nutrition Information Per Serving
Serving Size: ¼ of Recipe

Calories	150	Calories from Fat	45
		% Daily Value	
Total Fat	5g		8%
Saturated	2g		10%
Cholesterol	60mg		20%
Sodium	190mg		8%
Total Carbohydrate	3g		1%
Dietary Fiber	1g		4%
Sugars	0g		
Protein	22g		
Vitamin A	45%	Vitamin C	15%
Calcium	8%	Iron	15%

Dietary Exchanges: 1 Vegetable, 2½ Lean Meat

Beef and Spinach Roll-Ups

∙ ∙

PREP TIME: 25 MINUTES

1 (9-oz.) pkg. frozen spinach in a pouch, thawed, squeezed to drain*

½ teaspoon garlic powder

½ teaspoon salt-free lemon-pepper seasoning

1 lb. boneless beef sirloin steak (½ inch thick)

⅛ teaspoon pepper

4 pieces heavy thread or dental floss

1. In small bowl, combine spinach, garlic powder and lemon-pepper seasoning; mix well.

2. Place beef sirloin on cutting board. (Beef should be rectangular in shape.) Sprinkle with pepper. Spread spinach mixture evenly over beef. Beginning with long edge, roll up jelly-roll fashion. To secure roll-up, tie beef in 4 places with thread. With sharp knife, cut roll into 4 equal pieces.

3. Place rolls, cut side up, on broiler pan. Broil 4 to 6 inches from heat for 12 to 16 minutes or until beef is of desired doneness, turning once.

YIELD: 4 SERVINGS

Tip: * To quickly thaw spinach, cut small slit in cen-

meat tips for the **Hurried Cook**

∙ ∙

• For faster cooking, choose thin, boneless cuts, such as boneless pork chops, thin steaks, slices of lamb leg or pork tenderloin.

• Ground meat cooks quickly and is very versatile, but can be high in fat. Look for packages marked "extra lean" or choose a chunk of lean meat and ask the butcher to grind it for you. You'll probably pay a little more, but you will be paying for meat, not fat.

• Speed up cooking by butterflying meat (see "How to Butterfly Meats," page 186) or cutting it into strips or cubes. Many supermarkets sell strips or chunks of meat packaged for stewing or stir-frying.

Sweet 'n Spicy Meat and Potato Loaves

▪ ▪

PREP TIME: 15 MINUTES
(READY IN 45 MINUTES)

Sauce

1 (8-oz.) can (¾ cup) jellied cranberry sauce

¼ cup chili or barbecue sauce

2 tablespoons lemon juice

1 teaspoon dry mustard

Meat Loaves

1 lb. extra-lean ground beef

2 cups refrigerated shredded hash-brown potatoes (from 20-oz. pkg.)

½ cup finely chopped onion

2 egg whites

1 teaspoon Worcestershire sauce

½ teaspoon ground sage

1. Heat oven to 400°F. Place roasting rack in shallow pan; spray rack with nonstick cooking spray.*
2. In small bowl, combine all sauce ingredients; beat with wire whisk until smooth.
3. In large bowl, combine all meat loaf ingredients and ¼ cup of the sauce; mix well. Shape mixture into 6 oval loaves, about ¾ inch thick; place on sprayed rack in pan. Spoon about 1 teaspoon sauce over each loaf.
4. Bake at 400°F. for 15 minutes. Spoon an additional 1 teaspoon sauce over each loaf. Bake an additional 15 minutes or until no longer pink in center. Serve with remaining sauce.

YIELD: 6 SERVINGS

Tip: * A foil-lined 15 × 10 × 1-inch baking pan, sprayed with nonstick cooking spray, can be substituted for roasting pan and rack.

Nutrition Information Per Serving
Serving Size: ⅙ of Recipe

Calories 260		Calories from Fat 90	
		% Daily Value	
Total Fat 10g		.... 15%	
Saturated 4g		.... 20%	
Cholesterol 45mg		.... 15%	
Sodium 200mg		.... 8%	
Total Carbohydrate 26g		.... 9%	
Dietary Fiber 1g		.... 4%	
Sugars 15g			
Protein 17g			
Vitamin A 2%		Vitamin C 8%	
Calcium 0%		Iron 10%	

Dietary Exchanges: 1 Starch, ½ Fruit, 2 Medium-Fat Meat OR
1 ½ Carbohydrate, 2 Medium-Fat Meat

▼ Sweet 'n Spicy Meat and Potato Loaves

stretching the **Meat Loaf**

■ ■

Bread crumbs are traditional, but other fillers can extend a pound of ground meat destined for meat loaf. Try:

Purchased or homemade bread crumbs, plain or seasoned

Old-fashioned rolled oats

Cornmeal

Leftover cooked rice or mashed potatoes

Leftover cooked couscous or kasha

Refrigerated shredded hash-brown potatoes

Drained, chopped leftover cooked vegetables

Leftover mashed cooked winter squash

Speedy Meat Loaf

■ ■ ■ ■ ■ ■ ■ ■ ■ ■ ■ ■ ■ ■ ■ ■ ■ ■ ■

PREP TIME: 10 MINUTES
(READY IN 40 MINUTES)

¾ lb. extra-lean ground beef

½ cup Italian-style bread crumbs

⅓ cup chopped green bell pepper

¼ cup ketchup

1 tablespoon Worcestershire sauce

2 teaspoons onion powder

1 egg white

2 tablespoons ketchup

1. Heat oven to 475°F. Spray broiler pan rack with nonstick cooking spray; if desired, also line pan with foil.

2. In medium bowl, combine all ingredients except 2 tablespoons ketchup; mix well. Place mixture on sprayed broiler pan rack; shape mixture firmly into 8 × 4-inch rectangle.* Spread with 2 tablespoons ketchup.

3. Bake at 475°F. for 20 to 25 minutes or until center is no longer pink. Let stand 5 minutes before serving.

YIELD: 4 SERVINGS

Tip: * If desired, beef mixture can be shaped firmly into 8 × 4-inch rectangle on dinner plate or small plastic cutting board; invert onto sprayed broiler pan rack.

Nutrition Information Per Serving
Serving Size: ¼ of Recipe

Calories	250	Calories from Fat	100
			% Daily Value
Total Fat	11g		17%
Saturated	4g		20%
Cholesterol	55mg		18%
Sodium	580mg		24%
Total Carbohydrate	18g		6%
Dietary Fiber	1g		4%
Sugars	3g		
Protein	19g		
Vitamin A	6%	Vitamin C	15%
Calcium	4%	Iron	15%

Dietary Exchanges: 1 Starch, 2 Lean Meat, 1 Fat OR 1 Carbohydrate, 2 Lean Meat, 1 Fat

▲ Easy Steak Sandwiches

Easy Steak Sandwiches

PREP TIME: 10 MINUTES

⅓ cup beef broth

½ teaspoon garlic powder

1 teaspoon Worcestershire sauce

Dash pepper

¾ lb. beef round sandwich tip steaks
   (⅛ inch thick)

1 small onion, thinly sliced

4 (4- to 6-inch) French rolls, split

4 leaves romaine lettuce, if desired

1. In large nonstick skillet, combine broth, garlic powder, Worcestershire sauce and pepper. Bring to a boil. Add steaks and onion; cook over medium-high heat for 2 to 4 minutes or until beef is of desired doneness, turning once.

2. To serve, drizzle cooking liquid over cut surfaces of rolls. Layer lettuce, steak and onion in rolls.

YIELD: 4 SANDWICHES

Nutrition Information Per Serving
Serving Size: 1 Sandwich

Calories	300	Calories from Fat	50
		% Daily Value	
Total Fat	6g		9%
Saturated	2g		10%
Cholesterol	45mg		15%
Sodium	540mg		23%
Total Carbohydrate	38g		13%
Dietary Fiber	2g		8%
Sugars	4g		
Protein	23g		
Vitamin A	6%	Vitamin C	4%
Calcium	6%	Iron	20%

Dietary Exchanges: 2½ Starch, 2 Lean Meat OR 2½ Carbohydrate, 2 Lean Meat

Feta-Stuffed Burgers

PREP TIME: 35 MINUTES

4 Italian plum tomatoes, seeded, chopped

2 tablespoons finely chopped onion

1 tablespoon red wine vinegar

**2 teaspoons chopped fresh basil or ½ teaspoon
dried basil leaves**

⅛ teaspoon salt

Dash pepper

1 lb. ground beef top round*

2 teaspoons Dijon mustard

1½ oz. feta cheese, crumbled

4 burger buns, split

1. In medium bowl, combine tomatoes, onion, vinegar, basil, salt and pepper; mix well. Let stand at room temperature for 20 minutes to blend flavors.

2. Meanwhile, shape ground beef into 8 patties, 4 inches in diameter. Spread ½ teaspoon mustard on each of 4 patties; top mustard with feta cheese. Top each with remaining patty. Seal patties by pressing edges together.

3. Spray broiler pan with nonstick cooking spray. Place patties on pan. Broil 4 to 6 inches from heat for 3 minutes. Carefully turn burgers; broil an additional 3 to 5 minutes or until no longer pink in center.

4. To serve, place burgers on bottom halves of buns; spoon ¼ of tomato mixture over each burger. Cover with top halves of buns.

YIELD: 4 BURGERS

Tip: * For lowest fat content, ask butcher to grind beef top round. If desired, extra-lean ground beef can be substituted, but fat will increase to 10 grams of fat per serving.

Nutrition Information Per Serving
Serving Size: 1 Burger

Calories	290	Calories from Fat	70
		% Daily Value	
Total Fat	8g		12%
Saturated	4g		20%
Cholesterol	70mg		23%
Sodium	490mg		20%
Total Carbohydrate	25g		8%
Dietary Fiber	1g		4%
Sugars	7g		
Protein	29g		
Vitamin A	8%	Vitamin C	10%
Calcium	10%	Iron	20%

Dietary Exchanges: 1½ Starch, 1 Vegetable, 3 Lean Meat OR
1½ Carbohydrate, 1 Vegetable, 3 Lean Meat

tips for Great Burgers

- **Handle with care.** For juicy, good-textured burgers that don't emerge from the grill densely packed and "meat loafy," handle the ground beef mixture gently and as little as possible, and don't press burgers with a spatula while they're cooking.

- **Be prepared.** When ground beef is on sale, season a big batch and form it into patties. Wrap each patty individually in plastic wrap; store the wrapped patties in a labeled self-sealing heavy-duty freezer bag for easy defrosting and quick last-minute cooking.

- **Cleanliness is a virtue.** To avoid cross-contamination, remember to wash all surfaces that have come in contact with raw meat—including your hands—in hot soapy water.

- **Don't delay.** Wrap and freeze or cook ground beef, preferably the same day it's purchased or by the following day at latest.

- **Well done is done well.** Cook hamburgers until no trace of pink remains. Ground meat has so much exposed surface area that it is more prone to bacterial contamination than whole cuts of meat; thorough cooking ensures that any bacteria present will be destroyed.

Mini Cheesesteak Sandwiches

PREP TIME: 20 MINUTES

- **1 (20-inch) French bread baguette**
- **1 teaspoon olive oil**
- **2 garlic cloves, minced**
- **½ lb. beef sirloin sandwich steaks (¼ inch thick), cut into strips**
- **2 small onions, halved, sliced**
- **1 small green bell pepper, cut into strips**
- **1 teaspoon dried oregano leaves**
- **1 teaspoon dried basil leaves**
- **½ teaspoon salt**
- **1 (1½-oz.) slice mozzarella cheese, cut into 8 strips**

1. Cut V-shaped wedge from top of baguette the length of loaf. Set top wedge and loaf aside.

2. In large nonstick skillet, heat oil and garlic over medium-high heat until oil is hot. Add beef, onions and pepper strips; cook and stir about 4 minutes or until pepper strips are crisp-tender. Stir in oregano, basil and salt; cook and stir 1 minute.

3. Spoon beef mixture into loaf. Top with cheese strips. Place loaf on ungreased cookie sheet.

4. Broil 4 to 6 inches from heat for 1 to 2 minutes or until cheese is melted.* Place top wedge of bread on loaf; cut into 6 pieces. If desired, serve with hot pepperoncini salad peppers.

YIELD: 6 SANDWICHES

Tip: * Sandwich can be heated in 350°F. oven. Place top wedge of bread on loaf; place on ungreased cookie sheet. Bake about 5 minutes or until loaf is thoroughly heated and cheese is melted.

Nutrition Information Per Serving
Serving Size: 1 Sandwich

Calories	180	Calories from Fat	45
		% Daily Value	
Total Fat	5g		8%
Saturated	2g		10%
Cholesterol	25mg		8%
Sodium	450mg		19%
Total Carbohydrate	21g		7%
Dietary Fiber	2g		8%
Sugars	2g		
Protein	12g		
Vitamin A	2%	Vitamin C	10%
Calcium	10%	Iron	10%

Dietary Exchanges: 1½ Starch, 1 Lean Meat OR 1½ Carbohydrate, 1 Lean Meat

beyond the **Basic Bun**

Alternate breads that make good holders for hamburgers, hot dogs and other grilled meats include:

- **Pita (pocket) bread**
- **French, Portuguese or sourdough rolls**
- **Pumpernickel rolls**
- **French, Italian or sourdough bread slices**
- **French baguettes**
- **Sliced whole-grain or rye bread**
- **English muffins**
- **Bagels or bialys**
- **Focaccia**
- **Tortillas**

All-American Lean Burgers

■ ■

PREP TIME: 25 MINUTES

1 lb. extra-lean ground beef

¾ cup rolled oats

⅓ cup finely chopped onion

¼ teaspoon salt

⅛ teaspoon pepper

¼ cup skim milk

¼ cup barbecue sauce, if desired

Grill Directions: 1. Heat grill. In large bowl, combine all ingredients except barbecue sauce; mix well. Shape mixture into 6 patties, ¹/₂ inch thick.
2. When ready to grill, lightly oil grill rack. Place patties on gas grill over medium heat or on charcoal grill 4 to 6 inches from medium coals. Cook 10 to 12 minutes or until burgers are no longer pink in center, turning once and brushing each side occasionally with barbecue sauce.

Broiler Directions: 1. Prepare patties as directed above. Spray broiler pan with nonstick cooking spray. Place patties on sprayed pan.
2. Broil 4 to 6 inches from heat for 10 to 12 minutes or until burgers are no longer pink in center, turning once and brushing each side occasionally with barbecue sauce.

YIELD: 6 BURGERS

Nutrition Information Per Serving
Serving Size: 1 Burger

Calories	190	Calories from Fat	90

		% Daily Value
Total Fat	10g	15%
Saturated	4g	20%
Cholesterol	45mg	15%
Sodium	220mg	9%
Total Carbohydrate	9g	3%
Dietary Fiber	1g	4%
Sugars	1g	
Protein	16g	

Vitamin A	2%	Vitamin C	0%
Calcium	2%	Iron	10%

Dietary Exchanges: ¹/₂ Starch, 2 Medium-Fat Meat OR ¹/₂ Carbohydrate, 2 Medium-Fat Meat

Comparing Ground Meats

3-oz. Broiled	Calories	Fat (g)
85% lean/15% fat ground beef	205	12
80% lean/20% fat ground beef	230	15
73% lean/27% fat ground beef	250	18
93% fat-free ground turkey	170	8
100% ground turkey breast	110	1

Source: National Cattlemen's Beef Association, package labels

Pepper Steaks with Blackberry Glaze

■ ■ ■ ■ ■ ■ ■ ■ ■ ■ ■ ■ ■ ■ ■ ■

PREP TIME: 25 MINUTES

Glaze
½ cup blackberry jam

¼ cup red wine vinegar

Steaks
3 teaspoons coarse ground black pepper

4 (4-oz.) boneless beef strip steaks

½ cup fresh or frozen blackberries, thawed

Grill Directions: 1. Heat grill. In small saucepan, combine jam and vinegar. Cook over medium heat until jam is melted, stirring constantly. Remove from heat.

2. Rub pepper on both sides of each steak. When ready to grill, oil grill rack. Place steaks on gas grill over medium heat or on charcoal grill 4 to 6 inches from medium-high coals. Cook 8 to 12 minutes or until of desired doneness, turning once.

3. To serve, spread steaks with glaze; top with berries.

Broiler Directions: 1. Prepare glaze as directed above. Oil broiler pan. Rub pepper on both sides of each steak; place on oiled pan.

2. Broil 4 to 6 inches from heat for 7 to 10 minutes or until of desired doneness, turning once. Serve as directed above.

YIELD: 4 SERVINGS

Nutrition Information Per Serving
Serving Size: ¼ of Recipe

Calories 250	Calories from Fat 35
	% Daily Value
Total Fat 4g	...........6%
Saturated 1g	...........5%
Cholesterol 60mg	.........20%
Sodium 45mg	...........2%
Total Carbohydrate 30g	.........10%
Dietary Fiber 2g	...........8%
Sugars...........................21g	
Protein.............................24g	
Vitamin A 0%	Vitamin C 8%
Calcium 2%	Iron 15%

Dietary Exchanges: 2 Fruit, 3½ Very Lean Meat OR 2 Carbohydrate, 3½ Very Lean Meat

Milanese Beef Grill

■ ■ ■ ■ ■ ■ ■ ■ ■ ■ ■ ■ ■ ■ ■ ■

PREP TIME: 20 MINUTES

1 lb. boneless beef top round steak (¾ inch thick)

¼ teaspoon salt

⅛ to ¼ teaspoon pepper

⅓ cup finely chopped fresh parsley

2 tablespoons grated lemon peel

3 large garlic cloves, minced

¼ cup dry white wine or chicken broth

1 tablespoon Dijon mustard

Grill Directions: 1. Heat grill. Lightly sprinkle both sides of steak with salt and pepper. When ready to grill, place steak on gas grill over medium heat or on charcoal grill 4 to 6 inches from medium coals. Cook 8 to 11 minutes or until of desired doneness, turning once.

2. Meanwhile, on rimmed platter or in shallow baking dish, combine remaining ingredients; mix well.

3. Place hot grilled steak in sauce mixture. Cut steak diagonally across grain into slices. Coat each slice with sauce mixture before placing on individual plates. Spoon any remaining sauce over steak slices.

Broiler Directions: 1. Lightly sprinkle both sides of steak with salt and pepper; place on broiler pan.

2. Broil 4 to 6 inches from heat for 8 to 11 minutes or until of desired doneness, turning once. Continue as directed above.

YIELD: 4 SERVINGS

Nutrition Information Per Serving
Serving Size: ¼ of Recipe

Calories 150	Calories from Fat 35
	% Daily Value
Total Fat 4g	...........6%
Saturated 1g	...........5%
Cholesterol 60mg	.........20%
Sodium 260mg	.........11%
Total Carbohydrate 2g	...........1%
Dietary Fiber 0g	...........0%
Sugars 0g	
Protein.............................24g	
Vitamin A 6%	Vitamin C 8%
Calcium 2%	Iron 15%

Dietary Exchanges: 3 Lean Meat

Milanese Beef Grill ▶

Veal Marsala

Prep Time: 15 minutes

2 veal cutlets

⅛ teaspoon salt

⅛ teaspoon pepper

¼ cup skim milk

1 teaspoon all-purpose flour

1 tablespoon Marsala wine

1 tablespoon chopped fresh parsley

Dash salt

1. Spray small nonstick skillet with nonstick cooking spray. Heat over medium-high heat until hot. Sprinkle veal cutlets with ⅛ teaspoon salt and pepper. Cook cutlets 1 to 2 minutes on each side or until browned. Remove veal from skillet; cover to keep warm.

2. In same skillet, combine milk and flour; blend well. Cook over medium heat until thickened, stirring constantly. Stir in wine, parsley and dash of salt; cook until thoroughly heated. Serve sauce over veal.

Yield: 2 servings

Nutrition Information Per Serving
Serving Size: ½ of Recipe

Calories 120	Calories from Fat 35	
	% Daily Value	
Total Fat 4g	....6%	
Saturated 2g	....10%	
Cholesterol 60mg	....20%	
Sodium 270mg	....11%	
Total Carbohydrate 3g	....1%	
Dietary Fiber 0g	....0%	
Sugars 1g		
Protein 16g		
Vitamin A 4%	Vitamin C 4%	
Calcium 6%	Iron................................4%	

Dietary Exchanges: 2 Lean Meat

▼ Veal Marsala

Veal Chops with Creamy Mushroom Sauce

■ ■

PREP TIME: 20 MINUTES

2 (4- to 5-oz.) veal rib chops (¾ to 1 inch thick)

1 small onion, thinly sliced, separated into rings

1 garlic clove, minced

¼ cup dry white wine or chicken broth

¼ teaspoon dried rosemary leaves, crushed

¼ teaspoon salt

⅛ teaspoon pepper

¾ cup sliced fresh mushrooms

¼ cup nonfat sour cream

1 tablespoon dry white wine or water

1. Spray medium nonstick skillet with nonstick cooking spray. Add veal chops, onion and garlic; cook over medium heat about 2 minutes on each side or until veal is lightly browned.

2. Stir in ¼ cup wine, rosemary, salt and pepper. Reduce heat; cover and simmer 8 to 10 minutes or until veal is tender and of desired doneness. Place veal and onions on serving platter; cover to keep warm.

3. Add mushrooms to same skillet; cook over low heat until hot. Stir in sour cream and 1 tablespoon wine. Cook until thoroughly heated. Pour sauce over veal and onions.

YIELD: 2 SERVINGS

Nutrition Information Per Serving
Serving Size: ½ of Recipe

Calories	170	Calories from Fat	45
		% Daily Value	
Total Fat 5g			........8%
Saturated 1g			........5%
Cholesterol 80mg			......27%
Sodium 370mg			......15%
Total Carbohydrate 10g			........3%
Dietary Fiber 1g			........2%
Sugars 4g			
Protein 20g			
Vitamin A 4%		Vitamin C 4%	
Calcium 6%		Iron 8%	

Dietary Exchanges: 2 Vegetable, 2 Lean Meat

Roast Pork with Garlic Pepper Crust

■ ■

PREP TIME: 15 MINUTES (READY IN 1 HOUR)

4 to 6 garlic cloves, minced

1 tablespoon chopped fresh parsley or 1 teaspoon dried parsley flakes

1 teaspoon coarse ground black pepper

½ teaspoon dried thyme leaves

1 tablespoon lime or lemon juice

1 teaspoon olive oil

2 (½-lb.) pork tenderloins

1. Heat oven to 450°F. Line shallow roasting pan with foil; spray foil with nonstick cooking spray. In small bowl, combine garlic, parsley, pepper and thyme. In small cup, combine lime juice and oil.

2. Brush pork tenderloins with lime juice mixture, coating well. Rub garlic-pepper mixture over top and sides of tenderloins, pressing lightly. Place in sprayed foil-lined pan, garlic-pepper side up.

3. Bake at 450°F. for 25 to 35 minutes or until pork is no longer pink in center. Let stand 5 to 10 minutes before serving.

4. To serve, cut diagonally into ½-inch slices.

YIELD: 4 SERVINGS

Nutrition Information Per Serving
Serving Size: ¼ of Recipe

Calories	150	Calories from Fat	45
		% Daily Value	
Total Fat 5g			........8%
Saturated 2g			......10%
Cholesterol 65mg			......22%
Sodium 50mg			........2%
Total Carbohydrate 2g			........1%
Dietary Fiber 0g			........0%
Sugars 0g			
Protein 24g			
Vitamin A 0%		Vitamin C 4%	
Calcium 2%		Iron 10%	

Dietary Exchanges: 3 Lean Meat

Mustard *mania*

Dijon mustard, which originated in 1713 in Dijon, France, is a favorite mustard condiment, but there are now literally hundreds of mustard varieties available (hot, sweet, spicy, grainy and flavored), all produced from three types of mustard seeds: yellow, dark brown and the less common black. The darker the seed, the hotter the mustard.

Mustard's most appealing trait is its ability to add zest to a dish while contributing few calories and little fat (1 tablespoon of yellow mustard has about 12 calories and 0.6 grams of fat). Here's a look at the most common types:

English/Chinese Similar in potency, these two types are the most powerful mustards on the market. Use with caution; a little goes a long way.

Dijon Smooth and complex, this rich-tasting mustard, made with wine, is a standard in French and now American cupboards.

Coarse-Grained This mustard's mild and musty taste comes from the coarsely ground mustard seed it contains. This is how all mustards looked before smooth mustard was introduced in 1720.

German The Bavarian version's brown mustard seeds give a sweet flavor and dark color. The Düsseldorf variety is spicier.

Flavored Everything from honey to herbs has been added to mustard. A wide variety of flavored mustards are available in stores and from mail-order suppliers.

Ballpark The bright yellow color of this familiar, all-American mustard comes from the spice turmeric.

Dijon-Cranberry Pork Sandwiches

PREP TIME: 15 MINUTES

⅓ **cup unseasoned bread crumbs**

2 tablespoons pecans or walnuts, ground or finely chopped

4 (4-oz.) boneless pork loin chops, butterflied*

3 tablespoons Dijon mustard

8 slices pumpernickel bread, toasted

⅓ **cup purchased cranberry relish**

1. In small shallow bowl, combine bread crumbs and pecans; mix well. Spread both sides of pork chops with half of the mustard; coat with crumb mixture.

2. Spray large nonstick skillet with nonstick cooking spray. Heat over medium heat until hot. Add pork chops; cook 4 to 6 minutes or until no longer pink in center, turning once.

3. Spread remaining half of mustard on 4 slices of toast. Top with pork chops, cranberry relish and remaining toast slices.

YIELD: 4 SANDWICHES

Tip: * To butterfly pork chops, starting at long side of chop, cut chop in half horizontally, cutting almost but not completely through. Open chop and flatten to resemble butterfly shape.

Nutrition Information Per Serving
Serving Size: 1 Sandwich

Calories	380	Calories from Fat	100
		% Daily Value	
Total Fat	11g		17%
Saturated	4g		20%
Cholesterol	45mg		15%
Sodium	670mg		28%
Total Carbohydrate	48g		16%
Dietary Fiber	5g		20%
Sugars	13g		
Protein	23g		
Vitamin A	0%	Vitamin C	6%
Calcium	8%	Iron	15%

Dietary Exchanges: 2 Starch, 1 Fruit, 2 Lean Meat, 1 Fat OR
3 Carbohydrate, 2 Lean Meat, 1 Fat

Easy Pork Chow Mein

■ ■

PREP TIME: 20 MINUTES

4 cups hot cooked instant rice (cooked as directed on package, omitting margarine and salt)

½ cup purchased stir-fry sauce with ginger and garlic*

⅓ cup water

2 teaspoons cornstarch

1 (16-oz.) pkg. (6 cups) fresh cut stir-fry vegetables**

½ lb. pork tenderloin, cut into ½-inch cubes

2 tablespoons chow mein noodles, if desired

1. While rice is cooking, in small bowl, combine stir-fry sauce, water and cornstarch; blend well. Set aside.

2. In large saucepan, bring 6 cups water to a boil. Add vegetables; cook 1 minute or until green vegetables brighten. Drain.

3. Spray large nonstick wok or skillet with nonstick cooking spray. Heat over medium-high heat until hot. Add pork; cook and stir about 2 minutes or until pork is browned.

4. Stir in vegetables and cornstarch mixture. Reduce heat to medium-low; cover and cook 3 minutes or until vegetables are crisp-tender and sauce has thickened, stirring frequently. Serve over rice; top with chow mein noodles.

YIELD: 4 SERVINGS

Tips: * Stir-fry sauce can be found in the Asian foods section of large supermarkets or in Asian markets. If unavailable, use any other purchased oriental-style sauce.

** Fresh cut stir-fry vegetables (which may include broccoli, celery, cauliflower, snow pea pods, red bell pepper and/or carrots) can be found in the refrigerated fresh produce section of large supermarkets. If unavailable, use thawed frozen mixed vegetables; no need to cook 1 minute in boiling water.

Nutrition Information Per Serving
Serving Size: ¼ of Recipe

Calories.................................330	Calories from Fat 25	
	% Daily Value	
Total Fat 3g	....................................5%	
Saturated 1g	....................................5%	
Cholesterol 35mg	...................................12%	
Sodium 1,140mg	...................................48%	
Total Carbohydrate 58g	...................................19%	
Dietary Fiber.....................4g	...................................16%	
Sugars 2g		
Protein 18g		
Vitamin A......................130%	Vitamin C 35%	
Calcium 8%	Iron 20%	

Dietary Exchanges: 3 Starch, 2 Vegetable, 1 Lean Meat OR
3 Carbohydrate, 2 Vegetable, 1 Lean Meat

▼ Easy Pork Chow Mein

Southwest Pork and Black Bean Stir-Fry

▪▪▪▪▪▪▪▪▪▪▪▪▪▪▪▪▪▪▪

PREP TIME: 30 MINUTES

1 tablespoon olive or vegetable oil

¾ lb. pork tenderloin, cut into 2 × ½ × ¼-inch strips

1 medium onion, cut into thin wedges

1 small red bell pepper, cut into strips

2 garlic cloves, minced

2 cups frozen whole kernel corn, thawed*

1 (15-oz.) can black beans, drained, rinsed

1 small zucchini, chopped

½ cup chunky-style salsa

1. Heat oil in large nonstick skillet over medium-high heat until hot. Add pork, onion, bell pepper and garlic; cook and stir 6 to 8 minutes or until pork is no longer pink and vegetables are crisp-tender.

2. Stir in corn, beans, zucchini and salsa; cover and simmer 5 minutes or until zucchini is crisp-tender and flavors are blended. If desired, season with salt and pepper to taste.

YIELD: 4 (1½-CUP) SERVINGS

Tip: * To quickly thaw corn, place in colander or strainer; rinse with warm water until thawed. Drain well.

Nutrition Information Per Serving
Serving Size: 1½ Cups

Calories................................310	Calories from Fat 60
	% Daily Value
Total Fat ....7g 11%	
Saturated ....2g 10%	
Cholesterol ....50mg 17%	
Sodium ....480mg 20%	
Total Carbohydrate ....34g 11%	
Dietary Fiber ....8g 32%	
Sugars 7g	
Protein 27g	
Vitamin A.............................15%	Vitamin C 35%
Calcium................................6%	Iron 15%

Dietary Exchanges: 2 Starch, 1 Vegetable, 2½ Lean Meat OR
2 Carbohydrate, 1 Vegetable, 2½ Lean Meat

▼ Southwest Pork and Black Bean Stir-Fry

Orange Pork Sauté

....

PREP TIME: 20 MINUTES

2 cups hot cooked instant rice (cooked as directed on package, omitting margarine and salt)

¼ teaspoon grated orange peel

1 cup orange juice

1 tablespoon cornstarch

1 tablespoon brown sugar

¼ teaspoon salt

¼ teaspoon ginger

2 teaspoons olive oil

½ lb. pork tenderloin, cut into ½-inch cubes

½ cup drained mandarin orange segments

½ cup drained pineapple chunks

1. While rice is cooking, in small bowl, combine orange peel, orange juice, cornstarch, brown sugar, salt and ginger; mix well. Set aside.

2. Heat oil in medium nonstick skillet over medium-high heat until hot. Add pork; cook and stir 5 to 8 minutes or until pork is no longer pink.

3. Add orange segments, pineapple chunks and orange juice mixture; cook and stir gently until sauce is bubbly and thickened. Serve over rice.

YIELD: 2 SERVINGS

Nutrition Information Per Serving
Serving Size: ½ of Recipe

Calories	470	Calories from Fat	80
		% Daily Value	
Total Fat	9g		14%
Saturated	2g		10%
Cholesterol	65mg		22%
Sodium	320mg		13%
Total Carbohydrate	70g		23%
Dietary Fiber	3g		12%
Sugars	30g		
Protein	28g		
Vitamin A	10%	Vitamin C	80%
Calcium	6%	Iron	15%

Dietary Exchanges: 2½ Starch, 2 Fruit, 3 Lean Meat OR 4½ Carbohydrate, 3 Lean Meat

Sweet-and-Hot Peppered Pork on Rice

....

PREP TIME: 15 MINUTES

3 cups hot cooked instant rice (cooked as directed on package, omitting margarine and salt)

¼ cup firmly packed brown sugar

½ teaspoon crushed red pepper flakes

2 tablespoons soy sauce

2 teaspoons oil

1 lb. pork tenderloin, cut into thin strips

¼ teaspoon salt

⅛ teaspoon pepper

1 large onion, cut into thin wedges

1. While rice is cooking, in small bowl, combine brown sugar, crushed red pepper flakes and soy sauce; mix well. Set aside.

2. In large nonstick skillet, heat oil over high heat until hot. Sprinkle pork strips with salt and pepper. Add pork to skillet; cook and stir 3 to 4 minutes or until pork begins to brown.

3. Reduce heat to medium-high. Add onion; cook and stir 2 to 3 minutes or until tender. Stir in soy sauce mixture; cook an additional 2 minutes. Serve over rice.

YIELD: 4 SERVINGS

Nutrition Information Per Serving
Serving Size: ¼ of Recipe

Calories	350	Calories from Fat	50
		% Daily Value	
Total Fat	6g		9%
Saturated	2g		10%
Cholesterol	65mg		22%
Sodium	700mg		29%
Total Carbohydrate	48g		16%
Dietary Fiber	1g		4%
Sugars	16g		
Protein	27g		
Vitamin A	0%	Vitamin C	4%
Calcium	4%	Iron	20%

Dietary Exchanges: 3 Starch, 2 Lean Meat OR 3 Carbohydrate, 2 Lean Meat

▲ Oriental Pork Tortillas

Oriental Pork Tortillas

- -

PREP TIME: 15 MINUTES

⅓ **cup plum jam**

1 tablespoon cornstarch

½ **teaspoon ginger**

½ **teaspoon dry mustard**

¼ **teaspoon garlic powder**

2 tablespoons soy sauce

2 teaspoons red wine vinegar

4 (10-inch) flour tortillas

1 teaspoon oil

¾ **lb. boneless butterflied pork loin chops, cut into thin strips**

6 cups purchased coleslaw blend (from 16-oz. pkg.)

1. In small bowl, combine jam, cornstarch, ginger, dry mustard, garlic powder, soy sauce and vinegar;

mix well. Set aside. Heat tortillas as directed on package.

2. Meanwhile, heat oil in 12-inch nonstick skillet over medium-high heat until hot. Add pork; cook and stir 4 to 5 minutes or until no longer pink.

3. Add jam mixture and coleslaw blend; cook and stir until sauce is bubbly and thickened. Spoon mixture evenly down center of each warm tortilla; roll up.

YIELD: 4 SERVINGS

Nutrition Information Per Serving
Serving Size: ¼ of Recipe

Calories	420	Calories from Fat	100
		% Daily Value	
Total Fat	11g		17%
Saturated	3g		15%
Cholesterol	45mg		15%
Sodium	850mg		35%
Total Carbohydrate	57g		19%
Dietary Fiber	2g		8%
Sugars	19g		
Protein	24g		
Vitamin A	60%	Vitamin C	40%
Calcium	15%	Iron	20%

Dietary Exchanges: 3½ Starch, 1 Vegetable, 2 Lean Meat OR
3½ Carbohydrate, 1 Vegetable, 2 Lean Meat

Pork and Fettuccine with Light Tarragon Sauce

- - - - - - - - - - - - - - - - - -

PREP TIME: 25 MINUTES

8 oz. uncooked fettuccine

½ lb. pork tenderloin, cut into thin strips

1 cup thinly sliced carrots

1 (8-oz.) pkg. fresh whole mushrooms, quartered

1 cup evaporated skimmed milk

1 tablespoon all-purpose flour

½ teaspoon salt

⅛ teaspoon pepper

¼ cup tarragon vinegar

1. In Dutch oven or large saucepan, cook fettuccine to desired doneness as directed on package.

2. Meanwhile, spray large nonstick skillet with nonstick cooking spray. Heat over medium-high heat until hot. Add pork; cook and stir 3 to 5 minutes or until browned. Stir in carrots. Reduce heat to medium; cover and cook 1 minute. Stir in mushrooms. Cover; cook an additional 2 minutes.

3. In small bowl, combine milk, flour, salt and pepper; blend well. Add to pork mixture; cook and stir until thickened. Stir in vinegar.

4. Drain fettuccine; return to Dutch oven. Place over medium-low heat. Add pork mixture to fettuccine; toss to coat. If desired, garnish with fresh tarragon.

YIELD: 4 (1½-CUP) SERVINGS

Nutrition Information Per Serving
Serving Size: 1½ Cups

		% Daily Value
Calories	370	Calories from Fat 45
Total Fat	5g	8%
Saturated	1g	5%
Cholesterol	90mg	30%
Sodium	390mg	16%
Total Carbohydrate	56g	19%
Dietary Fiber	3g	12%
Sugars	12g	
Protein	26g	
Vitamin A	180%	Vitamin C 6%
Calcium	20%	Iron 25%

Dietary Exchanges: 3½ Starch, 1 Vegetable, 1½ Lean Meat OR 3½ Carbohydrate, 1 Vegetable, 1½ Lean Meat

Pork Chops in Country Onion Gravy

- - - - - - - - - - - - - - - - - -

PREP TIME: 30 MINUTES

4 (4-oz.) boneless pork loin chops

2 cups chopped onions

1 cup beef broth

⅛ teaspoon pepper

⅓ cup skim milk

2 tablespoons all-purpose flour

1. Generously spray 12-inch nonstick skillet with nonstick cooking spray. Heat over high heat until hot. Add pork chops; reduce heat to medium-high. Cook 3 minutes. Turn pork; cook an additional 2 to 3 minutes or until browned. Remove pork from skillet; cover to keep warm.

2. Reduce heat to medium. Add onions to same skillet; cook 3 minutes. Add broth and pepper; mix well. Add pork; spoon onion mixture over pork. Cover tightly; simmer 12 minutes or until pork is no longer pink in center.

3. In small bowl, combine milk and flour; blend well. Add to skillet; cook and stir 2 to 3 minutes or until thickened.

YIELD: 4 SERVINGS

Nutrition Information Per Serving
Serving Size: ¼ of Recipe

		% Daily Value
Calories	170	Calories from Fat 50
Total Fat	6g	9%
Saturated	2g	10%
Cholesterol	45mg	15%
Sodium	250mg	10%
Total Carbohydrate	11g	4%
Dietary Fiber	2g	8%
Sugars	5g	
Protein	19g	
Vitamin A	0%	Vitamin C 6%
Calcium	6%	Iron 6%

Dietary Exchanges: ½ Starch, 1 Vegetable, 2 Lean Meat OR ½ Carbohydrate, 1 Vegetable, 2 Lean Meat

Border Pork Roll-Ups

PREP TIME: 25 MINUTES
(READY IN 40 MINUTES)

Salsa
½ cup diced fresh pineapple*

¾ cup chunky-style salsa

Roll-Ups
1 lb. pork tenderloin

1 tablespoon brown sugar

2 teaspoons chili powder

2 tablespoons cider vinegar

1 medium onion, halved lengthwise, sliced

½ medium green bell pepper, cut into thin strips

4 (8- to 10-inch) fat-free flour tortillas, warmed

1. In small bowl, combine pineapple and salsa; mix well. Set aside.

2. Cut pork tenderloin in half lengthwise; cut into ¼-inch-thick slices. In medium bowl, combine brown sugar, chili powder and vinegar; mix well. Add pork; toss to coat. Let stand at room temperature for 15 minutes to marinate.

3. Spray large nonstick skillet with nonstick cooking spray. Heat over medium-high heat until hot. Add pork mixture to skillet; cook and stir 3 minutes. Add onion and bell pepper; cook and stir 2 to 4 minutes or until pork is no longer pink and vegetables are crisp-tender.

4. To serve, spoon ¼ of pork mixture onto each tortilla; roll up. Top with salsa.

YIELD: 4 SERVINGS

Tip: * One 8-oz. can crushed pineapple, drained, can be substituted for fresh pineapple.

Nutrition Information Per Serving
Serving Size: ¼ of Recipe

Calories	290	Calories from Fat	35
		% Daily Value	
Total Fat	4g		6%
Saturated	1g		5%
Cholesterol	65mg		22%
Sodium	610mg		25%
Total Carbohydrate	37g		12%
Dietary Fiber	2g		8%
Sugars	9g		
Protein	27g		
Vitamin A	15%	Vitamin C	25%
Calcium	0%	Iron	15%

Dietary Exchanges: 2 Starch, ½ Fruit, 2 Lean Meat OR 2½ Carbohydrate, 2 Lean Meat

■ **PRODUCE POINTERS**

cutting a Pineapple

With its spiky top and thorny-looking skin, this tropical fruit could well be called a "porcupineapple," but dealing with it is easy if you have a large, sharp knife:

1. Cut off and discard the spiky green top.

2. Cut the pineapple in half, top to bottom.

3. Cut each half into lengthwise wedges (as with a cantaloupe).

4. Lay each wedge on its side and trim away the tough central core.

5. Run the knife between the skin and the flesh to remove the skin.

6. Use the point of a potato peeler or a small paring knife to remove any "eyes" that still remain in the flesh.

7. Cut or chop the flesh as desired for the recipe.

Harvest Skillet Supper

. **.** **.** **.** **.** **.** **.** **.** **.** **.** **.** **.** **.** **.** **.** **.** **.** **.** **.**

PREP TIME: 25 MINUTES

2 teaspoons oil

¾ lb. pork tenderloin, cut into ¼-inch slices

¾ cup apple juice

2 tablespoons Dijon mustard

2 teaspoons cornstarch

2 teaspoons brown sugar

Dash salt

Dash pepper

1 sweet potato, peeled, cut into ¼-inch slices (2 cups)*

1 apple, cut into 16 wedges

½ cup coarsely chopped green bell pepper

1. Heat oil in large nonstick skillet over medium-high heat until hot. Add pork; cook until no longer pink and browned on each side. Remove pork from skillet; cover to keep warm. Drain drippings from skillet.

2. In small bowl, combine apple juice, mustard, cornstarch, brown sugar, salt and pepper; blend well. Add cornstarch mixture and sweet potato to skillet. Cover; cook over medium heat for 10 to 15 minutes or until sweet potato is crisp-tender, stirring occasionally.

3. Stir in apple, bell pepper and pork. Cover; cook an additional 5 minutes or until bell pepper is crisp-tender, stirring occasionally. If desired, serve with hot cooked rice sprinkled with chopped fresh parsley.

YIELD: 4 SERVINGS

Tip: * If desired, 2 cups sliced carrots can be substituted for the sweet potato.

Nutrition Information Per Serving
Serving Size: ¼ of Recipe

Calories 250		Calories from Fat 80	
		% Daily Value	
Total Fat 9g		.................14%	
Saturated 2g		.................10%	
Cholesterol 45mg		.................15%	
Sodium 260mg		.................11%	
Total Carbohydrate 24g		...................8%	
Dietary Fiber 2g		...................8%	
Sugars.............................14g			
Protein 18g			
Vitamin A 140%		Vitamin C 25%	
Calcium 4%		Iron.................................8%	

Dietary Exchanges: 1 Starch, ½ Fruit, 2 Lean Meat, ½ Fat OR
1½ Carbohydrate, 2 Lean Meat, ½ Fat

▼ Harvest Skillet Supper

Spicy Cumin Pork with Chili-Buttered Corn

PREP TIME: 30 MINUTES

4 medium ears fresh corn, halved*

1 tablespoon margarine or butter, softened

2 teaspoons chili powder

¼ teaspoon ground red pepper (cayenne)

¼ teaspoon salt

2 teaspoons fresh lime juice

1 teaspoon cumin

½ teaspoon dried thyme leaves

4 (4-oz.) boneless pork loin chops, butterflied**

Fresh lime wedges

1. In Dutch oven or large saucepan, bring 2 quarts (8 cups) water to a boil. Add corn; return to a boil. Cook over medium heat for 8 to 11 minutes or until tender.

2. Meanwhile, in small bowl, combine margarine, chili powder, ⅛ teaspoon of the ground red pepper, ⅛ teaspoon of the salt and lime juice; blend well. Set aside.

3. In another small bowl, combine cumin, thyme, remaining ⅛ teaspoon ground red pepper and remaining ⅛ teaspoon salt; mix thoroughly. Rub mixture evenly on both sides of pork chops.

4. Generously spray 12-inch nonstick skillet with nonstick cooking spray. Heat over high heat for 1 minute. Add pork; cook 2 minutes. Turn pork; reduce heat to medium-high. Cook an additional 2 to 3 minutes or until pork is no longer pink in center.

5. To serve, place pork in center of serving platter. Arrange ears of corn around pork. Spoon margarine mixture onto corn. Garnish platter with lime wedges.

YIELD: 4 SERVINGS

Tips: * One package (4 ears) frozen ears corn on the cob can be substituted for fresh corn. Cook as directed on package.

** To butterfly pork chops, starting at long side of chop, cut chop in half horizontally, cutting almost but not completely through. Open chop and flatten to resemble butterfly shape.

Nutrition Information Per Serving
Serving Size: ¼ of Recipe

Calories	260	Calories from Fat	90
		% Daily Value	
Total Fat	10g	15%	
Saturated	3g	15%	
Cholesterol	45mg	15%	
Sodium	230mg	10%	
Total Carbohydrate	24g	8%	
Dietary Fiber	3g	12%	
Sugars	2g		
Protein	19g		
Vitamin A	15%	Vitamin C	10%
Calcium	2%	Iron	10%

Dietary Exchanges: 1 ½ Starch, 2 Lean Meat, 1 Fat OR 1 ½ Carbohydrate, 2 Lean Meat, 1 Fat

How to Butterfly meats

Butterflying meats is both practical and attractive. The technique works best with a very sharp knife and with meat that is slightly frozen. Boneless chops, pork tenderloin, boneless chicken, shrimp and sea scallops all work well with this method.

Place the meat on a work surface or cutting board and cut the meat parallel to the surface, cutting almost but not quite all the way through. Separate the halves and flatten the meat into two connected sections that resemble a butterfly.

Since the meat is now half as thick, it cooks very quickly. Another benefit of the technique is that less meat seems like more. Because it covers double the surface area, butterflied meat gives the appearance of a more generous serving.

▲ Octoberfest Pork with Mushrooms

Octoberfest Pork with Mushrooms

■ ■ ■ ■ ■ ■ ■ ■ ■ ■ ■ ■ ■ ■ ■ ■ ■

PREP TIME: 30 MINUTES

4 (4-oz.) boneless pork loin chops

¼ teaspoon salt

¼ teaspoon pepper

⅓ cup chopped onion

4 tablespoons water

2 cups sliced fresh mushrooms

¼ teaspoon dried thyme leaves

⅓ cup beer

2 teaspoons all-purpose flour

1. Spray large nonstick skillet with nonstick cooking spray. Heat over high heat until hot. Sprinkle both sides of pork chops lightly with salt and pepper; add to skillet. Cook 2 minutes on each side or until browned.

Remove chops from skillet; cover to keep warm.

2. Add onion and 2 tablespoons of the water to same skillet; cook over medium heat for 2 minutes, stirring frequently. Add chops, mushrooms, thyme and beer. Reduce heat to medium-low; cover and cook 8 to 11 minutes or until chops are no longer pink in center.

3. In small bowl, combine remaining 2 tablespoons water and flour; blend well. Add to skillet; cook and stir until thickened. Serve mushroom mixture over chops.

YIELD: 4 SERVINGS

Nutrition Information Per Serving
Serving Size: ¼ of Recipe

Calories	150	Calories from Fat	50
			% Daily Value
Total Fat	6g		9%
Saturated	2g		10%
Cholesterol	50mg		17%
Sodium	170mg		7%
Total Carbohydrate	5g		2%
Dietary Fiber	1g		3%
Sugars	1g		
Protein	18g		
Vitamin A	0%	Vitamin C	2%
Calcium	0%	Iron	6%

Dietary Exchanges: 2 Lean Meat, 1 Vegetable

Barbecued Pork Tenderloin

■ ■ ■ ■ ■ ■ ■ ■ ■ ■ ■ ■ ■ ✕ ■ ■ ■ ■ ■ ■ ■

PREP TIME: 30 MINUTES

¼ cup ketchup

¼ cup chili sauce

1 tablespoon brown sugar

2 tablespoons finely chopped onion

⅛ teaspoon celery seed

Dash garlic powder

1½ teaspoons cider vinegar

1½ teaspoons Worcestershire sauce

1 teaspoon prepared mustard

⅛ teaspoon Liquid Smoke

2 (½-lb.) pork tenderloins

Grill Directions: 1. In small saucepan, combine all ingredients except pork; mix well. Bring to a boil. Reduce heat; simmer 5 minutes. Cool slightly.

2. Heat grill. Cut pork tenderloins in half lengthwise, cutting to but not through bottom; open and flatten.

3. When ready to grill, place flattened pork on gas grill over medium-high heat or on charcoal grill 4 to 6 inches from medium-high coals. Spoon half of sauce over pork. Cook 5 to 7 minutes. Turn pork; spoon remaining sauce over pork. Cook an additional 5 to 7 minutes or until pork is no longer pink in center.

Broiler Directions: 1. Prepare sauce and cut pork tenderloins as directed above. Line 15 × 10 × 1-inch baking pan with foil or spray broiler pan with nonstick cooking spray. Place pork on foil-lined pan; spoon half of sauce over pork.

2. Broil 4 to 6 inches from heat for 5 to 7 minutes. Turn pork; spoon remaining sauce over pork. Broil an additional 5 to 7 minutes or until pork is no longer pink in center.

YIELD: 4 SERVINGS

Nutrition Information Per Serving
Serving Size: ¼ of Recipe

Calories	180	Calories from Fat	35
		% Daily Value	
Total Fat	4g		6%
Saturated	1g		5%
Cholesterol	65mg		22%
Sodium	520mg		22%
Total Carbohydrate	13g		4%
Dietary Fiber	0g		0%
Sugars	9g		
Protein	24g		
Vitamin A	8%	Vitamin C	6%
Calcium	0%	Iron	10%

Dietary Exchanges: ½ Fruit, 3 Lean Meat OR ½ Starch, 3 Lean Meat

Canadian Bacon and Potato Frittata

■ ■ ■ ■ ■ ■ ■ ■ ■ ■ ■ ■ ■ ■ ■ ■ ■ ■ ■ ■

PREP TIME: 25 MINUTES

6 eggs or 1½ cups refrigerated or frozen fat-free egg product, thawed

2 tablespoons chopped fresh chives or 1 tablespoon freeze-dried chopped chives

2 tablespoons skim milk

¼ teaspoon salt

⅛ teaspoon dried thyme leaves

⅛ teaspoon pepper

¼ cup chopped red or green bell pepper

2 cups frozen southern-style hash-brown potatoes

½ cup coarsely chopped Canadian bacon or cooked ham

2 tablespoons shredded Cheddar cheese

1. In medium bowl, combine eggs, chives, milk, salt, thyme and pepper; beat well. Set aside.

2. Spray 10-inch nonstick skillet with nonstick cooking spray. Add bell pepper; cook and stir over medium heat for 1 minute. Add potatoes; cover and cook 8 to 10 minutes or until potatoes begin to brown, stirring frequently. Stir in Canadian bacon; cook and stir 1 to 2 minutes or until heated.

3. Add egg mixture to skillet; cover and cook over medium-low heat for 6 to 9 minutes or until set, lifting edges occasionally to allow uncooked egg mixture to flow to bottom of skillet.

4. Sprinkle with cheese. Cover; cook an additional 1 minute or until cheese is melted. To serve, cut into wedges.

YIELD: 4 SERVINGS

Nutrition Information Per Serving
Serving Size: 1/4 of Recipe

Calories	200	Calories from Fat	90
		% Daily Value	
Total Fat	10g		15%
Saturated	4g		20%
Cholesterol	330mg		110%
Sodium	520mg		22%
Total Carbohydrate	12g		4%
Dietary Fiber	1g		4%
Sugars	3g		
Protein	15g		
Vitamin A	20%	Vitamin C	25%
Calcium	8%	Iron	10%

Dietary Exchanges: 1/2 Starch, 2 Medium-Fat Meat OR 1/2 Carbohydrate, 2 Medium-Fat Meat

Mustard-Rosemary Pork and Apple Kabobs

■ ■ ■ ■ ■ ■ ■ ■ ■ ■ ■ ■ ■ ■ ■

PREP TIME: 35 MINUTES

Marinade
2 tablespoons brown sugar

2 tablespoons prepared mustard

2 tablespoons water

1 teaspoon dried rosemary leaves, crushed

Kabobs
6 oz. pork tenderloin, cut into 12 (1-inch) pieces

1 small red apple, cut into 12 pieces

1/2 medium onion, cut into 4 wedges, layers separated

Grill Directions: 1. In small bowl, combine all marinade ingredients; mix well. Add pork; toss gently to coat. Cover; let stand at room temperature for 10 minutes to marinate.

2. Heat grill. Drain pork, reserving marinade. Alternately thread apple, pork and onion onto each of two 14-inch or four 7- or 8-inch metal skewers.

today's meat:
A Leaner Profile

■ ■ ■ ■ ■ ■ ■ ■ ■ ■ ■ ■ ■ ■ ■ ■

Years ago, livestock was bred to produce animals heavily marbled with fat. As consciousness about the benefit of limiting dietary fat has grown, livestock producers have invested in research to improve genetics and feeding practices. The result: fresh beef products that average 27 percent leaner and pork products that average 31 percent leaner than those available in the early 1980s.

3. When ready to grill, place kabobs on gas grill over medium heat or on charcoal grill 4 to 6 inches from medium coals. Brush kabobs with reserved marinade; discard any remaining marinade. Cook 8 to 11 minutes or until pork is no longer pink and onion is crisp-tender, turning once.

Broiler Directions: 1. Prepare kabobs as directed above; place on broiler pan. Brush kabobs with reserved marinade; discard any remaining marinade. **2.** Broil 4 to 6 inches from heat for 8 to 11 minutes or until pork is no longer pink and onion is crisp-tender, turning once.

YIELD: 2 SERVINGS

Nutrition Information Per Serving
Serving Size: 1/2 of Recipe

Calories	160	Calories from Fat	35
		% Daily Value	
Total Fat	4g		6%
Saturated	1g		5%
Cholesterol	50mg		17%
Sodium	80mg		3%
Total Carbohydrate	14g		5%
Dietary Fiber	2g		8%
Sugars	12g		
Protein	18g		
Vitamin A	0%	Vitamin C	6%
Calcium	0%	Iron	6%

Dietary Exchanges: 1 Fruit, 2 Lean Meat OR 1 Carbohydrate, 2 Lean Meat

Grilled Lamb Chops with Rosemary and Black Pepper

PREP TIME: 30 MINUTES

8 (4-oz.) lamb loin chops

½ cup dry red wine

2 tablespoons Worcestershire sauce

1 teaspoon dried rosemary leaves

4 garlic cloves, minced

Freshly ground black pepper

¼ teaspoon salt

Grill Directions: 1. Heat grill. Generously pierce lamb chops with fork. Place in shallow dish; add wine. Let stand at room temperature for 15 minutes to marinate.

2. Meanwhile, in small bowl, combine Worcestershire sauce, rosemary and garlic; mix well. Set aside.

3. When ready to grill, remove lamb from marinade; discard marinade. Place lamb on gas grill over medium heat or on charcoal grill 4 to 6 inches from medium coals. Spoon half of sauce mixture evenly over chops; sprinkle generously with pepper. Cook 4 to 5 minutes or until browned.

4. Turn chops. Spoon remaining sauce over lamb; sprinkle with pepper. Cook an additional 4 to 5 minutes or to desired doneness. Sprinkle lamb with salt.

Broiler Directions: 1. Marinate lamb chops and prepare sauce as directed above.

2. Remove lamb from marinade; discard marinade. Place lamb on broiler pan. Spoon half of sauce mixture evenly over chops; sprinkle generously with pepper.

3. Broil 4 to 6 inches from heat for 4 to 5 minutes or until browned. Turn chops. Spoon remaining sauce over lamb; sprinkle with pepper. Cook an additional 4 to 5 minutes or to desired doneness. Sprinkle lamb with salt.

YIELD: 4 SERVINGS

Nutrition Information Per Serving
Serving Size: ¼ of Recipe

Calories	190	Calories from Fat	80
		% Daily Value	
Total Fat	9g		14%
Saturated	4g		20%
Cholesterol	85mg		28%
Sodium	220mg		9%
Total Carbohydrate	1g		1%
Dietary Fiber	0g		0%
Sugars	0g		
Protein	26g		
Vitamin A	0%	Vitamin C	0%
Calcium	0%	Iron	15%

Dietary Exchanges: 3½ Lean Meat

age makes a Difference

The word *lamb* refers to a sheep that is less than one year old; baby lamb is six to eight weeks old; spring lamb is three to five months old. Sheep ages twelve to twenty-four months old are called yearling, and sheep older than two years are referred to as mutton. While lamb, with its velvety, pale pink and mild-tasting flesh, is extremely tender, mutton has tougher, darker flesh and a much stronger flavor.

▲ Lamb and Asparagus Stir-Fry

Lamb and Asparagus Stir-Fry

PREP TIME: 20 MINUTES

13½ oz. (6 cups) uncooked medium egg noodles

½ cup vegetable broth

2 teaspoons cornstarch

¾ teaspoon dried rosemary leaves, crushed

¼ teaspoon salt

¼ teaspoon coarse ground black pepper

2 teaspoons olive oil

1 lb. boneless lean lamb sirloin or round steak, cut into thin strips

1 large onion, halved, thinly sliced

1 lb. fresh asparagus spears, cut diagonally into 1-inch pieces

1 small red bell pepper, cut into 2 × ¼ × ¼-inch strips

1. Cook noodles to desired doneness as directed on package.

2. Meanwhile, in small bowl or jar with tight-fitting lid, combine broth, cornstarch, rosemary, salt and pepper; blend or shake well. Set aside.

3. Heat oil in large nonstick skillet or wok over medium-high heat until hot. Add lamb; cook and stir 3 minutes. Add onion and asparagus; cook and stir an additional 3 minutes or until onion is tender and lamb is no longer pink. Add bell pepper; cook and stir 1 minute. Add broth mixture; cook and stir until thickened.

4. Drain noodles. Serve lamb mixture over noodles.

YIELD: 6 SERVINGS

Nutrition Information Per Serving
Serving Size: ⅙ of Recipe

Calories	330	Calories from Fat	50
		% Daily Value	
Total Fat	6g		9%
Saturated	2g		10%
Cholesterol	35mg		12%
Sodium	210mg		9%
Total Carbohydrate	48g		16%
Dietary Fiber	5g		20%
Sugars	6g		
Protein	20g		
Vitamin A	20%	Vitamin C	30%
Calcium	4%	Iron	20%

Dietary Exchanges: 3 Starch, 1 Vegetable, 1 Lean Meat OR
3 Carbohydrate, 1 Vegetable, 1 Lean Meat

Skewered Hot-Curry Lamb with Pineapple

■ ■

PREP TIME: 35 MINUTES

8 (7- to 10-inch) bamboo skewers

½ cup orange marmalade

1 (8-oz.) can pineapple chunks in unsweetened juice, drained, reserving ⅓ cup liquid

2 tablespoons soy sauce

1 teaspoon cornstarch

1 lb. ground lamb loin*

2 slices reduced-calorie bread, toasted, crumbled**

2 teaspoons curry powder

¼ to ½ teaspoon crushed red pepper flakes

1 medium green bell pepper, cut into 1-inch pieces

1. Soak bamboo skewers in water for 15 minutes. Meanwhile, in small bowl, combine orange marmalade and reserved ⅓ cup pineapple liquid; blend well. Set aside.

2. In medium bowl, combine soy sauce and cornstarch; blend well. Add lamb, bread crumbs, curry powder and crushed red pepper flakes; mix well. Shape mixture into 32 meatballs.

3. Spray broiler pan with nonstick cooking spray. Spray bamboo skewers with nonstick cooking spray. Alternately thread meatballs, bell pepper pieces and pineapple chunks onto skewers. Place kabobs on sprayed pan.

4. Broil 4 to 6 inches from heat for 3 to 4 minutes or until meatballs are browned. Turn kabobs; spoon some of marmalade mixture over meatballs. Broil an additional 3 to 4 minutes or until meatballs are no longer pink in center.

5. To serve, place kabobs on serving platter; spoon remaining marmalade mixture over meatballs, bell pepper and pineapple.

YIELD: 8 KABOBS; 4 SERVINGS

Tips: * Lamb loin has much less fat than regular ground lamb.
** If desired, coarsely chop bread in food processor or blender.

Nutrition Information Per Serving
Serving Size: ¼ of Recipe

Calories	270	Calories from Fat	45
		% Daily Value	
Total Fat	5g		8%
Saturated	2g		10%
Cholesterol	40mg		13%
Sodium	620mg		26%
Total Carbohydrate	42g		14%
Dietary Fiber	2g		8%
Sugars	28g		
Protein	15g		
Vitamin A	25%	Vitamin C	50%
Calcium	6%	Iron	15%

Dietary Exchanges: 2½ Fruit, 1 Vegetable, 1½ Lean Meat OR 2½ Carbohydrate, 1 Vegetable, 1½ Lean Meat

Fish and Seafood

Italian Barbecued Swordfish Steaks with Tomato Relish (page 217)

Halibut with Noodles in Ginger Soy Sauce

PREP TIME: 30 MINUTES

5 oz. (2½ cups) uncooked plain or spinach egg noodles

½ teaspoon coriander

⅛ teaspoon garlic powder

¼ teaspoon pepper

1 lb. halibut fillets

1 tablespoon chopped fresh cilantro

1 tablespoon chopped green onions

½ teaspoon sugar

½ teaspoon grated gingerroot

1 tablespoon rice vinegar

1 tablespoon soy sauce

1. In large saucepan, cook noodles to desired doneness as directed on package.

2. Meanwhile, in small bowl, combine coriander, garlic powder and pepper; sprinkle half of mixture on one side of halibut fillets.

3. Spray medium nonstick skillet with nonstick cooking spray. Heat over medium-high heat until hot. Place fish, seasoned side down, in hot skillet; cook 2 to 4 minutes. Sprinkle fish with remaining coriander mixture. Turn fish; cook an additional 2 to 4 minutes or until fish flakes easily with fork.

4. Drain noodles; return to saucepan. In small bowl, combine all remaining ingredients; mix well. Add to noodles; toss to coat. Serve noodles with fish.

YIELD: 4 SERVINGS

Nutrition Information Per Serving
Serving Size: ¼ of Recipe

Calories	270	Calories from Fat	35
		% Daily Value	
Total Fat	4g		6%
Saturated	1g		5%
Cholesterol	75mg		25%
Sodium	330mg		14%
Total Carbohydrate	27g		9%
Dietary Fiber	1g		4%
Sugars	2g		
Protein	31g		
Vitamin A	4%	Vitamin C	8%
Calcium	0%	Iron	15%

Dietary Exchanges: 2 Starch, 3 Very Lean Meat OR 2 Carbohydrate, 3 Very Lean Meat

▼ Halibut with Noodles in Ginger Soy Sauce

Lemony Salmon Fettuccine

- - - - - - - - - - - - - - - - -

PREP TIME: 25 MINUTES

1 (9-oz.) pkg. refrigerated spinach or plain fettuccine

1 teaspoon butter or margarine

2 garlic cloves, minced

2 cups skim milk

1 tablespoon all-purpose flour

¼ cup fat-free cream cheese (from 8-oz. tub)

2 tablespoons grated Parmesan cheese

1 (6⅛-oz.) can chunk-style water-packed boneless, skinless salmon, drained, flaked

½ teaspoon grated lemon peel

Chopped fresh parsley, if desired

1. Cook fettuccine to desired doneness as directed on package.

2. Meanwhile, spray large nonstick skillet with nonstick cooking spray. Add butter; melt over medium-high heat. Add garlic; cook until golden brown. Add milk and flour; mix with wire whisk until smooth. Cook and stir until mixture comes to a boil and thickens slightly.

3. Reduce heat to medium-low. Stir in cream cheese and Parmesan cheese; cook until mixture thickens and cream cheese melts. Stir in salmon and lemon peel.

4. Drain fettuccine. Add to cheese mixture; toss gently until well coated. Sprinkle with parsley.

YIELD: 3 (1½-CUP) SERVINGS

Nutrition Information Per Serving
Serving Size: 1½ Cups

Calories	410	Calories from Fat	50

		% Daily Value
Total Fat	6g	9%
Saturated	2g	10%
Cholesterol	35mg	12%
Sodium	720mg	30%
Total Carbohydrate	59g	20%
Dietary Fiber	3g	12%
Sugars	9g	
Protein	29g	

Vitamin A	20%	Vitamin C	6%
Calcium	35%	Iron	15%

Dietary Exchanges: 4 Starch, 2 Lean Meat OR 4 Carbohydrate, 2 Lean Meat

Peppery Halibut

- -

PREP TIME: 20 MINUTES

2 tablespoons all-purpose flour

½ teaspoon lemon-pepper seasoning

½ teaspoon dried parsley flakes

⅛ teaspoon garlic powder

1 (8-oz.) halibut steak (about ¾ inch thick), cut into 2 pieces

2 teaspoons olive oil

2 tablespoons lemon juice

⅛ teaspoon white pepper

⅛ teaspoon hot pepper sauce

1. In pie pan or shallow bowl, combine flour, lemon-pepper seasoning, parsley and garlic powder; mix well. Coat both sides of halibut with flour mixture, shaking off excess.

2. Heat oil in small nonstick skillet over medium-high heat until hot. Add fish; cook 1 to 2 minutes on each side or until browned. Reduce heat to medium; cook 5 to 7 minutes or until fish is firm and flakes easily with fork, turning once.

3. Meanwhile, in small bowl, combine lemon juice, pepper and hot pepper sauce; mix well. To serve, drizzle lemon juice mixture over fish.

YIELD: 2 SERVINGS

Nutrition Information Per Serving
Serving Size: ½ of Recipe

Calories	200	Calories from Fat	60

		% Daily Value
Total Fat	7g	11%
Saturated	1g	5%
Cholesterol	40mg	13%
Sodium	160mg	7%
Total Carbohydrate	7g	2%
Dietary Fiber	0g	0%
Sugars	1g	
Protein	27g	

Vitamin A	4%	Vitamin C	4%
Calcium	6%	Iron	8%

Dietary Exchanges: ½ Starch, 4 Very Lean Meat, ½ Fat OR ½ Carbohydrate, 4 Very Lean Meat, ½ Fat

Pan-Poached Salmon with Light Lemon Herb Sauce

■ ■ ■ ■ ■ ■ ■ ■ ■ ■ ■ ■ ■ ■ ■ ■

PREP TIME: 20 MINUTES

1 cup water

½ teaspoon vegetable-flavor instant bouillon

2 (8-oz.) salmon steaks (¾ to 1 inch thick), each cut into 2 pieces

1 tablespoon lemon juice

1 tablespoon chopped fresh parsley

1 tablespoon chopped fresh chives

1. In large nonstick skillet, combine water and bouillon. Bring to a boil. Arrange salmon steaks in skillet. Reduce heat; cover and simmer 6 minutes or until fish flakes easily with fork.

2. With slotted pancake turner, transfer fish to warm serving platter; cover loosely to keep warm.

3. Add lemon juice to liquid in skillet; cook over high heat for 2 to 5 minutes or until sauce is reduced to about ¼ cup, stirring frequently. Stir in parsley and chives. Spoon sauce over salmon.

YIELD: 4 SERVINGS

Nutrition Information Per Serving
Serving Size: ¼ of Recipe

Calories	190	Calories from Fat	90
		% Daily Value	
Total Fat	10g		15%
Saturated	2g		10%
Cholesterol	75mg		25%
Sodium	220mg		9%
Total Carbohydrate	0g		0%
Dietary Fiber	0g		0%
Sugars	0g		
Protein	24g		
Vitamin A	6%	Vitamin C	4%
Calcium	0%	Iron	4%

Dietary Exchanges: 3½ Lean Meat

poaching Fish

■ ■ ■ ■ ■ ■ ■ ■ ■ ■ ■ ■ ■ ■ ■ ■ ■ ■ ■ ■

Poaching is one of the easiest, no-fuss methods for cooking fish, and it requires no added fat. The poaching liquid used for Pan-Poached Salmon (above) works equally well for other types of fish. Thin fillets, such as sole or flounder, are great for poaching because they're done in a matter of minutes.

You can vary the poaching liquid if you like. Use white wine or orange juice in place of vegetable bouillon, or spike the bouillon or other liquid with some liqueur or soy sauce. Sprinkle in your favorite fresh herbs. For a traditional French *court bouillon,* cooks make a flavorful poaching broth by simmering aromatic ingredients such as chopped onion and julienned celery and carrots in water to infuse it with flavor before adding the fish.

Salmon Cakes with Dill Sauce

■ ■ ■ ■ ■ ■ ■ ■ ■ ■ ■ ■ ■ ■ ■ ■

PREP TIME: 25 MINUTES

Sauce
½ cup fat-free mayonnaise or salad dressing

1 teaspoon dried dill weed or 1 tablespoon chopped fresh dill

Salmon Cakes
1 (15- or 16-oz.) can red salmon, undrained

½ cup refrigerated or frozen fat-free egg product, thawed, or 2 eggs

¾ cup quick-cooking rolled oats

½ cup finely chopped celery

¼ teaspoon salt

¼ teaspoon pepper

¼ teaspoon hot pepper sauce, if desired

1. In small bowl, combine mayonnaise and dill; mix well. Set aside.

2. Place salmon and liquid from can in medium bowl; remove and discard any dark skin and large bones. Add all remaining salmon cake ingredients; mix thoroughly. Shape mixture into 6 patties, $^1/_2$ inch thick.

3. Spray large nonstick skillet with nonstick cooking spray. Place 3 patties in skillet; cook over medium heat for 5 to 6 minutes on each side or until thoroughly cooked and set. Repeat with remaining patties. Serve sauce with salmon cakes.

YIELD: 6 SERVINGS

Nutrition Information Per Serving
Serving Size: $^1/_6$ of Recipe

Calories	140	Calories from Fat	35

		% Daily Value
Total Fat	4g	6%
Saturated	0g	0%
Cholesterol	30mg	10%
Sodium	630mg	26%
Total Carbohydrate	10g	3%
Dietary Fiber	2g	8%
Sugars	1g	
Protein	17g	

Vitamin A	4%	Vitamin C	0%
Calcium	4%	Iron	8%

Dietary Exchanges: $^1/_2$ Starch, 2 Lean Meat OR $^1/_2$ Carbohydrate, 2 Lean Meat

about **Fresh Ginger**

Pungent fresh ginger is a key ingredient in many Asian meals and can transform a bland dish into a character-filled one. For sauces, ginger is usually best grated, as most people will not relish biting into a spicy-hot chunk. Fresh ginger is knobby; pare off the thin brown skin with a sharp paring knife or peeler before grating.

Cantonese Fish

PREP TIME: 30 MINUTES

2 tablespoons orange juice

1 tablespoon regular or lite soy sauce

2 teaspoons lemon juice

1 teaspoon brown sugar

1 teaspoon grated gingerroot

½ teaspoon vegetable or sesame oil

Dash pepper

2 (4-oz.) orange roughy fillets

1 teaspoon sesame seed, toasted, if desired*

1. In 8-inch square (2-quart) baking dish, combine all ingredients except orange roughy fillets and sesame seed; mix well. Place fish in soy sauce mixture; turn to coat. Let stand at room temperature for 15 minutes to marinate.

2. Meanwhile, heat oven to 375°F. Cover baking dish with foil. Bake 12 to 15 minutes or until fish flakes easily with fork. If desired, a small amount of sauce can be spooned over each serving. Place fish on serving platter; sprinkle with sesame seed.

YIELD: 2 SERVINGS

Tip: * To toast sesame seed, spread in small skillet; stir over medium heat for 2 to 3 minutes or until light golden brown.

Nutrition Information Per Serving
Serving Size: $^1/_2$ of Recipe

Calories	180	Calories from Fat	90

		% Daily Value
Total Fat	10g	15%
Saturated	0g	0%
Cholesterol	25mg	8%
Sodium	590mg	25%
Total Carbohydrate	5g	2%
Dietary Fiber	0g	0%
Sugars	4g	
Protein	18g	

Vitamin A	0%	Vitamin C	8%
Calcium	4%	Iron	4%

Dietary Exchanges: $^1/_2$ Starch, 3 Very Lean Meat, 1 Fat OR $^1/_2$ Carbohydrate, 3 Very Lean Meat, 1 Fat

▲ Broiled Salmon Steaks with Black Bean Salsa

Broiled Salmon Steaks with Black Bean Salsa

PREP TIME: 30 MINUTES

Salsa
1 (15-oz.) can black beans, drained, rinsed

½ cup diced orange sections

½ cup finely chopped tomato

1 tablespoon lime juice

1 teaspoon sugar

¾ teaspoon cumin

Fish
¾ teaspoon chili powder

½ teaspoon cumin

⅛ teaspoon garlic salt

⅛ teaspoon ground oregano

2 (8-oz.) salmon steaks (1 inch thick), each cut into 2 pieces

1. In medium bowl, combine all salsa ingredients; mix well. Let stand at room temperature for 15 to 30 minutes or refrigerate up to 2 hours to blend flavors. Stir before serving.

2. Spray broiler pan with nonstick cooking spray. In small bowl, combine chili powder, ½ teaspoon cumin, garlic salt and oregano; mix well. Lightly sprinkle both sides of salmon steaks with chili powder mixture; place on sprayed pan.

3. Broil 4 to 6 inches from heat for 8 to 12 minutes or until fish flakes easily with fork, turning once. Serve salsa with fish.

YIELD: 4 SERVINGS

Nutrition Information Per Serving
Serving Size: ¼ of Recipe

Calories	300	Calories from Fat	90
		% Daily Value	
Total Fat	10g		15%
Saturated	2g		10%
Cholesterol	75mg		25%
Sodium	90mg		4%
Total Carbohydrate	21g		7%
Dietary Fiber	7g		28%
Sugars	4g		
Protein	31g		
Vitamin A	8%	Vitamin C	20%
Calcium	4%	Iron	15%

Dietary Exchanges: 1½ Starch, 3½ Lean Meat OR 1½ Carbohydrate, 3½ Lean Meat

dressing up **Plain Fish**

Pan-fry or broil flounder, sole or other thin fillets for a supper that's ready in minutes. To dress up plain fish, try:

- A squeeze of fresh lemon or lime
- A dollop of purchased or homemade salsa
- A splash of bottled Italian dressing
- A sprinkle of minced fresh herbs, such as lemon basil and chives

- A topping of quick "cocktail sauce" made by blending ketchup, lemon juice and horseradish
- A spoonful of relish made by combining chopped ripe tomatoes, cooked corn kernels, minced red onion and fresh basil
- A bit of chutney

Broiled Red Snapper with Cucumber Salsa

PREP TIME: 15 MINUTES

Fish
1 lb. red snapper fillets

2 teaspoons oil

Salsa
½ cup finely chopped seeded and peeled cucumber

¼ cup chopped green bell pepper

2 tablespoons sliced green onions

1 tablespoon chopped fresh parsley or 1 teaspoon dried parsley flakes

1 teaspoon sugar

1 teaspoon grated lime peel, if desired

1 tablespoon lime juice

⅛ teaspoon hot pepper sauce

1. Line 15 × 10 × 1-inch baking pan with foil; spray with nonstick cooking spray. Pat red snapper fillets dry with paper towels; brush with oil. Place, skin side up, on sprayed foil-lined pan.

2. Broil 4 to 6 inches from heat for 10 to 12 minutes or until fish flakes easily with fork, turning once.

3. Meanwhile, in medium bowl, combine all salsa ingredients; mix well. Serve salsa over fish.

YIELD: 4 SERVINGS

Nutrition Information Per Serving
Serving Size: ¼ of Recipe

Calories.................................170	Calories from Fat 35	
		% Daily Value
Total Fat 4g	....6%	
Saturated 1g	....5%	
Cholesterol 55mg	....18%	
Sodium 70mg	....3%	
Total Carbohydrate............3g	....1%	
Dietary Fiber....................0g	....0%	
Sugars 2g		
Protein 30g		
Vitamin A 6%	Vitamin C 20%	
Calcium 6%	Iron..............................2%	

Dietary Exchanges: 1 Vegetable, 4 Very Lean Meat

about **Cucumbers**

To seed a cucumber, cut it in half lengthwise and scrape out the seeds with a teaspoon. The job is even easier with a serrated-tipped grapefruit spoon.

Fish Veracruz

■ ■ ■ ■ ■ ■ ■ ■ ■ ■ ■ ■ ■ ■ ■ ■

PREP TIME: 30 MINUTES

1 medium onion, halved, sliced

1 (14.5-oz.) can Mexican-style stewed tomatoes, undrained

⅓ cup dry red wine or chicken broth

3 tablespoons lemon juice

1 teaspoon cumin

⅛ to ¼ teaspoon cinnamon

¼ cup pimiento-stuffed olives, sliced

1 lb. red snapper, cod or orange roughy fillets

1. Heat oven to 400°F. Spray large nonstick skillet with nonstick cooking spray. Add onion; cook and stir over medium-high heat for 2 to 3 minutes. Stir in tomatoes, wine, lemon juice, cumin and cinnamon. Cook over medium heat for 5 to 7 minutes or until slightly thickened. Stir in olives.

2. Spray 13 × 9-inch (3-quart) baking dish with nonstick cooking spray. Arrange red snapper fillets in single layer in dish; spoon tomato mixture over top. Cover with foil.

3. Bake at 400°F. for 15 to 20 minutes or until fish flakes easily with fork.

YIELD: 4 SERVINGS

Nutrition Information Per Serving
Serving Size: ¼ of Recipe

Calories...............................190	Calories from Fat 45
	% Daily Value
Total Fat 5g	...............8%
Saturated 1g	...............5%
Cholesterol 25mg	...............8%
Sodium 1,070mg	.............45%
Total Carbohydrate 13g	...............4%
Dietary Fiber 2g	...............8%
Sugars 5g	
Protein 18g	
Vitamin A 8%	Vitamin C 8%
Calcium 10%	Iron 10%

Dietary Exchanges: 2 Vegetable, 2 Very Lean Meat, 1 ½ Fat

◀ Fish Veracruz

Swordfish Steaks with Fruit Salsa

■ ■ ■ ■ ■ ■ ■ ■ ■ ■ ■ ■ ■ ■ ■ ■

PREP TIME: 25 MINUTES

Salsa

1 (11-oz.) can pineapple and mandarin orange segments, drained, coarsely chopped

1 tablespoon chopped red onion

2 teaspoons chopped fresh cilantro

2 teaspoons fresh lime juice

⅛ teaspoon salt

½ to 1 jalapeño chile, seeded, chopped (2 to 3 teaspoons)

Fish

1 tablespoon brown sugar

1 tablespoon fresh lime juice

2 (4-oz.) swordfish steaks (¾ inch thick)

1. In medium microwave-safe bowl, combine all salsa ingredients; mix well. Microwave on HIGH for 1½ to 2 minutes or until thoroughly heated, stirring once halfway through cooking. Cover to keep warm.

2. In small bowl, combine brown sugar and 1 tablespoon lime juice; mix well. Spray broiler pan with nonstick cooking spray. Arrange swordfish steaks on sprayed pan; brush with brown sugar mixture.

3. Broil 4 to 6 inches from heat for 4 to 5 minutes on each side or until fish flakes easily with fork, brushing occasionally with brown sugar mixture. Serve salsa with fish.

YIELD: 2 SERVINGS

Nutrition Information Per Serving
Serving Size: ½ of Recipe

Calories...............................230	Calories from Fat 45
	% Daily Value
Total Fat 5g	...............8%
Saturated 1g	...............5%
Cholesterol 45mg	.............15%
Sodium 290mg	.............12%
Total Carbohydrate 22g	...............7%
Dietary Fiber 1g	...............4%
Sugars 20g	
Protein 23g	
Vitamin A 4%	Vitamin C 25%
Calcium 4%	Iron 10%

Dietary Exchanges: 1½ Fruit, 4 Very Lean Meat OR 1½ Carbohydrate, 4 Very Lean Meat

Lemon Butter Flounder Fillets

PREP TIME: 20 MINUTES

1 lb. flounder fillets

1 cup water

2 teaspoons cornstarch

½ teaspoon chicken-flavor instant bouillon

Dash pepper

2 tablespoons all-natural butter-flavor granules

1 teaspoon grated lemon peel

1 tablespoon chopped fresh chives

1. Line 15 × 10 × 1-inch baking pan with foil; spray foil with nonstick cooking spray. Pat flounder fillets dry with paper towels; place on sprayed foil-lined pan.

2. Broil 4 to 6 inches from heat for 6 to 8 minutes or until fish flakes easily with fork, turning once.

3. Meanwhile, in small saucepan, combine water, cornstarch, bouillon and pepper; blend well. Cook and stir over medium heat until bubbly and thickened. Reduce heat to low; stir in butter-flavor granules and lemon peel. Remove from heat; stir in chives. Serve sauce over fish.

YIELD: 4 SERVINGS

Nutrition Information Per Serving
Serving Size: ¼ of Recipe

Calories	140	Calories from Fat	20
		% Daily Value	
Total Fat	2g		3%
Saturated	1g		5%
Cholesterol	80mg		27%
Sodium	510mg		21%
Total Carbohydrate	3g		1%
Dietary Fiber	0g		0%
Sugars	0g		
Protein	28g		
Vitamin A	0%	Vitamin C	0%
Calcium	2%	Iron	2%

Dietary Exchanges: 4 Very Lean Meat

▼ Lemon Butter Flounder Fillets

The Right Fish *for the recipe*

Fish fall into three categories based on the texture of their flesh, each of which can be subgrouped as mild or stronger flavored.

Soft-Textured Fish

Soft-textured fish are delicate; handle gently so they don't fall apart.

- *Best cooking methods:* Baking, microwaving, sautéing, steaming
- *Mild flavor:* Flounder, sole, skate, sea trout
- *Stronger flavor:* Bluefish, herring

Flaky-Textured Fish

Fish in this group characteristically have flesh that separates into large flakes when cooked.

- *Best cooking methods:* Baking, broiling, grilling, microwaving, poaching, sautéing, steaming
- *Mild flavor:* Black sea bass, butterfish, cod, haddock, mullet, orange roughy, perch, pollack, pompano, porgy, red snapper, rockfish, shad, tilefish, trout, whitefish, whiting (hake)
- *Stronger flavor:* Mackerel, salmon, sardine, smelt

Firm-Textured Fish

Some of the fish in this group, notably swordfish and tuna, have flesh so firm that it resembles the texture of meat.

- *Best cooking methods:* Baking, broiling, grilling, microwaving, steaming, stir-frying
- *Mild flavor:* Carp, catfish, dolphinfish (mahi-mahi), grouper, halibut, shark, striped bass, swordfish, tilapia
- *Stronger flavor:* Monkfish, tuna

Parmesan-Topped Perch

PREP TIME: 20 MINUTES

¼ cup grated Parmesan cheese

¼ cup fat-free mayonnaise or salad dressing

1 tablespoon unseasoned bread crumbs

1 small garlic clove, minced

1 lb. perch fillets

1. Line 15 × 10 × 1-inch baking pan with foil; spray foil with nonstick cooking spray. In small bowl, combine cheese, mayonnaise, bread crumbs and garlic; blend well. Set aside.

2. Pat perch fillets dry with paper towels; place, skin side up, on sprayed foil-lined pan. Broil 4 to 6 inches from heat for 6 to 8 minutes, turning once.

3. Remove pan from oven; spread Parmesan mixture evenly over fish. Broil an additional 1 minute or until topping puffs and begins to brown and fish flakes easily with fork.

YIELD: 4 SERVINGS

Nutrition Information Per Serving
Serving Size: ¼ of Recipe

Calories	180	Calories from Fat	35
		% Daily Value	
Total Fat	4g		6%
Saturated	2g		10%
Cholesterol	135mg		45%
Sodium	390mg		16%
Total Carbohydrate	4g		1%
Dietary Fiber	1g		3%
Sugars	1g		
Protein	31g		
Vitamin A	0%	Vitamin C	2%
Calcium	20%	Iron	8%

Dietary Exchanges: ½ Starch, 4 Very Lean Meat OR ½ Carbohydrate, 4 Very Lean Meat

In Fish, *fat is not a dirty word*

A lean, high-quality protein source, fish contains omega-3 fatty acids, which may help lower blood cholesterol. Even butterfish, endowed with the rich flesh the name implies, contains far less fat than beef. Lean fish requires extra attention to prevent drying out when prepared by dry heat (baking, broiling, grilling).

Low-fat fish
(less than 5%)

- Black sea bass
- Catfish
- Cod
- Dolphinfish (mahimahi)
- Flounder
- Grouper
- Haddock
- Halibut
- Monkfish
- Orange roughy
- Perch
- Pollack
- Red snapper
- Rockfish
- Sea trout
- Shark
- Skate
- Smelt
- Sole
- Striped bass
- Swordfish
- Tilapia
- Tilefish
- Whiting (hake)

Moderately fat fish
(5 to 10%)

- Bluefish
- Butterfish
- Carp
- Trout
- Tuna
- Whitefish

Higher-fat fish (over 10%)
- Herring
- Mackerel
- Pompano
- Salmon
- Sardine

Source: USDA Handbook 8

Vegetable Tuna Casserole with Pretzel Topping

PREP TIME: 20 MINUTES
(READY IN 50 MINUTES)

3 oz. (1½ cups) uncooked wide egg noodles

1 (6-oz.) can water-packed tuna, drained, flaked

2 cups frozen broccoli florets, thawed*

½ cup finely chopped red or green bell pepper

¼ cup chopped green onions

1 (10¾-oz.) can condensed 98% fat-free cream of celery soup with 30% less sodium

¾ cup skim milk

½ teaspoon dried basil leaves

1 cup crushed pretzel twists or sticks

1. Cook noodles to desired doneness as directed on package. Drain.

2. Heat oven to 350°F. Spray 1½-quart casserole with nonstick cooking spray. In medium bowl, combine cooked noodles and all remaining ingredients except pretzels. Spoon mixture into sprayed casserole; top with pretzels.

3. Bake at 350°F. for 25 to 30 minutes or until thoroughly heated.

YIELD: 4 (1¼-CUP) SERVINGS

Tip: * To quickly thaw broccoli, place in colander; rinse with warm water until thawed. Pour cooked noodles into same colander with broccoli; drain well.

Nutrition Information Per Serving
Serving Size: 1¼ Cups

Calories	260	Calories from Fat	25
			% Daily Value
Total Fat	3g		5%
Saturated	1g		5%
Cholesterol	35mg		12%
Sodium	710mg		30%
Total Carbohydrate	39g		13%
Dietary Fiber	3g		12%
Sugars	7g		
Protein	18g		
Vitamin A	45%	Vitamin C	75%
Calcium	10%	Iron	15%

Dietary Exchanges: 2 Starch, 2 Vegetable, 1 Very Lean Meat OR
2 Carbohydrate, 2 Vegetable, 1 Very Lean Meat

Salmon with Leeks and Carrots in Parchment

PREP TIME: 25 MINUTES

1 cup (2 medium) thinly sliced carrots

4 (12-inch) circles parchment paper or heavy-duty foil

1 (1-lb.) salmon fillet, skin removed, cut into 4 pieces

2 medium leeks, white and pale green part thinly sliced (1½ cups), or 1 medium onion, halved, thinly sliced

2 tablespoons dry white wine or water

2 teaspoons olive oil

⅛ teaspoon salt

¼ teaspoon pepper

about Leeks

The leek, a mild member of the onion family, looks like a very fat, overgrown scallion. It's delicious, but it tends to hide a lot of grit inside its tightly rolled greens. Trim off the root end, then cut the leek lengthwise. Rinse the vegetable thoroughly, gently separating the green leaves to wash away dirt from all the crevices. The dark green part is rather tough and should be saved for flavoring stock.

smart Substitutions

It's safest to go with the fish that looks best in the market on shopping day. You can substitute freely among any of the subgroups. Replace any mild flaky fish, such as cod, with haddock or pollack or any other from that group. You can even try substitutions between groups—switch sole for cod, for example—as long as you take into consideration differences in texture and thickness of the fish and modify cooking times.

1. Heat oven to 450°F. Placing slightly off center, divide carrots evenly onto parchment circles.

2. Holding knife on a slant (45° angle), cut each salmon piece into 4 or 5 thin slices. Place salmon over carrots; sprinkle with leeks.

3. In small bowl, combine wine, oil, salt and pepper; mix well. Drizzle wine mixture evenly over fish and vegetables. Fold parchment in half; crimp edges to enclose fish and vegetables. Place on cookie sheet.

4. Bake at 450°F. for 10 to 12 minutes or until fish flakes easily with fork. To serve, place packets on serving plates and cut an X in each.

YIELD: 4 SERVINGS

Nutrition Information Per Serving
Serving Size: ¼ of Recipe

Calories	250	Calories from Fat	110
			% Daily Value
Total Fat	12g		18%
Saturated	2g		10%
Cholesterol	75mg		25%
Sodium	140mg		6%
Total Carbohydrate	9g		3%
Dietary Fiber	2g		8%
Sugars	3g		
Protein	25g		
Vitamin A	180%	Vitamin C	8%
Calcium	4%	Iron	8%

Dietary Exchanges: 1 Vegetable, 3 Lean Meat, 1 Fat

▲ Pecan-Crusted Catfish

Pecan-Crusted Catfish

PREP TIME: 25 MINUTES

½ cup corn flake crumbs

¼ cup (1 oz.) finely ground pecans

¼ teaspoon paprika

⅛ teaspoon garlic powder

⅛ teaspoon ground red pepper (cayenne)

1 lb. catfish fillets, cut into 4 pieces

1 egg white, slightly beaten

1. Heat oven to 450°F. Spray 15 × 10 × 1-inch baking pan with nonstick cooking spray. In large resealable plastic bag, combine crumbs, pecans, paprika, garlic powder and ground red pepper. Dip catfish fillets in egg white. Shake dipped fish in crumb mixture to coat. Place in sprayed pan.

2. Bake at 450°F. for 15 to 20 minutes or until fish flakes easily with fork. If desired, salt and pepper to taste.

YIELD: 4 SERVINGS

Nutrition Information Per Serving
Serving Size: ¼ of Recipe

Calories	200	Calories from Fat	60
			% Daily Value
Total Fat	7g		11%
Saturated	1g		5%
Cholesterol	50mg		17%
Sodium	220mg		9%
Total Carbohydrate	11g		4%
Dietary Fiber	1g		3%
Sugars	1g		
Protein	22g		
Vitamin A	20%	Vitamin C	6%
Calcium	0%	Iron	6%

Dietary Exchanges: ½ Starch, 3 Very Lean Meat, 1 Fat OR
½ Carbohydrate, 3 Very Lean Meat, 1 Fat

defrosting Frphu **Frozen Fish**

You don't need to defrost most frozen fish fillets before cooking—just cook them slightly longer.

If you're using commercially prepared fillets, follow the package instructions. If you can plan ahead, the best way to defrost home-frozen fish fillets is to leave them wrapped and on a plate in the refrigerator overnight or until completely defrosted. (Never defrost fish, chicken or meat at room temperature—the surface temperature rises to a point where bacteria can multiply before the center is thawed.)

If you're in a hurry, the microwave oven provides a good alternative; many ovens have programmed defrost cycles that automatically calculate thawing time. Arrange the fillets on a microwave-safe plate and cook at LOW (30% power) for about 3 minutes per pound, checking frequently to make sure the fish is not beginning to cook. Use microwave-defrosted fish at once.

Tuna Niçoise on French Bread

PREP TIME: 10 MINUTES

1 (8-oz.) loaf French bread

2 tablespoons reduced-fat margarine

1 (6-oz.) can water-packed chunk light tuna, drained, flaked

½ cup sliced ripe olives

½ medium tomato, chopped

½ to 1 cup shredded lettuce

1 tablespoon olive or vegetable oil

2 teaspoons red wine vinegar

Salt and pepper to taste

1. Cut bread in half lengthwise; spread lightly with margarine. On bottom half, layer tuna, olives, tomato and lettuce.

2. In small bowl, combine oil and vinegar; mix well. Drizzle over lettuce. Sprinkle with salt and pepper. Cover with top half of bread. To serve, cut into 4 sandwiches.

YIELD: 4 SANDWICHES

Nutrition Information Per Serving
Serving Size: 1 Sandwich

Calories	280	Calories from Fat	100

		% Daily Value	
Total Fat	11g		17%
Saturated	2g		10%
Cholesterol	10mg		3%
Sodium	690mg		29%
Total Carbohydrate	32g		11%
Dietary Fiber	2g		8%
Sugars	3g		
Protein	14g		

Vitamin A	10%	Vitamin C	4%
Calcium	6%	Iron	15%

Dietary Exchanges: 2 Starch, 1 Very Lean Meat, 2 Fat OR 2 Carbohydrate, 1 Very Lean Meat, 2 Fat

about Niçoise Ingredients

Recipes from Nice, the city on the Mediterranean in southeastern France, typically include garlic and tomato. A traditional *salade niçoise*, the inspiration for Tuna Niçoise on French Bread (above), combines tuna (or anchovies) with boiled potatoes, string beans, tomatoes, olives and hard-cooked eggs, all in a vinaigrette dressing.

Rush-Hour Tuna Melts

PREP TIME: 25 MINUTES

1 (6-oz.) can water-packed solid white tuna, drained, flaked

¾ cup chopped celery

2 tablespoons finely chopped onion

½ teaspoon grated lemon peel, if desired

⅓ cup fat-free mayonnaise or salad dressing

4 whole wheat English muffins, split, lightly toasted

8 slices tomato

4 oz. (1 cup) shredded reduced-fat Cheddar or Monterey Jack cheese

1. Heat oven to 350°F. In medium bowl, combine tuna, celery, onion, lemon peel and mayonnaise; mix well. Spread about 3 tablespoons tuna mixture on each English muffin half. Top each with tomato slice; sprinkle with cheese. Place on ungreased cookie sheet.

2. Bake at 350°F. for 8 to 10 minutes or until cheese is melted and sandwiches are thoroughly heated.

YIELD: 8 SANDWICHES; 4 SERVINGS

Nutrition Information Per Serving
Serving Size: ¼ of Recipe

Calories	280	Calories from Fat	60
		% Daily Value	
Total Fat	7g		11%
Saturated	3g		15%
Cholesterol	30mg		10%
Sodium	830mg		35%
Total Carbohydrate	31g		10%
Dietary Fiber	3g		12%
Sugars	5g		
Protein	23g		
Vitamin A	10%	Vitamin C	6%
Calcium	35%	Iron	15%

Dietary Exchanges: 2 Starch, 2 Lean Meat OR 2 Carbohydrate, 2 Lean Meat

about Catfish

Catfish, so named for its barbels that resemble feline whiskers, is a bottom feeder, and the wild fish is famous for its strong, "muddy" flavor. Most of the catfish you'll find in the market nowadays, however, has been farm raised and has a milder, "cleaner" flavor.

about Coleslaw Blend

Coleslaw mix saves the tedious task of grating by hand or fussing with the food processor. It's simply a mixture of preshredded, ready-to-dress cabbage and carrots. Use the mix in a traditional slaw, spiked with raisins in a sweet orange-juice dressing, or as a quick way to expand a stir-fry.

Cajun Fish Sandwiches with Slaw

PREP TIME: 15 MINUTES

Slaw

2 cups purchased coleslaw blend (from 16-oz. pkg.)

¼ cup reduced-calorie salad dressing or mayonnaise

2 tablespoons sweet pickle relish

Fish Sandwiches

1½ teaspoons Cajun or Creole seasoning

4 (about 5 × 3-inch) catfish fillets (¾ lb.)

4 large sesame sandwich buns, split

Grill Directions: 1. Heat grill. In medium bowl, combine all slaw ingredients; mix well. Set aside.

2. Sprinkle Cajun seasoning over both sides of catfish. If using grill basket, brush with oil. When ready to grill, place fish in basket. Place basket or fish fillets on gas grill over medium heat or on charcoal grill over medium coals. Cook 6 to 10 minutes or until fish flakes easily with fork, turning once.

3. Place buns, cut sides down, on grill rack. Cook about 30 seconds or until toasted. Place fish fillets on bottom halves of buns; top each with ¼ cup slaw. Cover with top halves of buns.

fish Buying and Storage Tips

A good fish market will:

- Display whole fish on or under crushed ice.

- Display fillets and steaks in a single layer in pans sunk into the ice.

A good fish market will not:

- Have raw fish sitting in puddles of water.

- Display raw and cooked seafood items side by side.

- Pile fillets and steaks. In piles, the top layers are too far from the cold surface and can spoil more rapidly.

- Smell "fishy."

When selecting whole fish, look for:

- Bright, bulging eyes. Dull, filmy or sunken eyes indicate fish past its prime.

- Bright red gills. Avoid gills that look brownish or slimy.

- Shiny, undamaged skin. Bypass fish with skin that looks wrinkled, dull or bruised or that is covered with brownish film.

When choosing fillets or steaks, look for:

- Flesh that is glossy, moist and intact. Avoid fish that looks dry, dull or slimy or whose flesh seems to be coming apart.

When purchasing frozen fish:

- Choose packages that are frozen solid and not mushy.

- Avoid packages that show signs of freezer burn (a dry-looking surface with white or gray spots).

- Skip packages that contain ice; the package was probably partially thawed and refrozen.

- Check the "sell by" date.

At home:

- Take the fish directly home, store it in the coldest part of your refrigerator and use it the same day.

- Thaw frozen fish in a dish in the refrigerator or in your microwave according to manufacturer's directions. Never thaw fish (or any meat or poultry) at room temperature; bacteria can multiply alarmingly fast.

- To avoid cross-contamination with other foods during preparation, thoroughly clean all surfaces that the raw fish touches; don't use a knife to cut up fish and then vegetables without washing it with soap and hot water first.

Broiler Directions: 1. Prepare slaw and season catfish as directed above. Place fish on broiler pan. **2.** Broil 4 to 6 inches from heat for 6 to 10 minutes or until fish flakes easily with fork, turning once. If desired, toast cut sides of buns under broiler. Place fish fillets on bottom halves of buns; top each with ¼ cup slaw. Cover with top halves of buns.

YIELD: 4 SANDWICHES

Nutrition Information Per Serving
Serving Size: 1 Sandwich

Calories	300	Calories from Fat	70

		% Daily Value
Total Fat	8g	12%
Saturated	1g	5%
Cholesterol	40mg	13%
Sodium	850mg	35%
Total Carbohydrate	36g	12%
Dietary Fiber	1g	4%
Sugars	13g	
Protein	20g	

Vitamin A	25%	Vitamin C	10%
Calcium	10%	Iron	10%

Dietary Exchanges: 2 Starch, 1 Vegetable, 2 Very Lean Meat, 1 Fat OR 2 Carbohydrate, 1 Vegetable, 2 Very Lean Meat, 1 Fat

Garden-Fresh Tuna Salad Sandwiches

PREP TIME: 15 MINUTES

1 (6-oz.) can water-packed tuna, drained, flaked

⅔ cup chopped seeded cucumber

½ cup shredded carrot

¼ cup chopped green onions

¼ cup fat-free mayonnaise or salad dressing

2 tablespoons nonfat sour cream

1 tablespoon lemon juice

4 leaves leaf lettuce

8 slices whole wheat bread, toasted if desired

1. In medium bowl, combine all ingredients except lettuce and bread; mix well.

2. Place 1 lettuce leaf on each of 4 slices of bread; spoon and spread ½ cup tuna mixture onto each. Top with remaining slices of bread.

YIELD: 4 SANDWICHES

Nutrition Information Per Serving
Serving Size: 1 Sandwich

Calories	220	Calories from Fat	25
		% Daily Value	
Total Fat	3g		5%
Saturated	1g		5%
Cholesterol	15mg		5%
Sodium	550mg		23%
Total Carbohydrate	32g		11%
Dietary Fiber	5g		20%
Sugars	5g		
Protein	16g		
Vitamin A	80%	Vitamin C	10%
Calcium	8%	Iron	15%

Dietary Exchanges: 2 Starch, 2 Very Lean Meat OR 2 Carbohydrate, 2 Very Lean Meat

Tuna *tips*

Canned tuna, while quite different from its fresh counterpart, offers an economical and easy main-dish selection. Tuna comes in three grades: solid or fancy contains the largest pieces, while flaked or grated contains the smallest. Chunk tuna falls between the two.

White tuna, slightly more expensive and firmer than regular or light tuna, comes from albacore, which is sometimes called "king of the tuna." White tuna is slightly richer (about 1 gram of fat per portion instead of ½ gram) and usually a little more expensive. To save fat, purchase tuna packed in water, not oil.

The recipe for Garden-Fresh Tuna Salad Sandwiches shows one way to liven up tuna. Here are some other ideas:

- Sprinkle some curry powder into your standard tuna salad.

- Instead of celery, mix in chopped water chestnuts.

- Layer a tuna sandwich with alfalfa sprouts and strips of roasted red pepper.

- Spoon tuna salad into a hollowed-out garden-ripe tomato.

- Combine tuna with potato or egg salad.

- Mix tuna with bottled nonfat or low-fat Italian salad dressing instead of the usual mayonnaise dressing.

◀ Garden-Fresh Tuna Salad Sandwiches

Grilled Fish with Corn Salsa

PREP TIME: 35 MINUTES

Fish

4 (4-oz.) red snapper fillets, or 1 lb. tuna steaks, cut into 4 pieces

⅛ teaspoon salt

Dash pepper

¼ cup chopped fresh basil

¼ cup chopped fresh cilantro

⅓ cup fresh lemon or lime juice

Salsa

1 (7-oz.) can vacuum-packed whole kernel corn, drained

¼ cup chopped red onion

¼ cup chopped fresh parsley

2 garlic cloves, minced

1 jalapeño chile, seeded, minced

2 tablespoons vinegar

1 tablespoon olive or vegetable oil

¼ teaspoon salt

⅛ teaspoon pepper

Grill Directions: 1. Heat grill. Sprinkle red snapper fillets with ⅛ teaspoon salt and dash of pepper. Pat basil and cilantro on 1 side of each fillet; place herb side up in shallow dish. Spoon lemon juice over herbs. Let stand at room temperature for 10 to 15 minutes to marinate.

2. Meanwhile, in large bowl, combine all salsa ingredients; mix well. Cover; refrigerate until serving time.

3. When ready to grill, lightly oil grill rack. Place fish, herb side up, on gas grill over medium heat or on charcoal grill 4 to 6 inches from medium coals. Cook 8 to 10 minutes or until fish flakes easily with fork, turning once.

4. To serve, spoon salsa over fish. If desired, garnish with additional fresh basil or cilantro.

Broiler Directions: 1. Marinate red snapper fillets and prepare salsa as directed above.

2. Spray broiler pan with nonstick cooking spray. Place fish, herb side up, on sprayed pan.

3. Broil 4 to 6 inches from heat for 8 to 10 minutes or until fish flakes easily with fork, turning once. Serve as directed above.

YIELD: 4 SERVINGS

Nutrition Information Per Serving
Serving Size: ¼ of Recipe

Calories	200	Calories from Fat	45
		% Daily Value	
Total Fat	5g		8%
Saturated	1g		5%
Cholesterol	40mg		13%
Sodium	420mg		18%
Total Carbohydrate	13g		4%
Dietary Fiber	2g		8%
Sugars	4g		
Protein	25g		
Vitamin A	10%	Vitamin C	30%
Calcium	6%	Iron	4%

Dietary Exchanges: 1 Starch, 3 Very Lean Meat OR 1 Carbohydrate, 3 Very Lean Meat

is it Done?

An easy way to estimate cooking time for fish is with the "10-minute rule." Measure the fish at its thickest part; allow about 10 minutes of cooking time for each inch of thickness. For example, a 1½-inch-thick salmon steak will take about 15 minutes to cook.

A few minutes before the estimated cooking time is up, check to see if the fish is opaque in the center and flakes easily when prodded with a fork. Because fish is low in fat, it can become tough and dry if overcooked, so remove it from the heat as soon as it loses the translucent appearance in the center.

Jerk Meats:
a Jamaican specialty

Many are the chile pepper aficionados who rank "jerk" preparations among the greatest of the world's spicy-hot dishes. Jerk refers to grilled meat that has been marinated in a piquant mixture that typically includes hot pepper, garlic, onions, sweet spices such as allspice and cinnamon and herbs such as thyme or bay leaf. Pork is traditional, but the marinade has inspired a wealth of spin-offs: jerk chicken, beef or even seafood dishes such as Grilled Jerk Fish.

Originally, cooking the meat over a smoky fire was a means of preserving it (much as sun-dried or smoked jerky was a staple for Native Americans). Modern versions are usually enjoyed hot off the grill.

Grilled Jerk Fish

PREP TIME: 25 MINUTES

Jerk Seasoning
½ teaspoon instant minced onion

½ teaspoon onion powder

¼ teaspoon sugar

⅛ teaspoon salt

¼ teaspoon allspice

¼ teaspoon freeze-dried chopped chives

¼ teaspoon ground thyme

⅛ teaspoon pepper

⅛ teaspoon ground red pepper (cayenne)

Dash cinnamon

Dash nutmeg

Fish
1 tablespoon oil

6 (4-oz.) halibut, grouper, swordfish or tilapia steaks (¾ inch thick)

Fresh chives or thyme, if desired

Grill Directions: 1. Heat grill. In small bowl, combine all jerk seasoning ingredients. Add oil; stir to combine. Spread mixture on both sides of halibut steaks.

2. When ready to grill, oil grill rack. Place fish on gas grill over medium heat or on charcoal grill 4 to 6 inches from medium-high coals. Cook 8 to 13 minutes or until fish flakes easily with fork, turning once. Garnish with fresh chives.

Broiler Directions: 1. Oil broiler pan. Prepare jerk seasoning and halibut steaks as directed above. Place fish on oiled pan.

2. Broil 4 to 6 inches from heat for 7 to 10 minutes or until fish flakes easily with fork, turning once. Garnish with fresh chives.

YIELD: 6 SERVINGS

Nutrition Information Per Serving
Serving Size: ⅙ of Recipe

Calories ...140	Calories from Fat ...45	
	% Daily Value	
Total Fat ...5g	...8%	
Saturated ...1g	...5%	
Cholesterol ...35mg	...12%	
Sodium ...105mg	...4%	
Total Carbohydrate ...1g	...1%	
Dietary Fiber ...0g	...0%	
Sugars ...1g		
Protein ...24g		
Vitamin A ...4%	Vitamin C ...0%	
Calcium ...6%	Iron ...6%	

Dietary Exchanges: 4 Very Lean Meat

Mahimahi with Pineapple Salsa

PREP TIME: 25 MINUTES

Salsa

½ medium fresh pineapple, peeled, cored and
finely chopped

1 red bell pepper, finely chopped

1 jalapeño chile, seeded, finely chopped

1 garlic clove, minced

¾ cup finely chopped red onion

¼ cup chopped fresh cilantro

▼ Mahimahi with Pineapple Salsa

Fish

½ cup pineapple juice

1 tablespoon grated lime peel

2 tablespoons lime juice

2 tablespoons rum, if desired

1 tablespoon olive oil

1 teaspoon paprika or ¼ teaspoon ground red
pepper (cayenne)

6 (4- to 6-oz.) mahimahi fillets*

Grill Directions: 1. In medium bowl, combine all salsa ingredients; mix well. Refrigerate until serving time or up to 4 days.

2. Heat grill. In shallow bowl, combine all fish ingredients except mahimahi fillets; mix well. Place fish in single layer in dish. Let stand 10 minutes at

mix-and-match Salsa Shop

■ ■

The following recipes all contain variations on salsa, which you can also use as dips or with other recipes. Try them with grilled chicken, as a dip for baked tortilla chips or pita triangles, or as a zesty garnish for a summer sandwich:

Broiled Red Snapper with Cucumber Salsa (page 199)

Broiled Salmon Steaks with Black Bean Salsa (198)

Grilled Fish with Corn Salsa (page 212)

Mahimahi with Pineapple Salsa (opposite)

Swordfish Steaks with Fruit Salsa (page 201)

Or invent your own salsa. The basic formula: a base of minced or chopped ingredients mixed with ingredients that contrast flavors and textures: sweet and tart, mild and spicy, crunchy and smooth.

room temperature to marinate.

3. When ready to grill, place fish on gas grill over medium heat or on charcoal grill 4 to 6 inches from medium-high coals. Cook 8 to 12 minutes or until fish flakes easily with fork, turning once. Serve salsa with fish.

Broiler Directions: 1. Prepare salsa and marinate mahimahi fillets as directed above. Spray broiler pan with nonstick cooking spray; place fish fillets on sprayed pan.

2. Broil 4 to 6 inches from heat for 8 to 10 minutes or until fish flakes easily with fork, turning once. Serve salsa with fish.

YIELD: 6 SERVINGS

Tip: * Other firm-textured fish (such as swordfish, halibut, shark, tuna or snapper) can be substituted for mahimahi.

removing Fish Bones

■ ■

Remove tiny pin bones from salmon or other fish fillets with tweezers or needle-nose pliers before cooking.

Nutrition Information Per Serving
Serving Size: 1/6 of Recipe

Calories	210	Calories from Fat	35
		% Daily Value	
Total Fat	4g		6%
Saturated	1g		5%
Cholesterol	100mg		33%
Sodium	120mg		5%
Total Carbohydrate	11g		4%
Dietary Fiber	1g		4%
Sugars	8g		
Protein	33g		
Vitamin A	20%	Vitamin C	45%
Calcium	8%	Iron	10%

Dietary Exchanges: 1/2 Fruit, 5 Very Lean Meat OR 1/2 Carbohydrate, 5 Very Lean Meat

Grilled Salmon Steaks with Basil Sauce

■ ■

PREP TIME: 20 MINUTES

Sauce

1 (8-oz.) container low-fat or nonfat plain yogurt

½ cup fresh basil leaves

1 tablespoon sliced green onions

1 teaspoon sugar

¼ teaspoon garlic powder

¼ teaspoon salt

Fish

2 (8-oz.) salmon steaks (1 inch thick), each cut into 2 pieces

Nonstick cooking spray

½ teaspoon lemon-pepper seasoning

Grill Directions: 1. In food processor bowl with metal blade or blender container, combine half of the yogurt and the remaining sauce ingredients. Process until smooth. Stir in remaining yogurt. Cover; refrigerate while preparing salmon.

2. Heat grill. Spray both sides of salmon steaks with nonstick cooking spray. Sprinkle with lemon-pepper seasoning.

3. When ready to grill, oil grill rack. Place fish on gas grill over medium heat or on charcoal grill 4 to 6 inches from medium-high coals. Cook 10 to 15 minutes or until fish flakes easily with fork, turning once. Serve sauce with fish.

Broiler Directions: 1. Prepare sauce and salmon steaks as directed above. Spray broiler pan with nonstick cooking spray. Place fish on sprayed pan.

2. Broil 4 to 6 inches from heat for 12 to 16 minutes or until fish flakes easily with fork, turning once. Serve sauce with fish.

YIELD: 4 SERVINGS

Nutrition Information Per Serving
Serving Size: ¼ of Recipe

Calories	250	Calories from Fat	110
		% Daily Value	
Total Fat	12g		18%
Saturated	2g		10%
Cholesterol	85mg		28%
Sodium	290mg		12%
Total Carbohydrate	6g		2%
Dietary Fiber	0g		0%
Sugars	4g		
Protein	30g		
Vitamin A	15%	Vitamin C	10%
Calcium	10%	Iron	6%

Dietary Exchanges: ½ Starch, 4 Lean Meat OR ½ Carbohydrate, 4 Lean Meat

Basil *basics*

■ ■ ■ ■ ■ ■ ■ ■ ■ ■ ■ ■ ■ ■ ■ ■ ■ ■ ■ ■

Basil's fragrant leaves send flavor to the very core of a dish. Sweet basil is the most popular of an herb family that includes basil varieties with a hint of lemon or anise flavor. It's easy to grow in a garden; if you keep pinching off leaves from the center of the plant, it will continue to grow all summer. The white flowers are edible, too, and they should be pinched off to prevent the plant from using its energies to go to seed instead of continuing to produce the tender leaves.

Once picked, basil becomes a little more fragile. To keep it freshest, trim the stems and put the "bouquet" into a jar or glass with an inch or so of water. Enclose the glass in a tightly sealed plastic bag and store in the refrigerator.

When you're ready to use it, pinch off the leaves and discard the fibrous stems. If basil will be sprinkled on top of a dish as a garnish, shred or chop the leaves just before serving time to prevent them from blackening at the edges.

Italian Barbecued Swordfish Steaks with Tomato Relish

■ ■ ■ ■ ■ ■ ■ ■ ■ ■ ■ ■ ■ ■ ■ ■ ■ ■

PREP TIME: 30 MINUTES

Fish

½ cup purchased fat-free Italian salad dressing

1 teaspoon paprika

¼ teaspoon coarse ground black pepper

4 (4- to 6-oz.) swordfish steaks (1 inch thick)

Relish

1 large tomato, seeded, chopped

1 (2¼-oz.) can sliced ripe olives, drained

1 to 2 tablespoons chopped fresh basil or parsley

Grill Directions: 1. In small bowl, combine dressing, paprika and pepper; mix well. Place swordfish steaks in large resealable plastic bag. Pour dressing mixture over fish; seal bag. Turn bag to coat both sides of fish. Refrigerate 15 minutes to marinate.

2. Meanwhile, heat grill. In medium bowl, combine tomato, olives and basil; mix well.

3. When ready to grill, oil grill rack. Place fish on gas grill over medium heat or on charcoal grill 4 to 6 inches from medium-high coals. Cook 10 to 13 minutes or until fish flakes easily with fork, turning once and brushing occasionally with marinade. Serve relish with fish.

Broiler Directions: 1. Marinate swordfish steaks and prepare relish as directed above. Spray broiler pan with nonstick cooking spray; place fish on sprayed pan.

2. Broil 4 to 6 inches from heat for 10 to 13 minutes or until fish flakes easily with fork, turning once and brushing occasionally with marinade. Serve relish with fish.

YIELD: 4 SERVINGS

Nutrition Information Per Serving
Serving Size: ¼ of Recipe

Calories...............................220	Calories from Fat 70	
	% Daily Value	
Total Fat 8g	.............12%	
Saturated 2g	.............10%	
Cholesterol 60mg	.............20%	
Sodium 570mg	.............24%	
Total Carbohydrate..............6g	.............2%	
Dietary Fiber.....................1g	.............4%	
Sugars 3g		
Protein 31g		
Vitamin A............................20%	Vitamin C 15%	
Calcium 2%	Iron 10%	

Dietary Exchanges: 1 Vegetable, 4 Very Lean Meat, 1 Fat

Fish on the Fire: *tips for grilling*

■ ■

Start with a very clean grill rack and heat it over the coals. Oil the rack *and* the fish to prevent your dinner from sticking to the grill and sending the menu up in smoke.

Firm-fleshed fish are the best candidates for grilling because they won't fall apart; for the same reason, steaks work better than fillets. Swordfish, tuna, shark and salmon steaks are all excellent choices. Chunks of "meaty" fish such as swordfish and tuna also make good kabobs.

A special long-handled grill basket that sandwiches fish securely between two wire grates simplifies turning and is indispensable for fillets. To improvise, place the fish between two wire cake-cooling racks and secure them with wire ties; flip with long-handled tongs. Spray the basekt or racks with nonstick cooking spray before grilling. Thin slices of lemon, lime or orange tucked between the fish and the grill rack or basket help minimize sticking, too. For sole and other delicate seafood, oil the fish and wrap in foil, or cook it in a pan set on the grill.

Asian Shrimp and Noodles

PREP TIME: 30 MINUTES

8 oz. uncooked linguine

⅓ cup water

1 tablespoon sugar

1 tablespoon rice or white vinegar

1 tablespoon lime juice

2 tablespoons fish sauce*

2 tablespoons ketchup

½ lb. shelled, deveined, uncooked medium shrimp, cut in half lengthwise**

2 teaspoons grated gingerroot

4 garlic cloves, minced

1 (8-oz.) pkg. (2 cups) fresh bean sprouts

4 green onions, sliced (½ cup)

¼ cup chopped fresh cilantro

2 tablespoons chopped dry-roasted peanuts

1. Cook linguine to desired doneness as directed on package.

2. Meanwhile, in small bowl, combine water, sugar, vinegar, lime juice, fish sauce and ketchup; mix well. Set aside.

3. Spray large nonstick skillet or wok with nonstick cooking spray. Heat over medium-high heat until hot. Add shrimp, gingerroot and garlic; cook and stir 2 to 3 minutes or until shrimp turn pink. Remove from skillet; cover to keep warm.

about Bean Sprouts

Bean sprouts are a great quick "filler" for stir-fries and salads. They add appealing crunch and require only a quick rinse. For hot dishes, stir in the sprouts shortly before serving, giving them just enough time to heat through without losing all their crispness.

4. Drain linguine; add to skillet. Cook and stir about 30 seconds. Stir in sauce mixture and bean sprouts; cook and stir until linguine is well coated and begins to absorb sauce. Stir in shrimp mixture, onions, cilantro and peanuts.

YIELD: 4 (1½-CUP) SERVINGS

Tips: * Three tablespoons lite soy sauce and 1 tablespoon dry sherry can be substituted for fish sauce. ** Small cooked bay shrimp can be substituted for halved medium shrimp. Cook gingerroot and garlic as directed. Stir shrimp in with sauce mixture.

Nutrition Information Per Serving
Serving Size: 1½ Cups

Calories	320	Calories from Fat	25
		% Daily Value	
Total Fat	3g		5%
Saturated	0g		0%
Cholesterol	80mg		27%
Sodium	800mg		33%
Total Carbohydrate	61g		20%
Dietary Fiber	2g		8%
Sugars	6g		
Protein	13g		
Vitamin A	6%	Vitamin C	15%
Calcium	6%	Iron	20%

Dietary Exchanges: 3½ Starch, 1 Vegetable, ½ Very Lean Meat OR 3½ Carbohydrate, 1 Vegetable, ½ Very Lean Meat

◄ Asian Shrimp and Noodles

▲ Asian-Style Shrimp and Pineapple Fried Rice

Asian-Style Shrimp and Pineapple Fried Rice

PREP TIME: 30 MINUTES

3 cups cooked long-grain white rice (cooked as directed on package, omitting margarine and salt)

1 (8-oz.) can pineapple tidbits in unsweetened juice, drained, reserving 1 tablespoon liquid

1 tablespoon soy sauce

1 teaspoon sugar

¼ teaspoon salt

¾ lb. shelled, deveined, uncooked medium shrimp*

1 tablespoon oil

½ medium red bell pepper, cut into thin strips

½ cup sliced green onions

½ jalapeño chile, seeded, minced

3 garlic cloves, minced

2 tablespoons chopped fresh cilantro

1. While rice is cooking, in small bowl, combine reserved tablespoon of pineapple liquid, soy sauce, sugar and salt; mix well. Set aside.

2. Heat large nonstick skillet over medium-high heat until hot. Add shrimp; cook and stir about 3

about Chiles

When working with jalapeño chiles or other hot chiles, wear rubber gloves or be sure to wash your hands carefully before touching your eyes or face. Chiles contain a substance called capsaicin, which can sting skin.

minutes or until shrimp turn pink. Remove from skillet; cover to keep warm.

3. Add oil to same skillet; heat over medium-high heat until hot. Add bell pepper, onions, chile and garlic; cook and stir 1 minute. Add cooked rice; cook and stir 1 to 2 minutes or until hot. Stir in pineapple, shrimp and sauce. Cook and stir 2 minutes or until thoroughly heated. Stir in cilantro.

YIELD: 4 (1½-CUP) SERVINGS

Tip: * One and one-half cups frozen uncooked medium shrimp can be substituted for fresh shrimp. Drain after cooking.

Nutrition Information Per Serving
Serving Size: 1½ Cups

Calories	330	Calories from Fat	45

		% Daily Value
Total Fat	5g	8%
Saturated	1g	5%
Cholesterol	130mg	43%
Sodium	550mg	23%
Total Carbohydrate	52g	17%
Dietary Fiber	2g	8%
Sugars	7g	
Protein	19g	

Vitamin A	15%	Vitamin C	35%
Calcium	6%	Iron	25%

Dietary Exchanges: 2 Starch, 1½ Fruit, 2 Very Lean Meat OR 3½ Carbohydrate, 2 Very Lean Meat

Asparagus-Scallop Stir-Fry

■ ■ ■ ■ ■ ■ ■ ■ ■ ■ ■ ■ ■ ■ ■ ■ ■ ■ ■ ■

PREP TIME: 20 MINUTES

2 tablespoons lemon juice

1 lb. bay scallops*

4 oz. uncooked angel hair pasta, broken into thirds

1 tablespoon oil

1 cup thinly sliced carrots

1 lb. fresh asparagus spears, cut into 1-inch pieces**

3 green onions, sliced

¼ cup purchased stir-fry sauce

about Angel Hair Pasta

Angel hair pasta (in Italian, *capelli d'angeli*) is a much thinner version of spaghetti. It cooks quickly, making it ideal for last-minute suppers. Don't overboil it, though, or like all pastas it will be mushy.

1. In medium bowl, drizzle lemon juice over scallops; set aside.

2. Cook pasta to desired doneness as directed on package.

3. Meanwhile, heat large nonstick skillet or wok over medium-high heat until hot. Add oil; heat until hot. Add carrots and asparagus; cook and stir 2 minutes. Add scallops with lemon juice; cook and stir 3 to 5 minutes or until scallops turn opaque. Add onions; cook and stir 1 minute.

4. Drain pasta; add to skillet. Stir in sauce; cook until thoroughly heated.

YIELD: 4 (1½-CUP) SERVINGS

Tips: * Larger sea scallops can be substituted for bay scallops; cut in half before cooking.
** One 9-oz. pkg. frozen asparagus cuts can be substituted; add at end of recipe with onions. Cook and stir 2 to 3 minutes or until thoroughly heated.

Nutrition Information Per Serving
Serving Size: 1½ Cups

Calories	270	Calories from Fat	45

		% Daily Value
Total Fat	5g	8%
Saturated	1g	5%
Cholesterol	25mg	8%
Sodium	670mg	28%
Total Carbohydrate	35g	12%
Dietary Fiber	4g	16%
Sugars	7g	
Protein	20g	

Vitamin A	180%	Vitamin C	25%
Calcium	6%	Iron	15%

Dietary Exchanges: 2 Starch, 1 Vegetable, 2 Very Lean Meat OR 2 Carbohydrate, 1 Vegetable, 2 Very Lean Meat

Creamy Seafood Omelet

PREP TIME: 20 MINUTES

Filling
⅓ cup frozen or canned cooked crabmeat, thawed, drained and chopped*

¼ cup sliced fresh mushrooms

1 tablespoon sliced green onions

2 tablespoons chopped tomato

⅛ teaspoon pepper

¼ cup light sour cream

Omelet
1 (8-oz.) carton (1 cup) refrigerated or frozen fat-free egg product, thawed, or 4 eggs

1 tablespoon skim milk

Topping
1 oz. (¼ cup) shredded colby–Monterey Jack cheese blend

1. Spray small nonstick saucepan with nonstick cooking spray. Combine all filling ingredients except sour cream in saucepan. Cook and stir over medium heat for 2 to 3 minutes or until thoroughly heated. Stir in sour cream. Remove from heat; cover to keep warm.

2. Spray 8- to 10-inch nonstick skillet with sloping sides (omelet pan) with nonstick cooking spray. In small bowl, combine egg product and milk; blend well. Pour egg mixture into skillet. Cook over medium heat without stirring, running spatula around edge of skillet and lifting egg mixture to allow uncooked portion to flow to bottom of skillet. Cook 3 to 4 minutes or until mixture is set but top is still moist.

3. Spoon filling over half of omelet. Sprinkle 2 tablespoons of the cheese over filling. With spatula, loosen edge of omelet and fold other half over filling. Sprinkle with remaining 2 tablespoons cheese. Cover; cook 1 minute.

YIELD: 2 SERVINGS

Tip: * One-third cup finely chopped imitation crabmeat (surimi) can be substituted for frozen or canned crabmeat.

Nutrition Information Per Serving
Serving Size: ½ of Recipe

Calories	180	Calories from Fat	60
			% Daily Value
Total Fat	7g		11%
Saturated	4g		20%
Cholesterol	35mg		12%
Sodium	580mg		24%
Total Carbohydrate	8g		3%
Dietary Fiber	0g		0%
Sugars	5g		
Protein	21g		
Vitamin A	20%	Vitamin C	6%
Calcium	20%	Iron	15%

Dietary Exchanges: ½ Starch, 2½ Lean Meat OR ½ Carbohydrate, 2½ Lean Meat

Seafood Pasta

PREP TIME: 30 MINUTES

12 oz. refrigerated linguine

1 tablespoon olive oil

2 cups chopped onions

3 cups (3 medium) chopped fresh tomatoes or 1 (28-oz.) can whole tomatoes, drained, cut up

1 cup chopped red or green bell pepper

½ cup chopped celery

3 large garlic cloves, minced

1 teaspoon dried Italian seasoning

½ teaspoon salt

¼ teaspoon crushed red pepper flakes

1 teaspoon honey or sugar

1 (8-oz.) can no-salt-added tomato sauce

9 oz. (about 1½ cups) shelled, deveined, uncooked small shrimp or uncooked scallops

1. In Dutch oven or large saucepan, cook linguine to desired doneness as directed on package.

2. Meanwhile, heat oil in large nonstick saucepan over medium heat until hot. Add onions; cook and stir 3 minutes. Add tomatoes, bell pepper, celery and

garlic; cook 5 minutes, stirring frequently. Add Italian seasoning, salt, red pepper flakes, honey and tomato sauce; simmer 15 minutes.

3. Drain linguine. Return to Dutch oven; cover to keep warm. Add shrimp to tomato mixture; cook 5 minutes or until shrimp turn opaque. Add shrimp mixture to cooked linguine; toss gently to coat.

YIELD: 6 (1½-CUP) SERVINGS

Nutrition Information Per Serving
Serving Size: 1½ Cups

Calories..............280		Calories from Fat..........35	
		% Daily Value	
Total Fat 4g		............6%	
Saturated 1g		............5%	
Cholesterol 105mg		............35%	
Sodium 290mg		............12%	
Total Carbohydrate............44g		............15%	
Dietary Fiber............4g		............16%	
Sugars 9g			
Protein 16g			
Vitamin A............35%		Vitamin C............70%	
Calcium............4%		Iron............20%	

Dietary Exchanges: 2½ Starch, 2 Vegetable, 1 Very Lean Meat OR 2½ Carbohydrate, 2 Vegetable, 1 Very Lean Meat

Shrimp Newburg Omelets

■ ■ ■ ■ ■ ■ ■ ■ ■ ■ ■ ■ ■ ■ ■ ■

PREP TIME: 20 MINUTES

Sauce
2 tablespoons all-purpose flour

½ teaspoon salt

1⅓ cups skim milk

1 tablespoon dry sherry

1 teaspoon margarine or butter, if desired

Omelets
1½ cups refrigerated or frozen fat-free egg product, thawed, or 6 eggs

3 tablespoons water

1 teaspoon dried dill weed

¼ teaspoon salt

⅛ teaspoon pepper

Filling
2 teaspoons olive oil

1½ cups sliced fresh mushrooms

½ lb. shelled, deveined, uncooked medium shrimp

1 small red bell pepper, cut into thin strips

1 tablespoon lemon juice

1. In medium nonstick saucepan, combine flour and ½ teaspoon salt. Gradually stir in milk with wire whisk; cook and stir over medium heat until bubbly and thickened. Remove from heat; stir in sherry and margarine. Cover to keep warm.

2. In small bowl, combine all omelet ingredients; mix well. Spray small nonstick skillet with nonstick cooking spray. Heat over medium-high heat until hot. Add ¼ of egg mixture to skillet. Cook 1½ to 2 minutes or until set. With pancake turner, loosen edge of omelet; gently shake pan and let omelet slide out onto serving plate. Repeat with remaining egg mixture.

3. Heat oil in medium nonstick skillet until hot. Add mushrooms, shrimp and bell pepper; cook 3 to 4 minutes or until shrimp turn pink. Add lemon juice; cook an additional 1 minute.

4. To serve, top each omelet with ¼ of shrimp mixture and 1 tablespoon sauce. Fold omelets in half over mixture; top each with ¼ cup sauce. If desired, sprinkle with paprika, chopped fresh parsley or dill.

YIELD: 4 SERVINGS

Nutrition Information Per Serving
Serving Size: ¼ of Recipe

Calories..............170		Calories from Fat..........35	
		% Daily Value	
Total Fat 4g		............6%	
Saturated 1g		............5%	
Cholesterol 80mg		............27%	
Sodium 690mg		............29%	
Total Carbohydrate............11g		............4%	
Dietary Fiber............1g		............3%	
Sugars 6g			
Protein 21g			
Vitamin A............25%		Vitamin C............30%	
Calcium............15%		Iron............20%	

Dietary Exchanges: ½ Starch, 1 Vegetable, 3 Very Lean Meat OR ½ Carbohydrate, 1 Vegetable, 3 Very Lean Meat

Monterey Grilled Shrimp

½ cup white wine

¼ cup purchased roasted red bell peppers (from 7.25-oz. jar), finely chopped

1 tablespoon finely chopped fresh lemon thyme*

1 teaspoon lemon juice

½ teaspoon hot pepper sauce

3 garlic cloves, minced

1¼ lb. shelled, deveined, uncooked large shrimp

1 teaspoon cornstarch

Grill Directions: 1. In medium bowl, combine wine, roasted bell peppers, lemon thyme, lemon juice, hot pepper sauce and garlic; mix well. Stir in shrimp. Refrigerate at least 20 minutes or up to 1 hour to marinate.

2. Heat grill. Thread shrimp onto 4 metal skewers; reserve marinade. When ready to grill, place skewered shrimp on gas grill over medium-high heat or on charcoal grill 4 to 6 inches from medium-high coals. Cook 2 to 3 minutes. Turn shrimp; cook an additional 2 to 3 minutes or until shrimp turn pink.

3. Meanwhile, pour marinade into small saucepan. Add cornstarch; blend well. Cook over medium heat until bubbly and thickened, stirring constantly. Place shrimp on serving platter; pour marinade mixture over shrimp.

Broiler Directions: 1. Marinate shrimp and thread on skewers as directed above; reserve marinade. Place skewered shrimp on broiler pan.

2. Broil 4 to 6 inches from heat for 2 to 3 minutes. Turn shrimp; broil an additional 2 to 3 minutes or until shrimp turn pink. Continue as directed above.

YIELD: 4 SERVINGS

Tip: * If lemon thyme is unavailable, substitute 1 teaspoon grated lemon peel plus 1 tablespoon chopped fresh thyme or 1 teaspoon dried thyme leaves.

Nutrition Information Per Serving
Serving Size: ¼ of Recipe

Calories	130	Calories from Fat	10
		% Daily Value	
Total Fat	1g		2%
Saturated	0g		0%
Cholesterol	200mg		67%
Sodium	240mg		10%
Total Carbohydrate	3g		1%
Dietary Fiber	0g		0%
Sugars	0g		
Protein	22g		
Vitamin A	10%	Vitamin C	20%
Calcium	6%	Iron	20%

Dietary Exchanges: 3½ Very Lean Meat

◄ Monterey Grilled Shrimp

Shrimp Jambalaya

PREP TIME: 30 MINUTES

1 tablespoon margarine or butter

3 stalks celery, chopped

1 medium onion, chopped

1 small green bell pepper, chopped

2 (14½-oz.) cans ready-to-serve fat-free chicken broth with ⅓ less sodium

2 cups uncooked instant rice

3 large tomatoes, coarsely chopped (about 3 cups)

¼ cup chopped fresh parsley

½ teaspoon dried thyme leaves

¼ teaspoon garlic powder

¼ teaspoon salt

¼ teaspoon pepper

⅛ teaspoon ground red pepper (cayenne)

1 lb. shelled, deveined, cooked medium shrimp

1. Melt margarine in nonstick Dutch oven or large nonstick saucepan over medium-high heat. Add celery, onion and bell pepper; cook 5 minutes, stirring occasionally.

2. Stir in all remaining ingredients except shrimp. Bring to a boil. Reduce heat; simmer 8 minutes.

3. Add shrimp; cook 2 minutes or until shrimp are thoroughly heated. To serve, spoon into 6 individual shallow bowls.

YIELD: 6 (1½-CUP) SERVINGS

Nutrition Information Per Serving
Serving Size: 1½ Cups

Calories	240	Calories from Fat	25
		% Daily Value	
Total Fat	3g		5%
Saturated	1g		5%
Cholesterol	150mg		50%
Sodium	630mg		26%
Total Carbohydrate	33g		11%
Dietary Fiber	2g		8%
Sugars	3g		
Protein	21g		
Vitamin A	15%	Vitamin C	30%
Calcium	6%	Iron	25%

Dietary Exchanges: 2 Starch, 1 Vegetable, 2 Very Lean Meat OR 2 Carbohydrate, 1 Vegetable, 2 Very Lean Meat

Spaghetti with Red Clam Sauce

PREP TIME: 20 MINUTES

8 oz. uncooked spaghetti

2 teaspoons olive oil

1 medium onion, chopped

4 garlic cloves, minced

1 (14.5-oz.) can no-salt-added whole tomatoes, undrained, cut up

1 (14.5-oz.) can no-salt-added stewed tomatoes, undrained

1 (6½-oz.) can minced clams, drained, reserving liquid

2 teaspoons dried Italian seasoning

¼ teaspoon salt

16 pitted medium ripe olives, halved

1. Cook spaghetti to desired doneness as directed on package.

2. Meanwhile, heat oil in large nonstick saucepan over medium-high heat until hot. Add onion and garlic; cook and stir 4 minutes.

3. Stir in tomatoes, reserved clam liquid, Italian seasoning and salt. Reduce heat; simmer 15 minutes.

4. Drain spaghetti. Stir clams and olives into sauce. Serve sauce over spaghetti.

YIELD: 4 SERVINGS

Nutrition Information Per Serving
Serving Size: ¼ of Recipe

Calories	330	Calories from Fat	45
		% Daily Value	
Total Fat	5g		8%
Saturated	1g		5%
Cholesterol	15mg		5%
Sodium	380mg		16%
Total Carbohydrate	57g		19%
Dietary Fiber	4g		16%
Sugars	8g		
Protein	15g		
Vitamin A	15%	Vitamin C	45%
Calcium	15%	Iron	60%

Dietary Exchanges: 4 Starch, ½ Very Lean Meat OR 4 Carbohydrate, ½ Very Lean Meat

Meatless 8 Entrees

Spicy Rigatoni, Beans and Greens (page 236)

Asian-Style Two-Rice Stir-Fry

■ ■

PREP TIME: 30 MINUTES

1½ cups uncooked instant brown rice

1 cup instant wild rice*

1½ cups refrigerated or frozen fat-free egg product, thawed, or 6 eggs

1 tablespoon oil

1 stalk celery, thinly sliced (½ cup)

1 small red bell pepper, cut into long, thin strips

2 (8-oz.) cans sliced water chestnuts, well drained

1 (9-oz.) pkg. frozen sweet peas in a pouch, thawed**

¼ cup lite soy or tamari sauce

¼ teaspoon pepper

½ cup thinly sliced green onions

1. In medium saucepan, combine amount of water specified on both rice packages (about 2½ cups water); omit margarine and salt. Bring to a boil. Stir in brown and wild rice. Reduce heat; cover and simmer 5 minutes. Remove from heat; let stand, covered, for 5 minutes.

2. Meanwhile, spray large nonstick skillet with nonstick cooking spray. Add egg product; cook over medium-low heat, without stirring, until top is no longer wet. Do not turn. Remove egg from skillet; cut into thin strips. Set aside.

3. Heat oil in same skillet or nonstick wok over high heat until hot. Add celery, bell pepper and water chestnuts; cook and stir 2 minutes. Stir in peas; cook and stir an additional 2 minutes. Add cooked rice; toss lightly to combine. Add soy sauce; toss and cook until thoroughly heated. Sprinkle with pepper.

4. To serve, fluff rice with fork. Place rice and vegetable mixture on serving platter; sprinkle with egg strips and onions. If desired, serve with additional soy sauce.

YIELD: 6 (1½-CUP) SERVINGS

Tips: * Two cups cooked wild rice can be substituted for the instant wild rice.
** To quickly thaw peas, place in colander or strainer; rinse with warm water until thawed. Drain well.

Nutrition Information Per Serving
Serving Size: 1½ Cups

Calories	300	Calories from Fat	35
		% Daily Value	
Total Fat	4g		6%
Saturated	0g		0%
Cholesterol	0mg		0%
Sodium	580mg		24%
Total Carbohydrate	53g		18%
Dietary Fiber	6g		24%
Sugars	7g		
Protein	14g		
Vitamin A	25%	Vitamin C	30%
Calcium	6%	Iron	20%

Dietary Exchanges: 3 Starch, 1 Vegetable, 1 Very Lean Meat OR
3 Carbohydrate, 1 Vegetable, 1 Very Lean Meat

refrigerated Fresh Pasta

■ ■ ■ ■ ■ ■ ■ ■ ■ ■ ■ ■ ■ ■ ■ ■ ■ ■ ■ ■

In old Italy, there was no refrigeration, so fresh pasta was made each day and sold in bakeries, to be eaten the same day. Today, fresh pasta has made a comeback. Many grocery stores have added fresh egg pasta to their refrigerated sections.

Among the offerings are ravioli or tortellini made with egg and filled with meat and cheese, egg fettuccine and other soft noodles. Refrigerated pasta is more expensive than dried, but it takes less time to cook and has a nice texture. Be careful not to overcook refrigerated pasta; it quickly becomes gummy.

Fresh Pasta with Skinny Tomato Sauce

PREP TIME: 35 MINUTES

1 medium onion, finely chopped

1 garlic clove, minced

2 tablespoons water

2 (9-oz.) pkg. refrigerated linguine

1 (28-oz.) can crushed tomatoes with Italian herbs, undrained

1 tablespoon olive oil

2 teaspoons sugar

¼ teaspoon salt

¼ teaspoon freshly ground black pepper

1 bay leaf

1. In nonstick Dutch oven or large saucepan, combine onion, garlic and water. Bring to a boil. Reduce heat to low; cover and cook 10 minutes or until onion is tender and translucent, stirring occasionally and adding additional water if necessary to prevent scorching.

2. Meanwhile, cook linguine to desired doneness as directed on package.

3. Add all remaining ingredients except linguine to onion mixture. Bring to a boil. Reduce heat; cover and simmer 10 minutes to blend flavors.

4. Drain linguine. Remove and discard bay leaf from sauce. Serve sauce over linguine.

YIELD: 4 SERVINGS

Nutrition Information Per Serving
Serving Size: ¼ of Recipe

Calories	480	Calories from Fat	60
		% Daily Value	
Total Fat	7g		11%
Saturated	1g		5%
Cholesterol	95mg		32%
Sodium	670mg		28%
Total Carbohydrate	87g		29%
Dietary Fiber	6g		24%
Sugars	10g		
Protein	17g		
Vitamin A	25%	Vitamin C	35%
Calcium	10%	Iron	30%

Dietary Exchanges: 5½ Starch, 1 Fat OR 5½ Carbohydrate, 1 Fat

Perfect Pasta,
every time

Before you begin to cook pasta, have a warmed serving bowl ready, as well as the sauce.

For every pound of pasta, bring 4 quarts of water to a full, rolling boil. Add 1 tablespoon of salt, if desired, then the pasta. Use a fork to stir the pasta, separating the shapes or strands. Cover the pot.

When the water has returned to a boil, uncover the pot and begin checking for doneness: bite into a piece and see how it tastes. Let personal preference, not the clock, be your guide. Fresh egg pasta will become soft in just a minute or so, while thick shapes may need 10 minutes. Stir the pasta occasionally to help it cook evenly and to prevent sticking on the bottom of the pot.

Once you like what you taste, drain the pasta into a colander. Do not rinse the pasta unless it will be used in a cold salad. Shake excess water from the pasta, taking care to leave a little moisture behind. This helps pasta carry sauce without absorbing too much of it.

Place hot pasta in a warmed serving bowl, toss with sauce and serve at once. Or add cooked pasta to your pot of simmering sauce, toss and then arrange on a serving dish.

Lean Pasta Primavera

PREP TIME: 30 MINUTES

16 oz. refrigerated fettuccine

1 (12-oz.) can evaporated skimmed milk

½ cup water

3 tablespoons cornstarch

1 tablespoon chopped fresh basil or 1 teaspoon dried basil leaves

½ teaspoon salt

¼ teaspoon pepper

1 cup light ricotta cheese

3 tablespoons grated Parmesan cheese

⅓ cup chicken broth

⅓ cup finely chopped onion

4 garlic cloves, minced

2 cups sliced fresh mushrooms

1½ cups fresh broccoli florets

2 medium zucchini, cut in half lengthwise, sliced (1½ cups)

1 cup halved fresh snow pea pods

1 cup halved cherry tomatoes

1. Cook fettuccine to desired doneness as directed on package.

pasta **Primavera**

Traditional pasta primavera ("springtime pasta"), with its colorful assortment of vegetables, looks and tastes beautiful, but its cream sauce is no friend of the low-fat diner. Evaporated skimmed milk in Lean Pasta Primavera (above) mimics the creamy texture of the original's sauce at a fraction of the calories and fat.

about **Sugar Snap Peas**

With their edible pods and sweet, meaty peas, sugar snaps have gained tremendous popularity since their introduction fifteen years ago. To prepare them, trim or snap off the stem end, then pull off the strings on either side.

2. Meanwhile, in medium nonstick saucepan, combine milk, water, cornstarch, basil, salt and pepper; blend well. Bring to a boil. Reduce heat to medium; simmer 5 to 8 minutes or until bubbly and thickened, stirring constantly. Remove from heat.

3. In blender container or food processor bowl with metal blade, combine ½ cup sauce, ricotta cheese and Parmesan cheese; blend until smooth. Add mixture to remaining sauce in saucepan. Set aside. Drain fettuccine; set aside.

4. In nonstick Dutch oven over medium-high heat, bring broth to a boil. Add onion and garlic; cook 3 minutes, stirring occasionally. Add mushrooms, broccoli and zucchini; cover and cook 4 minutes.

5. Add pea pods and tomatoes; cook an additional 1 minute. Add sauce and cooked fettuccine; cook until thoroughly heated.

YIELD: 6 (1½-CUP) SERVINGS

Nutrition Information Per Serving
Serving Size: 1½ Cups

Calories	410	Calories from Fat	70
		% Daily Value	
Total Fat	8g		12%
Saturated	4g		20%
Cholesterol	95mg		32%
Sodium	440mg		18%
Total Carbohydrate	62g		21%
Dietary Fiber	4g		16%
Sugars	12g		
Protein	23g		
Vitamin A	30%	Vitamin C	50%
Calcium	40%	Iron	25%

Dietary Exchanges: 4 Starch, 1 Vegetable, 1 Medium-Fat Meat OR
4 Carbohydrate, 1 Vegetable, 1 Medium-Fat Meat

Low-Fat Linguine Vegetable Toss

. . . .

PREP TIME: 25 MINUTES

8 oz. uncooked linguine

1 tablespoon olive oil

3 large garlic cloves, minced

2 cups fresh sugar snap peas

1½ cups cut (1-inch pieces) fresh asparagus spears

4 Italian plum tomatoes, diced

⅓ cup chopped fresh basil or 4½ teaspoons dried basil leaves

¼ teaspoon salt

⅛ teaspoon coarse ground black pepper

2 tablespoons finely shredded fresh Parmesan cheese

1. In Dutch oven or large saucepan, cook linguine to desired doneness as directed on package.

2. Meanwhile, heat oil in large nonstick skillet over medium-high heat until hot. Add garlic; cook about 30 seconds, stirring constantly. Reduce heat to medium; add sugar snap peas and asparagus. Cover; cook 3 minutes. (If vegetables begin to stick, add 1 to 2 tablespoons water to skillet.)

3. Add tomatoes; cook an additional 2 to 4 minutes or until vegetables are crisp-tender, stirring occasionally. Stir in basil, salt and pepper.

4. Drain linguine; return to Dutch oven. Add vegetable mixture; toss to mix. Sprinkle with cheese.

YIELD: 4 (1¾-CUP) SERVINGS

Nutrition Information Per Serving
Serving Size: 1¾ Cups

Calories 310	Calories from Fat 50	
	% Daily Value	
Total Fat 6g	...................................9%	
Saturated 1g	...................................5%	
Cholesterol 2mg	...................................1%	
Sodium 200mg	...................................8%	
Total Carbohydrate 53g	.................................18%	
Dietary Fiber 5g	.................................20%	
Sugars 7g		
Protein 12g		
Vitamin A 15%	Vitamin C 70%	
Calcium 10%	Iron 25%	

Dietary Exchanges: 3 Starch, 1 Vegetable, 1 Fat OR 3 Carbohydrate, 1 Vegetable, 1 Fat

▼ Low-Fat Linguine Vegetable Toss

Pasta Cannellini

PREP TIME: 25 MINUTES

5½ oz. (2 cups) uncooked pasta nuggets (radiatore)

2 teaspoons olive or vegetable oil

1 cup thinly sliced onions

1 garlic clove, minced

1 (28-oz.) can whole tomatoes, undrained, cut up

1 (15-oz.) can cannellini beans, drained, rinsed

1 teaspoon dried oregano leaves

1. Cook pasta to desired doneness as directed on package.

2. Meanwhile, heat oil in large nonstick skillet over medium heat until hot. Add onions and garlic; cook and stir about 6 minutes or until onions are tender. Add tomatoes, beans and oregano; mix well. Bring to a boil. Reduce heat; simmer 5 to 10 minutes to blend flavors.

3. Drain pasta. Serve sauce over pasta. If desired, sprinkle with grated or shredded Parmesan cheese.

YIELD: 4 SERVINGS

Nutrition Information Per Serving
Serving Size: ¼ of Recipe

Calories	300	Calories from Fat	35
		% Daily Value	
Total Fat	4g		6%
Saturated	1g		5%
Cholesterol	0mg		0%
Sodium	450mg		19%
Total Carbohydrate	55g		18%
Dietary Fiber	7g		28%
Sugars	9g		
Protein	12g		
Vitamin A	25%	Vitamin C	0%
Calcium	10%	Iron	20%

Dietary Exchanges: 3 Starch, 2 Vegetable OR 3 Carbohydrate, 2 Vegetable

Pasta with Olives and Fresh Tomatoes

PREP TIME: 15 MINUTES

8 oz. uncooked spaghetti

4 large tomatoes

1 (4-oz.) can sliced ripe olives, drained

1½ teaspoons dried basil leaves or 2 tablespoons chopped fresh basil

¼ teaspoon garlic powder

¼ teaspoon salt

⅛ teaspoon pepper

2 teaspoons olive oil

2 oz. (½ cup) shredded fresh Parmesan cheese

1. Cook spaghetti to desired doneness as directed on package.

2. Meanwhile, chop tomatoes; place in large bowl. Stir in all remaining ingredients except cheese.

3. Drain spaghetti. Add to tomato mixture; toss gently to mix. Sprinkle with cheese.

YIELD: 4 (2-CUP) SERVINGS

Nutrition Information Per Serving
Serving Size: 2 Cups

Calories	350	Calories from Fat	80
		% Daily Value	
Total Fat	9g		14%
Saturated	3g		15%
Cholesterol	5mg		2%
Sodium	560mg		23%
Total Carbohydrate	54g		18%
Dietary Fiber	5g		20%
Sugars	7g		
Protein	13g		
Vitamin A	30%	Vitamin C	45%
Calcium	15%	Iron	25%

Dietary Exchanges: 3 Starch, 2 Vegetable, 1½ Fat OR 3 Carbohydrate, 2 Vegetable, 1½ Fat

◄ Pasta Cannellini

Ravioli with Zucchini

PREP TIME: 25 MINUTES

1 (9-oz.) pkg. refrigerated cheese-filled ravioli

3 cups julienne-cut (2 × ⅛ × ⅛-inch) zucchini

½ cup sliced green onions

1 medium red bell pepper, coarsely chopped

½ teaspoon garlic powder

½ teaspoon dried basil leaves

¼ teaspoon salt

⅛ teaspoon pepper

¼ cup water

½ teaspoon chicken-flavor instant bouillon

1 oz. (¼ cup) shredded reduced-fat mozzarella cheese

1. Cook ravioli to desired doneness as directed on package.

2. Meanwhile, spray large nonstick skillet with nonstick cooking spray. Heat over medium-high heat until hot. Add zucchini, onions, bell pepper, garlic powder, basil, salt and pepper. Cook and stir 3 to 5 minutes or until vegetables are crisp-tender.

3. Drain ravioli; rinse with hot water. Add ravioli, water and bouillon to vegetable mixture; mix gently. Cook over medium-low heat for an additional 3 to 5 minutes or until thoroughly heated, stirring occasionally. Add cheese; toss gently to combine.

YIELD: 4 (1-CUP) SERVINGS

Nutrition Information Per Serving
Serving Size: 1 Cup

Calories	250	Calories from Fat	80
		% Daily Value	
Total Fat	9g		14%
Saturated	6g		30%
Cholesterol	60mg		20%
Sodium	510mg		21%
Total Carbohydrate	28g		9%
Dietary Fiber	3g		12%
Sugars	6g		
Protein	13g		
Vitamin A	30%	Vitamin C	50%
Calcium	20%	Iron	10%

Dietary Exchanges: 1½ Starch, 1 Vegetable, 1 High-Fat Meat OR
1½ Carbohydrate, 1 Vegetable, 1 High-Fat Meat

▼ Ravioli with Zucchini

Italian *mini quiz*

Can you match the words below at left with the correct definitions at right?

1. Canile

A. Crisp sweet pastry cylinder dusted with powdered sugar and filled with a mixture of sweetened ricotta, sometimes studded with miniature chocolate chips

2. Cannèlla

B. Sheets of pasta topped with a filling, rolled up, topped with a sauce and baked

3. Cannellini

C. Doghouse or kennel

4. Cannelloni

D. White kidney beans, important for Tuscan white bean soup

5. Cannoli

E. Cinnamon

ANSWERS: 1-C, 2-E, 3-D, 4-B, 5-A

Fettuccine in Corn Sauce with Green Chiles

PREP TIME: 15 MINUTES

1 (9-oz.) pkg. refrigerated fettuccine

1½ teaspoons oil

3 tablespoons finely chopped onion

2 garlic cloves, minced

1 (15-oz.) can cream-style corn

1 (4.5-oz.) can chopped green chiles, undrained

⅔ cup skim milk

3 to 4 drops hot pepper sauce

2 firm, ripe Italian plum tomatoes, finely chopped

⅓ cup sliced green onions

¼ cup sliced ripe olives

1. Cook fettuccine to desired doneness as directed on package.

2. Meanwhile, in large nonstick skillet, heat oil over medium heat until hot. Add chopped onion and garlic; cook and stir 2 minutes. Set aside.

3. In blender container or food processor bowl with metal blade, combine corn, chiles, milk and hot pepper sauce; blend or process until smooth.

4. Pour corn mixture over onion and garlic into skillet; heat over medium heat until hot. Drain fettuccine. Add fettuccine, tomatoes, green onions and olives to corn mixture; toss to coat. Cook until thoroughly heated.

YIELD: 4 (1-CUP) SERVINGS

Nutrition Information Per Serving
Serving Size: 1 Cup

Calories	330	Calories from Fat	45
		% Daily Value	
Total Fat	5g		8%
Saturated	1g		5%
Cholesterol	45mg		15%
Sodium	800mg		33%
Total Carbohydrate	60g		20%
Dietary Fiber	6g		24%
Sugars	13g		
Protein	11g		
Vitamin A	10%	Vitamin C	35%
Calcium	8%	Iron	15%

Dietary Exchanges: 3½ Starch, 1 Vegetable, 1 Fat OR 3½ Carbohydrate, 1 Vegetable, 1 Fat

Spicy Rigatoni, Beans and Greens

■ ■ ■ ■ ■ ■ ■ ■ ■ ■ ■ ■ ■ ■ ■ ■ ■

PREP TIME: 30 MINUTES

8 oz. (3¼ cups) uncooked rigatoni (pasta tubes with ridges)

1 teaspoon olive oil

1 medium onion, sliced

3 garlic cloves, minced

1 (14.5-oz.) can diced tomatoes with Italian-style herbs, undrained

1 (15.5-oz.) can great northern beans, drained, rinsed

2 tablespoons thinly sliced fresh sage leaves or 1 teaspoon dried sage leaves

¼ teaspoon crushed red pepper flakes

6 cups thinly sliced fresh spinach leaves

1. Cook rigatoni to desired doneness as directed on package.

2. Meanwhile, spray large nonstick skillet with non-stick cooking spray. Add oil; heat over medium-high heat until hot. Add onion and garlic; cook 3 to 4 minutes or until onion begins to brown, stirring frequently.

3. Stir in tomatoes; simmer 2 minutes. Stir in beans, sage and red pepper flakes; cook until thoroughly heated. Add spinach; mix well.

4. Drain rigatoni. Serve tomato mixture over rigatoni.

YIELD: 4 SERVINGS

Nutrition Information Per Serving
Serving Size: ¼ of Recipe

Calories	370	Calories from Fat	25
		% Daily Value	
Total Fat	3g		5%
Saturated	0g		0%
Cholesterol	0mg		0%
Sodium	680mg		28%
Total Carbohydrate	69g		23%
Dietary Fiber	10g		40%
Sugars	10g		
Protein	16g		
Vitamin A	120%	Vitamin C	45%
Calcium	20%	Iron	35%

Dietary Exchanges: 4 Starch, 2 Vegetable OR 4 Carbohydrate, 2 Vegetable

Bean-Friendly
cooking

■ ■ ■ ■ ■ ■ ■ ■ ■ ■ ■ ■ ■ ■ ■ ■ ■

Tips for cooking beans from the dried state:

• Beans left uncovered during cooking will be more firm than those covered during cooking.

• Resist the old tip about adding baking soda to soften the beans. Baking soda actually keeps beans from absorbing moisture and may destroy some nutrients.

• Add salt and acidic ingredients such as tomatoes, lemon juice and vinegar near the end of the cooking time. Otherwise, beans may not soften during cooking.

• Store dried beans in a tightly sealed container or a bag in a cool, dry place for up to a year. It's not necessary to refrigerate or freeze dried beans.

• Cooked beans, stored in a sealed container, keep 2 to 3 days in the refrigerator or up to 2 months in the freezer.

Spaghetti Squash with Fresh Mushroom Sauce

■ ■

PREP TIME: 25 MINUTES

1 medium spaghetti squash (about 3 lb.)

Sauce
1 cup sliced fresh mushrooms

1 small onion, chopped

2 garlic cloves, minced

1 (26-oz.) jar reduced-fat tomato and herb spaghetti sauce

1. Cut squash in half lengthwise; remove and discard seeds. Place, cut side down, in ungreased 13 × 9-inch (3-quart) microwave-safe dish. Add ¼ cup water to dish. Cover with microwave-safe plastic wrap.

Microwave on HIGH for 8 to 13 minutes or until tender.

2. Meanwhile, spray large nonstick skillet with nonstick cooking spray. Add mushrooms, onion and garlic; cook and stir over medium heat for 3 to 5 minutes or until tender. Add sauce; bring to a boil. Simmer 2 to 3 minutes or until thoroughly heated.

3. While sauce is simmering, use fork to remove spaghetti-like strands of cooked squash; place in serving bowl. Serve sauce over squash.

YIELD: 4 SERVINGS

Nutrition Information Per Serving
Serving Size: ¼ of Recipe

Calories	160	Calories from Fat	10
		% Daily Value	
Total Fat	1g		2%
Saturated	0g		0%
Cholesterol	0mg		0%
Sodium	620mg		26%
Total Carbohydrate	33g		11%
Dietary Fiber	7g		28%
Sugars	22g		
Protein	5g		
Vitamin A	15%	Vitamin C	40%
Calcium	10%	Iron	15%

Dietary Exchanges: 2 Starch OR 2 Carbohydrate

▼ Spaghetti Squash with Fresh Mushroom Sauce

Does Vegetarianism *equal good health?*

Eating vegetarian doesn't guarantee good nutrition. While a vegetarian diet can offer more fiber and less cholesterol, fat and animal protein, it also may include many high-fat foods, such as nuts, oil and full-fat dairy products. In addition, avoidance of animal foods may result in low intakes of certain nutrients. Vegetarians need to take special care to get enough of these:

- **Calcium** is abundant in dairy products. Plant foods, including dark green leafy vegetables, also have calcium, but it's not as easily absorbed. Boost calcium intake by eating foods such as broccoli and kale, and tofu processed with calcium sulfate. Eat at least three servings of low-fat dairy products daily. If you don't eat dairy foods, take a calcium supplement. Soy milk fortified with calcium also can help.

- **Vitamin D** is produced by the body in response to sunlight. Production is limited, however, anytime you wear sunscreen and during winter months if you live in northern climates. Vitamin D is also found naturally in egg yolks, liver and sardines, and it's added to milk. If you're a milk drinker, two glasses a day will ensure adequate vitamin D intake. Take a multivitamin with vitamin D if you're a vegan.

- **Iron** is found in animal foods and a variety of plant foods including legumes and dried fruit. Plant iron is less easily absorbed by the body; this improves when plant iron is eaten with vitamin C. Combine cereals, breads, grains and dried beans with vitamin C–rich foods such as orange juice, strawberries or tomatoes. Women of childbearing age and teenagers have higher iron needs.

- **Vitamin B$_{12}$** is unique to animal foods and seafood. If you don't eat animal foods, look for foods such as breakfast cereal and soy milk that are fortified with B$_{12}$, or take a B$_{12}$ supplement.

- **Protein** is present in animal and plant foods, including legumes, grains, nuts and seeds. Protein is important because it provides amino acids, which are needed to build, repair and maintain body tissues. Most animal foods contain nearly all the essential amino acids for good health; all plant foods lack a sufficient amount of one or more essential amino acids. If you don't eat animal products, ensure adequate protein intake by eating a variety of plant foods daily.

▲ Tortellini with Tomato Sauce

Tortellini with Tomato Sauce

∎ ∎ ∎ ∎ ∎ ∎ ∎ ∎ ∎ ∎ ∎ ∎ ∎ ∎ ∎ ∎ ∎

PREP TIME: 20 MINUTES

1½ teaspoons olive oil

1 medium onion, chopped

1 (10½-oz.) can condensed beef consommé*

1 (8-oz.) can no-salt-added tomato sauce

2 teaspoons brown sugar

½ teaspoon dried Italian seasoning

¼ teaspoon garlic powder

1 (9-oz.) pkg. refrigerated cheese-filled tortellini

½ medium green bell pepper, chopped

1½ cups chopped seeded tomatoes

1. Heat oil in large nonstick skillet over medium heat until hot. Add onion; cook 2 minutes. Stir in consommé, tomato sauce, brown sugar, Italian seasoning and garlic powder. Bring to a boil. Cook over medium heat for 2 minutes.

2. Add tortellini and bell pepper; simmer 5 minutes, stirring occasionally. Add tomatoes; cook an additional 3 minutes or until thoroughly heated.

YIELD: 4 (1-CUP) SERVINGS

Tip: * For a vegetarian version, 1 cup water can be substituted for the consommé.

Nutrition Information Per Serving
Serving Size: 1 Cup

Calories	320	Calories from Fat	80
		% Daily Value	
Total Fat	9g		14%
Saturated	3g		15%
Cholesterol	35mg		12%
Sodium	650mg		27%
Total Carbohydrate	44g		15%
Dietary Fiber	5g		20%
Sugars	10g		
Protein	15g		
Vitamin A	20%	Vitamin C	30%
Calcium	15%	Iron	15%

Dietary Exchanges: 2½ Starch, 1 Vegetable, 1 High-Fat Meat OR
2½ Carbohydrate, 1 Vegetable, 1 High-Fat Meat

getting enough protein **Without Meat**

How much protein do you need to maintain good health? The Recommended Daily Allowance (RDA) is 50 grams for women and 63 for men. Most foods have some protein, and unless your diet is very calorie deficient or contains only alcohol, sugar, fat and fruit—all poor sources of protein—you won't have trouble reaching the recommended amount of protein.

Vegetable and Grain Sources of Protein

Baked potato with skin	5 g
Barley, 1 cup, cooked	5 g
Broccoli, ½ cup, cooked	3 g
Brown rice, 1 cup, cooked	5 g
Corn, ½ cup, cooked	3 g
Kidney beans, 1 cup	15 g
Spaghetti, 1 cup, cooked	5 g
Spinach, ½ cup, cooked	3 g

White rice, 1 cup, cooked	4 g
Whole wheat bread, 1 slice	2 g

Dairy and Egg Sources of Protein

Egg, 1 large	6 g
Egg substitute, ¼ cup	6 g
Nonfat cottage cheese, ½ cup	14 g
Nonfat plain yogurt, 1 cup	13 g
Reduced-fat cheddar cheese, 1 oz.	7 g
Skim milk, 1 cup	8 g

Tomato, Garlic and Spinach Pasta

PREP TIME: 20 MINUTES

8 oz. uncooked fettuccine

1 tablespoon olive oil

4 garlic cloves, finely chopped

1 (28-oz.) can crushed tomatoes, undrained

1 (15½-oz.) can navy beans, drained, rinsed

¾ cup water

¼ teaspoon coarse ground black pepper

1 cup chopped fresh spinach leaves

1 oz. (¼ cup) finely shredded fresh Parmesan cheese

1. In Dutch oven or large saucepan, cook fettuccine to desired doneness as directed on package.

2. Meanwhile, heat oil in large nonstick skillet over medium heat until hot. Add garlic; cook 30 to 60 sec-

onds, stirring constantly. Stir in tomatoes, beans, water and pepper. Bring to a boil. Reduce heat to medium-low; simmer 8 to 10 minutes or until slightly thickened.

3. Add spinach; cook and stir 20 to 30 seconds or until spinach is wilted but still bright green.

4. Drain fettuccine; return to Dutch oven. Add sauce; toss to combine. Sprinkle with cheese.

YIELD: 4 SERVINGS

Nutrition Information Per Serving
Serving Size: ¼ of Recipe

Calories	460	Calories from Fat	60
		% Daily Value	
Total Fat	7g		11%
Saturated	2g		10%
Cholesterol	5mg		2%
Sodium	880mg		37%
Total Carbohydrate	79g		26%
Dietary Fiber	9g		36%
Sugars	10g		
Protein	21g		
Vitamin A	40%	Vitamin C	35%
Calcium	25%	Iron	35%

Dietary Exchanges: 5 Starch, 1 Vegetable, 1 Fat OR 5 Carbohydrate, 1 Vegetable, 1 Fat

Vegetable Ragu

· ·

PREP TIME: 35 MINUTES

6 cups hot cooked instant rice (cooked as directed on package, omitting margarine and salt)

1 medium eggplant, peeled, seeded and chopped

2 teaspoons olive oil

2 cups chopped onions

1 cup finely chopped carrots

1 cup finely chopped zucchini

2 garlic cloves, minced

3 teaspoons dried basil leaves

1 teaspoon fennel seed

2 teaspoons red wine vinegar

1 (14.5-oz.) can diced tomatoes, undrained

1 (19-oz.) can cannellini beans, drained

¼ cup finely chopped fresh parsley

1. While rice is cooking, place eggplant in nonstick Dutch oven; add ¹/₂ cup water. Bring to a boil. Reduce heat; simmer 8 to 10 minutes or until eggplant is tender, stirring occasionally. Remove eggplant from Dutch oven; set aside.

2. Wipe Dutch oven dry with paper towels. Heat oil in same Dutch oven over medium-high heat until hot. Stir in onions, carrots, zucchini, garlic, basil and fennel seed. Reduce heat to medium; cook and stir 7 to 9 minutes or until vegetables are tender.

3. Add eggplant and vinegar; cook and stir over high heat until all liquid evaporates, about 1 minute. Add tomatoes and beans; cook an additional 3 to 5 minutes or until thickened. Stir in parsley. Serve over rice.

YIELD: 6 SERVINGS

Nutrition Information Per Serving
Serving Size: ¹/₆ of Recipe

Calories	360	Calories from Fat	25
		% Daily Value	
Total Fat	3g		5%
Saturated	0g		0%
Cholesterol	0mg		0%
Sodium	230mg		10%
Total Carbohydrate	72g		24%
Dietary Fiber	8g		32%
Sugars	9g		
Protein	11g		
Vitamin A	130%	Vitamin C	25%
Calcium	10%	Iron	25%

Dietary Exchanges: 4 Starch, 2 Vegetable OR 4 Carbohydrate, 2 Vegetable

▼ Vegetable Ragu

▲ Scrambled Tostadas

Scrambled Tostadas
■ ■ ■ ■ ■ ■ ■ ■ ■ ■ ■ ■ ■ ■ ■ ■ ■ ■ ■ ■

PREP TIME: 25 MINUTES

4 tostada shells

1½ cups refrigerated or frozen fat-free egg product, thawed, or 6 eggs

¼ cup skim milk

¼ teaspoon salt

¼ teaspoon pepper

1 teaspoon olive oil

½ cup chopped onion

½ cup chopped green bell pepper

½ cup vegetarian refried beans

¼ cup purchased spicy red chili sauce or enchilada sauce

4 oz. (1 cup) shredded reduced-fat Monterey Jack cheese

1. Heat oven to 375°F. Spray cookie sheet with non-stick cooking spray. Place tostada shells on sprayed sheet. Bake at 375°F. for 5 to 6 minutes or until hot and crisp, turning once.

2. Meanwhile, in medium bowl, combine egg product, milk, salt and pepper; mix well.

3. Heat oil in medium nonstick skillet over medium heat until hot. Add onion and bell pepper; cook 4 to 5 minutes or until tender. Add egg product mixture; cook until set, stirring occasionally.

4. Top each warm tostada shell on cookie sheet with 2 tablespoons refried beans, ¼ of scrambled egg mixture, 1 tablespoon red chili sauce and ¼ cup cheese.

5. Bake at 375°F. for 8 to 10 minutes or until cheese is melted.

YIELD: 4 TOSTADAS

Nutrition Information Per Serving
Serving Size: 1 Tostada

Calories...............................240	Calories from Fat 90	
	% Daily Value	
Total Fat............................10g	....15%	
Saturated 3g	....15%	
Cholesterol 20mg	....7%	
Sodium 660mg	....28%	
Total Carbohydrate 17g	....6%	
Dietary Fiber 3g	....12%	
Sugars 4g		
Protein 21g		
Vitamin A...........................20%	Vitamin C 15%	
Calcium 30%	Iron.................................15%	

Dietary Exchanges: 1 Starch, 3 Lean Meat OR 1 Carbohydrate, 3 Lean Meat

Skillet-Roasted Vegetable Tacos

■ ■ ■ ■ ■ ■ ■ ■ ■ ■ ■ ■ ■ ■ ■ ■ ■ ■

PREP TIME: 25 MINUTES

1 (4.6-oz.) pkg. (12) taco shells

1 tablespoon olive oil

1 small eggplant (1 lb.), peeled, cut into ¼-inch cubes

1 large red bell pepper, finely chopped

1 small onion, coarsely chopped

2 garlic cloves, minced

2 to 3 tablespoons taco sauce

¼ teaspoon salt

⅛ teaspoon pepper

½ cup light sour cream

about **Crisp Taco Shells**

Taco shells always taste best, with the nicest crisp texture and most intense corn flavor, if they're briefly reheated in the oven prior to filling.

1. If desired, heat taco shells as directed on package.

2. Heat oil in large nonstick skillet over high heat until hot. Add eggplant, bell pepper, onion and garlic; cook and stir 3 to 5 minutes or until vegetables begin to brown. Cover; remove from heat. Let stand 5 minutes to soften vegetables. Stir in taco sauce, salt and pepper.

3. To serve, spoon about 2 tablespoons vegetable mixture into each taco shell. Top each with sour cream and, if desired, additional taco sauce.

YIELD: 12 TACOS; 6 SERVINGS

Nutrition Information Per Serving
Serving Size: ⅙ of Recipe

Calories...............................190	Calories from Fat 90	
	% Daily Value	
Total Fat............................10g	....15%	
Saturated 2g	....10%	
Cholesterol 5mg	....2%	
Sodium 250mg	....10%	
Total Carbohydrate 21g	....7%	
Dietary Fiber 4g	....16%	
Sugars 5g		
Protein 3g		
Vitamin A...........................25%	Vitamin C 40%	
Calcium 6%	Iron.................................4%	

Dietary Exchanges: 1 Starch, 1 Vegetable, 2 Fat OR 1 Carbohydrate, 1 Vegetable, 2 Fat

Grain *guide*

Barley The characteristic ovals, an important component in many hearty European soups, are sold in whole or "pearl" forms or ground into flour. For pearl barley, the hull is removed, reducing nutrition but speeding up cooking time.

Bulgur Commonly used in pilafs and salads, bulgur is wheat kernels that have been steamed, dried and crushed.

Hominy A type of corn that has been dried and hulled, hominy is available ground as grits, canned or finely ground for masa harina, the principal ingredient of corn tortillas and tamales.

Quinoa (*KEEN-wah*) Mild flavored and light textured, quinoa is a good source of protein. The Incas used the grain extensively; modern shoppers can find it in larger supermarkets and health food stores. It tends to be pricier than most other grains.

Wild rice Harvested primarily in Minnesota and California, "wild rice" is a misnomer because the grain is actually a kind of grass. It costs more than ordinary rice, but can be blended with other rices and even a little bit will impart nutty flavor to a dish.

Creole-Style Beans and Rice

PREP TIME: 20 MINUTES
(READY IN 40 MINUTES)

2 teaspoons oil

1 cup chopped celery

1 medium onion, chopped

1 small red or green bell pepper, chopped

2 jalapeño chiles, seeded, finely chopped

2 (8-oz.) cans no-salt-added tomato sauce

1 (15.5-oz.) can red beans or kidney beans, drained, rinsed

1 (15-oz.) can black beans, drained, rinsed

1 (14½-oz.) can ready-to-serve vegetable broth

½ cup uncooked long-grain white rice

¼ to ½ teaspoon hot pepper sauce

1. Heat oil in large nonstick saucepan or Dutch oven over medium heat until hot. Add celery, onion, bell pepper and chiles; cook and stir 6 to 8 minutes or until tender.

2. Add all remaining ingredients; mix well. Bring to a boil. Reduce heat; cover and simmer 20 minutes or until rice is tender.

YIELD: 4 (1½-CUP) SERVINGS

Nutrition Information Per Serving
Serving Size: 1½ Cups

Calories	330	Calories from Fat	35
		% Daily Value	
Total Fat	4g		6%
Saturated	0g		0%
Cholesterol	0mg		0%
Sodium	900mg		38%
Total Carbohydrate	59g		20%
Dietary Fiber	10g		40%
Sugars	9g		
Protein	14g		
Vitamin A	20%	Vitamin C	70%
Calcium	8%	Iron	20%

Dietary Exchanges: 4 Starch, ½ Fat OR 4 Carbohydrate, ½ Fat

Eggplant and Zucchini with Pasta in a Greek Red Sauce

PREP TIME: 25 MINUTES

5 oz. (2 cups) uncooked mini lasagna noodles (mafalda)

1 small zucchini, cut into short julienne strips

1 small Japanese eggplant, cut into ½-inch cubes

⅓ cup chopped green onions

2 garlic cloves, minced

1 (14.5-oz.) can stewed tomatoes, undrained

¾ cup drained canned dark red kidney beans, rinsed

1 teaspoon dried oregano leaves

¼ teaspoon dried thyme leaves

1. Cook noodles to desired doneness as directed on package.

2. Meanwhile, spray medium nonstick skillet with nonstick cooking spray. Add zucchini, eggplant, onions and garlic; cook over medium heat for about 10 minutes or until lightly browned, stirring occasionally.

3. Add tomatoes, beans, oregano and thyme; cook until thoroughly heated. Drain noodles. Serve sauce over noodles.

YIELD: 2 SERVINGS

Nutrition Information Per Serving
Serving Size: ½ of Recipe

Calories...............................440	Calories from Fat 20	
	% Daily Value	
Total Fat 2g	...................3%	
Saturated 0g	...................0%	
Cholesterol 0mg	...................0%	
Sodium 660mg	.................28%	
Total Carbohydrate.............87g	.................29%	
Dietary Fiber 10g	.................40%	
Sugars 12g		
Protein 18g		
Vitamin A..........................30%	Vitamin C 45%	
Calcium 15%	Iron 35%	

Dietary Exchanges: 5 Starch, 2 Vegetable OR 5 Carbohydrate, 2 Vegetable

---

■ PRODUCE POINTERS

spotlight on **Eggplant**

Eggplant comes in a rainbow of colors, but flavor, texture and quality are quite similar. Any variety will work fine for most recipes. The most common eggplant in the United States is the large, bulbous-shaped dark purple variety. Chinese cooks prefer a long, narrow type that is called Japanese or Oriental in the United States. It ranges from solid purple to striped in appearance. The best eggplant selection comes during the harvest months of August and September.

- Choose plump eggplant heavy for their size and with satiny, firm skin.

- Use eggplant within a day or two of purchase. Refrigerate eggplant whole in a loosely closed plastic bag or uncovered in the crisper section. Don't cut eggplant until ready to use.

- To prepare eggplant, wash and trim both ends. Then slice, chop or stuff it. In all except large eggplant, the skin is quite thin so there's no need to peel it first.

- Eggplant tastes best when thoroughly cooked, not raw or al dente.

- One-half cup of cooked eggplant has about 20 calories.

- One pound of eggplant yields 3 to 4 cups diced. One pound uncooked eggplant yields about ½ pound cooked.

Herbed Mac 'n' Cheese

PREP TIME: 25 MINUTES

12 oz. (about 5 cups) rigatoni (pasta tubes with ridges), ziti (long tubular pasta) or large elbow macaroni

2 tablespoons all-purpose flour

1 tablespoon spicy brown mustard

1½ teaspoons dried basil leaves

¼ teaspoon garlic powder

1½ cups skim milk

6 oz. (1½ cups) shredded reduced-fat Cheddar cheese

1 tablespoon grated Parmesan cheese

1. Cook rigatoni to desired doneness as directed on package.

2. Meanwhile, in large nonstick saucepan, combine flour, mustard, basil and garlic powder. Gradually stir in milk with wire whisk. Cook and stir over medium-high heat for about 4 minutes or until bubbly and thickened. Reduce heat to low; stir in Cheddar and Parmesan cheeses until melted.

3. Drain rigatoni. Stir into cheese sauce until well mixed.

YIELD: 4 (1½-CUP) SERVINGS

Nutrition Information Per Serving
Serving Size: 1½ Cups

Calories................500	Calories from Fat..........90
	% Daily Value
Total Fat................10g	................15%
Saturated................5g	................25%
Cholesterol................35mg	................12%
Sodium................510mg	................21%
Total Carbohydrate................73g	................24%
Dietary Fiber................2g	................8%
Sugars................8g	
Protein................29g	
Vitamin A................15%	Vitamin C................0%
Calcium................50%	Iron................20%

Dietary Exchanges: 5 Starch, 1½ Medium-Fat Meat OR 5 Carbohydrate, 1½ Medium-Fat Meat

◀ Herbed Mac 'n' Cheese

Garbanzo Couscous Pilaf

PREP TIME: 25 MINUTES

1 tablespoon margarine or butter

1 small onion, halved, thinly sliced

1 (14½-oz.) can ready-to-serve vegetable broth

1 teaspoon cumin

¼ teaspoon salt

⅛ teaspoon white pepper

2 cups carrot sticks (1 × ¼ × ¼ inches)

1 small white turnip, peeled, cut into sticks (1 × ¼ × ¼ inches)

1 red bell pepper, cut into ¾-inch pieces

1 medium zucchini, cut lengthwise into quarters and sliced into 1-inch chunks

1 (15-oz.) can garbanzo beans, drained, rinsed

1⅓ cups uncooked couscous

1. Melt margarine in medium saucepan over medium heat. Add onion; cook 2 to 3 minutes or until light golden brown. Stir in broth, cumin, salt and pepper. Bring to a boil. Add carrot sticks; cover and cook over medium heat for 2 minutes.

2. Add turnip and bell pepper; cover and cook 1 minute. Stir in zucchini, beans and couscous. Reduce heat to low; cover and cook 5 to 10 minutes or until couscous is tender.

3. To serve, toss with fork to distribute vegetables. If desired, sprinkle with chopped fresh cilantro.

YIELD: 6 (1⅓-CUP) SERVINGS

Nutrition Information Per Serving
Serving Size: 1⅓ Cups

Calories................270	Calories from Fat..........35
	% Daily Value
Total Fat................4g	................6%
Saturated................1g	................5%
Cholesterol................0mg	................0%
Sodium................630mg	................26%
Total Carbohydrate................49g	................16%
Dietary Fiber................7g	................28%
Sugars................7g	
Protein................10g	
Vitamin A................250%	Vitamin C................35%
Calcium................6%	Iron................10%

Dietary Exchanges: 3 Starch, 1 Vegetable OR 3 Carbohydrate, 1 Vegetable

Garden Variety Omelet

Filling

¼ cup thinly sliced (¼ inch) onion

¼ cup chopped red bell pepper

¼ cup chopped yellow or green bell pepper

¼ cup sliced zucchini, cut into quarters

¼ cup sliced fresh mushrooms

¼ teaspoon salt

Dash pepper

Omelet

1 (8-oz.) carton (1 cup) refrigerated or frozen fat-free egg product, thawed, or 4 eggs

1 tablespoon skim milk

Toppings

1 oz. (¼ cup) shredded reduced-fat Swiss cheese

2 slices tomato

2 sprigs parsley

1. Spray 8- to 10-inch nonstick skillet with sloping sides (omelet pan) with nonstick cooking spray. Add all filling ingredients; cook over medium heat for 7 to 9 minutes or until tender, stirring occasionally. Remove mixture from skillet; cover to keep warm. Let skillet cool 1 minute; wipe clean with paper towel.

2. In small bowl, combine egg product and milk; blend well. Spray same skillet with nonstick cooking spray. Heat over medium heat until hot. Pour egg mixture into skillet. Cook without stirring, lifting edges occasionally to allow uncooked egg mixture to flow to bottom of skillet. Cook 3 to 4 minutes or until mixture is set but top is still moist.

3. Spoon cooked vegetables over half of omelet; sprinkle with half of cheese. With pancake turner, loosen edge of omelet and fold over vegetables. Sprinkle with remaining cheese. Cover; cook 1 minute. Place tomato slices on top of omelet; garnish with parsley.

YIELD: 2 SERVINGS

Nutrition Information Per Serving
Serving Size: ½ of Recipe

Calories	130	Calories from Fat	35
		% Daily Value	
Total Fat	4g		6%
Saturated	3g		15%
Cholesterol	15mg		5%
Sodium	500mg		21%
Total Carbohydrate	7g		2%
Dietary Fiber	1g		4%
Sugars	5g		
Protein	16g		
Vitamin A	30%	Vitamin C	60%
Calcium	20%	Iron	15%

Dietary Exchanges: 1 Vegetable, 2 Lean Meat

how to make a Great Omelet

Here's how to make sure your omelet is all it's cracked up to be:

- Use a skillet with sloping, rather than straight sides, to ease both cooking and sliding the finished omelet onto a plate.

- Spray the skillet with nonstick cooking spray and heat the pan before adding the egg mixture.

- After the bottom of the omelet begins to set, loosen the edges gently with a spatula to let the uncooked egg mixture from the top flow underneath to cook.

- Cover the skillet at the end of the cooking time to trap heat and allow the top of the omelet to cook through.

- Spread any filling ingredients onto the cooked omelet and fold over. Cut the omelet in half and slide each half onto a warmed plate.

Cuban-Style Stuffed Chiles

PREP TIME: 35 MINUTES

1 ⅓ cups cooked instant brown rice (cooked as directed on package, omitting margarine and salt)

8 large (5-inch) Anaheim chiles or 4 medium poblano chiles

1 (15-oz.) can black beans, drained, rinsed

⅓ cup frozen whole kernel corn, thawed*

4 green onions, sliced (½ cup)

½ cup salsa

4 oz. (1 cup) shredded colby–Monterey Jack cheese blend

1. Heat oven to 400°F. Spray large cookie sheet with nonstick cooking spray.

2. While rice is cooking, in Dutch oven, bring 2 quarts (8 cups) water to a boil. Slit each chile lengthwise on 1 side from stem to within ½ inch of tip. At stem end of slit, cut crosswise forming a T-shaped cut with stem still attached. Cook chiles in boiling water for 4 to 8 minutes or just until tender. Rinse with cold water. Remove seeds and veins with tip of knife.

3. In medium bowl, combine cooked rice, beans, corn, onions, salsa and ½ cup of the cheese; mix well. Fill each Anaheim chile with about ⅓ cup filling or each poblano chile with about ¾ cup filling. Place peppers on sprayed cookie sheet; cover with foil.

flavorful **Grains**

To impart additional flavor to vegetarian grain dishes, cook them in liquids other than water—try vegetable stock, tomato juice, apple juice or wine.

4. Bake at 400°F. for 10 to 12 minutes or until hot. Remove foil; sprinkle with remaining ½ cup cheese. Bake an additional 2 to 3 minutes or until cheese is melted.

YIELD: 4 SERVINGS

Tip: * To quickly thaw corn, place in colander or strainer; rinse with warm water until thawed. Drain well.

Nutrition Information Per Serving
Serving Size: ¼ of Recipe

Calories	370	Calories from Fat	90
		% Daily Value	
Total Fat	10g		15%
Saturated	6g		30%
Cholesterol	25mg		8%
Sodium	530mg		22%
Total Carbohydrate	52g		17%
Dietary Fiber	11g		44%
Sugars	11g		
Protein	19g		
Vitamin A	35%	Vitamin C	455%
Calcium	25%	Iron	25%

Dietary Exchanges: 3 Starch, 1 Vegetable, 1 High-Fat Meat OR 3 Carbohydrate, 1 Vegetable, 1 High-Fat Meat

Corn and Chive Omelet with Mushroom Filling

■ ■

PREP TIME: 25 MINUTES

Filling and Garnish
1 teaspoon margarine or butter

1½ cups sliced fresh mushrooms

1 tablespoon chopped fresh parsley

Omelet
1½ cups refrigerated or frozen fat-free egg product, thawed, or 6 eggs

1 (8.5-oz.) can cream-style corn

1 tablespoon chopped fresh chives

⅛ teaspoon pepper

1. Melt margarine in medium nonstick skillet or saucepan over medium heat. Add mushrooms; cook 4 to 6 minutes or until tender, stirring occasionally. Remove from heat; cover to keep warm.

2. In medium bowl, combine all omelet ingredients; mix well.

▼ Corn and Chive Omelet with Mushroom Filling

Chive *talk*

Chives, a member of the onion family, resemble hollow blades of green grass. The flavor is neutral enough that you can safely combine chives with just about any other herb.

- Snip or chop chives for a garnish or to distribute distinctive flavor throughout a dish.

- For greatest impact, use chives uncooked. Add them to warm dishes just before serving.

- Chives blend well with almost any other herb. Chop them with fresh parsley, dill or oregano for an all-purpose garnish for soups or salads.

- Blend minced chives into softened butter to make a savory spread for bread or baked potatoes.

- Onion chives (usually referred to simply as "chives") are the most common variety.

Mature chives sport edible pink-purple flower heads, which have also have an onion flavor and add a splash of color to a salad. The stalks of the flowers, however, are fibrous and tough.

- Chinese chives, a more pungent cousin, are larger and flatter than the onion chives and can range from green to yellowish. Use them in the same ways as common chives, though perhaps with a less generous hand.

- Dried chives are at best a pale imitation of the fresh variety.

- Chives are perennials and flourish in a garden even with benign neglect. In fact, they can become invasive, and you may find yourself dividing the mass and sharing clumps with anyone who will take them.

3. Spray 10- to 12-inch nonstick skillet with sloping sides (omelet pan) with nonstick cooking spray. Heat skillet over medium-high heat until hot. Reduce heat to medium; pour egg mixture into skillet. Cook about 1 minute or until mixture starts to cook around edges. Reduce heat to medium-low; cover and cook 3 minutes. Uncover; lift edges to allow uncooked egg mixture to flow to bottom of skillet. Cover; cook an additional 3 to 7 minutes or until set.
4. Spoon mushroom filling over half of omelet. Carefully fold other half of omelet over filling. Cut omelet into 3 pieces; slide each piece onto individual plate. Sprinkle with parsley.

YIELD: 3 SERVINGS

Nutrition Information Per Serving
Serving Size: 1/3 of Recipe

Calories	150	Calories from Fat	20
		% Daily Value	
Total Fat	2g		3%
Saturated	0g		0%
Cholesterol	0mg		0%
Sodium	490mg		20%
Total Carbohydrate	18g		6%
Dietary Fiber	1g		4%
Sugars	9g		
Protein	14g		
Vitamin A	15%	Vitamin C	6%
Calcium	4%	Iron	15%

Dietary Exchanges: 1 Starch, 2 Very Lean Meat OR 1 Carbohydrate, 2 Very Lean Meat

Italian Vegetarian Lasagna

PREP TIME: 25 MINUTES
(READY IN 1 HOUR 5 MINUTES)

12 uncooked lasagna noodles

½ cup dry sherry or unsweetened apple juice

1 medium onion, finely chopped

1 (8-oz.) pkg. (3 cups) sliced fresh mushrooms

2 large zucchini, coarsely grated (about 4 cups)

2 medium red or green bell peppers, chopped

2 cups chopped fresh spinach

1 teaspoon dried basil leaves

½ teaspoon dried oregano leaves

1 (15-oz.) container light ricotta cheese

1 cup nonfat cottage cheese

¼ cup grated Parmesan cheese

1 (8-oz.) can tomato sauce

4 oz. (1 cup) shredded mozzarella cheese

1. Heat oven to 425°F. Spray 13 × 9-inch (3-quart) baking dish with nonstick cooking spray. Cook lasagna noodles to desired doneness as directed on package.

lasagna *Tips*

- Drain lasagna noodles while they are still a bit more al dente than other noodles. They will soften further as they bake in the oven.

- Reserve unbroken lasagna noodles for the top of the casserole; use broken ones in lower layers.

2. Meanwhile, bring sherry to a boil in large non-stick skillet or Dutch oven over medium-high heat. Add onion; cook 3 minutes, stirring frequently. Add mushrooms, zucchini and bell peppers; cook 5 minutes, stirring occasionally. Add spinach, basil and oregano; cook 2 minutes. Remove from heat; drain well.

3. In medium bowl, combine ricotta cheese, cottage cheese and Parmesan cheese; mix well.

4. Drain lasagna noodles. Place 3 noodles in bottom of sprayed baking dish. Top with ⅓ of ricotta mixture and ⅓ of vegetable mixture. Repeat layering 2 more times. Top with remaining 3 lasagna noodles, tomato sauce and mozzarella cheese. Cover dish tightly with sprayed foil.

5. Bake at 425°F. for 25 to 30 minutes or until bubbly around edges. Remove foil; bake an additional 5 minutes or until top is light golden brown. Let stand 5 minutes before serving.

YIELD: 10 SERVINGS

Nutrition Information Per Serving
Serving Size: ¹/₁₀ of Recipe

Calories	250	Calories from Fat	60
		% Daily Value	
Total Fat	7g		11%
Saturated	4g		20%
Cholesterol	20mg		7%
Sodium	400mg		17%
Total Carbohydrate	29g		10%
Dietary Fiber	3g		12%
Sugars	6g		
Protein	17g		
Vitamin A	45%	Vitamin C	50%
Calcium	30%	Iron	15%

Dietary Exchanges: 1½ Starch, 1 Vegetable, 2 Lean Meat OR
1½ Carbohydrate, 1 Vegetable, 2 Lean Meat

Spinach Rice Pie

PREP TIME: 10 MINUTES
(READY IN 45 MINUTES)

1½ cups skim milk

1 (9-oz.) pkg. frozen spinach in a pouch, thawed, squeezed to drain*

1 cup uncooked instant white or brown rice

2 oz. (½ cup) shredded Swiss cheese

2 tablespoons finely chopped onion

1 teaspoon salt

¼ teaspoon nutmeg

1 tablespoon fresh lemon juice

2 eggs, beaten

1. Heat oven to 350°F. Spray 9-inch pie pan with nonstick cooking spray. In large saucepan, heat milk until very hot but not boiling. Add all remaining ingredients; mix well. Pour into sprayed pan.

2. Bake at 350°F. for 25 to 35 minutes or until knife inserted in center comes out clean.

YIELD: 6 SERVINGS

Tip: * To quickly thaw spinach, cut small slit in center of pouch; microwave on HIGH for 2 to 3 minutes or until thawed. Remove spinach from pouch; squeeze dry with paper towels.

Nutrition Information Per Serving
Serving Size: ⅙ of Recipe

Calories	170	Calories from Fat	50
		% Daily Value	
Total Fat	6g		9%
Saturated	3g		15%
Cholesterol	85mg		28%
Sodium	530mg		22%
Total Carbohydrate	19g		6%
Dietary Fiber	1g		4%
Sugars	4g		
Protein	9g		
Vitamin A	35%	Vitamin C	15%
Calcium	20%	Iron	8%

Dietary Exchanges: 1 Starch, 1 Vegetable, 1 Medium-Fat Meat OR 1 Carbohydrate, 1 Vegetable, 1 Medium-Fat Meat

Teriyaki Tofu and Onions

PREP TIME: 20 MINUTES
(READY IN 35 MINUTES)

¼ cup lite teriyaki sauce

3 tablespoons water

4 teaspoons soy sauce

1 (10.5-oz.) pkg. extra-firm lite tofu*

⅓ cup ready-to-serve vegetable broth

2 cups sliced fresh mushrooms

½ large red onion, thinly sliced

1. In 12 × 8-inch (2-quart) baking dish, combine 2 tablespoons of the teriyaki sauce, water and soy sauce; mix well. Cut tofu into 8 slices, ¼ to ½ inch thick. Place tofu in dish; turn to coat with sauce mixture. Let stand at room temperature for 15 minutes to marinate, turning occasionally.

2. Heat oven to 375°F. Cover dish loosely with foil. Bake at 375°F. for 10 to 15 minutes or until thoroughly heated.

3. Meanwhile, combine remaining 2 tablespoons teriyaki sauce and broth in large nonstick skillet. Add mushrooms and onion; cook over medium heat for 8 to 10 minutes or until vegetables are tender. Serve mushroom mixture over tofu.

YIELD: 4 SERVINGS

Tip: * Lite tofu can be purchased at health food stores or some large supermarkets.

Nutrition Information Per Serving
Serving Size: ¼ of Recipe

Calories	70	Calories from Fat	10
		% Daily Value	
Total Fat	1g		2%
Saturated	0g		0%
Cholesterol	0mg		0%
Sodium	830mg		35%
Total Carbohydrate	8g		3%
Dietary Fiber	2g		8%
Sugars	5g		
Protein	7g		
Vitamin A	0%	Vitamin C	2%
Calcium	2%	Iron	8%

Dietary Exchanges: ½ Starch, 1 Very Lean Meat OR ½ Carbohydrate, 1 Very Lean Meat

what is Tofu, Anyway?

A staple in Asian cuisines, tofu has caught on in the American market in the last twenty years or so. It's a white or off-white protein-packed meat alternative made from soybeans, with a bland, very neutral flavor that takes on the character of whatever it's mixed with. It's an ideal low-fat extender for meat and meatless main dishes and salads: Three ounces of light tofu have just 1 gram of fat, while three ounces of 80% lean ground beef weigh in with about 11 grams of fat.

In a process similar to the way that dairy milk becomes cheese, tofu is made from soy milk curds that are pressed into a wooden container to set until they become a soft but cohesive block.

Tofu falls into two main categories. Soft (silken) tofu has an almost creamy texture and works well in desserts, dips and dressings. Firm and extra-firm tofu holds its shape and can be diced, sliced or broken into pieces for stir-fries, soups and pasta dishes. Try cubing and adding it to "stretch" egg or chicken salad, or blend it with sprouts, chopped tomato and onion for a high-protein, low-fat sandwich filling.

Tofu is sold in Asian markets and is also readily available in the refrigerated section of most supermarkets, with packages dated for freshness. At home, store tofu in the refrigerator; cover it with fresh water daily once opened. It should retain its mild fresh flavor for more than a week; if it becomes tangy or sour, you've kept it too long and should discard it.

Tofu-Vegetable Frittata

PREP TIME: 30 MINUTES

1½ cups sliced fresh mushrooms

½ cup shredded carrot

1 garlic clove, minced

1 tablespoon water

¾ cup refrigerated or frozen fat-free egg product, thawed, or 3 eggs

½ (10.5-oz.) pkg. firm lite tofu, squeezed dry*

½ cup nonfat sour cream

1 teaspoon dried Italian seasoning

1 oz. (¼ cup) shredded reduced-fat Cheddar cheese

1 teaspoon finely chopped fresh parsley or ½ teaspoon dried parsley flakes, if desired

1. Spray 9- to 10-inch nonstick skillet with nonstick cooking spray. Heat over medium heat until hot. Add mushrooms, carrot, garlic and water; cover and cook 3 to 5 minutes or until mushrooms soften, stirring occasionally.

2. In blender container or food processor bowl with metal blade, combine egg product, tofu and sour cream; blend until smooth. Add Italian seasoning; blend with on-off pulses just until mixed. Pour over vegetables. Reduce heat to low; cover and cook 12 to 15 minutes or until eggs are set.

3. Sprinkle with cheese and parsley; cook an additional 1 to 2 minutes or until cheese is melted. Cut into wedges to serve.

YIELD: 4 SERVINGS

Tip: * Lite tofu can be purchased at health food stores or some large supermarkets.

Sweet-and-Sour Tofu

■ ■ ■ ■ ■ ■ ■ ■ ■ ■ ■ ■ ■ ■ ■ ■ ■ ■ ■

PREP TIME: 25 MINUTES

4 cups hot cooked instant rice (cooked as directed on package, omitting margarine and salt)

½ (10.5-oz.) pkg. firm lite tofu*

1 teaspoon cornstarch

1 medium green bell pepper, cut into squares

½ large onion, cut into 8 wedges

1 (8-oz.) can pineapple chunks in unsweetened juice, undrained

1 (9-oz.) jar sweet-and-sour sauce

1. While rice is cooking, cut tofu into small bite-sized cubes; toss with cornstarch. Spray large non-stick skillet with nonstick cooking spray. Heat over medium-high heat until hot. Add tofu; cook 5 to 8 minutes or until golden brown, stirring frequently. Place tofu on plate.

2. Add bell pepper, onion and pineapple (with juice) to same skillet. Bring to a boil. Reduce heat; simmer 7 to 10 minutes or until onion is tender and liquid has been reduced.

3. Add cooked tofu and sweet-and-sour sauce; stir gently to mix. Cover; cook 1 minute or until bubbly and thickened. Serve over rice.

YIELD: 4 SERVINGS

Tip: * Lite tofu can be purchased in health food stores or some large supermarkets.

vegetarianism
Defined

▪ ▪ ▪ ▪ ▪ ▪ ▪ ▪ ▪ ▪ ▪ ▪ ▪ ▪ ▪ ▪ ▪ ▪ ▪

Vegetarians dine mainly on grains, vegetables, nuts, seeds and fruits. Yet vegetarianism is not confined to a single eating pattern.

Vegans Strict vegetarians. They avoid meat, poultry, seafood, eggs, dairy products and other foods containing animal products, such as honey and lard.

Lacto-vegetarians Eat dairy products but not meat, poultry, seafood or eggs.

Lacto-ovo vegetarians Exclude only meat, poultry and seafood, and include eggs and dairy products. This is the most popular form of vegetarianism among Americans.

Spicy Tofu, Cheese and Green Chile Enchiladas

PREP TIME: 30 MINUTES

1 (10.5-oz.) pkg. extra-firm lite tofu, cut into small cubes*

2 oz. (½ cup) shredded mozzarella cheese

1 (4.5-oz.) can chopped green chiles

¼ cup taco sauce

6 (7- or 8-inch) flour tortillas

1 (10-oz.) can enchilada sauce

1 to 2 tablespoons sliced ripe olives, if desired

▼ Spicy Tofu, Cheese and Green Chile Enchiladas

1. Heat oven to 425°F. Spray 13 × 9-inch (3-quart) baking dish with nonstick cooking spray. In medium bowl, combine tofu, cheese, chiles and taco sauce; mash and mix until well combined. Spoon mixture evenly onto tortillas; roll up. Place seam side down in sprayed baking dish. Top with enchilada sauce.

2. Bake at 425°F. for 15 to 20 minutes or until bubbly and lightly browned. Sprinkle with olives.

YIELD: 6 SERVINGS

Tip: * Lite tofu can be purchased at health food stores or some large supermarkets.

Nutrition Information Per Serving
Serving Size: ⅙ of Recipe

Calories	200	Calories from Fat	50
		% Daily Value	
Total Fat	6g		9%
Saturated	2g		10%
Cholesterol	5mg		2%
Sodium	810mg		34%
Total Carbohydrate	26g		9%
Dietary Fiber	2g		8%
Sugars	3g		
Protein	10g		
Vitamin A	6%	Vitamin C	15%
Calcium	15%	Iron	15%

Dietary Exchanges: 1½ Starch, 1 Medium-Fat Meat OR
1½ Carbohydrate, 1 Medium-Fat Meat

California White Pizza

PREP TIME: 25 MINUTES

1 whole bulb garlic

½ cup nonfat sour cream

⅓ cup crumbled feta cheese

1 teaspoon olive oil

1 large sweet onion, halved, sliced (about 2 cups)

1 (10-oz.) prebaked thin-crust Italian bread shell

1 (9-oz.) pkg. frozen artichoke hearts, thawed, chopped*

4 oz. (1 cup) shredded mozzarella cheese

2 oz. (½ cup) finely shredded Asiago or Parmesan cheese

1. Heat oven to 425°F. Place garlic bulb in small microwave-safe bowl; cover with microwave-safe waxed paper. Microwave on HIGH for 1 to 2 minutes or until very soft. Break garlic cloves apart; set aside to cool slightly.

2. Press garlic cloves lightly to squeeze out soft garlic into small bowl; mash with fork. Add sour cream; mix well. Gently stir in feta cheese.

3. Heat oil in medium nonstick skillet over high heat until hot. Add onion; cook and stir until onion begins to brown, adding 1 tablespoon water if necessary to prevent scorching.

4. Place bread shell on ungreased cookie sheet. Bake at 425°F. for 2 minutes. Remove bread shell from oven; spread with garlic mixture. Top with artichokes, onion and shredded cheeses. Return to oven; bake an additional 10 minutes or until cheese is melted.

YIELD: 6 SERVINGS

Tip: * To quickly thaw artichoke hearts, place in colander or strainer; rinse with warm water until thawed. Drain well.

Nutrition Information Per Serving
Serving Size: ⅙ of Recipe

Calories	310	Calories from Fat	100
		% Daily Value	
Total Fat	11g		17%
Saturated	6g		30%
Cholesterol	25mg		8%
Sodium	640mg		27%
Total Carbohydrate	33g		11%
Dietary Fiber	3g		12%
Sugars	6g		
Protein	19g		
Vitamin A	8%	Vitamin C	8%
Calcium	40%	Iron	10%

Dietary Exchanges: 2 Starch, 2 Medium-Fat Meat OR 2 Carbohydrate, 2 Medium-Fat Meat

Fresh Vegetable Pizza Wedges

■ ■

PREP TIME: 35 MINUTES

Filling
¾ cup low-fat cottage cheese

4 oz. ⅓-less-fat cream cheese (Neufchâtel)

1 teaspoon dried dill weed

⅛ teaspoon garlic powder

Vegetables
1 medium tomato, chopped

1 cup chopped fresh broccoli florets

¼ cup sliced green onions

½ cup chopped yellow summer squash

½ cup chopped carrot

Crust
1 (10-oz.) can refrigerated pizza crust

1. Heat oven to 425°F. Spray 12-inch pizza pan with nonstick cooking spray. Unroll dough; place in sprayed pan. Starting at center, press out dough with hands, forming ½-inch rim. Prick dough generously with fork.

2. Bake at 425°F. for 12 to 14 minutes or until golden brown. Place in refrigerator or freezer to cool while preparing filling and vegetables.

3. In blender container or food processor bowl with metal blade, combine all filling ingredients; blend or process until smooth. Spread over cooled crust.

4. Sprinkle tomato on filling along edge of crust. Continue forming rings of vegetables using broccoli, onions, squash and carrot, covering all of filling. To serve, cut into wedges.

YIELD: 6 SERVINGS

Nutrition Information Per Serving
Serving Size: ⅙ of Recipe

Calories	210	Calories from Fat	45
		% Daily Value	
Total Fat	5g		8%
Saturated	3g		15%
Cholesterol	10mg		3%
Sodium	470mg		20%
Total Carbohydrate	28g		9%
Dietary Fiber	2g		8%
Sugars	5g		
Protein	11g		
Vitamin A	70%	Vitamin C	25%
Calcium	6%	Iron	10%

Dietary Exchanges: 1½ Starch, 1 Vegetable, 1 Very Lean Meat, 1 Fat OR 1½ Carbohydrate, 1 Vegetable, 1 Very Lean Meat, 1 Fat

Asparagus Veggie Melts

PREP TIME: 20 MINUTES

6 oz. fresh asparagus spears

¼ cup water

2 tablespoons fat-free mayonnaise or salad dressing

½ teaspoon Dijon mustard or brown mustard

¼ teaspoon dried dill weed

½ (16-inch) or 1 (8-inch) loaf French bread, split lengthwise

1 cup sliced fresh mushrooms

½ small red bell pepper, cut into thin rings

2 (1½-oz.) slices reduced-fat mozzarella cheese

1. Break or cut off tough ends of asparagus. In 12 × 8-inch (2-quart) microwave-safe dish, arrange spears with tips in center. Add water; cover with microwave-safe plastic wrap. Microwave on HIGH for 3 to 4 minutes or until asparagus is crisp-tender.*

2. Meanwhile, in small bowl, combine mayonnaise, mustard and dill; mix well. Spread mayonnaise mixture evenly over cut side of each half of bread. Top each sandwich with mushrooms, cooked asparagus and bell pepper rings. Cut cheese into 1-inch-wide strips; arrange over peppers. Place on ungreased broiler pan or cookie sheet.

3. Broil 4 to 6 inches from heat for 1 to 2 minutes or until cheese is melted.

YIELD: 2 SANDWICHES

▼ Asparagus Veggie Melts

Tip: * To cook asparagus in steamer basket, arrange spears in basket in skillet; add water. Cover; steam 3 to 5 minutes or until crisp-tender. Remove from steamer; continue as directed above.

Nutrition Information Per Serving
Serving Size: 1 Sandwich

Calories................................290	Calories from Fat 80	
		% Daily Value
Total Fat 9g	.......................14%	
Saturated 5g	.......................25%	
Cholesterol 25mg	........................8%	
Sodium 740mg	.......................31%	
Total Carbohydrate 34g	.......................11%	
Dietary Fiber 4g	.......................16%	
Sugars 5g		
Protein 18g		
Vitamin A...........................25%	Vitamin C 40%	
Calcium 35%	Iron 15%	

Dietary Exchanges: 2 Starch, 1 Vegetable, 1½ Medium-Fat Meat OR 2 Carbohydrate, 1 Vegetable, 1½ Medium-Fat Meat

Eggsceptional Potato Squares

■ ■

PREP TIME: 35 MINUTES
(READY IN 1 HOUR 5 MINUTES)

1 tablespoon butter or margarine

1 garlic clove, minced

2½ cups frozen southern-style hash-brown potatoes

2 tablespoons chopped green onions

2 tablespoons chopped red or green bell pepper

¼ teaspoon salt

⅛ teaspoon pepper

6 eggs

¼ cup skim milk

2 tablespoons grated Parmesan cheese

⅛ teaspoon dry mustard

1. In large nonstick skillet over low heat, combine butter and garlic; heat until butter is melted. Add potatoes, onions, bell pepper, salt and pepper; cook 5 minutes, stirring occasionally.

2. Gently pat potato mixture into single layer. Cover; cook over low heat for 10 minutes.

3. Meanwhile, heat oven to 350°F. Spray 12 × 8-inch (2-quart) baking dish with nonstick cooking spray. Remove skillet from heat. Spoon potatoes into sprayed dish, spreading evenly.*

4. In blender container or in bowl with electric mixer, combine eggs and all remaining ingredients; blend at high speed until well mixed and slightly frothy. Pour over potato mixture.

5. Bake at 350°F. for 20 to 30 minutes or until knife inserted in center comes out clean. To serve, cut into squares. If desired, garnish with green onions or bell pepper curls.

YIELD: 6 SERVINGS

Tip: * Recipe can be prepared to this point, cooled slightly, covered with foil and refrigerated for up to 1 day. To bake, uncover dish and continue as directed above.

Nutrition Information Per Serving
Serving Size: ⅙ of Recipe

Calories................................180	Calories from Fat 70	
		% Daily Value
Total Fat 8g	.......................12%	
Saturated 3g	.......................15%	
Cholesterol 220mg	.......................73%	
Sodium 240mg	.......................10%	
Total Carbohydrate 17g	........................6%	
Dietary Fiber 2g	........................8%	
Sugars 2g		
Protein 9g		
Vitamin A...........................15%	Vitamin C 15%	
Calcium 8%	Iron 10%	

Dietary Exchanges: 1 Starch, 1 Medium-Fat Meat, ½ Fat OR 1 Carbohydrate, 1 Medium-Fat Meat, ½ Fat

Zucchini *tips*

- Smaller is better when it comes to zucchini. The ideal zucchini is 1 to 2 inches in diameter and 4 to 6 inches long.

- Look for zucchini with a firm texture and glossy, bright color. If you plan to stuff zucchini, choose ones that are a little bigger, with a firm rind. Any zucchini that feels limp has lost flavor and texture.

- In addition to green zucchini, you may find yellow, green-striped or even round varieties of these summer squashes. They can be used interchangeably.

- Refrigerate zucchini unwashed in the crisper drawer or in vented plastic vegetable bags and plan to use it as soon as possible (preferably within a day or so). Wash it just before using. There's no need to peel zucchini.

Light Zucchini Bake

PREP TIME: 25 MINUTES
(READY IN 1 HOUR 10 MINUTES)

Nonstick cooking spray

1 cup chopped peeled zucchini

1 (8-oz.) carton (1 cup) refrigerated or frozen fat-free egg product, thawed, or 4 eggs

2 tablespoons margarine or butter, melted

½ teaspoon dried parsley flakes

¼ teaspoon salt

⅛ teaspoon pepper

½ cup grated Parmesan cheese

3 cups diced unpeeled zucchini

1 small onion, finely chopped

1 cup reduced-fat baking mix

1. Heat oven to 350°F. Spray 13 × 9-inch (3-quart) baking dish with nonstick cooking spray. In food processor bowl with metal blade, puree zucchini to make ½ cup.

2. In medium bowl, combine pureed zucchini, egg product, margarine, parsley, salt, pepper and 6 tablespoons of the Parmesan cheese; blend well. Stir in diced zucchini and onion. Add baking mix; mix well. Pour into sprayed baking dish. Sprinkle with remaining 2 tablespoons Parmesan cheese. Spray cheese with nonstick cooking spray to lightly coat top.

3. Bake at 350°F. for 35 to 45 minutes or until casserole is golden brown and toothpick inserted in center comes out clean.

YIELD: 8 SERVINGS

Nutrition Information Per Serving
Serving Size: ⅛ of Recipe

Calories	140	Calories from Fat	50
		% Daily Value	
Total Fat	6g		9%
Saturated	2g		10%
Cholesterol	5mg		2%
Sodium	440mg		18%
Total Carbohydrate	14g		5%
Dietary Fiber	1g		4%
Sugars	3g		
Protein	7g		
Vitamin A	10%	Vitamin C	8%
Calcium	10%	Iron	8%

Dietary Exchanges: ½ Starch, 1 Vegetable, 1 Very Lean Meat, 1 Fat OR ½ Carbohydrate, 1 Vegetable, 1 Very Lean Meat, 1 Fat

Spinach and Cabbage Frittata

■ ■ ■ ■ ■ ■ ■ ■ ■ ■ ■ ■ ■ ■ ■ ■ ■ ■

PREP TIME: 20 MINUTES
(READY IN 35 MINUTES)

1 teaspoon oil

2 cups finely shredded cabbage

1 medium onion, thinly sliced

1 teaspoon dried oregano leaves

½ cup refrigerated or frozen fat-free egg product, thawed, or 2 eggs

½ cup skim milk

2 oz. (½ cup) shredded reduced-fat Cheddar cheese

¼ teaspoon salt

½ cup all-purpose or whole wheat flour

1 (9-oz.) pkg. frozen spinach in a pouch, thawed, squeezed to drain*

1. Heat oven to 450°F. Heat oil in large nonstick skillet over medium-high heat until hot. Stir in cabbage, onion and oregano. Reduce heat to medium; cook and stir about 7 minutes or until vegetables soften.

2. In large bowl, combine egg product, milk, cheese and salt; mix well. Add flour; stir until well blended. Stir in spinach and cooked cabbage mixture. Pour into ungreased ovenproof 9-inch nonstick skillet or 9-inch round nonstick cake pan.

3. Bake at 450°F. for 13 to 15 minutes or until puffed and golden brown. If desired, serve with warm spaghetti sauce.

YIELD: 4 SERVINGS

Tip: * To quickly thaw spinach, cut small slit in center of pouch; microwave on HIGH for 2 to 3 minutes or until thawed. Remove spinach from pouch; squeeze dry with paper towels.

Nutrition Information Per Serving
Serving Size: ¼ of Recipe

Calories	180	Calories from Fat	45
		% Daily Value	
Total Fat	5g		8%
Saturated	2g		10%
Cholesterol	10mg		3%
Sodium	350mg		15%
Total Carbohydrate	21g		7%
Dietary Fiber	4g		16%
Sugars	4g		
Protein	12g		
Vitamin A	110%	Vitamin C	35%
Calcium	25%	Iron	15%

Dietary Exchanges: 1 Starch, 1 Vegetable, 1 Medium-Fat Meat OR
1 Carbohydrate, 1 Vegetable, 1 Medium-Fat Meat

▼ Spinach and Cabbage Frittata

Polenta Wedges with Spaghetti Sauce

PREP TIME: 40 MINUTES

Polenta

1 cup yellow cornmeal

1 cup water

1 (14½-oz.) can ready-to-serve chicken broth

⅓ cup grated Parmesan cheese

¼ cup chopped fresh parsley

1 (2-oz.) jar diced pimientos, drained

Sauce

¾ cup spaghetti sauce

2 teaspoons olive oil

1. Line cookie sheet with foil. In medium nonstick saucepan, combine cornmeal and water; beat with wire whisk until well blended. Add broth; bring to a boil over medium-high heat. Cook 10 to 15 minutes, stirring constantly with wire whisk, until mixture is very thick and begins to pull away from sides of pan while stirring.

2. Remove saucepan from heat. Reserve 1 tablespoon of the Parmesan cheese for topping; stir remaining Parmesan cheese, parsley and pimientos into cornmeal mixture until well mixed. Spread evenly in ungreased 9-inch round cake pan. Cover; refrigerate 10 minutes or until set.

3. Meanwhile, heat spaghetti sauce in small saucepan; cover to keep warm.

4. Turn polenta out onto foil-lined cookie sheet, tapping bottom of pan to release. Cut into 6 wedges; separate slightly. Brush tops with oil; sprinkle with

reserved tablespoon of Parmesan cheese.

5. Broil 4 to 6 inches from heat for 3 to 5 minutes or until thoroughly heated. To serve, spoon spaghetti sauce over polenta wedges.

YIELD: 6 SERVINGS

Nutrition Information Per Serving
Serving Size: ⅙ of Recipe

Calories...............160		Calories from Fat...........50
		% Daily Value
Total Fat 6g		.........9%
Saturated 2g		........10%
Cholesterol 4mg		.........1%
Sodium 480mg		........20%
Total Carbohydrate......21g		.........7%
Dietary Fiber 3g		........12%
Sugars 2g		
Protein 6g		
Vitamin A......15%		Vitamin C 15%
Calcium 10%		Iron 8%

Dietary Exchanges: 1½ Starch, 1 Fat OR 1½ Carbohydrate, 1 Fat

French Bread Pizza with Beans and Chunky Vegetables

PREP TIME: 30 MINUTES

Crust
4 (5-inch-long) pieces French bread

Topping
2 cups reduced-fat, reduced-sodium chunky vegetable spaghetti sauce

1 (15.5-oz.) can pinto or pink beans, drained, rinsed

½ small red onion, halved, thinly sliced

⅛ teaspoon garlic powder

¼ teaspoon pepper

8 oz. (2 cups) shredded reduced-fat mozzarella cheese

6 fresh basil leaves, chopped, or ½ teaspoon dried basil leaves, if desired

1. Heat oven to 425°F. Line large cookie sheet with foil; spray with nonstick cooking spray.

2. Cut each bread piece in half horizontally. Hollow out center of each to form ¾-inch-thick shell; discard bread crumbs or save for another use. If necessary,

about **Polenta**

Made from cornmeal, polenta is a northern Italian preparation that can resemble either cornmeal mush or a very simple dense cornbread.

cut thin slice off rounded bottom of each piece so it will sit firmly while baking. Place, hollowed side up, on sprayed foil-lined cookie sheet. Set aside.

3. In large bowl, combine spaghetti sauce, beans, onion, garlic powder and pepper; mix well. Spoon mixture evenly into bread shells, spreading almost to edges. Sprinkle each with cheese and basil.

4. Bake at 425°F. for 15 minutes or until cheese is melted and filling is hot.

YIELD: 8 SANDWICHES

Nutrition Information Per Serving
Serving Size: 1 Sandwich

Calories	280	Calories from Fat	50
		% Daily Value	
Total Fat	6g		9%
Saturated	4g		20%
Cholesterol	10mg		3%
Sodium	820mg		34%
Total Carbohydrate	42g		14%
Dietary Fiber	3g		12%
Sugars	6g		
Protein	15g		
Vitamin A	15%	Vitamin C	8%
Calcium	25%	Iron	15%

Dietary Exchanges: 3 Starch, 1 Lean Meat OR 3 Carbohydrate, 1 Lean Meat

Bean Burgers with Oregano–Sour Cream Sauce

PREP TIME: 25 MINUTES

½ **cup nonfat sour cream**

2 tablespoons chopped green onions

¼ **teaspoon dried oregano leaves**

⅛ **teaspoon salt**

1 (15.5-oz.) can kidney beans, drained, rinsed

3 tablespoons unseasoned bread crumbs

¼ **teaspoon garlic powder**

Dash ground red pepper (cayenne)

Dash pepper

1 egg, beaten

1 teaspoon margarine or butter

4 burger buns, split

capital Grains

Grain has become a dietary buzzword, as if it were a recent discovery. Truth is, grains have been culinary staples since ancient times. What is new is the realization that grains contribute significant nutritional impact to daily meals and are not simply a filler to bulk up recipes or stretch more expensive ingredients. Best of all, there's the wonderful range of flavor nuances, some bordering almost on nutty—an ideal take-off point for any number of meatless main dishes.

1. In small bowl, combine sour cream, onions, oregano and salt; mix well. Refrigerate until serving time.

2. In medium bowl with fork or in food processor bowl with metal blade, mash beans well. Add bread crumbs, garlic powder, ground red pepper, pepper and egg; mix well. Mixture will be soft. With wet hands, shape mixture into 4 patties, ½ inch thick.

3. Melt margarine in medium nonstick skillet over medium heat. Cook bean patties 5 minutes. Turn and flatten slightly; cook an additional 5 minutes or until thoroughly heated and set. Serve in buns with sour cream sauce.

YIELD: 4 SANDWICHES

Nutrition Information Per Serving
Serving Size: 1 Sandwich

Calories	270	Calories from Fat	45
		% Daily Value	
Total Fat	5g		9%
Saturated	1g		5%
Cholesterol	55mg		18%
Sodium	560mg		23%
Total Carbohydrate	43g		14%
Dietary Fiber	5g		20%
Sugars	8g		
Protein	13g		
Vitamin A	8%	Vitamin C	0%
Calcium	15%	Iron	15%

Dietary Exchanges: 3 Starch, ½ Lean Meat OR 3 Carbohydrate, ½ Lean Meat

Swiss Apple Bagelwiches

PREP TIME: 20 MINUTES

- **2 oz. ⅓-less-fat cream cheese (Neufchâtel), softened**

- **1 teaspoon Dijon mustard**

- **1 teaspoon chopped fresh chives or ½ teaspoon freeze-dried chopped chives**

- **2 whole wheat or pumpernickel bagels, split, toasted**

- **1 apple**

- **2 (7 × 3½-inch) slices wafer-thin low-sodium, reduced-fat Swiss cheese, each cut in half**

1. Heat oven to 350°F. In small bowl, combine cream cheese, mustard and chives; blend well. Spread on cut sides of bagels. Place on ungreased cookie sheet.

2. Core apple; cut into ½-inch-thick rings. Place 1 apple ring on each bagel half; top each with piece of cheese.

3. Bake at 350°F. for 5 to 6 minutes or until cheese is melted and sandwiches are warm.

YIELD: 4 SANDWICHES

Nutrition Information Per Serving
Serving Size: 1 Sandwich

Calories	210	Calories from Fat	60
		% Daily Value	
Total Fat	7g		11%
Saturated	4g		20%
Cholesterol	20mg		7%
Sodium	310mg		13%
Total Carbohydrate	26g		9%
Dietary Fiber	3g		12%
Sugars	5g		
Protein	10g		
Vitamin A	6%	Vitamin C	2%
Calcium	15%	Iron	8%

Dietary Exchanges: 2 Starch, ½ Lean Meat, ½ Fat OR 2 Carbohydrate, ½ Lean Meat, ½ Fat

Grilled Cheese and Vegetable Sandwiches

PREP TIME: 35 MINUTES

- **Olive oil nonstick cooking spray**

- **8 thin slices zucchini (¼ cup)**

- **½ small onion, thinly sliced**

- **¼ medium red bell pepper, thinly sliced**

- **¼ teaspoon dried basil leaves**

- **¾ teaspoon rice vinegar**

- **4 (½-inch-thick) slices sourdough bread**

- **2 oz. reduced-fat sharp Cheddar cheese, cut into 4 slices**

- **4 thin slices tomato**

1. Spray medium nonstick skillet with nonstick cooking spray. Add zucchini, onion and bell pepper; cook over medium-high heat for 2 to 3 minutes or until vegetables begin to soften. Remove skillet from heat. Add basil and vinegar; toss gently.

2. Spray 1 side of each slice of bread with cooking spray. Turn 2 bread slices over; top each with 1 cheese slice, 2 tomato slices, half of the cooked vegetables and a second cheese slice. Top each with second slice of bread, sprayed side up.

3. Cook sandwiches in same nonstick skillet over medium heat for 3 to 4 minutes on each side or until bread is golden brown and cheese is melted, covering skillet loosely during last half of cooking time.

YIELD: 2 SANDWICHES

Nutrition Information Per Serving
Serving Size: 1 Sandwich

Calories	260	Calories from Fat	80
		% Daily Value	
Total Fat	9g		14%
Saturated	4g		20%
Cholesterol	20mg		7%
Sodium	530mg		22%
Total Carbohydrate	30g		10%
Dietary Fiber	2g		8%
Sugars	4g		
Protein	14g		
Vitamin A	20%	Vitamin C	25%
Calcium	30%	Iron	8%

Dietary Exchanges: 2 Starch, 1 Medium-Fat Meat, ½ Fat OR 2 Carbohydrate, 1 Medium-Fat Meat, ½ Fat

Side Dishes

9

Pearl Onion, Carrot and Zucchini Sauté (page 280)

Caribbean Rice and Beans

■ ■

PREP TIME: 20 MINUTES

2 cups flaked coconut

2 cups water

2 green onions, thinly sliced

1 garlic clove, minced

½ to 1 teaspoon dried thyme leaves

½ teaspoon salt

½ teaspoon sugar

2 cups uncooked instant rice

1 (15.5-oz.) can kidney beans, drained, rinsed

1. In medium saucepan, combine coconut and water. Bring to a boil; boil 1 minute. Place strainer over 2-cup measuring cup. Pour coconut mixture into strainer; press out all liquid. Measure liquid and add water to make 2 cups. Discard coconut.

2. Return coconut liquid to same saucepan. Stir in onions, garlic, thyme, salt and sugar. Bring to a boil. Add rice; cook 1 to 2 minutes or until liquid is absorbed.

3. Add beans; cook until thoroughly heated.

YIELD: 8 (¾-CUP) SERVINGS

Nutrition Information Per Serving
Serving Size: ¾ Cup

Calories	220	Calories from Fat	50
		% Daily Value	
Total Fat	6g		9%
Saturated	5g		25%
Cholesterol	0mg		0%
Sodium	250mg		10%
Total Carbohydrate	36g		12%
Dietary Fiber	3g		12%
Sugars	7g		
Protein	5g		
Vitamin A	0%	Vitamin C	0%
Calcium	4%	Iron	10%

Dietary Exchanges: 2½ Starch, 1 Fat OR 2½ Carbohydrate, 1 Fat

Wild Rice with Apples

■ ■

PREP TIME: 30 MINUTES

2 teaspoons olive oil

3 shallots, minced

3 garlic cloves, minced

2¼ cups uncooked instant wild rice*

2¼ cups ready-to-serve fat-free chicken broth with ⅓ less sodium

1½ cups chopped unpeeled red apple

⅛ teaspoon pepper

3 tablespoons chopped fresh parsley

1. Heat oil in large nonstick saucepan over medium heat until hot. Add shallot and garlic; cook about 1 minute, stirring constantly. Stir in rice, broth, apple and pepper. Bring to a boil. Reduce heat to low; cover and cook 10 to 15 minutes or until rice is tender.

2. Remove saucepan from heat; let stand 5 minutes. Drain and discard any excess liquid. Stir in parsley.

YIELD: 6 (¾-CUP) SERVINGS

Tip: * If instant wild rice is unavailable, 2¼ cups uncooked instant brown rice can be used.

Nutrition Information Per Serving
Serving Size: ¾ Cup

Calories	270	Calories from Fat	20
		% Daily Value	
Total Fat	2g		3%
Saturated	0g		0%
Cholesterol	0mg		0%
Sodium	220mg		9%
Total Carbohydrate	52g		17%
Dietary Fiber	5g		20%
Sugars	6g		
Protein	10g		
Vitamin A	20%	Vitamin C	6%
Calcium	2%	Iron	8%

Dietary Exchanges: 3½ Starch OR 3½ Carbohydrate

Rice *varieties*

Thousands of rice varieties are grown throughout the world. But shopping for rice is relatively easy because just a handful of choices are widely available. Texture, flavor and even fragrance vary widely, but the rice you choose depends more on your taste preferences than the recipe.

Brown Rice

Brown rice is any rice that's still encased in its rough bran layer, which gives it a tan color. It has a slightly nutlike flavor from the endosperm. Brown rice takes 45 to 50 minutes to cook and can be used in any recipe that calls for rice. Instant brown rice has been partially cooked and then dehydrated. It takes 5 to 15 minutes to prepare, depending on the brand.

Long-Grain Rice

Long-grain rice is America's most popular rice and comes in several forms. Long-grain rice is good for pilafs and side dishes and in salads and stuffings.

- Regular enriched long-grain rice has long kernels that stay separate during the 15-minute cooking time, giving rice a fluffy texture. It's enriched after the milling process to restore lost nutrients.

- Converted, or parboiled, rice is processed to keep grains even more separate and fluffy than regular long-grain rice. Converted rice isn't enriched because processing seals in nutrients. It cooks in about 25 minutes.

- Instant rice is cooked and then dehydrated. It takes just 5 minutes to prepare.

- Basmati rice is grown in India and Pakistan and is a specialty long-grain rice with rich taste and aroma. Serve it with curry recipes for an authentic flavor. White basmati rice cooks in about 15 minutes.

Medium and Short-Grain Rices

Medium and short-grain rices are softer and stickier than long-grain rice and are good in Italian risotto and Spanish paella, as well as in rice molds and rice pudding.

Arborio rice is a short-grain rice imported from Italy. During cooking, its white ovals become creamy, soft and smooth and are delicious with various risotto seasonings. Arborio rice absorbs much liquid—usually water, wine or broth—during its 20-minute cooking.

Wild Rice

Wild rice is actually a grass that grows in marshy areas. Native to the northern lakes of Minnesota and Wisconsin, most wild rice is no longer "wild" and much of it is now grown in California. This nutty grain has a smoky taste and is excellent for salads, main dishes and pilafs. Wild rice cooks in 45 minutes to 1 hour.

Herb Vegetable Couscous

．．．．．．．．．．．．．．．．．．．．．．．．

PREP TIME: 15 MINUTES

1 cup chicken broth

⅔ cup frozen early June peas

⅛ teaspoon salt

⅛ teaspoon pepper

**1 teaspoon chopped fresh thyme or
⅓ teaspoon dried thyme leaves**

1 garlic clove, minced

¾ cup uncooked couscous

1 medium tomato, seeded, chopped

1. In medium saucepan, combine broth, peas, salt, pepper, thyme and garlic. Bring to a boil.

2. Remove saucepan from heat; stir in couscous and tomato. Cover; let stand 5 minutes. Fluff with fork before serving.

YIELD: 6 (½-CUP) SERVINGS

Nutrition Information Per Serving
Serving Size: ½ Cup

Calories 100	Calories from Fat 0
	% Daily Value
Total Fat ....0g 0%	
Saturated ....0g 0%	
Cholesterol ....0mg 0%	
Sodium ....200mg 8%	
Total Carbohydrate.............21g 7%	
Dietary Fiber ....2g 8%	
Sugars 1g	
Protein..............................5g	
Vitamin A 4%	Vitamin C 6%
Calcium 0%	Iron................................4%

Dietary Exchanges: 1½ Starch OR 1½ Carbohydrate

▼ Herb Vegetable Couscous

all about **Potatoes**

Selecting Choose firm, clean potatoes free of breaks in the skin or green spots. If green spots develop, trim just before cooking. Remove any "eyes" or sprouts just before cooking.

Storing Remove store-bought potatoes from plastic bags; trapped moisture can result in rotting. Do not wash potatoes before storing. Store potatoes at 45 to 50°F. in a dark, well-ventilated place to keep them fresh for several weeks. Light and refrigeration cause potatoes to turn green and develop a bitter flavor.

Preparing Toss peeled potatoes with a little lemon juice to prevent browning if you're not cooking them immediately. Soaking them in cold water results in nutrient loss.

Mashing Russet potatoes are the favored variety for mashed potatoes. Or try Yukon Gold potatoes for a richer, sweeter flavor and creamy yellow color.

To help potatoes hold their heat, add heated milk to mashed potatoes rather than cold milk straight from the refrigerator. Serve potatoes immediately after mashing; they don't reheat well. If potatoes must be kept warm until serving time, place them in an uncovered double boiler or in a covered casserole dish in a warm oven.

Perfect Mashed Potatoes

PREP TIME: 20 MINUTES
(READY IN 45 MINUTES)

4 medium russet potatoes (about 1½ lb.), peeled, cut into quarters

¾ teaspoon salt

1 to 2 tablespoons margarine or butter, if desired

Dash pepper

¼ to ⅓ cup hot skim milk

1. Place potatoes in large saucepan; add enough water to cover. Add ½ teaspoon of the salt. Bring to a boil. Reduce heat; cover loosely and boil gently for 15 to 20 minutes or until potatoes break apart easily when pierced with fork. Drain well.

2. Return potatoes to saucepan; shake saucepan gently over low heat for 1 to 2 minutes to evaporate any excess moisture.

3. Mash potatoes with potato masher until no lumps remain. Add margarine, pepper and remaining ¼ teaspoon salt; continue mashing, gradually adding enough milk to make potatoes smooth and creamy.

YIELD: 8 (½-CUP) SERVINGS

Nutrition Information Per Serving
Serving Size: ½ Cup

Calories	80	Calories from Fat	25
		% Daily Value	
Total Fat	3g		5%
Saturated	1g		5%
Cholesterol	0mg		0%
Sodium	180mg		8%
Total Carbohydrate	13g		4%
Dietary Fiber	1g		3%
Sugars	1g		
Protein	1g		
Vitamin A	2%	Vitamin C	8%
Calcium	0%	Iron	0%

Dietary Exchanges: 1 Starch OR 1 Carbohydrate

Italian Parmesan Potatoes

■ ■

PREP TIME: 15 MINUTES
(READY IN 1 HOUR)

3 medium russet potatoes, unpeeled, cut lengthwise into 8 wedges

2 teaspoons olive or vegetable oil

¼ teaspoon dried Italian seasoning

⅛ teaspoon salt

⅛ teaspoon garlic powder

⅛ teaspoon paprika

2 to 3 tablespoons shredded fresh Parmesan cheese

Grill Directions: 1. Heat grill. Cut 14-inch-square sheet of heavy-duty foil. Place potatoes in center. In small bowl, combine oil, Italian seasoning, salt, garlic powder and paprika. Drizzle over potatoes; stir gently to coat. Wrap securely using double-fold seals.
2. Place foil packet on gas grill over medium heat or on charcoal grill 4 to 6 inches from medium-high coals. Cook 30 to 40 minutes or until potatoes are tender.

3. Remove packet from grill; open packet. Stir gently; sprinkle with cheese. Return packet to grill; cook an additional 3 to 5 minutes or until cheese is melted.

Oven Directions: 1. Heat oven to 450°F. Prepare potatoes in foil packet as directed above; place on cookie sheet.
2. Bake at 450°F. for 40 to 50 minutes or until potatoes are tender.
3. Remove packet from oven; open packet. Stir gently; sprinkle with cheese. Return packet to oven; bake an additional 3 to 5 minutes or until cheese is melted.

YIELD: 4 SERVINGS

Nutrition Information Per Serving
Serving Size: ¼ of Recipe

Calories	230	Calories from Fat	45
		% Daily Value	
Total Fat	5g		8%
Saturated	2g		10%
Cholesterol	5mg		2%
Sodium	250mg		10%
Total Carbohydrate	39g		13%
Dietary Fiber	4g		16%
Sugars	2g		
Protein	7g		
Vitamin A	2%	Vitamin C	25%
Calcium	15%	Iron	10%

Dietary Exchanges: 2½ Starch, 1 Fat OR 2½ Carbohydrate, 1 Fat

▼ Italian Parmesan Potatoes

Sweet Potato *facts*

- Sweet potatoes and yams look and taste somewhat alike, but they're actually from unrelated botanical families. Neither is related to the white potato, either. Sweet potatoes have smooth skins, while yams are rough and scaly. Yams are rarely available in the United States (even when the produce sign says "yams"), except in specialty markets.

- Per serving, the sweet potato is the richest vegetable source of vitamin A, supplying more than twice the Recommended Daily Allowance. It's also a good source of antioxidant vitamins C and E. And it's one of the few good sources of vitamin E that's not loaded with fat. A medium sweet potato has 140 to 160 calories, no fat and little sodium.

- Sweet potatoes can be divided into two basic types: dry and moist. The dry varieties have pale skin and dry, pale yellow flesh when cooked. The moist varieties are dense textured and deep orange after cooking. These moist varieties are sometimes mistakenly called yams.

- Choose small to medium sweet potatoes that are firm and have no discolored patches. Store them in a cool, dry place (55 to 60°F.) with good air circulation. Raw sweet potatoes will spoil faster if stored in the refrigerator or a sealed plastic bag.

Maple Pecan–Glazed Sweet Potatoes

PREP TIME: 25 MINUTES

1 cup apple juice

4 teaspoons cornstarch

½ cup maple-flavored syrup

½ teaspoon cinnamon

1 tablespoon margarine or butter

⅛ teaspoon salt

2 lb. sweet potatoes (about 3 large), peeled, cut into ¾-inch cubes (about 5 cups)

2 tablespoons chopped pecans

1. In small bowl, combine 2 tablespoons of the apple juice and cornstarch; mix well. Set aside.

2. In large nonstick skillet or Dutch oven, combine remaining apple juice, syrup, cinnamon, margarine and salt; mix well. Bring to a boil. Add potatoes; stir to coat well. Return to a boil. Reduce heat; cover and simmer 8 to 10 minutes or just until potatoes are tender.

3. Stir cornstarch mixture into potato mixture; cook and stir over medium-high heat until bubbly and thickened. Spoon into serving bowl. Sprinkle with pecans.

YIELD: 8 (½-CUP) SERVINGS

Nutrition Information Per Serving
Serving Size: ½ Cup

Calories	200	Calories from Fat	25
		% Daily Value	
Total Fat	3g		5%
Saturated	0g		0%
Cholesterol	0mg		0%
Sodium	80mg		3%
Total Carbohydrate	40g		13%
Dietary Fiber	3g		12%
Sugars	17g		
Protein	2g		
Vitamin A	330%	Vitamin C	20%
Calcium	2%	Iron	4%

Dietary Exchanges: 1½ Starch, 1 Fruit, ½ Fat
OR 2½ Carbohydrate, ½ Fat

▲ Skillet Acorn Squash

Skillet Acorn Squash

■ ■ ■ ■ ■ ■ ■ ■ ■ ■ ■ ■ ■ ■ ■ ■ ■ ■ ■

PREP TIME: 25 MINUTES

1 large acorn squash (2 lb.)

½ cup apple juice

1 tablespoon margarine or butter

¼ teaspoon cinnamon

1. Trim ends off squash. Stand squash on end; cut in half. Remove and discard seeds and fiber. Cut each squash half crosswise into ½-inch-thick slices.

2. In 12-inch nonstick skillet, combine apple juice, margarine and cinnamon; mix well. Add squash.

Bring to a boil. Reduce heat; cover and simmer 10 minutes.

3. Turn slices; cover and simmer an additional 5 to 8 minutes or until squash is tender.

YIELD: 4 SERVINGS

Nutrition Information Per Serving
Serving Size: ¼ of Recipe

Calories	120	Calories from Fat	25
			% Daily Value
Total Fat	3g		5%
Saturated	1g		5%
Cholesterol	0mg		0%
Sodium	40mg		2%
Total Carbohydrate	22g		7%
Dietary Fiber	3g		12%
Sugars	7g		
Protein	1g		
Vitamin A	15%	Vitamin C	20%
Calcium	6%	Iron	8%

Dietary Exchanges: 1½ Starch OR 1½ Carbohydrate

about **Acorn Squash**

Acorn squash is identifiable by its sharply ridged, dark green skin, splashed with orange. It is shaped like a very big acorn and its flesh is a pale gold color with a mild, sweet flavor.

- Squash is one of the richest vegetable sources of vitamin A and is a good source of vitamin C and dietary fiber.

- Choose squash that's heavy for its size with a firm shell and no cracks or soft spots.

- At home, store the squash in a cool place (50°F.) with good air circulation. Refrigerate only after cutting; wrap and store for up to five days.

Caraway Brussels Sprouts

PREP TIME: 20 MINUTES

1 teaspoon olive oil

3 tablespoons finely chopped red onion

¼ teaspoon caraway seed

1 lb. (4 cups) fresh Brussels sprouts, halved vertically*

⅓ cup water

½ teaspoon chicken-flavor instant bouillon

2 teaspoons lemon juice

Dash pepper

1. Heat oil in large nonstick skillet over medium heat until hot. Add onion and caraway seed; cook and stir 1 minute. Add Brussels sprouts; cook and stir an additional 1 minute.

2. Add water and bouillon. Reduce heat to low; cover and cook 6 to 10 minutes or until Brussels sprouts are crisp-tender. Stir in lemon juice and pepper.

YIELD: 6 (½-CUP) SERVINGS

Tip: * One 1-lb. pkg. frozen Brussels sprouts can be substituted for fresh. Place Brussels sprouts in colander or large strainer; rinse with warm water until partially thawed. Halve Brussels sprouts vertically.

Nutrition Information Per Serving
Serving Size: ½ Cup

Calories	50	Calories from Fat	10
		% Daily Value	
Total Fat	1g		2%
Saturated	0g		0%
Cholesterol	0mg		0%
Sodium	25mg		1%
Total Carbohydrate	7g		2%
Dietary Fiber	3g		12%
Sugars	2g		
Protein	3g		
Vitamin A	15%	Vitamin C	80%
Calcium	4%	Iron	6%

Dietary Exchanges: 2 Vegetable

about **Brussels Sprouts**

Brussels sprouts resemble their larger cousin, the green cabbage. To prepare them, trim off the stems and remove any tough outer leaves.

Asparagus with Orange-Chive Sauce

■■■■■■■■■■■■■■■■■■■■

PREP TIME: 15 MINUTES

1 lb. fresh asparagus spears, trimmed

¼ cup orange juice

1 teaspoon grated orange peel

½ teaspoon cornstarch

Dash pepper

1 tablespoon chopped fresh chives

1. In large skillet, bring ¹/₂ inch water to a boil. Add asparagus; return to a boil. Cover; cook 3 to 5 minutes or until asparagus is tender.*

2. Meanwhile, in small nonstick saucepan, combine orange juice, orange peel, cornstarch and pepper; mix well. Cook over medium heat until mixture boils and begins to thicken. Remove from heat; stir in chives.

3. Drain asparagus; place on serving platter. Top with chive sauce.

YIELD: 4 SERVINGS

Tip: * If desired, place asparagus spears in steamer basket over boiling water. Cover; steam 3 to 5 minutes or until asparagus is tender.

Nutrition Information Per Serving
Serving Size: ¹/₄ of Recipe

Calories	35	Calories from Fat	0
		% Daily Value	
Total Fat	0g		0%
Saturated	0g		0%
Cholesterol	0mg		0%
Sodium	0mg		0%
Total Carbohydrate	7g		2%
Dietary Fiber	2g		8%
Sugars	4g		
Protein	2g		
Vitamin A	10%	Vitamin C	25%
Calcium	2%	Iron	4%

Dietary Exchanges: 1 Vegetable

■ PRODUCE POINTERS

choosing and using **Asparagus**

Choose firm, unwrinkled spears with tight tips; the cut ends should be moist, preferably standing in a tray of water. Asparagus is best eaten right away, but if you must store it, wrap it tightly in plastic and refrigerate up to 3 or 4 days.

- To prepare asparagus, snap off the tough ends by hand near the bottom of the stalk. There's a natural breaking point an inch or two from the bottom. Rinse thoroughly. If the stalks still seem sandy, use a paring knife or peeler to remove the triangular "leaves" below the tip. If the stems are tough, peel the skin off the bottom third or so of the spear.

- To cook on the stovetop, lay the spears flat in a skillet filled with simmering water or in a steamer basket over boiling water. Cook, uncovered, about 4 to 8 minutes per pound, depending on thickness.

- To microwave, fill a shallow microwave-safe dish with ¹/₄ cup of water and arrange the asparagus with the tips toward the center. Cover with plastic wrap, leaving one corner folded back for venting, and cook 2 to 4 minutes, depending on the thickness, rearranging the stalks once for even cooking. Let the dish stand for 3 minutes.

  One pound of asparagus yields two to three servings. Asparagus is a good source of vitamin C and potassium; four large spears contain about 20 calories.

◀ Asparagus with Orange-Chive Sauce

Apple-Glazed Carrots

2 cups fresh baby carrots

¼ cup unsweetened apple juice or apple cider

¼ cup apple jelly

1½ teaspoons Dijon mustard

1. In medium nonstick skillet, combine carrots and apple juice. Bring to a boil. Reduce heat; cover and simmer 10 to 14 minutes or until carrots are crisp-tender.

2. Uncover skillet; cook over medium heat until liquid evaporates. Stir in jelly and mustard; cook and stir until jelly is melted and carrots are glazed.

YIELD: 4 (½-CUP) SERVINGS

Nutrition Information Per Serving
Serving Size: ½ Cup

Calories	90	Calories from Fat	0
		% Daily Value	
Total Fat	0g		0%
Saturated	0g		0%
Cholesterol	0mg		0%
Sodium	90mg		4%
Total Carbohydrate	22g		7%
Dietary Fiber	2g		8%
Sugars	14g		
Protein	1g		
Vitamin A	170%	Vitamin C	0%
Calcium	4%	Iron	0%

Dietary Exchanges: 1 Fruit, 1 Vegetable OR 1 Carbohydrate, 1 Vegetable

Cauliflower Parmesan

4 cups fresh cauliflower florets (1 medium head)

1 tablespoon olive oil

2 tablespoons all-purpose flour

½ cup skim milk

⅓ cup water

½ teaspoon chicken-flavor instant bouillon

¼ cup grated Parmesan cheese

¼ cup fresh bread crumbs

¼ teaspoon paprika

1. In medium nonstick saucepan, combine cauliflower and ¼ cup water. Bring to a boil. Reduce heat; cover and simmer 5 to 6 minutes or until cauliflower is crisp-tender. Drain; spoon cauliflower into ungreased 1-quart ovenproof casserole. Set aside.

2. Heat oil in same saucepan over medium heat until hot. With wire whisk, stir in flour; cook and stir 1 minute. Add milk, ⅓ cup water and bouillon; blend well. Cook 3 minutes or until sauce boils and thickens, stirring constantly. Stir in cheese; cook and stir until cheese is melted. Pour sauce over cauliflower. Sprinkle with bread crumbs and paprika.

3. Broil 4 to 6 inches from heat for 2 minutes or until bread crumbs are golden brown.

YIELD: 6 (½-CUP) SERVINGS

Nutrition Information Per Serving
Serving Size: ½ Cup

Calories	80	Calories from Fat	35
		% Daily Value	
Total Fat	4g		6%
Saturated	1g		5%
Cholesterol	4mg		1%
Sodium	125mg		5%
Total Carbohydrate	8g		3%
Dietary Fiber	2g		8%
Sugars	3g		
Protein	4g		
Vitamin A	2%	Vitamin C	35%
Calcium	10%	Iron	4%

Dietary Exchanges: 1 Vegetable, 1 Fat

Herbed Chickpeas and Carrots

■ ■ ■ ■ ■ ■ ■ ■ ■ ■ ■ ■ ■ ■ ■ ■ ■ ■ ■ ■

PREP TIME: 20 MINUTES

1 teaspoon olive oil

¼ cup chopped onion

¼ cup sliced celery

1 medium carrot, thinly sliced (½ cup)

1 (15-oz.) can chickpeas or garbanzo beans, drained, rinsed

¼ cup water

½ teaspoon dried Italian seasoning

Dash pepper

1. Heat oil in medium nonstick saucepan over medium heat until hot. Add onion, celery and carrot; cook and stir until carrot is crisp-tender.

2. Stir in all remaining ingredients. Bring to a boil. Reduce heat; simmer an additional 5 minutes.

YIELD: 4 (½-CUP) SERVINGS

Nutrition Information Per Serving
Serving Size: ½ Cup

Calories 120	Calories from Fat 25	
	% Daily Value	
Total Fat 3g	....5%	
Saturated 0g	....0%	
Cholesterol 0mg	....0%	
Sodium 160mg	....7%	
Total Carbohydrate 18g	....6%	
Dietary Fiber 6g	....24%	
Sugars 2g		
Protein 5g		
Vitamin A 100%	Vitamin C 4%	
Calcium 4%	Iron..............................4%	

Dietary Exchanges: 1 Starch, 1 Fat OR 1 Carbohydrate, 1 Fat

▼ Herbed Chickpeas and Carrots

Corn and Salsa Stuffed Peppers

PREP TIME: 10 MINUTES
(READY IN 40 MINUTES)

- **2 cups frozen whole kernel corn, thawed***

- **¼ cup sliced green onions**

- **⅓ cup chunky-style salsa**

- **2 green bell peppers, halved lengthwise, seeds removed**

- **1 oz. (¼ cup) shredded mozzarella cheese**

- **2 slices bacon, crisply cooked, crumbled, if desired****

Grill Directions: 1. Heat grill. Cut four 14 × 12-inch sheets of heavy-duty foil. In medium bowl, combine corn, onions and salsa; blend well. Spoon into bell pepper halves. Place 1 stuffed pepper in center of each sheet of foil. Wrap each packet securely using double-fold seals.

2. Place foil packets on gas grill over medium heat or on charcoal grill 4 to 6 inches from medium-high coals. Cook 20 to 25 minutes or until peppers are crisp-tender.

3. Remove packets from grill; open packets. Sprinkle each stuffed pepper with 1 tablespoon cheese. Reseal packets; let stand 3 to 5 minutes or until cheese is melted. Sprinkle with bacon.

Oven Directions: 1. Heat oven to 425°F. Prepare stuffed peppers in foil packets as directed above; place on cookie sheet.

2. Bake at 425°F. for 25 to 30 minutes or until peppers are crisp-tender.

3. Remove packets from oven; open packets. Sprinkle each stuffed pepper with 1 tablespoon cheese. Reseal packets; let stand 3 to 5 minutes or until cheese is melted. Sprinkle with bacon.

YIELD: 4 SERVINGS

▼ Corn and Salsa Stuffed Peppers

Tip: * To quickly thaw corn, place in colander or strainer; rinse with warm water until thawed. Drain well.

** To cook bacon in microwave, place bacon on microwave-safe dish lined with microwave-safe paper towel. Microwave on HIGH for 1 to 3 minutes or until bacon is crisp.

Nutrition Information Per Serving
Serving Size: ¼ of Recipe

Calories 150	Calories from Fat 35
	% Daily Value
Total Fat 4g	......6%
Saturated 2g	.....10%
Cholesterol 5mg	......2%
Sodium 330mg	.....14%
Total Carbohydrate 22g	......7%
Dietary Fiber 3g	.....12%
Sugars 4g	
Protein 6g	
Vitamin A...........................10%	Vitamin C 50%
Calcium 6%	Iron..............................4%

Dietary Exchanges: 1 Starch, 1 Vegetable, 1 Fat OR 1 Carbohydrate, 1 Vegetable, 1 Fat

Okra-Corn Medley

▪ ▪ ▪ ▪ ▪ ▪ ▪ ▪ ▪ ▪ ▪ ▪ ▪ ▪ ▪ ▪

PREP TIME: 20 MINUTES

3 slices bacon

1 lb. fresh okra, sliced crosswise

1 (1-lb.) pkg. frozen whole kernel corn, thawed*

½ cup chopped red bell pepper

¼ teaspoon salt

⅛ teaspoon pepper

1. In large nonstick skillet, cook bacon until crisp. Remove bacon from skillet; crumble. Set aside.

2. Drain all but 1 tablespoon bacon drippings from skillet, *or* drain off all drippings and add ¼ cup water to skillet. Add okra; cook over medium heat for 4 to 6 minutes or until crisp-tender, stirring frequently.

3. Stir in crumbled bacon, corn, bell pepper, salt and pepper; cook until thoroughly heated, stirring occasionally.

YIELD: 10 (½-CUP) SERVINGS

Tip: * To quickly thaw corn, place in colander or strainer; rinse with warm water until thawed. Drain well.

Nutrition Information Per Serving
Serving Size: ½ Cup

Calories 90	Calories from Fat 25
	% Daily Value
Total Fat 3g	......5%
Saturated 1g	......5%
Cholesterol 3mg	......1%
Sodium 90mg	......4%
Total Carbohydrate 13g	......4%
Dietary Fiber 2g	......8%
Sugars 3g	
Protein 3g	
Vitamin A...........................15%	Vitamin C 25%
Calcium 4%	Iron..............................4%

Dietary Exchanges: ½ Starch, 1 Vegetable, ½ Fat OR ½ Carbohydrate, 1 Vegetable, ½ Fat

Fiber *guide*

Food	Fiber (g)
Asparagus, ½ cup, cooked	1.9
Bell pepper, ½ cup, raw	0.9
Broccoli, ½ cup, cooked	2.0
Brussels sprouts, ½ cup, cooked	3.4
Carrot, 1 medium, raw	2.3
Cauliflower, ½ cup, cooked	1.7
Celery, 1 stalk, raw	0.6
Corn, ½ cup, cooked	3.0
Garbanzo beans, ½ cup, cooked	7.0
Green beans, ½ cup, cooked	0.6
Kidney beans, ½ cup, cooked	8.0
Mushrooms, ½ cup, raw	0.4
Okra, ½ cup, cooked	2.0
Peas, ½ cup, cooked	2.2
Potato with skin, 1 medium, baked	2.9
Spinach, 1 cup, raw	1.5
Sweet potato, ½ cup, cooked	3.0
Swiss chard, ½ cup, cooked	1.4
Tomato, 1 medium, raw	1.4
Water chestnuts, ½ cup, sliced	3.0
Winter squash, ½ cup, cooked	2.9
Zucchini, ½ cup, raw	0.8

all about **Onions**

Onions, chives, leeks and shallots are all members of the genus *allium,* bulbous herbs of the lily family.

Dry onions Mature onions encased in dry, papery skin are referred to as dry onions. The common cooking onion comes in many shapes and sizes. Those available in the spring and summer tend to be milder, and some special varieties like Maui, Vidalia, Texas Sweet and Walla Walla are especially sweet. The fall and winter onions are firmer and more pungent.

Boilers Dry onions smaller than $1^1/_2$ inches. They're usually cooked as a side dish.

Pearl onions Very tiny dry onions. Available in red, white or yellow.

Scallions and green onions Can be used interchangeably and are often called for synonymously in recipes, although they are not the same thing. The scallion is actually an immature form of a regular onion and is milder in flavor. Its white base has straight sides, while the green onion's base is more bulblike in shape.

Chives Used most often as an herb to season or garnish soups, salads and spreads.

Leeks Mild in flavor, the flat, tightly rolled leaves of leeks are served on their own or sliced or chopped and used in soups, stews and salads. Trim and discard the root and the green leafy ends before using.

Shallots Arranged in cloves tucked in a single head, the mild-flavored shallot is formed in the same way as garlic. You'll most often find the cloves already separated when you buy shallots.

Pearl Onion, Carrot and Zucchini Sauté

■ ■

PREP TIME: 20 MINUTES

1½ cups frozen small whole onions, thawed*

1½ cups julienne-cut (2½ × ⅛ × ⅛-inch) carrot

1½ cups sliced halved zucchini

1 tablespoon rice or cider vinegar

¼ teaspoon lemon-pepper seasoning

1. In large nonstick skillet, combine onions, carrots and $^1/_3$ cup water. Bring to a boil. Reduce heat; cover and simmer 4 to 6 minutes or until carrots are crisp-tender.

2. Add zucchini; cover and cook an additional 1 to 2 minutes or until zucchini is crisp-tender, stirring occasionally. Drain; stir in vinegar and lemon-pepper seasoning.

YIELD: 6 (1-CUP) SERVINGS

Tip: * To quickly thaw onions, place in colander or strainer; rinse with warm water until thawed. Drain well.

Nutrition Information Per Serving
Serving Size: 1 Cup

Calories 35	Calories from Fat 0
	% Daily Value
Total Fat 0g	...........0%
Saturated 0g	...........0%
Cholesterol 0mg	...........0%
Sodium 35mg	...........1%
Total Carbohydrate...............8g	...........3%
Dietary Fiber 2g	...........8%
Sugars 4g	
Protein..................................1g	
Vitamin A...........................170%	Vitamin C 8%
Calcium 2%	Iron...............................2%

Dietary Exchanges: 1½ Vegetable

Crumb-Topped Green Beans and Mushrooms

■ ■ ■ ■ ■ ■ ■ ■ ■ ■ ■ ■ ■ ■ ■ ■

PREP TIME: 15 MINUTES

1 (1-lb.) pkg. frozen cut green beans, thawed*

2 cups sliced fresh mushrooms

¼ cup finely chopped shallots or onion

2 tablespoons water

¼ teaspoon salt, if desired

⅛ teaspoon pepper, if desired

1 tablespoon margarine or butter

1 tablespoon olive oil

1 cup fresh white bread crumbs**

1 teaspoon dried basil leaves

1. In large nonstick skillet, combine green beans, mushrooms, shallots and water; cook over medium-high heat for 3 to 4 minutes or until vegetables are crisp-tender and liquid evaporates. Stir in salt and pepper. Spoon into serving dish; cover to keep warm.

2. In same skillet, melt margarine in oil. Add bread crumbs and basil; cook and stir over medium-high heat until light brown. Sprinkle over vegetables.

YIELD: 7 (½-CUP) SERVINGS

Tips: * To quickly thaw green beans, place in colander or strainer; rinse with warm water until thawed. Drain well.

** Bread crumbs can be made by placing pieces of fresh bread in blender container or food processor bowl with metal blade; blend or process until coarsely chopped.

Nutrition Information Per Serving
Serving Size: ½ Cup

Calories 80	Calories from Fat 35
	% Daily Value
Total Fat 4g	...........6%
Saturated 1g	...........5%
Cholesterol 0mg	...........0%
Sodium 135mg	...........6%
Total Carbohydrate 10g	...........3%
Dietary Fiber 2g	...........8%
Sugars 2g	
Protein..................................2g	
Vitamin A...........................20%	Vitamin C 10%
Calcium 4%	Iron...............................6%

Dietary Exchanges: 2 Vegetable, 1 Fat

Onion *equivalents*

■ ■ ■ ■ ■ ■ ■ ■ ■ ■ ■ ■ ■ ■

**1 1b. dry onions = 3 large or
4 medium onions
1 large onion = about 1 cup chopped
1 medium onion = about ¾ cup chopped
1 small onion = about ⅓ cup chopped**

Mushroom *guide*

- **Storing** Mushrooms keep best with good air circulation. If the mushrooms you buy are sealed in plastic, remove the plastic and place the mushrooms in a paper bag before refrigerating.

- **Cleaning** Mushrooms need only be wiped with a soft cloth or a mushroom brush, available from kitchen specialty stores. If you do decide to rinse mushrooms, do it quickly. A fresh mushroom, already 90 percent water, absorbs even more and its flavor will diminish.

- **Trimming** For most mushrooms, you need trim off the stem end only if it's dried and shriveled. Shiitake mushrooms are the exception; their stems are tough and should be discarded.

- **Measuring** One pound of fresh mushrooms equals 6 cups sliced. One pound of fresh mushrooms equals 2 cups sliced and cooked.

Creamed Onions and Mushrooms

PREP TIME: 25 MINUTES

1 (1-lb.) pkg. frozen small whole onions

1 (8-oz.) pkg. (3 cups) sliced fresh mushrooms

2 tablespoons dry sherry or chicken broth

½ teaspoon dried tarragon leaves, crushed

2 tablespoons all-purpose flour

¾ cup skim milk

2 tablespoons light sour cream

1. In large nonstick saucepan, combine onions and ½ cup water. Bring to a boil. Cover; cook 3 minutes. Drain well. Remove onions from saucepan; set aside.

2. In same saucepan, combine mushrooms, sherry and tarragon. Cook over medium heat for 7 to 8 minutes or until most of liquid has evaporated.

3. Remove saucepan from heat; stir in flour until combined. Add milk; stir to blend. Cook over medium heat for 3 to 5 minutes or until slightly thickened, stirring occasionally.

4. Stir in onions; cook until thoroughly heated. Remove from heat; stir in sour cream. If desired, season to taste with salt and pepper.

YIELD: 5 (½-CUP) SERVINGS

Nutrition Information Per Serving
Serving Size: ½ Cup

Calories	90	Calories from Fat	10
		% Daily Value	
Total Fat	1g		2%
Saturated	0g		0%
Cholesterol	3mg		1%
Sodium	35mg		1%
Total Carbohydrate	15g		5%
Dietary Fiber	2g		8%
Sugars	7g		
Protein	4g		
Vitamin A	2%	Vitamin C	10%
Calcium	8%	Iron	6%

Dietary Exchanges: ½ Starch, 2 Vegetable OR ½ Carbohydrate, 2 Vegetable

▲ Basil Sugar Snap Peas with Mushrooms

Basil Sugar Snap Peas with Mushrooms

PREP TIME: 15 MINUTES

1 tablespoon olive oil

1 cup sliced fresh mushrooms

1 garlic clove, minced

3 cups frozen sugar snap peas

½ cup halved cherry tomatoes

2 teaspoons chopped fresh basil or ½ teaspoon dried basil leaves

1 tablespoon grated Parmesan cheese

1. Heat oil in medium nonstick saucepan over medium heat until hot. Add mushrooms and garlic; cook until tender, stirring occasionally. Remove from saucepan; cover to keep warm.

2. Add ⅓ cup water to same saucepan; bring to a boil. Add sugar snap peas; return to a boil. Stir; reduce heat. Cover; simmer $2\frac{1}{2}$ to $4\frac{1}{2}$ minutes or until crisp-tender.

3. Drain sugar snap peas; return to saucepan. Stir in mushroom mixture, tomatoes and basil. Spoon into serving bowl; sprinkle with cheese.

YIELD: 5 (½-CUP) SERVINGS

Nutrition Information Per Serving
Serving Size: ½ Cup

Calories 70		Calories from Fat 25	
		% Daily Value	
Total Fat 3g		.....5%	
Saturated......................1g		.....5%	
Cholesterol 0mg		....0%	
Sodium 25mg		.....1%	
Total Carbohydrate.............8g		.....3%	
Dietary Fiber.....................3g		....12%	
Sugars 3g			
Protein................................3g			
Vitamin A 4%		Vitamin C 25%	
Calcium 6%		Iron 10%	

Dietary Exchanges: 1 Vegetable, 1 Fat

Zucchini with Tomatoes and Basil

■ ■ ■ ■ ■ ■ ■ ■ ■ ■ ■ ■ ■ ■ ■ ■ ■ ■ ■

PREP TIME: 15 MINUTES

4 small zucchini (½ lb.), cut into ½-inch-thick slices

1 cup coarsely chopped tomatoes

2 tablespoons chopped fresh basil

¼ teaspoon salt

⅛ teaspoon pepper

2 teaspoons lemon juice

2 tablespoons shredded fresh Parmesan cheese, if desired

1. In medium saucepan, combine zucchini and ¼ cup water. Cook over medium heat for 3 to 4 minutes or until crisp-tender. Drain well.

2. Add tomatoes, basil, salt, pepper and lemon juice; mix well. Cook and stir about 1 minute or until thoroughly heated. Sprinkle with cheese.

YIELD: 5 (½-CUP) SERVINGS

Nutrition Information Per Serving
Serving Size: ½ Cup

Calories	35	Calories from Fat	10
			% Daily Value
Total Fat	1g		2%
Saturated	0g		0%
Cholesterol	0mg		0%
Sodium	160mg		7%
Total Carbohydrate	5g		2%
Dietary Fiber	2g		8%
Sugars	3g		
Protein	2g		
Vitamin A	10%	Vitamin C	20%
Calcium	4%	Iron	4%

Dietary Exchanges: 1 Vegetable

Swiss Chard Italiano

■ ■ ■ ■ ■ ■ ■ ■ ■ ■ ■ ■ ■ ■ ■ ■ ■ ■ ■

PREP TIME: 20 MINUTES

1 teaspoon olive oil

1 garlic clove, minced

7 cups chopped fresh Swiss chard or spinach

2 tablespoons finely chopped red onion

1 (14.5- or 16-oz.) can whole tomatoes, drained, cut up

½ teaspoon dried marjoram leaves

1. Heat oil in large nonstick skillet over medium heat until hot. Add garlic; cook and stir 1 to 2 minutes.

2. Add all remaining ingredients; cook 10 minutes, stirring occasionally. If desired, season to taste with salt and pepper.

YIELD: 4 (½-CUP) SERVINGS

Nutrition Information Per Serving
Serving Size: ½ Cup

Calories	40	Calories from Fat	10
			% Daily Value
Total Fat	1g		2%
Saturated	0g		0%
Cholesterol	0mg		0%
Sodium	240mg		10%
Total Carbohydrate	6g		2%
Dietary Fiber	2g		8%
Sugars	2g		
Protein	2g		
Vitamin A	50%	Vitamin C	35%
Calcium	6%	Iron	8%

Dietary Exchanges: 1 Vegetable

about Swiss Chard

Swiss chard is a mild-flavored leafy green with red or white stalks and ribs. It has a heartier texture than that of spinach, but is more tender than kale or broccoli rabe.

10 Breads

Carrot Zucchini Muffins (page 293)

Spiced Apple Bread

	Small Loaf (8 slices)	Large Loaf (12 slices)
Unsweetened apple juice, room temperature	½ cup	¾ cup
Natural applesauce, room temperature	¼ cup	½ cup
Margarine or butter, room temperature	1 tablespoon	2 tablespoons
Bread flour	1⅔ cups	2½ cups
Rolled oats	⅓ cup	¾ cup
Sugar	4 teaspoons	¼ cup
Salt	½ teaspoon	1 teaspoon
Cinnamon	¾ teaspoon	1 teaspoon
Ginger	⅛ teaspoon	¼ teaspoon
Active dry yeast	1¼ teaspoons	2½ teaspoons

1. If bread machine typically uses 2 cups flour, use small loaf recipe. If machine uses 3 cups flour, use large loaf recipe.

2. Follow manufacturer's directions for loading ingredients into machine. Measure ingredients carefully.

3. Select regular, rapid or delayed-time bake cycle and follow manufacturer's directions for starting machine.

HIGH ALTITUDE (ABOVE 3500 FEET): For small loaf, increase apple juice by 1 to 2 tablespoons and decrease yeast by ¼ to ½ teaspoon. For large loaf, increase apple juice by 1½ to 3 tablespoons and decrease yeast by ¼ to ¾ teaspoon. Continue as directed above.

Nutrition Information Per Serving
Serving Size: 1 Slice

Calories	180	Calories from Fat	25

		% Daily Value
Total Fat	3g	5%
Saturated	0g	0%
Cholesterol	0mg	0%
Sodium	200mg	8%
Total Carbohydrate	32g	11%
Dietary Fiber	2g	8%
Sugars	7g	
Protein	5g	

Vitamin A	0%	Vitamin C	0%
Calcium	0%	Iron	10%

Dietary Exchanges: 2 Starch, ½ Fat OR 2 Carbohydrate, ½ Fat

▼ Spiced Apple Bread

Bread Machine *tips*

■ ■

While old-fashioned bread making is largely art, in which the experienced baker judges proportions from the feel of the dough, making loaves with a modern bread machine is more science. You'll achieve best results if you stick to the rules:

- Have all ingredients at room temperature and add them in the order specified.

- Measure carefully. The machine requires precise and consistent amounts to turn out a consistent loaf.

- Machine baking requires less yeast per loaf than traditional methods. Buy yeast in jars or transfer it to a wide-mouth container to make measuring easier.

- Keep the bread machine free of crumbs and spills.

- Use bread flour not all-purpose.

- Remember that the machine is actually a small oven and can get hot. Use pot holders and keep the machine out of the reach of children.

- Some machines are not suited to recipes that call for whole-grain flour exclusively, because the machine has to work harder to raise the dough; check manufacturer's instructions for suggestions.

- Remove the baked loaf promptly to avoid sogginess.

Delicious Grain Bread

■ ■

	Small Loaf (8 slices)	Large Loaf (12 slices)
Water, room temperature	¾ cup	1 cup plus 2 tablespoons
Margarine or butter, room temperature	1 tablespoon	2 tablespoons
Honey	1 tablespoon	2 tablespoons
Bread flour	1 cup	1¾ cups
Whole wheat flour	½ cup	¾ cup
Shreds of whole bran cereal	⅓ cup	½ cup
Cracked wheat (not bulgur)	2 tablespoons	2 tablespoons
Instant nonfat dry milk	1 tablespoon	2 tablespoons
Salt	½ teaspoon	1 teaspoon
Active dry yeast	1¼ teaspoons	2 teaspoons

1. If bread machine typically uses 2 cups flour, use small loaf recipe. If machine uses 3 cups flour, use large loaf recipe.

2. Follow manufacturer's directions for loading ingredients into machine. Measure ingredients carefully.

3. Select regular, rapid or delayed-time bake cycle and follow manufacturer's directions for starting machine.

HIGH ALTITUDE (ABOVE 3500 FEET): For small loaf, increase water by 1 to 2 tablespoons and decrease yeast by ¼ to ½ teaspoon. For large loaf, increase water by 1½ to 3 tablespoons and decrease yeast by ¼ to ¾ teaspoon. Continue as directed above.

Nutrition Information Per Serving
Serving Size: 1 Slice

Calories...............150	Calories from Fat...........2	
	% Daily Value	
Total Fat 2g	..........5%	
Saturated 0g	..........0%	
Cholesterol 0mg	..........0%	
Sodium 250mg	..........10%	
Total Carbohydrate...........27g	..........9%	
Dietary Fiber...............3g	..........12%	
Sugars 4g		
Protein...............5g		
Vitamin A 4%	Vitamin C...............2%	
Calcium 0%	Iron...............10%	

Dietary Exchanges: 2 Starch OR 2 Carbohydrate

Buttermilk Cornmeal Biscuits

■ ■

PREP TIME: 30 MINUTES

3½ cups all-purpose flour

½ cup cornmeal

5 teaspoons baking powder

1 teaspoon baking soda

½ teaspoon salt

½ cup margarine or butter

1½ to 1¾ cups buttermilk*

1. Heat oven to 400°F. Grease cookie sheet. In large bowl, combine flour, cornmeal, baking powder, baking soda and salt; mix well.

2. With pastry blender or fork, cut in margarine until mixture resembles coarse crumbs. Stir in enough buttermilk to form a soft dough.

3. On lightly floured surface, shape dough into ball. Roll dough to 1-inch thickness; cut with floured 2-inch round cutter. Place biscuits on greased cookie sheet.

4. Bake at 400°F. for 10 to 15 minutes or until light golden brown. Serve warm.

YIELD: 20 BISCUITS

Biscuit *basics*

■ ■ ■ ■ ■ ■ ■ ■ ■ ■ ■ ■ ■ ■ ■ ■ ■ ■

For the most tender biscuits, mix the ingredients gently and work quickly. For drop biscuits, which will have a rougher top and slightly coarser texture, simply drop spoonfuls of the mixed dough onto the baking sheet. For smoother biscuits, pat the dough into shape for gentle rolling, but avoid heavy-duty kneading. Cut biscuits with a sharp-edged cutter or knife; a dull edge may pinch the top and bottom together and prevent the biscuits from rising properly. Scraps may be rerolled, although the additional handling may make biscuits slightly less tender.

Buttermilk
in the batter

■ ■ ■ ■ ■ ■ ■ ■ ■ ■ ■ ■ ■ ■ ■ ■ ■ ■ ■ ■

Buttermilk is a great secret ingredient in the low-fat cook's arsenal, improving flavor and texture of many baked recipes. Despite its rich thickness and its name, buttermilk has only 100 calories and just 2.5 grams of fat per cup. (Nonfat buttermilk also is available in some areas.) Because it's slightly tart and tangy, it sharpens flavors. Its acidity helps to tenderize baked goods, too. This is an especially desirable feature in low-fat baking, which sometimes loses tenderness when fat is cut.

If you don't have buttermilk on hand, you can improvise by adding 1 tablespoon of lemon juice, white vinegar or cider vinegar to a cup of skim milk. Let the mixture stand for 10 minutes or so, until the milk looks slightly lumpy and thickened.

Tip: * To substitute for buttermilk, use $4^{1}/_{2}$ to $4^{3}/_{4}$ teaspoons vinegar or lemon juice plus skim milk to make $1^{1}/_{2}$ to $1^{3}/_{4}$ cups.

HIGH ALTITUDE (ABOVE 3500 FEET): No change.

Nutrition Information Per Serving
Serving Size: 1 Biscuit

Calories	140	Calories from Fat	45
		% Daily Value	
Total Fat	5g		8%
Saturated	1g		5%
Cholesterol	0mg		0%
Sodium	270mg		11%
Total Carbohydrate	20g		7%
Dietary Fiber	1g		3%
Sugars	1g		
Protein	3g		
Vitamin A	4%	Vitamin C	0%
Calcium	8%	Iron	6%

Dietary Exchanges: 1 Starch, 1 Fat OR 1 Carbohydrate, 1 Fat

Golden Pineapple Carrot Coffee Cake

PREP TIME: 25 MINUTES
(READY IN 1 HOUR)

Cake

⅓ cup sugar

¼ cup refrigerated or frozen fat-free egg product, thawed, or 1 egg

3 tablespoons oil

1 cup shredded carrots

1 (8-oz.) can crushed pineapple in unsweetened juice, undrained

⅓ cup orange juice

1½ cups all-purpose flour

1½ teaspoons baking soda

1 teaspoon cinnamon

¼ teaspoon salt

Topping

⅓ cup sugar

⅓ cup finely chopped walnuts

¾ teaspoon cinnamon

1. Heat oven to 350°F. Spray 9-inch round cake pan with nonstick cooking spray.

2. In medium bowl, combine ⅓ cup sugar, egg product and oil; mix well. Add carrots, pineapple and orange juice; blend well.

3. In small bowl, combine flour, baking soda, 1 teaspoon cinnamon and salt; mix well. Add to carrot-pineapple mixture; stir just until dry ingredients are moistened. Spread batter evenly in sprayed pan.

4. In another small bowl, combine all topping ingredients; mix well. Sprinkle over batter.

5. Bake at 350°F. for 25 to 35 minutes or until toothpick inserted in center comes out clean. Cool 10 minutes before serving.

YIELD: 8 SERVINGS
HIGH ALTITUDE (ABOVE 3500 FEET): No change.

Nutrition Information Per Serving
Serving Size: ⅛ of Recipe

Calories	270	Calories from Fat	80
		% Daily Value	
Total Fat	9g		14%
Saturated	1g		5%
Cholesterol	0mg		0%
Sodium	320mg		13%
Total Carbohydrate	43g		14%
Dietary Fiber	2g		8%
Sugars	23g		
Protein	4g		
Vitamin A	80%	Vitamin C	10%
Calcium	2%	Iron	10%

Dietary Exchanges: 2 Starch, 1 Fruit, 1 Fat OR 3 Carbohydrate, 1 Fat

note about Nuts

If you are trying to reconcile a love of nuts with a healthy diet, take a cue from Golden Pineapple Carrot Coffee Cake. Chop a small quantity of nuts and sprinkle them on top of the batter instead of mixing them with the other ingredients. This gives some nutty crunch in every bite and fools the eye into seeing a generous quantity of nuts, even if the amount has been greatly reduced from the original recipe.

Lemony Raspberry Coffee Cake

PREP TIME: 25 MINUTES
(READY IN 1 HOUR)

⅓ cup sugar

¼ cup refrigerated or frozen fat-free egg product, thawed, or 1 egg

¼ cup oil

2 tablespoons grated lemon peel

1 tablespoon lemon juice

1 (8-oz.) container low-fat lemon yogurt

1¾ cups all-purpose flour

2 teaspoons baking powder

½ teaspoon baking soda

¼ teaspoon salt

⅔ cup low-sugar red raspberry preserves

1. Heat oven to 350°F. In medium bowl, combine sugar, egg product and oil; beat well. Stir in lemon peel, lemon juice and yogurt.

2. Add flour, baking powder, baking soda and salt; stir just until dry ingredients are moistened. Spread half of batter in ungreased 9-inch round cake pan.

3. Reserve ⅓ cup preserves for top of cake. Carefully spread remaining ⅓ cup preserves over batter to within ¼ inch of edge of pan. Spoon remaining batter over top, spreading to cover preserves completely.

▼ Golden Pineapple Carrot Coffee Cake (page 289)/Passover Apple Lemon Coffee Cake/ Lemony Raspberry Coffee Cake

4. Bake at 350°F. for 25 to 35 minutes or until toothpick inserted in center comes out clean. Spread reserved ⅓ cup preserves over top of cake. Cool 10 minutes before serving. Serve warm.

YIELD: 8 SERVINGS

HIGH ALTITUDE (ABOVE 3500 FEET): No change.

Nutrition Information Per Serving
Serving Size: ⅛ of Recipe

Calories	260	Calories from Fat	70
		% Daily Value	
Total Fat	8g		12%
Saturated	1g		5%
Cholesterol	0mg		0%
Sodium	380mg		16%
Total Carbohydrate	43g		14%
Dietary Fiber	1g		2%
Sugars	21g		
Protein	5g		
Vitamin A	0%	Vitamin C	6%
Calcium	15%	Iron	10%

Dietary Exchanges: 2 Starch, 1 Fruit, 1 Fat OR 3 Carbohydrate, 1 Fat

Passover Apple Lemon Coffee Cake

■ ■ ■ ■ ■ ■ ■ ■ ■ ■ ■ ■ ■ ■ ■ ■

PREP TIME: 15 MINUTES
(READY IN 50 MINUTES)

2 cups (2 medium) finely chopped peeled baking apples

1 tablespoon grated lemon peel

3 tablespoons lemon juice

⅓ cup sugar

2 eggs

¼ cup oil

½ cup matzo meal

⅓ cup potato starch

½ teaspoon cinnamon

¼ teaspoon salt

Glaze
1 tablespoon sugar

1 tablespoon lemon juice

1. Heat oven to 350°F. Spray 8-inch square pan with nonstick cooking spray. In small bowl, combine apples, lemon peel and 3 tablespoons lemon juice; mix well. Set aside.

2. In large bowl, combine ⅓ cup sugar and eggs; beat at medium speed with electric mixer until thick and lemon colored. Slowly add oil, beating until well mixed. Stir in matzo meal.

3. Sift potato starch over apple mixture. Add cinnamon and salt; mix well. Fold into matzo mixture. Spread batter evenly in sprayed pan.

4. Bake at 350°F. for 25 to 35 minutes or until cake springs back when touched lightly in center. In small bowl, combine glaze ingredients; stir until sugar is dissolved. Brush over top of warm cake. Serve warm.

YIELD: 9 SERVINGS

HIGH ALTITUDE (ABOVE 3500 FEET): No change.

Nutrition Information Per Serving
Serving Size: ⅑ of Recipe

Calories	160	Calories from Fat	60
		% Daily Value	
Total Fat	7g		11%
Saturated	1g		5%
Cholesterol	45mg		15%
Sodium	75mg		3%
Total Carbohydrate	23g		8%
Dietary Fiber	1g		2%
Sugars	13g		
Protein	0g		
Vitamin A	0%	Vitamin C	6%
Calcium	6%	Iron	0%

Dietary Exchanges: 1 Starch, ½ Fruit, 1½ Fat

about Passover Ingredients

Matzo meal is coarsely crushed matzo (thin unleavened bread), which substitutes for bread crumbs or flour. It is often used as a breading, a binder for gefilte fish (seasoned ground fish patties) and for matzo balls.

Potato starch, which resembles powdered sugar in appearance, is the sediment collected after potatoes are grated. With a deftly wielded whisk, it stands in for cornstarch in baking (most observant Jews do not use corn or derivative products at Passover) and to thicken sauces and gravies.

Carrot Zucchini Muffins

PREP TIME: 10 MINUTES
(READY IN 35 MINUTES)

2 cups all-purpose flour

1 cup rolled oats

¾ cup firmly packed brown sugar

3 teaspoons baking powder

½ teaspoon cinnamon

¼ teaspoon salt

⅔ cup skim milk

3 tablespoons oil

2 egg whites

1 cup finely shredded carrots

½ cup shredded unpeeled zucchini (1 small)

1. Heat oven to 400°F. Spray 12 muffin cups with nonstick cooking spray, or line muffin cups with paper baking cups and spray paper cups with nonstick cooking spray.

2. In large bowl, combine flour, oats, brown sugar, baking powder, cinnamon and salt; mix well.

3. In small bowl, combine milk, oil and egg whites; blend well. Add to dry ingredients all at once; stir just until dry ingredients are moistened. Stir in carrots and zucchini just until blended. Spoon batter evenly into sprayed muffin cups.

4. Bake at 400°F. for 16 to 21 minutes or until muffins are golden brown and toothpick inserted in center comes out clean. Immediately remove from pan. Serve warm.

YIELD: 12 MUFFINS

HIGH ALTITUDE (ABOVE 3500 FEET): Decrease brown sugar to ⅔ cup. Bake at 400°F. for 18 to 22 minutes.

Nutrition Information Per Serving
Serving Size: 1 Muffin

Calories	200	Calories from Fat	35

		% Daily Value
Total Fat	4g	6%
Saturated	1g	5%
Cholesterol	0mg	0%
Sodium	150mg	6%
Total Carbohydrate	36g	12%
Dietary Fiber	2g	8%
Sugars	15g	
Protein	4g	

Vitamin A	50%	Vitamin C	0%
Calcium	8%	Iron	10%

Dietary Exchanges: 2 Starch, 1 Fat OR 2 Carbohydrate, 1 Fat

muffin *Magic*

Follow these tips for successful muffins.

- To keep the muffins tender, measure ingredients carefully and mix gently, just enough to moisten. Overbeating develops the gluten, a protein in flour that provides structure. Gluten development is a key for yeast bread but will toughen muffins.

- Reduced-fat muffins are more likely to stick to muffin papers than some conventional recipes. For best results, spray muffin tins with nonstick cooking spray instead of using paper liners, or spray the paper liners. Remove the papers while the muffins are still warm.

- Don't overbake the muffins.

- Most homemade muffins, and most reduced-fat baked goods, taste best while still warm. To rejuvenate muffins that have been sitting around for a while, heat them in the microwave oven just long enough to warm them.

◀ Carrot Zucchini Muffins/Cranberry Upside-Down Muffins (page 298)

Cheese-Topped Pumpkin Muffins

■ ■ ■ ■ ■ ■ ■ ■ ■ ■ ■ ■ ■ ■ ■ ■ ■ ■ ■

PREP TIME: 30 MINUTES

1¾ cups all-purpose flour

½ cup sugar

3 teaspoons baking powder

1 teaspoon pumpkin pie spice

¼ teaspoon salt

¾ cup canned pumpkin

½ cup skim milk

¼ cup oil

2 egg whites

4 oz. fat-free cream cheese (from 8-oz. pkg.), cut into 12 cubes*

2 tablespoons brown sugar

1. Heat oven to 400°F. Spray 12 muffin cups with nonstick cooking spray, or line muffin cups with paper baking cups and spray paper cups with nonstick cooking spray.

2. In large bowl, combine flour, sugar, baking powder, pumpkin pie spice and salt; mix well.

---

muffin toppings to add **Before Baking**

Add flavor and texture to a dozen muffins by sprinkling one of these simple topping mixtures over the batter just before baking.

Cinnamon Hazelnut Streusel

2 tablespoons all-purpose flour
2 tablespoons brown sugar
2 tablespoons finely chopped hazelnuts (filberts) or pecans
1 tablespoon oil
½ teaspoon cinnamon

In small bowl, combine all ingredients. Sprinkle 1½ teaspoons mixture over batter in each muffin cup; gently press into batter. Bake. Per serving: 30 calories, 2 g fat.

Savory Streusel Topping

2 tablespoons all-purpose flour
3 tablespoons wheat germ
1 teaspoon dried Italian seasoning
⅛ teaspoon salt
1 tablespoon oil

In small bowl, combine all ingredients; mix well. Sprinkle 1½ teaspoons mixture over batter in each muffin cup; gently press into batter. Bake. Per serving: 20 calories, 1 g fat.

Cinnamon Sugar Topping

5½ teaspoons sugar
½ teaspoon cinnamon

In small bowl, combine sugar and cinnamon. Sprinkle ½ teaspoon mixture over batter in each muffin cup. Bake. Per serving: 6 calories, 0 g fat.

Oat Almond Topping

5 tablespoons rolled oats
1 tablespoon chopped almonds

In small bowl, combine oats and almonds. Sprinkle 1½ teaspoons mixture over batter in each muffin cup; gently press into batter. Bake. Per serving: 12 calories, 1 g fat.

Raspberry Crumble Topping

¾ cup fresh raspberries or frozen unsweetened raspberries
2 tablespoons brown sugar
¼ teaspoon cinnamon

Press raspberries into batter in muffin cups. In small bowl, combine brown sugar and cinnamon. Sprinkle ½ teaspoon mixture over batter in each muffin cup. Bake. Per serving: 12 calories, 0 g fat.

3. In small bowl, combine pumpkin, milk, oil and egg whites; blend well. Add to dry ingredients all at once; stir just until dry ingredients are moistened. Spoon batter evenly into sprayed muffin cups. Press 1 cube cream cheese into center of each muffin. Top each with ½ teaspoon brown sugar.

4. Bake at 400°F. for 14 to 18 minutes or until toothpick inserted near center, but not into cream cheese, comes out clean. Immediately remove from pan. Serve warm. Store in refrigerator.

YIELD: 12 MUFFINS

Tip: * Fat-free cream cheese in a tub can be used. Make indentation in center of each muffin with tip of spoon; place 1½ teaspoons cream cheese in each indentation.

HIGH ALTITUDE (ABOVE 3500 FEET): Increase flour to 1¾ cups plus 2 tablespoons. Divide batter into 14 sprayed muffin cups. Bake at 400°F. for 16 to 20 minutes.

Nutrition Information Per Serving
Serving Size: 1 Muffin

Calories...............170	Calories from Fat.........45	
	% Daily Value	
Total Fat..............5g	...........8%	
Saturated............1g	...........5%	
Cholesterol..........0mg	...........0%	
Sodium................200mg	...........8%	
Total Carbohydrate.....27g	...........9%	
Dietary Fiber.........1g	...........4%	
Sugars...............12g		
Protein..............4g		
Vitamin A............70%	Vitamin C............0%	
Calcium..............10%	Iron.................6%	

Dietary Exchanges: 1½ Starch, 1 Fat OR 1½ Carbohydrate, 1 Fat

about Canned Pumpkin

Canned pumpkin, a convenient year-round alternative to fresh pumpkin puree, makes short work of baking pumpkin recipes. Read the label and make sure you are buying what you want. Pureed or "solid pack" pumpkin is simply unseasoned pumpkin that has been cooked and pureed; "pumpkin pie" preparations are presweetened and spiced. If you are making pie, the latter may serve your purposes, but you'll be better off with plain pumpkin puree for most other dishes.

▲ Coriander Corn Muffins (page 296)/Cheese-Topped Pumpkin Muffins

Coriander Corn Muffins

1½ cups all-purpose flour

½ cup yellow cornmeal

¼ cup sugar

¼ cup firmly packed brown sugar

3 teaspoons baking powder

½ teaspoon coriander

¼ teaspoon salt

½ cup skim milk

¼ cup oil

2 egg whites

1 cup frozen whole kernel corn, thawed*

1. Heat oven to 400°F. Spray 12 muffin cups with nonstick cooking spray, or line muffin cups with paper baking cups and spray paper cups with non-stick cooking spray.

2. In large bowl, combine flour, cornmeal, sugar, brown sugar, baking powder, coriander and salt; mix well.

3. In small bowl, combine milk, oil and egg whites; blend well. Add to dry ingredients all at once; stir just until dry ingredients are moistened. Gently stir in corn. Spoon batter evenly into sprayed muffin cups.

4. Bake at 400°F. for 14 to 19 minutes or until muffins are light golden brown and toothpick inserted in center comes out clean. Immediately remove from pan. Serve warm.

YIELD: 12 MUFFINS

Tip: * To quickly thaw corn, place in colander or strainer; rinse with warm water until thawed. Drain well.

HIGH ALTITUDE (ABOVE 3500 FEET): Decrease baking powder to 2 teaspoons. Bake as directed above.

Nutrition Information Per Serving
Serving Size: 1 Muffin

Calories	170	Calories from Fat	45
		% Daily Value	
Total Fat	5g		8%
Saturated	1g		5%
Cholesterol	0mg		0%
Sodium	140mg		6%
Total Carbohydrate	28g		9%
Dietary Fiber	1g		4%
Sugars	10g		
Protein	3g		
Vitamin A	0%	Vitamin C	0%
Calcium	6%	Iron	6%

Dietary Exchanges: 1½ Starch, 1 Fat OR 1½ Carbohydrate, 1 Fat

about **Coriander Seed**

Dried coriander seed comes from the same plant that produces the citrusy-tasting green herb (also called cilantro) that's a favorite flavor in Asian, Indian, Latin American and American Southwest cooking. The seeds, however, have a sweet flavor more reminiscent of orange-caraway-nutmeg and are often used in baking or in curry and other spice blends.

Refrigerator Apple Bran Muffins

2 cups shreds of whole bran cereal

1½ cups buttermilk*

2 cups all-purpose flour

½ cup whole wheat flour

1 cup sugar

1 teaspoon baking powder

1 teaspoon baking soda

1 teaspoon cinnamon

1 teaspoon ginger

¼ teaspoon salt

½ cup raisins

1 cup unsweetened applesauce

½ cup oil

4 egg whites

muffin toppings to add **After Baking**

Dress up a dozen muffins warm from the oven with one of these simple topping combos.

Honey Sunflower Nut Topping

¼ cup honey, heated
2 tablespoons unsalted shelled
sunflower seeds, toasted

Brush each warm muffin with 1 teaspoon honey; sprinkle each with ½ teaspoon sunflower seeds. Per serving: 30 calories, 1 g fat.

Maple Walnut Topping

¾ cup powdered sugar
2 to 3 tablespoons maple-flavored syrup,
heated
2 tablespoons finely chopped walnuts

In small bowl, combine powdered sugar and syrup; stir until smooth. Drizzle 1 teaspoon mix-ture over each warm muffin; sprinkle each with ½ teaspoon walnuts. Per serving: 50 calories, 1 g fat.

Fruit and Preserves Topping

¼ cup light peach or apricot syrup
¼ cup dried mixed fruit bits, finely
chopped

Brush each warm muffin with 1 teaspoon peach syrup; sprinkle each with 1 teaspoon fruit bits. Per serving: 18 calories, 0 g fat.

Lemon Drizzle Topping

⅔ cup powdered sugar
2 to 3 teaspoons lemon juice
Grated lemon peel

In small bowl, combine powdered sugar and lemon juice; stir until smooth. Drizzle 1 teaspoon mixture over each warm muffin; sprinkle each with lemon peel. Per serving: 25 calories, 0 g fat.

1. In medium bowl, combine cereal and buttermilk; let stand 5 minutes or until cereal is softened.

2. Meanwhile, in large bowl, combine all-purpose flour, whole wheat flour, sugar, baking powder, baking soda, cinnamon, ginger, salt and raisins; mix well.

3. To cereal mixture, add applesauce, oil and egg whites; blend well. Add to dry ingredients all at once; stir just until dry ingredients are moistened. Batter can be baked immediately or stored for up to 2 weeks in tightly covered container in refrigerator.

4. When ready to bake, heat oven to 400°F. Spray desired number of muffin cups with nonstick cooking spray or line with paper baking cups. Stir batter; fill sprayed muffin cups ¾ full. If desired, sprinkle with sugar.

5. Bake at 400°F. for 15 to 20 minutes or until toothpick inserted in center comes out clean. Immediately remove from pan. Serve warm.

YIELD: 30 MUFFINS

Tip: * To substitute for buttermilk, use 4½ teaspoons vinegar or lemon juice plus skim milk to make 1½ cups.

HIGH ALTITUDE (ABOVE 3500 FEET): Increase all-purpose flour to 2¼ cups. Bake as directed above.

Nutrition Information Per Serving
Serving Size: 1 Muffin

Calories	130	Calories from Fat	35
		% Daily Value	
Total Fat	4g		6%
Saturated	1g		5%
Cholesterol	0mg		0%
Sodium	140mg		6%
Total Carbohydrate	21g		7%
Dietary Fiber	2g		8%
Sugars	10g		
Protein	3g		
Vitamin A	4%	Vitamin C	2%
Calcium	4%	Iron	6%

Dietary Exchanges: 1 Starch, ½ Fruit, ½ Fat OR 1½ Carbohydrate, ½ Fat

Cranberry Upside-Down Muffins

■ ■ ■ ■ ■ ■ ■ ■ ■ ■ ■ ■ ■ ■ ■ ■ ■ ■

PREP TIME: 15 MINUTES
(READY IN 35 MINUTES)

¾ cup whole berry cranberry sauce

¼ cup firmly packed brown sugar

2 cups all-purpose flour

2 tablespoons sugar

3 teaspoons baking powder

½ teaspoon salt

1 cup skim milk

¼ cup oil

1 teaspoon grated orange peel

2 egg whites

1. Heat oven to 400°F. Spray 12 muffin cups with nonstick cooking spray. Spoon 1 tablespoon cranberry sauce into each muffin cup; top each with 1 teaspoon brown sugar.

2. In large bowl, combine flour, sugar, baking powder and salt; mix well.

3. In small bowl, combine milk, oil, orange peel and egg whites; blend well. Add to dry ingredients all at once; stir just until dry ingredients are moistened. Spoon batter evenly over cranberries and brown sugar in muffin cups.

4. Bake at 400°F. for 14 to 18 minutes or until toothpick inserted in center comes out clean. Cool in pan 1 minute. Loosen muffin edges with knife; invert onto wire rack set over sheet of waxed paper. Cool 5 minutes before serving.

YIELD: 12 MUFFINS

HIGH ALTITUDE (ABOVE 3500 FEET): No change.

Nutrition Information Per Serving
Serving Size: 1 Muffin

Calories	180	Calories from Fat	45
		% Daily Value	
Total Fat	5g		8%
Saturated	1g		5%
Cholesterol	0mg		0%
Sodium	200mg		8%
Total Carbohydrate	31g		10%
Dietary Fiber	1g		3%
Sugars	14g		
Protein	3g		
Vitamin A	0%	Vitamin C	0%
Calcium	8%	Iron	6%

Dietary Exchanges: 1 Starch, 1 Fruit, 1 Fat OR 2 Carbohydrate, 1 Fat

using Citrus Peel

■ ■ ■ ■ ■ ■ ■ ■ ■ ■ ■ ■ ■ ■ ■ ■

Citrus skin contains oils that have intense flavor that can brighten up many sweet or savory recipes. In recipes that call for the zest or peel of an orange, lemon or lime (rarely grapefruit), make sure to use the very thin outer colored layer of the peel, not the bitter white pith.

The easiest ways to remove the zest are with a sharp, fine-holed grater or with a tool called a zester. A zester has a handle like a potato peeler but a small metal head (rather than a long blade) with several sharp holes that remove fine strands of zest. You also can remove thin pieces of zest with a sharp vegetable peeler or paring knife and then shred or mince the pieces with a knife.

Cheese Latkes with Fruit Topping

■ ■ ■ ■ ■ ■ ■ ■ ■ ■ ■ ■ ■ ■ ■ ■ ■ ■

PREP TIME: 30 MINUTES

Pancakes
1 (8-oz.) carton (1 cup) refrigerated or frozen fat-free egg product, thawed, or 4 eggs

1 (15-oz.) container light ricotta cheese

⅓ cup all-purpose flour

¼ cup sugar

1 teaspoon baking powder

2 tablespoons oil

2 teaspoons vanilla

Topping
1 cup low-fat plain yogurt

1 cup sliced banana, berries or other fruit

▲ Cheese Latkes with Fruit Topping

1. In medium bowl with wire whisk or in food processor bowl with metal blade, combine all pancake ingredients; beat or process until smooth and well blended.

2. Heat nonstick griddle or large skillet to medium-low heat (325°F.). Lightly oil griddle. Spoon rounded tablespoons of batter onto hot griddle, spreading to form 3-inch pancakes. Cook until bubbles form on tops, and bottoms are golden brown. Carefully loosen with pancake turner; turn and brown other side.

3. Place pancakes on cookie sheet; keep warm in 250°F. oven. Repeat with remaining batter, coating griddle with oil between batches. Serve warm pancakes with yogurt and fruit.

YIELD: 42 PANCAKES; 14 SERVINGS

Tip: If pancakes stick to griddle, add 1 to 2 tablespoons water to batter.

Nutrition Information Per Serving
Serving Size: 1 Pancake

Calories	100	Calories from Fat	25
		% Daily Value	
Total Fat	3g		5%
Saturated	1g		5%
Cholesterol	4mg		1%
Sodium	200mg		8%
Total Carbohydrate	11g		4%
Dietary Fiber	0g		0%
Sugars	7g		
Protein	7g		
Vitamin A	2%	Vitamin C	0%
Calcium	8%	Iron	4%

Dietary Exchanges: ½ Starch, 1 Lean Meat OR ½ Carbohydrate, 1 Lean Meat

Oat and Wheat Pancakes with Cherry-Berry Sauce

▪ ▪

PREP TIME: 40 MINUTES

Sauce

½ cup water

1 tablespoon cornstarch

¼ cup sugar

2 teaspoons fresh lemon juice

2 teaspoons vanilla

¼ teaspoon ginger

1½ cups frozen unsweetened pitted dark sweet cherries

1½ cups frozen unsweetened raspberries or blueberries

▼ Oat and Wheat Pancakes with Cherry-Berry Sauce

Pancakes

¾ cup uncooked oat bran hot cereal

½ cup whole wheat flour

3 tablespoons dark brown sugar

2 tablespoons wheat germ

2 ¼ teaspoons baking powder

¼ teaspoon salt

1¼ cups skim milk

1 tablespoon oil

2 egg whites or ⅓ cup refrigerated or frozen fat-free egg product, thawed

1. In medium saucepan, combine water and corn-starch; stir until cornstarch is dissolved. Stir in all remaining sauce ingredients. Cook over medium-high heat for 10 to 15 minutes or until mixture comes to a boil, stirring occasionally. Boil 1 minute. Set aside.

2. In medium bowl, combine oat bran, flour, brown sugar, wheat germ, baking powder and salt; mix well.

Pancake *stir-ins*

It's easy to transform plain pancakes into better-tasting, better for you versions. For a recipe that yields 8 to 10 (4-inch) pancakes, stir any of these whole-grain or fruit additions into packaged mix or your favorite basic recipe.

- $1/3$ cup wheat bran, $1/4$ cup unsweetened applesauce and 2 tablespoons chopped walnuts

- $1/2$ cup cooked brown rice, wild rice or barley and $1/4$ teaspoon almond extract

- $1/2$ cup chopped fresh fruit (pears, apples, peaches, bananas) and $1/8$ teaspoon powdered ginger or coconut extract

- 2 tablespoons yellow cornmeal and $1/4$ cup chopped lean ham or shredded reduced-fat cheddar cheese

- $1/4$ cup quick-cooking rolled oats, $1/2$ teaspoon cinnamon and 2 tablespoons additional water

- $1/2$ cup wheat germ and $1/4$ cup low-fat cottage cheese

- $1/4$ cup dried fruit (chopped apricots or dates, cranberries, raisins) and 1 teaspoon grated lemon peel

- $1/2$ cup blueberries (sprinkle 1 to 2 tablespoons on top of each pancake before turning)

- $1/2$ cup low-fat granola cereal, $1/4$ cup orange juice and 1 teaspoon grated orange peel

- $1/3$ cup uncooked multigrain oatmeal hot cereal mix, 2 teaspoons instant coffee granules or crystals, 2 tablespoons hot cocoa mix and 3 tablespoons water

3. In small bowl, combine milk, oil and egg whites; beat until well blended. Add to dry ingredients; stir just until dry ingredients are moistened and large lumps disappear.

4. Heat nonstick griddle or large skillet to medium-high heat (375°F.). Pour scant $1/4$ cup batter onto hot griddle, spreading to form 4-inch pancakes. Cook $1^1/2$ to 2 minutes, turning when edges look cooked and bubbles begin to break on surface. Continue to cook $1^1/2$ to 2 minutes or until golden brown. Serve warm sauce over pancakes.

YIELD: 12 PANCAKES; 4 SERVINGS

Nutrition Information Per Serving
Serving Size: $1/4$ of Recipe

Calories	370	Calories from Fat	50

		% Daily Value
Total Fat	6g	9%
Saturated	1g	5%
Cholesterol	0mg	0%
Sodium	480mg	20%
Total Carbohydrate	68g	23%
Dietary Fiber	9g	36%
Sugars	39g	
Protein	11g	

Vitamin A	6%	Vitamin C	20%
Calcium	30%	Iron	15%

Dietary Exchanges: 3 Starch, $1^1/2$ Fruit, 1 Fat OR $4^1/2$ Carbohydrate, 1 Fat

what's Egg Substitute?

Egg substitute is pasteurized egg white plus a trace of vegetable gums (less than 1%) and a bit of coloring. It comes frozen or refrigerated in boxes that resemble milk cartons. Simply pour the amount needed in a recipe: $1/4$ cup egg substitute = 1 whole fresh egg.

Nutrition Comparison

	1 Large Egg	$1/4$ cup Egg Substitute*
Calories	80	30
Protein	6 g	6 g
Carbohydrate	1 g	1 g
Fat	6 g	0 g
Cholesterol	270 mg	0 mg
Sodium	70 mg	100 mg

Source: Egg Beaters package label

Whole-Grain Waffles

■ ■ ■ ■ ■ ■ ■ ■ ■ ■ ■ ■ ■ ■ ■ ■

PREP TIME: 20 MINUTES

½ **cup all-purpose flour**

½ **cup whole wheat flour**

½ **cup quick-cooking rolled oats**

2 **teaspoons baking powder**

1¼ **cups skim milk**

1 **tablespoon oil**

¼ **cup refrigerated or frozen fat-free egg product, thawed, or 1 egg**

1. Heat nonstick waffle iron. In large bowl, combine all-purpose flour, whole wheat flour, oats and baking powder; mix well.

2. In small bowl, combine milk, oil and egg product; blend well. Add to dry ingredients all at once; stir just until large lumps disappear. Spread batter in hot waffle iron; bake until waffle is golden brown and steaming stops.

YIELD: 6 (4-INCH) WAFFLES; 3 SERVINGS

HIGH ALTITUDE (ABOVE 3500 FEET): No change.

Nutrition Information Per Serving
Serving Size: ⅓ of Recipe

Calories................280	Calories from Fat..........50	
		% Daily Value
Total Fat.....................6g	.........9%	
Saturated.....................1g	.........5%	
Cholesterol................0mg	.........0%	
Sodium.....................300mg	.........13%	
Total Carbohydrate..........45g	.........15%	
Dietary Fiber.................4g	.........16%	
Sugars........................6g		
Protein.......................12g		
Vitamin A..................6%	Vitamin C....................0%	
Calcium....................25%	Iron.........................15%	

Dietary Exchanges: 3 Starch, 1 Fat OR 3 Carbohydrate, 1 Fat

make-ahead **Waffles**

■ ■ ■ ■ ■ ■ ■ ■ ■ ■ ■ ■ ■ ■ ■ ■

Double the waffle recipe on a leisurely weekend. Individually wrap and freeze leftovers. For a quick midweek breakfast, just pop a waffle into the toaster.

Rosemary Bell Pepper Bread

■ ■ ■ ■ ■ ■ ■ ■ ■ ■ ■ ■ ■ ■ ■ ■ ■ ■

PREP TIME: 10 MINUTES
(READY IN 35 MINUTES)

1¾ **cups all-purpose flour**

1½ **teaspoons baking powder**

½ **teaspoon baking soda**

¼ **teaspoon salt**

2 **tablespoons margarine or butter**

⅔ **cup skim milk**

½ **cup chopped red, yellow or green bell pepper**

1 **teaspoon chopped fresh rosemary or**
   ½ **teaspoon dried rosemary leaves, crushed**

1 **egg or 2 egg whites**

2 **tablespoons grated Parmesan cheese**

1. Heat oven to 400°F. Spray 8- or 9-inch round cake pan with nonstick cooking spray.

2. In large bowl, combine flour, baking powder, baking soda and salt; mix well.

3. Using pastry blender or fork, cut in margarine until well mixed. Stir in milk, bell pepper, rosemary and egg until soft dough forms. Spread dough evenly in sprayed pan. Sprinkle with Parmesan cheese.

4. Bake at 400°F. for 16 to 22 minutes or until center is firm to the touch and cheese is golden brown. Cut into wedges. Serve warm or cool.

YIELD: 12 SERVINGS

HIGH ALTITUDE (ABOVE 3500 FEET): No change.

Nutrition Information Per Serving
Serving Size: 1/12 of Recipe

Calories................100	Calories from Fat..........25	
		% Daily Value
Total Fat.....................3g	.........5%	
Saturated.....................1g	.........5%	
Cholesterol................20mg	.........7%	
Sodium.....................210mg	.........9%	
Total Carbohydrate..........15g	.........5%	
Dietary Fiber.................1g	.........2%	
Sugars........................1g		
Protein.......................3g		
Vitamin A..................8%	Vitamin C...................10%	
Calcium.....................8%	Iron..........................6%	

Dietary Exchanges: 1 Starch, ½ Fat OR 1 Carbohydrate, ½ Fat

▲ Southwest Salsa Cornbread/Zucchini Bread with Dried Cranberries (page 305)/Tomato Basil Dinner Bread (page 304)

Southwest Salsa Cornbread

PREP TIME: 10 MINUTES
(READY IN 35 MINUTES)

1 ¼ cups all-purpose flour

¾ cup cornmeal

2 teaspoons baking powder

¼ teaspoon salt

1 cup frozen whole kernel corn or 7-oz. can vacuum-packed whole kernel corn, drained

¾ cup skim milk

½ cup chunky-style salsa

3 tablespoons oil

1 egg

1. Heat oven to 400°F. Spray 9-inch square pan with nonstick cooking spray.

2. In large bowl, combine flour, cornmeal, baking powder and salt; mix well. Add all remaining ingredients; stir just until well mixed. Spoon batter evenly into sprayed pan.

3. Bake at 400°F. for 18 to 23 minutes or until toothpick inserted in center comes out clean. Cut into squares. Serve warm.

YIELD: 12 SERVINGS
HIGH ALTITUDE (ABOVE 3500 FEET): No change.

Nutrition Information Per Serving
Serving Size: 1/12 of Recipe

Calories	130	Calories from Fat	35
		% Daily Value	
Total Fat	4g		6%
Saturated	1g		5%
Cholesterol	20mg		7%
Sodium	260mg		11%
Total Carbohydrate	20g		7%
Dietary Fiber	1g		4%
Sugars	2g		
Protein	4g		
Vitamin A	4%	Vitamin C	10%
Calcium	8%	Iron	6%

Dietary Exchanges: 1 ½ Starch, ½ Fat OR 1 ½ Carbohydrate, ½ Fat

Spicy Sweet Potato Bread

PREP TIME: 30 MINUTES

½ cup sugar

½ cup mashed canned or cooked sweet potatoes

⅓ cup skim milk

1 tablespoon oil

1 egg or 2 egg whites

1 cup all-purpose flour

2 teaspoons baking powder

¼ teaspoon nutmeg

¼ teaspoon allspice

½ cup dried currants

1. Heat oven to 400°F. Spray 8- or 9-inch square pan with nonstick cooking spray.

2. In large bowl, combine sugar and sweet potatoes; blend well. Add milk, oil and egg; mix well.

3. Add flour, baking powder, nutmeg and allspice; stir until well combined. Stir in currants. Pour batter into sprayed pan.

4. Bake at 400°F. for 12 to 19 minutes or until bread is light golden brown and center is firm to the touch. Cut into squares. Serve warm or cool.

YIELD: 12 SERVINGS

HIGH ALTITUDE (ABOVE 3500 FEET): No change.

Nutrition Information Per Serving
Serving Size: 1/12 of Recipe

Calories	120	Calories from Fat	20
		% Daily Value	
Total Fat	2g		3%
Saturated	0g		0%
Cholesterol	20mg		7%
Sodium	95mg		4%
Total Carbohydrate	24g		8%
Dietary Fiber	1g		4%
Sugars	14g		
Protein	2g		
Vitamin A	20%	Vitamin C	4%
Calcium	6%	Iron	6%

Dietary Exchanges: 1 Starch, ½ Fruit OR 1½ Carbohydrate

Tomato Basil Dinner Bread

PREP TIME: 10 MINUTES
(READY IN 40 MINUTES)

2 cups all-purpose flour

1½ teaspoons baking powder

½ teaspoon baking soda

¼ teaspoon salt

1 cup (3 medium) chopped Italian plum tomatoes

¾ cup nonfat plain yogurt

¼ cup chopped fresh basil

2 tablespoons margarine or butter, softened

1 egg or 2 egg whites

1. Heat oven to 400°F. Spray 9-inch round cake pan with nonstick cooking spray. In large bowl, combine flour, baking powder, baking soda and salt; mix well.

2. In small bowl, combine tomatoes, yogurt, basil, margarine and egg; blend well. Add to flour mixture; stir just until dry ingredients are moistened. Spoon dough evenly into sprayed pan.

3. Bake at 400°F. for 22 to 28 minutes or until bread is golden brown and center is firm to the touch. Cut into wedges. Serve warm.

YIELD: 12 SERVINGS

HIGH ALTITUDE (ABOVE 3500 FEET): No change.

Nutrition Information Per Serving
Serving Size: 1/12 of Recipe

Calories	120	Calories from Fat	25
		% Daily Value	
Total Fat	3g		5%
Saturated	1g		5%
Cholesterol	20mg		7%
Sodium	200mg		8%
Total Carbohydrate	18g		6%
Dietary Fiber	1g		3%
Sugars	2g		
Protein	4g		
Vitamin A	4%	Vitamin C	4%
Calcium	8%	Iron	6%

Dietary Exchanges: 1 Starch, ½ Fat OR 1 Carbohydrate, ½ Fat

Zucchini Bread with Dried Cranberries

■ ■

PREP TIME: 15 MINUTES
(READY IN 35 MINUTES)

½ **cup sugar**

½ **cup shredded unpeeled zucchini (1 small)**

⅓ **cup skim milk**

1 **tablespoon oil**

1 **egg or 2 egg whites**

1 **cup all-purpose flour**

2 **teaspoons baking powder**

½ **teaspoon cinnamon**

¼ **teaspoon cloves**

½ **cup sweetened dried cranberries**

1 **tablespoon sugar, if desired**

1. Heat oven to 400°F. Spray 8- or 9-inch round cake pan with nonstick cooking spray. In large bowl, combine ½ cup sugar, zucchini, milk, oil and egg; mix well.

2. Add flour, baking powder, cinnamon, cloves and dried cranberries; mix just until combined. Pour into sprayed pan; sprinkle with 1 tablespoon sugar.

3. Bake at 400°F. for 12 to 19 minutes or until light golden brown. Cool 5 minutes before serving. Cut into wedges. Serve warm.

YIELD: 12 SERVINGS

HIGH ALTITUDE (ABOVE 3500 FEET): No change.

Nutrition Information Per Serving
Serving Size: 1/12 of Recipe

Calories..............................120	Calories from Fat 20
	% Daily Value
Total Fat 2g	...........3%
Saturated 0g	...........0%
Cholesterol 20mg	...........7%
Sodium 90mg	...........4%
Total Carbohydrate.............23g	...........8%
Dietary Fiber 1g	...........4%
Sugars................................15g	
Protein................................2g	
Vitamin A 0%	Vitamin C 0%
Calcium 6%	Iron................................4%

Dietary Exchanges: 1 Starch, ½ Fruit OR 1½ Carbohydrate

Miniature Quick Cherry Pecan Scones

■ ■

PREP TIME: 25 MINUTES

2 **cups all-purpose flour**

1 **tablespoon sugar**

3 **teaspoons baking powder**

¾ **to 1 cup skim milk**

2 **tablespoons oil**

2 **tablespoons finely chopped maraschino cherries, well drained on paper towel**

2 **tablespoons finely chopped pecans**

1. Heat oven to 450°F. In medium bowl, combine flour, sugar and baking powder; blend well. Add ¾ cup milk and oil; stir just until dry ingredients are moistened, adding additional milk, 1 tablespoon at a time, if necessary to form a soft dough. Stir in cherries and pecans.

2. On generously floured surface with floured hands, knead dough 15 to 20 times. Pat into 1-inch-thick round; cut with floured 1½-inch round cutter.* Place scones on ungreased cookie sheet.

3. Bake at 450°F. for 8 to 9 minutes or until light golden brown. Serve warm.

YIELD: 20 SCONES

Tip: * If desired, pat dough into 1-inch-thick 5 × 4-inch rectangle; cut into 20 squares.

HIGH ALTITUDE (ABOVE 3500 FEET): No change.

Nutrition Information Per Serving
Serving Size: 1 Scone

Calories..................................70	Calories from Fat 20
	% Daily Value
Total Fat 2g	...........3%
Saturated 0g	...........0%
Cholesterol 0mg	...........0%
Sodium 80mg	...........3%
Total Carbohydrate.............11g	...........4%
Dietary Fiber 0g	...........0%
Sugars 2g	
Protein................................2g	
Vitamin A 0%	Vitamin C 0%
Calcium 6%	Iron................................4%

Dietary Exchanges: 1 Starch OR 1 Carbohydrate

Moist Spiced Apple Scones

■ ■ ■ ■ ■ ■ ■ ■ ■ ■ ■ ■ ■ ■ ■ ■ ■ ■ ■

PREP TIME: 15 MINUTES
(READY IN 40 MINUTES)

Scones
2 cups all-purpose flour

½ cup firmly packed brown sugar

2 teaspoons baking powder

½ teaspoon cinnamon

¼ teaspoon nutmeg

¼ teaspoon ginger

⅛ teaspoon salt

2 tablespoons margarine or butter

1 cup chopped dried apples

½ cup unsweetened applesauce

¼ cup buttermilk*

1 egg

Topping
1 teaspoon sugar

⅛ teaspoon cinnamon

1. Heat oven to 375°F. Spray large cookie sheet with nonstick cooking spray. In medium bowl, combine flour, brown sugar, baking powder, ½ teaspoon cinnamon, nutmeg, ginger and salt; mix well.

2. Using pastry blender or fork, cut in margarine until mixture resembles coarse crumbs. Stir in apples.

3. In small bowl, combine applesauce, buttermilk and egg; mix well. Add to dry ingredients; stir just until dry ingredients are moistened. (Dough will be sticky.) Place dough on sprayed cookie sheet. With wet fingers, shape into 8-inch round, about ¾ inch thick.

4. In another small bowl, combine topping ingredients; sprinkle over top of dough. With sharp knife, score top surface into 8 wedges, cutting about ¼ inch deep.

5. Bake at 375°F. for 18 to 22 minutes or until scones are golden brown and toothpick inserted in center comes out clean. Cut into wedges. Serve warm.

YIELD: 8 SCONES

Tip: * To substitute for buttermilk, use ¾ teaspoon vinegar or lemon juice plus skim milk to make ¼ cup.

HIGH ALTITUDE (ABOVE 3500 FEET): No change.

Nutrition Information Per Serving
Serving Size: 1 Scone

Calories	240	Calories from Fat	35
		% Daily Value	
Total Fat	4g		6%
Saturated	1g		5%
Cholesterol	25mg		8%
Sodium	180mg		8%
Total Carbohydrate	47g		16%
Dietary Fiber	2g		8%
Sugars	23g		
Protein	4g		
Vitamin A	4%	Vitamin C	0%
Calcium	8%	Iron	10%

Dietary Exchanges: 2 Starch, 1 Fruit, ½ Fat OR 3 Carbohydrate, ½ Fat

about Scones

Scones, a British favorite for teatime, are a sweetened baking powder biscuit. They're often spiked with raisins, currants or dried fruit and cut into circles, wedges or triangles.

Desserts

11

Luscious Berry Lemon Tart (page (page 332)

Black Forest Cherry-Cranberry Cake

PREP TIME: 25 MINUTES
(READY IN 55 MINUTES)

Cake

1 (1 lb. 2.25-oz.) pkg. devil's food cake mix

2 tablespoons all-purpose flour

1¾ cups water

¾ cup refrigerated or frozen fat-free egg product, thawed, or 3 eggs

▼ Black Forest Cherry-Cranberry Cake

Filling and Topping

1 (21-oz.) can cherry-cranberry or cherry pie filling

¾ teaspoon almond extract

2 cups frozen light whipped topping, thawed

1. Heat oven to 350°F. Spray 15 × 10 × 1-inch baking pan with nonstick cooking spray. Line bottom with waxed paper; spray paper. Prepare cake mix as directed on package using flour, water and egg product. Pour into sprayed paper-lined pan.

2. Bake at 350°F. for 18 to 20 minutes or until cake springs back when touched lightly in center. Remove cake from pan; remove waxed paper. Cool 15 minutes.

3. In small bowl, combine pie filling and ½ teaspoon of the almond extract; mix well.

4. Cut cake in half crosswise to form two 10 × 7-inch layers. Place 1 cake layer on serving platter or tray; spread pie filling mixture over top. Top with remaining cake layer.

5. Stir remaining ¼ teaspoon almond extract into whipped topping. Spread mixture over top and sides of cake. Serve immediately or refrigerate until serving time. If desired, garnish each serving with maraschino or candied cherry and chocolate curls. Store in refrigerator.

YIELD: 12 SERVINGS

HIGH ALTITUDE (ABOVE 3500 FEET): Increase flour to ⅓ cup.
Bake as directed above.

Nutrition Information Per Serving
Serving Size: 1/12 of Recipe

Calories	270	Calories from Fat	45
		% Daily Value	
Total Fat	5g		8%
Saturated	3g		15%
Cholesterol	0mg		0%
Sodium	370mg		15%
Total Carbohydrate	51g		17%
Dietary Fiber	2g		8%
Sugars	31g		
Protein	4g		
Vitamin A	4%	Vitamin C	2%
Calcium	4%	Iron	10%

Dietary Exchanges: 1½ Starch, 2 Fruit, 1 Fat OR 3½ Carbohydrate, 1 Fat

Almond extract imparts a nutty nuance that's especially good in combination with fruit desserts. It's made from bitter almonds because their more intense flavor holds up better in processing than that of the sweet almonds that we eat raw. Bitter almonds aren't sold raw in the United States because they contain a substance that's poisonous in all but small quantities. (Heat during processing destroys the substance, prussic acid, and renders them safe for extracts and other flavorings.)

Sugar-Crusted Lime Cake

■ ■ ■ ■ ■ ■ ■ ■ ■ ■ ■ ■ ■ ■ ■

PREP TIME: 15 MINUTES
(READY IN 1 HOUR 20 MINUTES)

Cake

2 egg whites, room temperature*

½ teaspoon baking powder

1 cup all-purpose flour

¾ cup sugar

1 tablespoon grated lime peel

1 teaspoon baking powder

¼ teaspoon salt

⅓ cup skim milk

¼ cup shortening

2 tablespoons lime juice

Topping

¼ cup sugar

1 tablespoon lime juice

1. Heat oven to 350°F. Spray 9-inch round cake pan with nonstick cooking spray; sprinkle lightly with flour.

2. In small bowl, combine egg whites and ½ teaspoon baking powder; beat until stiff peaks form. Set aside.

3. In large bowl, combine flour and all remaining cake ingredients; beat at low speed until moistened. Beat 2 minutes at medium speed. Gently fold stiffly beaten egg whites into batter. Pour into sprayed and floured pan.

4. Bake at 350°F. for 27 to 35 minutes or until toothpick inserted in center comes out clean.

5. In small bowl, combine topping ingredients; spread over hot cake. Cool cake in pan on wire rack for 30 minutes or until completely cooled.

YIELD: 8 SERVINGS

Tip: * For higher volume, bring egg whites to room temperature before beating. Set bowl of egg whites in large bowl of very warm water; stir gently for 2 to 3 minutes.

HIGH ALTITUDE (ABOVE 3500 FEET): Decrease sugar in cake to ⅔ cup. Bake as directed above.

Nutrition Information Per Serving
Serving Size: ⅛ of Recipe

Calories	220	Calories from Fat	50
		% Daily Value	
Total Fat	6g		9%
Saturated	2g		10%
Cholesterol	0mg		0%
Sodium	180mg		8%
Total Carbohydrate	38g		13%
Dietary Fiber	1g		2%
Sugars	26g		
Protein	3g		
Vitamin A	0%	Vitamin C	0%
Calcium	6%	Iron	4%

Dietary Exchanges: 1 Starch, 1½ Fruit, 1 Fat OR 2½ Carbohydrate, 1 Fat

Gingerbread Streusel Cake

Streusel

1 tablespoon all-purpose flour

2 tablespoons quick-cooking rolled oats

2 tablespoons brown sugar

⅛ teaspoon ginger

⅛ teaspoon cinnamon

1 tablespoon margarine or butter

Cake

1¾ cups all-purpose flour

1 teaspoon baking powder

1 teaspoon ginger

¼ teaspoon baking soda

¼ teaspoon salt

½ cup skim milk

½ cup light molasses

3 tablespoons oil

1 egg

1. Heat oven to 350°F. Spray bottom and sides of 9-inch square pan with nonstick cooking spray.

2. In small bowl, combine all streusel ingredients except margarine; mix well. Using fork or pastry blender, cut in margarine until mixture resembles coarse crumbs. Set aside.

3. In large bowl, combine 1¾ cups flour, baking powder, 1 teaspoon ginger, baking soda and salt; mix well. Add milk, molasses, oil and egg; beat with wire whisk about 1 minute or until smooth. Pour batter evenly into sprayed pan. Sprinkle with streusel mixture.

4. Bake at 350°F. for 18 to 23 minutes or until center is firm to the touch. Cut into squares; serve warm or cool. If desired, serve topped with light whipped topping or nonfat vanilla yogurt.

YIELD: 9 SERVINGS
HIGH ALTITUDE (ABOVE 3500 FEET): No change.

Nutrition Information Per Serving
Serving Size: ⅑ of Recipe

Calories	220	Calories from Fat	60
			% Daily Value
Total Fat	7g		11%
Saturated	1g		5%
Cholesterol	25mg		8%
Sodium	190mg		8%
Total Carbohydrate	36g		12%
Dietary Fiber	1g		3%
Sugars	15g		
Protein	4g		
Vitamin A	2%	Vitamin C	0%
Calcium	10%	Iron	15%

Dietary Exchanges: 1½ Starch, 1 Fruit, 1 Fat OR 2½ Carbohydrate, 1 Fat

Blackberry-Topped Angel Food Dessert

½ cup blackberry jam

1 tablespoon crème de cassis liqueur*

1 (16½-oz.) can blackberries in syrup, drained

6 (¾-inch-thick) slices angel food cake

3 cups nonfat vanilla frozen yogurt

2 tablespoons powdered sugar

1. In medium bowl, combine jam and liqueur; mix well. Fold in blackberries.

2. Place 1 slice of cake on each of 6 individual dessert plates. Top each with ½ cup frozen yogurt; spoon about ¼ cup blackberry mixture over each. Sprinkle desserts with powdered sugar.

YIELD: 6 SERVINGS

Tip: * Two teaspoons brandy or ½ teaspoon brandy extract can be substituted for the crème de cassis liqueur.

vanilla *Forms*

Vanilla Bean Vanilla bean is the costliest way to buy vanilla. Prices range from 50 cents to several dollars a bean. Beans usually come individually packaged in glass tubes; look for whitish crystals on the outside of the bean. Use the bean whole to flavor sauces or custards, then rinse it off, dry it and store it again in the tube; one bean can be used again several times for such uses. Or, break off and use a small piece at a time. Or, split the bean open and use a tiny spoon to scrape out the little seeds inside. One bean scraping equals about $1\frac{1}{2}$ to 2 tablespoons of extract, so you probably only need a portion of a bean for a recipe. Use the scraped-out pod to make "vanilla sugar" by burying the pod in granulated sugar; use the flavored sugar for baking.

Pure Vanilla Extract Pure vanilla extract is the next costliest form. The law requires that pure extracts contain at least 13.5 ounces of beans to each gallon of liquid and a 35 percent alcohol level.

Vanilla Flavoring Vanilla flavoring contains less than 35 percent alcohol and a lower bean-to-liquid ratio.

Imitation Vanilla Imitation vanilla is the least costly flavoring because it is synthetic. It contains no vanilla beans.

Nutrition Information Per Serving
Serving Size: $\frac{1}{6}$ of Recipe

Calories................................330	Calories from Fat 0	
	% Daily Value	
Total Fat 0g	....0%	
Saturated 0g	....0%	
Cholesterol 0mg	....0%	
Sodium 370mg	....15%	
Total Carbohydrate 75g	....25%	
Dietary Fiber 3g	....12%	
Sugars............................69g		
Protein 6g		
Vitamin A 2%	Vitamin C 6%	
Calcium 15%	Iron 4%	

Dietary Exchanges: 2 Starch, 3 Fruit OR 5 Carbohydrate

Grandma's Apricot Kuchen

PREP TIME: 10 MINUTES
(READY IN 40 MINUTES)

5 tablespoons margarine or butter, softened

⅓ cup sugar

1 teaspoon vanilla

1 egg

1 cup all-purpose flour

½ teaspoon baking powder

¼ teaspoon salt

1 (16-oz.) can apricot halves, well drained

2 tablespoons sugar

½ teaspoon cinnamon

1. Heat oven to 375°F. Spray 9-inch round cake pan or springform pan with nonstick cooking spray.

2. In large bowl, combine margarine and $\frac{1}{3}$ cup sugar; beat until well blended. Add vanilla and egg; beat well. Stir in flour, baking powder and salt. Spread dough evenly in bottom of sprayed pan.

3. Arrange apricot halves over dough. In small bowl, combine 2 tablespoons sugar and cinnamon; sprinkle over apricots.

4. Bake at 375°F. for 20 to 25 minutes or until edges are golden brown. Cool 5 minutes.

YIELD: 8 SERVINGS

HIGH ALTITUDE (ABOVE 3500 FEET): No change.

Nutrition Information Per Serving
Serving Size: $\frac{1}{8}$ of Recipe

Calories................................190	Calories from Fat 70	
	% Daily Value	
Total Fat 8g	....12%	
Saturated 2g	....10%	
Cholesterol 25mg	....8%	
Sodium 180mg	....8%	
Total Carbohydrate 27g	....9%	
Dietary Fiber 1g	....4%	
Sugars............................14g		
Protein 3g		
Vitamin A 20%	Vitamin C 2%	
Calcium 2%	Iron 6%	

Dietary Exchanges: 1 Starch, 1 Fruit, 1 Fat OR 2 Carbohydrate, 1 Fat

▲ Mocha Cappuccino Pudding Cake

Mocha Cappuccino Pudding Cake

PREP TIME: 10 MINUTES
(READY IN 55 MINUTES)

Cake

1¼ cups all-purpose flour

¾ cup sugar

2 tablespoons unsweetened cocoa

1 tablespoon instant espresso powder

1½ teaspoons baking powder

½ teaspoon salt

½ cup skim milk

2 tablespoons margarine or butter, melted

1 teaspoon vanilla

Pudding

1 cup sugar

2 tablespoons unsweetened cocoa

1 teaspoon instant espresso powder

1½ cups skim milk heated to 120 to 130° F.

1. Heat oven to 350° F. In medium bowl, combine flour, ¾ cup sugar, 2 tablespoons cocoa, 1 tablespoon espresso powder, baking powder and salt; mix well. Add all remaining cake ingredients; mix until well blended. Spread in ungreased 9-inch square pan.

2. In small bowl, combine all pudding ingredients except milk; mix well. Sprinkle evenly over cake batter. Pour hot milk over sugar mixture.

3. Bake at 350° F. for 35 to 45 minutes or until center is set and firm to the touch. If desired, place foil or cookie sheet on lower oven rack under cake to catch any spills. To serve, spoon warm cake into dessert dishes.

YIELD: 9 SERVINGS

HIGH ALTITUDE (ABOVE 3500 FEET): Increase flour to 1⅓ cups. Bake as directed above.

Nutrition Information Per Serving
Serving Size: ⅑ of Recipe

Calories	270	Calories from Fat	25
		% Daily Value	
Total Fat	3g		5%
Saturated	1g		5%
Cholesterol	0mg		0%
Sodium	260mg		11%
Total Carbohydrate	57g		19%
Dietary Fiber	1g		4%
Sugars	42g		
Protein	4g		
Vitamin A	4%	Vitamin C	0%
Calcium	10%	Iron	8%

Dietary Exchanges: 1 Starch, 3 Fruit OR 4 Carbohydrate

Sour Cream and Raisin Pudding Cakes

■ ■

PREP TIME: 15 MINUTES
(READY IN 45 MINUTES)

1 cup all-purpose flour

⅔ cup sugar

2 teaspoons baking powder

¼ teaspoon salt

¾ cup light sour cream

2 tablespoons margarine or butter, melted

1 cup raisins

¾ cup firmly packed brown sugar

1½ cups water heated to 120 to 130°F.

1. Heat oven to 350°F. Place eight 8- to 10-oz. custard cups or individual ovenproof bowls in 15 × 10 × 1-inch baking pan.

2. Lightly spoon flour into measuring cup; level off. In medium bowl, combine flour, sugar, baking powder, salt, sour cream and margarine; mix well. Stir in raisins. Spoon and spread about ⅓ cup batter in each custard cup.

3. In small bowl, combine brown sugar and hot water; mix well. Pour 3 to 4 tablespoons brown sugar mixture evenly over batter in each cup.

4. Bake at 350°F. for 20 to 30 minutes or until tops are light golden brown and toothpick inserted in center comes out clean. Serve warm.

YIELD: 8 SERVINGS

HIGH ALTITUDE (ABOVE 3500 FEET): Bake at 350°F. for 25 to 35 minutes.

Nutrition Information Per Serving
Serving Size: ⅛ of Recipe

Calories	320	Calories from Fat	45
		% Daily Value	
Total Fat	5g		8%
Saturated	2g		10%
Cholesterol	5mg		2%
Sodium	250mg		10%
Total Carbohydrate	66g		22%
Dietary Fiber	1g		4%
Sugars	50g		
Protein	3g		
Vitamin A	6%	Vitamin C	0%
Calcium	15%	Iron	10%

Dietary Exchanges: 1 Starch, 3½ Fruit, 1 Fat OR 4½ Carbohydrate, 1 Fat

Cherry and Peach Cream Cakes

■ ■

PREP TIME: 20 MINUTES

2 cups fresh sweet cherries, pitted

1 medium peach, peeled, cut into 1-inch pieces

⅓ cup peach spreadable fruit, melted

¾ cup low-fat peach yogurt

¼ cup nonfat sour cream

8 individual sponge shortcake cups

3 tablespoons peach-flavored schnapps, rum or orange juice

1. In medium bowl, combine cherries, peach and spreadable fruit; toss to coat. In small bowl, combine yogurt and sour cream; blend well.

2. Place shortcake cups on 8 individual dessert plates. Sprinkle each with about 1 teaspoon schnapps. Spread about 1 to 2 tablespoons yogurt mixture evenly in each cup. Spoon fruit over yogurt mixture. Store in refrigerator.

YIELD: 8 SERVINGS

Nutrition Information Per Serving
Serving Size: ⅛ of Recipe

Calories	210	Calories from Fat	10
		% Daily Value	
Total Fat	1g		2%
Saturated	0g		0%
Cholesterol	30mg		10%
Sodium	100mg		4%
Total Carbohydrate	43g		14%
Dietary Fiber	1g		4%
Sugars	35g		
Protein	4g		
Vitamin A	4%	Vitamin C	6%
Calcium	8%	Iron	6%

Dietary Exchanges: 1 Starch, 2 Fruit OR 3 Carbohydrate

Strawberry-Rhubarb Shortcakes

■ ■ ■ ■ ■ ■ ■ ■ ■ ■ ■ ■ ■ ■ ■ ■ ■ ■ ■ ■

PREP TIME: 30 MINUTES

Topping

4 cups fresh or frozen sliced rhubarb

½ cup sugar

2 tablespoons grated orange peel

1 pint (2 cups) fresh strawberries, sliced

Shortcakes

1¾ cups all-purpose flour

1 tablespoon sugar

3 teaspoons baking powder

¼ cup margarine or butter, cut into pieces

1 cup skim milk

1. In medium saucepan, combine rhubarb, ½ cup sugar and orange peel; mix well. Cook over medium heat for 8 to 10 minutes or until rhubarb is tender, stirring occasionally. Cool slightly. Stir in strawberries.

2. Heat oven to 450°F. Spray cookie sheet with nonstick cooking spray. In medium bowl, combine flour, 1 tablespoon sugar and baking powder; mix well. Using pastry blender or fork, cut in margarine until mixture resembles coarse crumbs. Add milk; stir just until all dry ingredients are moistened. Drop dough by about ¼ cupfuls onto sprayed cookie sheet; flatten slightly.

3. Bake at 450°F. for 9 to 12 minutes or until light golden brown. Immediately remove from cookie sheet. Split shortcakes; place 2 halves on each individual dessert plate. Spoon about ⅓ cup topping over each shortcake.

YIELD: 8 SERVINGS

HIGH ALTITUDE (ABOVE 3500 FEET): No change.

Nutrition Information Per Serving
Serving Size: ⅛ of Recipe

Calories................................250		Calories from Fat 50	
		% Daily Value	
Total Fat 6g	..........................9%		
Saturated 1g	..........................5%		
Cholesterol 0mg	..........................0%		
Sodium 270mg	..........................11%		
Total Carbohydrate 43g	..........................14%		
Dietary Fiber 3g	..........................12%		
Sugars............................19g			
Protein...............................5g			
Vitamin A 8%		Vitamin C 35%	
Calcium 20%		Iron 10%	

Dietary Exchanges: 1 Starch, 2 Fruit, 1 Fat OR 3 Carbohydrate, 1 Fat

▼ Strawberry-Rhubarb Shortcakes

Rhubarb *Facts*

- Though rhubarb's reputation has been made as a dessert ingredient, it's actually a vegetable, a member of the buckwheat family. In the United States, rhubarb's most often used in pies, desserts, sauces, preserves or quick breads. But in parts of Europe and the Middle East, it's often used as a savory ingredient with roasted meats and poultry.

- One pound of fresh rhubarb equals about 4 cups of chopped rhubarb.

- Choose fresh rhubarb that's firm and crisp. If the leaves are attached, discard them; they're poisonous. Stalks range from rose pink to bright pink-red. Thinner stalks tend to be slightly sweeter and more tender. Avoid wilted or thick stalks.

- Rhubarb keeps in the refrigerator, loosely wrapped in plastic, for at least a week. When ready to use, rinse the stalks, but there's no need to peel them unless there are especially tough strings on some stalks. If you have an abundance of rhubarb, slice and freeze it, with or without sugar, for up to six months.

- Rhubarb is most plentiful in May and June but is available fresh from January through June and frozen throughout the year.

- 12 ounces of frozen rhubarb equal about $1\frac{1}{2}$ cups of sliced rhubarb.

- Rhubarb contains vitamins A and C; it has about 20 calories per cup.

Cranberry-Orange Drop Cookies

PREP TIME: 45 MINUTES

Cookies
1 (15.6-oz.) pkg. cranberry bread mix

⅓ cup orange juice

¼ cup oil

1 teaspoon grated orange peel

1 egg

Frosting
1½ cups powdered sugar

½ teaspoon grated orange peel

5 to 6 teaspoons orange juice

1. Heat oven to 350°F. In large bowl, combine all cookie ingredients. Stir 50 to 75 strokes until dry particles are moistened. Drop by teaspoonfuls 2 inches apart onto ungreased cookie sheets.

2. Bake at 350°F. for 10 to 13 minutes or until cookies are set and edges are light golden brown. Immediately remove from cookie sheets. Cool completely.

3. In small bowl, combine all frosting ingredients; beat until smooth. Frost cooled cookies. Let stand until frosting is set. Store between sheets of waxed paper in loosely covered container.

YIELD: 3 DOZEN COOKIES

HIGH ALTITUDE (ABOVE 3500 FEET): Add 1 tablespoon flour to dry bread mix. Bake as directed above.

Nutrition Information Per Serving
Serving Size: 1 Cookie

Calories	80	Calories from Fat	20
		% Daily Value	
Total Fat	2g		3%
Saturated	0g		0%
Cholesterol	5mg		2%
Sodium	50mg		2%
Total Carbohydrate	15g		5%
Dietary Fiber	0g		0%
Sugars	11g		
Protein	1g		
Vitamin A	0%	Vitamin C	2%
Calcium	0%	Iron	0%

Dietary Exchanges: 1 Starch OR 1 Carbohydrate

Cocoa Mocha Brownies

■ ■ ■ ■ ■ ■ ■ ■ ■ ■ ■ ■ ■ ■ ■ ■ ■

PREP TIME: 30 MINUTES

⅔ cup all-purpose flour

¾ cup sugar

¼ cup unsweetened cocoa

2 teaspoons instant coffee granules or crystals

¼ teaspoon baking powder

⅛ teaspoon salt

⅓ cup margarine or butter, melted

2 teaspoons vanilla

1 egg, slightly beaten

1 teaspoon powdered sugar

1. Heat oven to 350°F. Spray 8-inch square pan with nonstick cooking spray.
2. In large bowl, combine flour, sugar, cocoa, instant coffee, baking powder and salt; blend well. Add margarine, vanilla and egg; stir just to combine. Spread evenly in sprayed pan.
3. Bake at 350°F. for 18 minutes or until set. DO NOT OVERBAKE. Sprinkle with powdered sugar. Cut into bars. Serve warm or cool.

YIELD: 16 BARS

HIGH ALTITUDE (ABOVE 3500 FEET): Decrease sugar to ⅔ cup. Bake as directed above.

Nutrition Information Per Serving
Serving Size: 1 Bar

Calories	100	Calories from Fat	35
		% Daily Value	
Total Fat	4g		6%
Saturated	1g		5%
Cholesterol	15mg		5%
Sodium	75mg		3%
Total Carbohydrate	14g		5%
Dietary Fiber	1g		2%
Sugars	10g		
Protein	1g		
Vitamin A	4%	Vitamin C	0%
Calcium	0%	Iron	2%

Dietary Exchanges: 1 Starch, ½ Fat OR \ Carbohydrate, ½ Fat

Double Chocolate Chip Cookies

■ ■ ■ ■ ■ ■ ■ ■ ■ ■ ■ ■ ■ ■ ■ ■ ■

PREP TIME: 30 MINUTES

½ cup firmly packed brown sugar

¼ cup margarine or butter, softened

½ teaspoon vanilla

1 egg white

1 cup all-purpose flour

3 tablespoons unsweetened cocoa

½ teaspoon baking soda

⅛ teaspoon salt

½ cup semi-sweet chocolate chips

1. Heat oven to 375°F. In large bowl, combine brown sugar and margarine; beat until light and fluffy. Add vanilla and egg white; blend well.
2. Add flour, cocoa, baking soda and salt; mix well. Stir in chocolate chips. Drop dough by teaspoonfuls 2 inches apart onto ungreased cookie sheets.
3. Bake at 375°F. for 8 to 9 minutes or until set. DO NOT OVERBAKE. Cool 1 minute; remove from cookie sheets.

YIELD: 24 COOKIES

chocolate **Bloom**

■ ■ ■ ■ ■ ■ ■ ■ ■ ■ ■ ■ ■ ■

The harmless grayish coating that forms on chocolate is called "bloom" and is just the cocoa butter coming to the surface. It appears after chocolate has been stored in a too warm place and will disappear once you melt chocolate. To prevent bloom, store chocolate at cool room temperature in a dry place.

chocolate *Choices*

All chocolate starts out as chocolate liquor, which has been extracted from hulled cocoa beans and then molded into solid cakes. Cocoa butter is either removed or added to make the numerous varieties of chocolate. Here are the most common types:

Bitter, unsweetened or baking chocolate The solid cakes of chocolate liquor with no sugar added. It smells wonderful as it melts, belying its unpalatably bitter flavor. It must be combined with a sweetener of some sort in baked goods.

Bittersweet or semi-sweet chocolate Contains at least 35 percent chocolate liquor, as well as additional cocoa butter, milk solids, butterfat, sweetener and flavorings.

Semi-sweet chocolate chips Semi-sweet chocolate formed into pieces. When melted, they hold their shape and should be stirred until smooth. The first "chips" for cookies were diced from a solid bar. Later, the Nestlé Company began commercially packaging chips.

Unsweetened cocoa powder Pure chocolate with most of the cocoa butter removed. The solids are then ground into powder. Dutch-process cocoa is treated with alkali, which makes the cocoa darker and slightly less bitter.

Milk chocolate Contains at least 10 percent pure chocolate, 12 percent whole milk solids and at least 3.66 percent butterfat. Flavorings, sugar, cocoa butter and emulsifiers may also be added.

White chocolate Not really chocolate because it doesn't contain any chocolate liquor. Also called white confectionery coating or confectioner's chocolate, it's used in almond bark and "white chocolate" chips and as a coating for candies. A blend of sugar, cocoa butter, milk solids, butterfat, emulsifiers and flavorings, white chocolate varies in quality and is available in a range of colors from ivory to bright white to pastels.

Tip: If desired, cookies can be glazed. In small bowl, combine $^{1}/_{2}$ cup powdered sugar, $1^{1}/_{2}$ teaspoons skim milk, 2 drops vanilla and, if desired, 2 drops butter flavor. Stir to blend; drizzle glaze over cookies.

HIGH ALTITUDE (ABOVE 3500 FEET): Increase flour to 1 cup plus 2 tablespoons. Bake as directed above.

Nutrition Information Per Serving
Serving Size: 1 Cookie

Calories	70	Calories from Fat	25
			% Daily Value
Total Fat	3g		5%
Saturated	1g		5%
Cholesterol	0mg		0%
Sodium	65mg		3%
Total Carbohydrate	11g		4%
Dietary Fiber	1g		2%
Sugars	7g		
Protein	1g		
Vitamin A	0%	Vitamin C	0%
Calcium	0%	Iron	2%

Dietary Exchanges: $^{1}/_{2}$ Starch, $^{1}/_{2}$ Fat OR $^{1}/_{2}$ Carbohydrate, $^{1}/_{2}$ Fat

healthy *Baking Tips*

I want to reduce the fat in my baking. Where do I start?

First, identify high-fat ingredients in the recipe such as butter (or margarine or shortening) and eggs. Less obvious sources include nuts, peanut butter, coconut, chocolate, sour cream and cream cheese.

How do I adapt the recipe once I know where its fat comes from?

There are three primary methods:

- Use smaller amounts of high-fat ingredients. Try reducing the butter, for example, by 25 percent or 50 percent and see if you like the result. Home-baked recipes will usually be best if you don't make more than a 50 percent reduction in fat.

- Substitute a low-fat version for a high-fat ingredient. With a sour cream cake, for example, try nonfat or reduced-fat sour cream.

- Add moisture to compensate for reduced fat. Try replacing about half of the fat with an equal measure of applesauce or plain nonfat yogurt, which will boost moisture but not alter the recipe's flavor (though the texture will be more cakelike).

Since reduced-fat baking yields slightly different results, you'll like some modified recipes better than others. Often the hardest recipe to change is one that people know and love, such as Toll House cookies. Also, if you're working with a recipe that's already fat-reduced, you may not have success with further substitutions.

I've purchased packages of fat-free Danish and coffee cakes that were delicious. Why can't I duplicate these recipes at home?

Commercial bakers have access to certain gums and preservatives that help create good moisture and texture, but these ingredients are not available to home cooks.

How can I prevent low-fat baked goods from being tough?

Do not overmix batters and doughs. Bake with cake flour, which has less gluten than all-purpose flour. Do not overbake.

Low-fat cookies often taste dry. What can I do about that?

Serve them warm, either straight from the oven or briefly reheated in the microwave. Since low-fat products can become stale faster, bake small batches and refrigerate or freeze the extra dough for later use. Store leftovers in airtight containers, or freeze them.

Do light products (such as margarine) work in baking?

Often, yes. In general, batters will be thinner and doughs a little softer than those made with regular fats. The resulting baked goods will have a more cakelike texture and a smoother, less "pebbly" top. They also will be more likely to stick to the baking pan—use nonstick pans and spray them with nonstick cooking spray. As with other low-fat baked goods, they dry out more quickly and, as a result, taste best soon after being baked.

How can I achieve the best flavor in low-fat cookies?

Boost ginger, lemon, nutmeg, vanilla or other spices or extracts by about 25 percent. If a recipe calls for a teaspoon of cinnamon, for example, try using 1 ¼ teaspoons.

Ginger Orange Bars

■ ■

PREP TIME: 25 MINUTES
(READY IN 1 HOUR 15 MINUTES)

Bars

½ **cup sugar**

½ **cup margarine or butter, softened**

½ **cup molasses**

1 egg

1½ **cups all-purpose flour**

½ **cup whole wheat flour**

1 teaspoon baking soda

¼ **teaspoon ginger**

⅔ **cup buttermilk***

2 teaspoons grated orange peel

Frosting

2 cups powdered sugar

1 tablespoon margarine or butter, softened

½ **teaspoon grated orange peel**

2 to 4 tablespoons orange juice

1. Heat oven to 350°F. Spray 15 × 10 × 1-inch baking pan with nonstick cooking spray.

2. In large bowl, combine sugar and ½ cup margarine; beat until light and fluffy. Add molasses and egg; beat well.

3. In small bowl, combine all-purpose flour, whole wheat flour, baking soda and ginger; blend well. Add to sugar mixture alternately with buttermilk; mix well. Stir in 2 teaspoons orange peel. Spread evenly in sprayed pan.

4. Bake at 350°F. for 15 to 20 minutes or until toothpick inserted in center comes out clean. Cool 30 minutes or until completely cooled.

5. In small bowl, combine all frosting ingredients, adding enough orange juice for desired spreading consistency; beat until smooth. Spread over cooled bars. Cut into bars.

YIELD: 48 BARS

Tip: * To substitute for buttermilk, use 2 teaspoons vinegar or lemon juice plus skim milk to make ⅔ cup.

HIGH ALTITUDE (ABOVE 3500 FEET): No change.

Nutrition Information Per Serving
Serving Size: 1 Bar

Calories	80	Calories from Fat	20
		% Daily Value	
Total Fat	2g		3%
Saturated	0g		0%
Cholesterol	5mg		2%
Sodium	60mg		3%
Total Carbohydrate	14g		5%
Dietary Fiber	0g		0%
Sugars	9g		
Protein	1g		
Vitamin A	0%	Vitamin C	0%
Calcium	0%	Iron	2%

Dietary Exchanges: 1 Starch OR 1 Carbohydrate

▼ Ginger Orange Bars

Caramel Chocolate Crunch Bars

- - - - - - - - - - - - - - - - -

PREP TIME: 15 MINUTES
(READY IN 45 MINUTES)

⅓ cup firmly packed brown sugar

¼ cup margarine or butter, softened

½ cup all-purpose flour

½ cup quick-cooking rolled oats

½ cup Grape-Nuts® cereal

¼ cup caramel ice cream topping

¼ cup miniature chocolate chips

1. Heat oven to 425°F. Line 8-inch square pan with foil; spray foil with nonstick cooking spray.*
2. In medium bowl, combine brown sugar and margarine; blend well. Add flour, oats and cereal to sugar mixture; mix well. Press in bottom of sprayed foil-lined pan. Drizzle caramel topping to within $1/2$ inch of edges.
3. Bake at 425°F. for 10 minutes or until edges are light golden brown. Immediately sprinkle bars with chocolate chips; let stand 1 to 2 minutes to melt. Spread melted chips evenly over bars; cool 5 minutes. Remove bars from pan by carefully lifting foil. Cool in freezer for 15 minutes. Cut into bars.

YIELD: 16 BARS

Tip: * To easily line pan, shape foil over inverted pan. Turn pan upright; fit foil into pan.

Nutrition Information Per Serving
Serving Size: 1 Bar

Calories	110	Calories from Fat	35
		% Daily Value	
Total Fat	4g		6%
Saturated	1g		5%
Cholesterol	0mg		0%
Sodium	80mg		3%
Total Carbohydrate	17g		6%
Dietary Fiber	1g		3%
Sugars	9g		
Protein	2g		
Vitamin A	6%	Vitamin C	0%
Calcium	0%	Iron	4%

Dietary Exchanges: 1 Starch, 1 Fat OR 1 Carbohydrate, 1 Fat

Lemon Squares

- - - - - - - - - - - - - - - - - - -

PREP TIME: 30 MINUTES
(READY IN 1 HOUR 25 MINUTES)

Base
1⅔ cups all-purpose flour

½ cup powdered sugar

¾ cup margarine or butter, cut into pieces

Filling
1 (8-oz.) carton (1 cup) refrigerated or frozen fat-free egg product, thawed, or 4 eggs

2 cups sugar

¼ cup all-purpose flour

1 teaspoon baking powder

¼ cup lemon juice

1 tablespoon grated lemon peel

Garnish
2 tablespoons powdered sugar

1. Heat oven to 375°F. In large bowl, combine 1⅔ cups flour and ½ cup powdered sugar; mix well. Using pastry blender or fork, cut in margarine until mixture resembles coarse crumbs. Press mixture in bottom of ungreased 13 × 9-inch pan.
2. Bake at 375°F. for 14 to 17 minutes or until edges are light golden brown.
3. Meanwhile, in medium bowl, combine all filling ingredients except lemon juice and lemon peel; blend well with wire whisk or fork. Stir in lemon juice and lemon peel. Pour filling over base.
4. Bake an additional 18 to 25 minutes or until center is just set. Cool 30 minutes or until completely cooled. Sprinkle with 2 tablespoons powdered sugar. Cut into bars.

YIELD: 36 BARS

HIGH ALTITUDE (ABOVE 3500 FEET): NO CHANGE.

Nutrition Information Per Serving

Serving Size: 1 Bar

Calories	120	Calories from Fat	35

% Daily Value

Total Fat	4g	6%
Saturated	1g	5%
Cholesterol	0mg	0%
Sodium	70mg	3%
Total Carbohydrate	19g	6%
Dietary Fiber	0g	0%
Sugars	13g	
Protein	1g	

Vitamin A	4%	Vitamin C	0%
Calcium	0%	Iron	2%

Dietary Exchanges: 1 Starch, 1 Fat OR 1 Carbohydrate, 1 Fat

▼ Lemon Squares/Caramel Chocolate Crunch Bars

Minted Watermelon Granita

■ ■

PREP TIME: 10 MINUTES
(READY IN 3 HOURS 10 MINUTES)

⅓ **cup sugar**

½ **cup water**

¼ **cup mint-flavored apple jelly**

4 cups seeded watermelon cubes

2 tablespoons fresh lemon juice

1. In small saucepan, combine sugar, water and jelly; mix well. Cook over medium-high heat about 4 minutes or until sugar is completely dissolved and jelly is melted, stirring occasionally. Cool 5 minutes.

2. Meanwhile, place watermelon in blender container or food processor bowl with metal blade. Cover; blend until smooth. Add cooled syrup and lemon juice; blend until mixed. Pour into 13 × 9-inch (3-quart) baking dish. Freeze at least 1 hour or until icy around edges.

3. Stir and mash with fork to break up ice crystals. Freeze about 2 hours or until all liquid is frozen, breaking up mixture with fork every 30 minutes. Serve immediately or let stand at room temperature 5 to 15 minutes before serving. To serve, stir with fork; spoon into 6 individual dessert dishes.

YIELD: 6 (½-CUP) SERVINGS

Nutrition Information Per Serving
Serving Size: ½ Cup

Calories	110	Calories from Fat	0
			% Daily Value
Total Fat	0g		0%
Saturated	0g		0%
Cholesterol	0mg		0%
Sodium	5mg		0%
Total Carbohydrate	28g		9%
Dietary Fiber	1g		2%
Sugars	27g		
Protein	1g		
Vitamin A	8%	Vitamin C	20%
Calcium	0%	Iron	0%

Dietary Exchanges: 2 Fruit OR 2 Carbohydrate

Plum Crisp

■ ■

PREP TIME: 15 MINUTES
(READY IN 1 HOUR)

Fruit Mixture
4 cups sliced fresh plums (6 to 8 medium)

½ **cup sugar**

¼ **cup all-purpose flour**

¼ **teaspoon cinnamon**

Topping
⅓ **cup all-purpose flour**

⅓ **cup rolled oats**

⅓ **cup firmly packed brown sugar**

¼ **cup margarine or butter, cut into pieces**

1. Heat oven to 375°F. In large bowl, combine plums, sugar, ¼ cup flour and cinnamon; toss to mix. Spoon into ungreased 8-inch square pan.

2. In medium bowl, combine ⅓ cup flour, oats and brown sugar; mix well. Using fork or pastry blender, cut in margarine until mixture resembles coarse crumbs. Sprinkle evenly over plum mixture.

3. Bake at 375°F. for 35 to 45 minutes or until golden brown. Serve warm or cool.

YIELD: 6 SERVINGS

Nutrition Information Per Serving
Serving Size: ⅙ of Recipe

Calories	310	Calories from Fat	80
			% Daily Value
Total Fat	9g		14%
Saturated	2g		10%
Cholesterol	0mg		0%
Sodium	95mg		4%
Total Carbohydrate	55g		18%
Dietary Fiber	3g		12%
Sugars	37g		
Protein	3g		
Vitamin A	15%	Vitamin C	10%
Calcium	2%	Iron	6%

Dietary Exchanges: 1½ Starch, 2 Fruit, 2 Fat OR 3½ Carbohydrate, 2 Fat

Apples *for baking*

Cortland Round, red-skinned apples with a flavor somewhat like that of a milder McIntosh, Cortlands are a good choice for cooking, especially in recipes where a soft texture is desirable.

Golden Delicious With their lovely, tender yellow skin, golden delicious apples look beautiful in a fruit bowl. They have a mellow, sweet flavor that may need picking up with a bit of lemon juice or another tart flavor for pie.

Granny Smith Green skinned and firm textured, with a slightly tart flavor and a profile similar to that of a Delicious apple, Granny Smith apples are equally fine for eating out of hand and baking. Granny Smiths retain more shape and often some crispness after cooking. Cut them very thin if you prefer a softer baked apple.

Greening Covered with somewhat coarse green skin, Greenings are not the best to eat out of hand. Cooking brings out the sweetness of the flavor, with enough tartness for contrast.

McIntosh Readily available and an all-around good choice for cooking and eating, McIntosh apples have shiny red skin with some green patches and juicy, crisp flesh that becomes very tender when cooked. Larger apples are best for cooking, since there's a higher flesh-to-skin ratio and therefore less peeling.

Rome Fat, deep red Rome apples have a firm texture and mild flavor. Choose the huge ones and you'll need only a few for baked recipes.

Ginger Apple Crisp

PREP TIME: 15 MINUTES
(READY IN 45 MINUTES)

⅓ **cup corn flake crumbs**

¼ **cup firmly packed brown sugar**

3 **tablespoons all-purpose flour**

2 **tablespoons crystallized ginger, chopped, or**
   1 teaspoon ginger

2 **tablespoons margarine or butter, melted**

6 **medium apples, peeled, thinly sliced (6 cups)**

2 **tablespoons sugar**

2 **teaspoons lemon juice**

1½ **cups nonfat vanilla frozen yogurt or ice milk**

1. Heat oven to 400°F. Spray 8-inch square (2-quart) baking dish with nonstick cooking spray.

2. In small bowl, combine corn flake crumbs, brown sugar, flour and ginger; mix well. Stir in margarine until well mixed.

3. Place apples in sprayed baking dish. Add sugar and lemon juice; toss to coat. Sprinkle apples with crumb mixture; press gently.

4. Bake at 400°F. for 25 to 30 minutes or until apples are tender and mixture is bubbly. Cool slightly. Serve warm with frozen yogurt.

YIELD: 6 SERVINGS

Nutrition Information Per Serving
Serving Size: ⅙ of Recipe

Calories	260	Calories from Fat	35
		% Daily Value	
Total Fat	4g		6%
Saturated	1g		5%
Cholesterol	0mg		0%
Sodium	125mg		5%
Total Carbohydrate	54g		18%
Dietary Fiber	4g		16%
Sugars	43g		
Protein	3g		
Vitamin A	8%	Vitamin C	15%
Calcium	6%	Iron	6%

Dietary Exchanges: 1 Starch, 2½ Fruit, 1 Fat OR 3½ Carbohydrate, 1 Fat

Peach-Cranberry Crunch Cups

PREP TIME: 10 MINUTES
(READY IN 35 MINUTES)

Fruit Mixture
1 (29-oz.) can peach slices, well drained

1 cup fresh or frozen cranberries

2 tablespoons sugar

Topping
⅓ cup all-purpose flour

⅓ cup rolled oats

⅓ cup firmly packed brown sugar

½ teaspoon cinnamon

3 tablespoons margarine or butter, melted

1. Heat oven to 375°F. Spray six 6-oz. custard cups with nonstick cooking spray; place on cookie sheet.

2. In medium bowl, combine peaches, cranberries and sugar; toss lightly. Spoon about ½ cup fruit mixture into each sprayed custard cup.

3. In medium bowl, combine all topping ingredients; mix until crumbly. Sprinkle over fruit mixture.

4. Bake at 375°F. for 20 to 25 minutes or until golden brown.

YIELD: 6 SERVINGS

Nutrition Information Per Serving
Serving Size: ⅙ of Recipe

Calories	200	Calories from Fat	50
		% Daily Value	
Total Fat	6g		9%
Saturated	1g		5%
Cholesterol	0mg		0%
Sodium	75mg		3%
Total Carbohydrate	35g		12%
Dietary Fiber	3g		12%
Sugars	24g		
Protein	2g		
Vitamin A	20%	Vitamin C	8%
Calcium	2%	Iron	8%

Dietary Exchanges: 1 Starch, 1 Fruit, 1 Fat OR 2 Carbohydrate, 1 Fat

■ PRODUCE POINTERS

Cranberry *facts*

- Cranberries are cultivated in huge sandy bogs and are harvested in September and October. The peak season for fresh berries runs from October through December.

- Cranberries are sold in 12- or 16-ounce bags. Look for plump, firm berries with no bruising or soft spots.

- Cranberries keep well. Refrigerate fresh bagged cranberries for two months or freeze for up to a year.

- Cranberries are good sources of vitamin C and fiber; one cup of cranberries has about 45 calories.

Fruit with Caramel Sauce

PREP TIME: 10 MINUTES

1 medium nectarine or peach, cut into wedges

1 kiwi fruit, peeled, sliced

1 cup fresh strawberries, halved

1 cup fresh blueberries

⅔ cup caramel ice cream topping

¼ teaspoon rum extract

1. Arrange fruit on 6 individual dessert plates or in 6 dishes.

2. In small saucepan, combine ice cream topping and rum extract; heat over medium heat until warm, stirring occasionally. Drizzle 1 heaping tablespoon topping mixture over each serving of fruit.

YIELD: 6 SERVINGS

Nutrition Information Per Serving

Serving Size: 1/6 of Recipe

Calories..................................140	Calories from Fat 0
	% Daily Value
Total Fat ....0g 0%	
Saturated ....0g 0%	
Cholesterol ....0mg 0%	
Sodium ....125mg 5%	
Total Carbohydrate.............34g 11%	
Dietary Fiber ....2g 8%	
Sugars..............................25g	
Protein.................................1g	
Vitamin A 6%	Vitamin C 40%
Calcium 2%	Iron..................................0%

Dietary Exchanges: 2 1/2 Fruit OR 2 1/2 Carbohydrate

Caramel Yogurt and Apples

■ ■

PREP TIME: 25 MINUTES

Topping

4 oz. 1/3-less-fat cream cheese (Neufchâtel), softened

2 tablespoons powdered sugar

1/4 cup low-fat vanilla yogurt

Caramel Yogurt

1 tablespoon margarine or butter

1/2 cup firmly packed brown sugar

1 tablespoon light corn syrup

1/4 cup evaporated skimmed milk or half-and-half

1/2 cup low-fat vanilla yogurt

Apples

3 medium apples, coarsely chopped

1. In small bowl, beat cream cheese about 30 seconds or until fluffy. Add powdered sugar; gradually add 1/4 cup yogurt, beating until smooth. Refrigerate while preparing caramel yogurt.

2. Melt margarine in small saucepan. Stir in brown sugar and corn syrup. Bring to a boil over medium heat, stirring constantly. Stir in milk. Return to a boil; boil 1 minute. Remove from heat; cool 5 minutes, stirring occasionally. With wire whisk, beat in 1/2 cup yogurt until smooth.

3. Divide chopped apples evenly into 6 individual dessert dishes. Spoon warm caramel yogurt over apples; top with topping. If desired, sprinkle with nutmeg.

YIELD: 6 SERVINGS

Nutrition Information Per Serving

Serving Size: 1/6 of Recipe

Calories..................................200	Calories from Fat 50
	% Daily Value
Total Fat ....6g 9%	
Saturated ....3g 15%	
Cholesterol ....10mg 3%	
Sodium ....150mg 6%	
Total Carbohydrate.............32g 11%	
Dietary Fiber ....2g 8%	
Sugars..............................29g	
Protein.................................4g	
Vitamin A 8%	Vitamin C 6%
Calcium 10%	Iron..................................2%

Dietary Exchanges: 1 Starch, 1 Fruit, 1 Fat OR 2 Carbohydrate, 1 Fat

measuring **Apples**

■ ■ ■ ■ ■ ■ ■ ■ ■ ■ ■ ■ ■ ■ ■ ■ ■ ■ ■ ■

- 3 medium apples = 1 pound

- 6 to 8 medium apples (2 pounds) make a 9-inch pie

- 1 pound of apples makes 1 1/2 cups of applesauce

- 1 bushel of apples makes 16 to 20 quarts of juice

Kiwi Fruit Pavlova with Raspberry Sauce

■ ■ ■ ■ ■ ■ ■ ■ ■ ■ ■ ■ ■ ■ ■ ■ ■ ■ ■ ■

PREP TIME: 25 MINUTES
(READY IN 1 HOUR 55 MINUTES)

6 egg whites

1 teaspoon cream of tartar

1 cup sugar

1 (10-oz.) pkg. frozen raspberries in light syrup, thawed

4 kiwi fruit, peeled, sliced

1. Heat oven to 275°F. Line cookie sheet with parchment paper.

2. In large bowl, beat egg whites and cream of tartar at medium speed until soft peaks form. Gradually add 1 cup sugar, beating at high speed until stiff glossy peaks form and sugar is almost dissolved. Spoon meringue onto paper-lined cookie sheet; spread into 12-inch round.

3. Bake at 275°F. for 1 hour. DO NOT OPEN OVEN. Turn oven off; leave meringue in oven with door closed for 30 minutes.

4. Meanwhile, in blender container or food processor bowl with metal blade, puree raspberries until smooth.

5. To serve, cut meringue into 8 wedges; place on individual dessert plates. Top wedges with kiwi fruit slices and raspberry sauce.

YIELD: 8 SERVINGS

Nutrition Information Per Serving
Serving Size: $1/8$ of Recipe

Calories	170	Calories from Fat	0
		% Daily Value	
Total Fat	0g		0%
Saturated	0g		0%
Cholesterol	0mg		0%
Sodium	45mg		2%
Total Carbohydrate	40g		13%
Dietary Fiber	3g		12%
Sugars	37g		
Protein	3g		
Vitamin A	0%	Vitamin C	70%
Calcium	0%	Iron	2%

Dietary Exchanges: 1 Starch, 1 $1/2$ Fruit OR 2 $1/2$ Carbohydrate

Meringues: *the best and the lightest*

■ ■

- Use a glass or metal bowl, not plastic, for beating egg whites.

- Eggs separate most easily straight from the refrigerator but whip up best at room temperature. Separate carefully and make sure the mixing bowl (or saucepan) and beaters are absolutely clean before starting—even the smallest bit of grease or yolk will inhibit whipping.

- Partially beat the egg whites with cream of tartar, which acts as a stabilizer, and then beat in sugar a little at a time.

- Bake meringues on a sheet of parchment paper (heavier than waxed paper and mois-ture resistant). Parchment paper is available in specialty kitchen stores and many supermarkets. Do NOT substitute waxed paper.

- Beaten egg whites react to moisture in the air, so you will have best results baking meringues on a dry day; in very humid weather, the peaks may not hold or the baked meringue may "weep" droplets of liquid.

- Be patient. Most meringues require an hour of baking and then additional time in the oven with the thermostat turned off. *Do not open the oven door* before the total time has elapsed.

- Store the baked meringues in an airtight container at room temperature, or in the freezer.

Strawberry *facts*

- Look for plump strawberries with a natural shine, bright red color and fresh-looking green hull. Ripe berries are red throughout. Avoid berries with white "shoulders" (stem ends) and white centers; they're not fully ripe. Unlike tomatoes or many other fruits, strawberries do not ripen after being picked.

- Strawberries are available most of the year. Peak season is May through September.

- To store strawberries, loosely cover them with plastic wrap and refrigerate for up to two days. Do not wash the berries until you're ready to use them.

- Don't toss those less than perfect looking strawberries. Instead wash them, trim off any blemishes, cut them up and sprinkle with sugar; refrigerate. Serve them solo or over cereal, frozen yogurt or fat-free pound cake.

- Just before using, rinse strawberries with the hulls still attached. Don't remove the hulls before washing; they prevent the water from breaking down the texture and flavor inside the berries.

- Strawberries taste best when served at room temperature.

- Strawberries are an excellent source of vitamin C and contain about 45 calories per cup.

Cream-Filled Strawberries

PREP TIME: 15 MINUTES

6 large fresh strawberries

¼ cup ⅓-less-fat cream cheese (Neufchâtel), softened

¼ cup light ricotta cheese

2 teaspoons powdered sugar

¼ teaspoon almond extract or vanilla

2 teaspoons chocolate-flavored syrup, if desired

2 fresh mint leaves, if desired

1. Wash and drain strawberries; remove stems if desired. Stand strawberries up on stem end; cut strawberries into quarters, cutting down to but not completely through stem end. Set aside.

2. In small bowl, combine cream cheese, ricotta cheese, powdered sugar and almond extract; blend well. Pipe about 1 tablespoon cheese mixture into each cut strawberry.* Serve immediately, or cover and refrigerate until serving time.

3. To serve, drizzle each of 2 individual serving plates with 1 teaspoon syrup. Place 3 strawberries on each plate; garnish with mint leaf.

YIELD: 2 SERVINGS

Tip: * Use decorating bag or make a small cut in corner of small plastic bag. Fill bag with cheese mixture; twist or seal top. Gently squeeze mixture into strawberries.

Nutrition Information Per Serving
Serving Size: ½ of Recipe

Calories	160	Calories from Fat	80
		% Daily Value	
Total Fat	9g		14%
Saturated	6g		30%
Cholesterol	30mg		10%
Sodium	160mg		7%
Total Carbohydrate	13g		4%
Dietary Fiber	2g		8%
Sugars	11g		
Protein	7g		
Vitamin A	10%	Vitamin C	70%
Calcium	10%	Iron	4%

Dietary Exchanges: 1 Fruit, 1 Very Lean Meat, 1 Fat OR 1 Carbohydrate, 1 Very Lean Meat, 1 Fat

▲ Frosty Margarita Pie

Frosty Margarita Pie

PREP TIME: 15 MINUTES
(READY IN 1 HOUR 45 MINUTES)

Crust
½ cup finely chopped strawberries

½ cup sugar

¾ cup graham cracker crumbs (12 squares)

Filling
1 quart (4 cups) nonfat vanilla frozen yogurt

1 tablespoon grated lime peel

⅓ cup fresh lime juice

2 to 4 tablespoons tequila, if desired

Topping
1 cup frozen light whipped topping, thawed,
    if desired

Lime and strawberry slices, if desired

1. In small bowl, combine all crust ingredients; mix well.
Press in bottom and up sides of 9-inch pie pan. Set aside.

2. In large bowl with electric mixer, combine all filling ingredients. Mix at high speed just until combined. Spoon into crust. Freeze at least $1\frac{1}{2}$ hours or until firm enough to cut. Serve topped with whipped topping; garnish with lime and strawberry slices.

YIELD: 8 SERVINGS

Tip: Filling can be prepared in food processor bowl with metal blade or blender container. Process 10 to 15 seconds or just until combined.

Nutrition Information Per Serving
Serving Size: ⅛ of Recipe

Calories	220	Calories from Fat	20
		% Daily Value	
Total Fat	2g		3%
Saturated	1g		5%
Cholesterol	0mg		0%
Sodium	105mg		4%
Total Carbohydrate	43g		14%
Dietary Fiber	1g		3%
Sugars	33g		
Protein	4g		
Vitamin A	0%	Vitamin C	25%
Calcium	8%	Iron	2%

Dietary Exchanges: 2 Starch, 1 Fruit OR 3 Carbohydrate

Fresh Pineapple Tart

■ ■

PREP TIME: 25 MINUTES
(READY IN 40 MINUTES)

6 soft coconut macaroon cookies (about 5 oz.)

¼ cup unseasoned bread crumbs

1 egg white, slightly beaten

½ cup sugar

3 tablespoons cornstarch

3 cups chopped fresh pineapple (from 1½ pineapples) or drained canned crushed pineapple in unsweetened juice

1 tablespoon lemon juice

1. Heat oven to 400°F. Spray 9-inch tart pan with removable bottom with nonstick cooking spray.

2. Place cookies in food processor bowl with metal blade; process 10 to 15 seconds or until fine crumbs form. (There should be about 1⅓ cups crumbs.) Add bread crumbs; process until mixed. Add egg white; mix well. Press mixture in bottom and up sides of sprayed pan to form crust.

3. Bake at 400°F. for 7 to 9 minutes or until golden brown. Place in refrigerator or freezer until cooled.

4. Meanwhile, in medium saucepan, combine sugar and cornstarch; mix well. Add pineapple and lemon juice; blend well. Cook over medium-high heat for about 5 minutes or until mixture thickens, stirring constantly. Place saucepan in pan of cold water; stir 2 to 3 minutes or until cooled.

▼ Fresh Pineapple Tart

5. Pour pineapple mixture into cooled baked crust. Place in freezer for 15 minutes or until set. Store in refrigerator.

YIELD: 8 SERVINGS

Nutrition Information Per Serving
Serving Size: 1/8 of Recipe

Calories	190	Calories from Fat	25
		% Daily Value	
Total Fat	3g		5%
Saturated	2g		10%
Cholesterol	0mg		0%
Sodium	80mg		3%
Total Carbohydrate	38g		13%
Dietary Fiber	1g		4%
Sugars	29g		
Protein	2g		
Vitamin A	0%	Vitamin C	10%
Calcium	0%	Iron	4%

Dietary Exchanges: 1 Starch, 1 1/2 Fruit, 1/2 Fat OR 2 1/2 Carbohydrate, 1/2 Fat

Frozen Cranberry-Raspberry Chiffon Pie

PREP TIME: 25 MINUTES
(READY IN 2 HOURS 25 MINUTES)

Crust

1¼ cups chocolate wafer cookie crumbs (20 to 22 cookies)

3 tablespoons margarine or butter, melted

Filling

1 (12-oz.) container crushed cranberry-raspberry sauce

1 (8-oz.) can jellied cranberry sauce (¾ cup)

1 teaspoon grated lemon peel

1 (7-oz.) jar marshmallow creme

2½ cups frozen light whipped topping, thawed

1. Heat oven to 375°F. Spray 9-inch pie pan with nonstick cooking spray.

2. In small bowl, combine crust ingredients; mix well. Press firmly in bottom and up sides of sprayed pan. Bake at 375°F. for 10 minutes. Cool.

■ PRODUCE POINTERS

picking Pineapple

To choose a pineapple, close your eyes and smell. The sweetest pineapples have the sweetest aroma, and that's the single best predictor of flavor. A pineapple's sweetness doesn't continue to develop after the fruit is picked.

Choose large, plump pineapple with bright color, fresh green leaves and no soft spots, decay on the bottom or fermented odor. Pineapples are available year-round, but the best prices generally can be found between April and June.

3. Meanwhile, in large bowl, combine cranberry sauces and lemon peel; reserve and refrigerate 1/3 cup for garnish. Stir marshmallow creme into remaining cranberry mixture until well blended. Gently fold in whipped topping. Spoon mixture evenly into cooled baked crust. Freeze 2 hours for a soft, creamy dessert, or cover with foil and freeze longer for a firmer texture.

4. To serve, spoon reserved 1/3 cup cranberry mixture in ring near outer edge of pie. If desired, garnish with fresh raspberries and mint leaves.

YIELD: 8 SERVINGS

Nutrition Information Per Serving
Serving Size: 1/8 of Recipe

Calories	350	Calories from Fat	80
		% Daily Value	
Total Fat	9g		14%
Saturated	4g		20%
Cholesterol	0mg		0%
Sodium	200mg		8%
Total Carbohydrate	65g		22%
Dietary Fiber	2g		8%
Sugars	53g		
Protein	2g		
Vitamin A	6%	Vitamin C	4%
Calcium	2%	Iron	4%

Dietary Exchanges: 1 Starch, 3 Fruit, 2 Fat OR 4 Carbohydrate, 2 Fat

Luscious Berry Lemon Tart

PREP TIME: 25 MINUTES
(READY IN 55 MINUTES)

1 refrigerated pie crust (from 15-oz. pkg.)

1 tablespoon sugar

1 (2.9-oz.) pkg. lemon pudding and pie filling mix (not instant)

½ cup sugar

2¼ cups water

2 egg yolks

2 cups sliced fresh strawberries

¾ cup fresh blueberries

3 tablespoons red currant jelly

1 teaspoon orange-flavored liqueur or orange juice

Fresh mint leaves, if desired

1. Heat oven to 450°F. Microwave pie crust pouch on DEFROST for 20 to 40 seconds, or let stand at room temperature for 15 minutes. Remove crust from pouch. Unfold crust; peel off plastic sheets. Sprinkle crust with 1 tablespoon sugar. Place crust, sugar side up, in 10-inch tart pan with removable bottom. Press in bottom and up sides of pan. Trim edges if necessary. Generously prick crust with fork. Bake at 450°F. for 9 to 11 minutes or until light golden brown. Cool.

2. Meanwhile, in medium saucepan, combine pudding mix, ½ cup sugar, ¼ cup of the water and egg yolks; blend well. Stir in remaining 2 cups water. Cook over medium heat until mixture comes to a boil, stirring constantly. Cool 5 minutes, stirring twice. Pour into cooled baked crust. Refrigerate 30 minutes or until set.

3. Just before serving, remove sides of pan; place tart on serving plate. Arrange strawberries and blueberries over lemon filling.

4. In small saucepan, heat jelly and liqueur; cool slightly. Drizzle over fruit. Garnish with mint leaves, if desired. Store in refrigerator.

YIELD: 10 SERVINGS

Nutrition Information Per Serving
Serving Size: ¹⁄₁₀ of Recipe

Calories	220	Calories from Fat	60
		% Daily Value	
Total Fat	7g		11%
Saturated	3g		15%
Cholesterol	50mg		17%
Sodium	150mg		6%
Total Carbohydrate	37g		12%
Dietary Fiber	1g		4%
Sugars	24g		
Protein	2g		
Vitamin A	0%	Vitamin C	30%
Calcium	0%	Iron	2%

Dietary Exchanges: 1 Starch, 1½ Fruit, 1 Fat OR 2½ Carbohydrate, 1 Fat

using nonstick Cooking Spray

Skip the shortening and use nonstick cooking spray to coat cookie sheets—it's quicker and saves on fat. To prevent spray buildup, wipe cookie sheets with a paper towel between batches.

Cooking spray is made from regular vegetable oil with ingredients such as lecithin to improve dispersal and propellants that make it possible to spread a much thinner layer of oil than you could otherwise.

Pumpkin Cheese Tart

PREP TIME: 20 MINUTES
(READY IN 1 HOUR)

Crust
1 cup crushed gingersnaps (about 20 cookies)

⅓ cup rolled oats, ground if desired*

¼ teaspoon cinnamon

3 tablespoons margarine or butter, melted

Cream Cheese Filling
2 (8-oz.) containers light cream cheese, softened

⅓ cup sugar

1 tablespoon all-purpose flour

2 tablespoons skim milk

½ teaspoon vanilla

1 egg

Pumpkin Filling
1 cup canned pumpkin

⅓ cup firmly packed brown sugar

½ teaspoon pumpkin pie spice

¼ cup skim milk

Caramel Sauce
½ cup firmly packed brown sugar

¼ cup corn syrup

2 tablespoons water

1 tablespoon margarine or butter

¼ teaspoon vanilla

1. Heat oven to 375°F. Spray 10-inch tart pan with removable bottom with nonstick cooking spray.

2. In small bowl, combine all crust ingredients; mix well. Press in bottom and up sides of sprayed pan. Bake at 375°F. for 6 to 8 minutes or until set.

3. Meanwhile, in large bowl, combine all cream cheese filling ingredients. Beat at medium speed until smooth and creamy. Reserve ⅔ cup cream cheese filling; set aside.

4. In small bowl, combine all pumpkin filling ingredients; blend well. Add to remaining cream cheese filling; mix well. Spoon into partially baked crust.

Spoon dollops of reserved cream cheese filling randomly over pumpkin filling. With table knife, swirl mixtures to marble.

5. Bake at 375°F. for 25 to 30 minutes or until set. Cool 10 minutes. Remove sides of pan. Serve warm, or cool completely and refrigerate until serving time.

6. Just before serving, in small saucepan, combine all caramel sauce ingredients. Cook over medium heat until mixture comes to a boil, stirring constantly. Boil 1 minute. Remove from heat. To serve, cut tart into wedges; place on individual dessert plates. Top with warm caramel sauce. Store in refrigerator.

YIELD: 12 SERVINGS

Tip: * To grind rolled oats, place in food processor bowl with metal blade or blender container; process until smooth.

Nutrition Information Per Serving
Serving Size: 1/12 of Recipe

Calories	280	Calories from Fat	100
			% Daily Value
Total Fat	11g		17%
Saturated	5g		25%
Cholesterol	35mg		12%
Sodium	320mg		13%
Total Carbohydrate	40g		13%
Dietary Fiber	1g		4%
Sugars	31g		
Protein	6g		
Vitamin A	20%	Vitamin C	0%
Calcium	8%	Iron	8%

Dietary Exchanges: 2½ Starch, 2 Fat OR 2½ Carbohydrate, 2 Fat

Lemon-Orange Meringue Tarts

PREP TIME: 25 MINUTES
(READY IN 3 HOURS 25 MINUTES)

Meringues
3 egg whites

¼ teaspoon cream of tartar

½ cup sugar

Filling
¼ cup sugar

4 teaspoons cornstarch

1 cup orange juice

1 tablespoon lemon juice

1 teaspoon grated lemon peel

Garnish
1 tablespoon powdered sugar, if desired

Fresh mint leaves, if desired

1. Heat oven to 250°F. Line cookie sheet with parchment paper. Draw six 4-inch circles on paper.
2. In large bowl, beat egg whites and cream of tartar at medium speed until soft peaks form. Gradually add ½ cup sugar, beating at high speed until stiff glossy peaks form and sugar is almost dissolved. Spoon meringue onto circles on paper-lined cookie sheet, building up edges to form 1-inch-high sides.
3. Bake at 250°F. for 1 hour. DO NOT OPEN OVEN. Turn oven off; leave meringues in oven with door closed for 2 hours.
4. Meanwhile, in medium saucepan, combine ¼ cup sugar and cornstarch. Slowly stir in orange juice. Cook and stir over medium-low heat until mixture thickens. Stir in lemon juice and lemon peel. Cool completely. Store filling in refrigerator.
5. To serve, spoon lemon filling into meringue shells. Sprinkle with powdered sugar. If desired, garnish with mint leaves.

YIELD: 6 SERVINGS

Cinnamon's *story*

Cinnamon is one of the world's oldest spices. It was used in China in 2500 B.C., and it's still one of the essentials in Chinese five-spice powder. Early Egyptians used cinnamon for everything from perfumes to embalming; the Romans included it in their love potions. Later, cinnamon was among the spices that sent explorers in search of sea routes to the Far East.

There are two types of cinnamon. Cassia is the dark red or brown variety that's most familiar in the United States, harvested primarily in Indonesia. It's pungent and bittersweet. Ceylon cinnamon is buff colored and mildly sweet, usually more expensive than Cassia cinnamon.

The spice is actually the inner bark of a tropical evergreen tree. It is harvested during the rainy season, when the wood is more pliable. When the bark is dried, it curls into long quills that are cut into sticks or ground into powder.

Chocolate Cinnamon Flans

■ ■ ■ ■ ■ ■ ■ ■ ■ ■ ■ ■ ■ ■ ■ ■ ■

PREP TIME: 10 MINUTES
(READY IN 50 MINUTES)

4 tablespoons fat-free hot fudge topping

1 (14-oz.) can fat-free or low-fat sweetened condensed milk (not evaporated)

½ cup refrigerated or frozen fat-free egg product, thawed, or 2 eggs

2 tablespoons unsweetened cocoa

1 teaspoon cinnamon

1. Heat oven to 350°F. Spray four 6-oz. custard cups with nonstick cooking spray; place in 13 × 9-inch pan. Place 1 tablespoon hot fudge topping in bottom of each cup.

2. In medium saucepan, combine all remaining ingredients; mix well. Cook over medium heat for 2 to 3 minutes or until warm to the touch (110 to 115°F.). Divide mixture evenly into custard cups. Pour boiling water into pan around custard cups to a depth of 1 inch.

3. Bake at 350°F. for 22 to 30 minutes or until edges are set and centers are slightly soft. Cool in pan of water for 10 minutes. Remove cups from water. Run sharp knife around top edge of each flan; turn upside down to unmold onto 4 individual serving plates. Serve warm or refrigerate until cool. Store in refrigerator.

YIELD: 4 SERVINGS

Nutrition Information Per Serving
Serving Size: ¼ of Recipe

Calories 350	Calories from Fat 0

	% Daily Value
Total Fat 0g	0%
Saturated 0g	0%
Cholesterol 15mg	5%
Sodium 180mg	8%
Total Carbohydrate 76g	25%
Dietary Fiber 1g	4%
Sugars 71g	
Protein 12g	

Vitamin A 4%	Vitamin C 0%
Calcium 30%	Iron 8%

Dietary Exchanges: 3½ Starch, 1½ Fruit OR 5 Carbohydrate

▼ Chocolate Cinnamon Flans

tips for making
Less Chocolate Taste Like More

- **Chocolate extract.** Chocolate extract is much like vanilla extract—flavored essence dissolved in alcohol. It provides the flavor of chocolate without any of the fat or caffeine and almost none of the calories (just 8 per teaspoon). While it's not a substitute for chocolate in baking, it can be used to enhance the chocolate flavor in reduced-chocolate baked goods. Or use it to give reduced-calorie yogurt, shakes, puddings and ice cream toppings a chocolate boost.

- **Chocolate garnishes.** Use chocolate-covered coffee beans, chocolate curls, grated chocolate or even just a sprinkling of cocoa to garnish lower-calorie desserts or fruit.

- **Cooking with cocoa.** Unsweetened cocoa powder, which is considerably lower in fat than chocolate, can be used in place of chocolate, especially when flavoring toppings, sauces or dips. But remember that the fat in chocolate plays a role in the success of baked goods, so you can't do away with all of it. One square of chocolate is equivalent to 3 tablespoons of cocoa powder plus 1 tablespoon of butter, margarine or oil.

- **Complementary flavors.** Enhance the flavor of chocolate by combining it with other flavors such as cherry, orange, cinnamon, coconut, almond, coffee, mint or peanut butter.

Chocolate Almond Mousse

PREP TIME: 15 MINUTES
(READY IN 35 MINUTES)

¾ **cup sugar**

⅓ **cup unsweetened cocoa**

3 **tablespoons cornstarch**

Dash salt

2 **cups skim milk**

⅛ **to ¼ teaspoon almond extract**

1 **cup frozen light whipped topping, thawed**

1. In medium nonstick saucepan, combine sugar, cocoa, cornstarch and salt; mix well. With wire whisk, stir in milk. Cook over medium heat until mixture comes to a boil, stirring constantly with wire whisk. Boil 1 minute, stirring constantly. Remove from heat; stir in almond extract. Pour into 13 × 9-inch pan. Cover surface with plastic wrap. Place in freezer for 15 to 20 minutes or just until cool.

2. Place chocolate mixture in medium bowl; fold in whipped topping. Serve immediately or refrigerate until serving time. Store in refrigerator.

YIELD: 6 (½-CUP) SERVINGS

Nutrition Information Per Serving
Serving Size: ½ Cup

Calories	190	Calories from Fat	20
		% Daily Value	
Total Fat	2g		3%
Saturated	2g		10%
Cholesterol	0mg		0%
Sodium	65mg		3%
Total Carbohydrate	38g		13%
Dietary Fiber	2g		8%
Sugars	30g		
Protein	4g		
Vitamin A	4%	Vitamin C	0%
Calcium	10%	Iron	4%

Dietary Exchanges: 1½ Starch, 1 Fruit OR 2½ Carbohydrate

Eggnog Bread Pudding with Rum Sauce

■ ■ ■ ■ ■ ■ ■ ■ ■ ■ ■ ■ ■ ■ ■ ■ ■ ■ ■ ■

PREP TIME: 20 MINUTES
(READY IN 1 HOUR)

Bread Pudding
1 cup sugar

1 teaspoon nutmeg

2 cups skim milk

1 teaspoon vanilla

2 eggs

10 cups French bread cubes (1-inch)

⅔ cup raisins

Sauce
1 cup firmly packed brown sugar

½ cup light corn syrup

2 tablespoons rum*

2 tablespoons margarine or butter

½ teaspoon vanilla

1. Heat oven to 350°F. Spray 13 × 9-inch (3-quart) baking dish with nonstick cooking spray.

2. In large bowl, combine sugar, nutmeg, milk, 1 teaspoon vanilla and eggs; beat with wire whisk until smooth. Fold in bread cubes and raisins. Pour into sprayed baking dish.

3. Bake at 350°F. for 40 to 45 minutes or until knife inserted in center comes out clean.

4. Meanwhile, in small saucepan, combine all sauce ingredients. Cook over medium heat until mixture comes to a boil, stirring constantly. Boil 1 minute. Remove from heat; cool slightly. Serve warm sauce over warm bread pudding.

YIELD: 16 SERVINGS

Tip: * To substitute for rum, use ½ teaspoon rum extract plus water to make 2 tablespoons.

Nutrition Information Per Serving

Serving Size: ¹/₁₆ of Recipe		
Calories 260	Calories from Fat 25	
	% Daily Value	
Total Fat 3g	...... 5%	
Saturated 1g	...... 5%	
Cholesterol 25mg	...... 8%	
Sodium 210mg	...... 9%	
Total Carbohydrate 53g	...... 18%	
Dietary Fiber 1g	...... 4%	
Sugars 36g		
Protein 4g		
Vitamin A 4%	Vitamin C 0%	
Calcium 8%	Iron 6%	

Dietary Exchanges: 2 Starch, 1 ½ Fruit OR 3 ½ Carbohydrate

about **Bread Pudding**

Because it's traditionally made with no preservatives and little or no fat, French bread can become stale pretty quickly, making it a perfect candidate for bread pudding. If you have French bread that's too hard to cut easily into cubes, break it into chunks to get an approximate measurement, and then soak it in the milk mixture until it's soft enough to mush up a bit.

Phyllo Cheesecakes
with Raspberry Sauce

■ ■ ■ ■ ■ ■ ■ ■ ■ ■ ■ ■ ■ ■ ■ ■ ■ ■ ■

PREP TIME: 20 MINUTES
(READY IN 1 HOUR 5 MINUTES)

Cheesecakes

Butter-flavor nonstick cooking spray

**1 (8-oz.) pkg. ⅓-less-fat cream cheese
(Neufchâtel), softened**

⅓ cup sugar

**⅓ cup refrigerated or frozen fat-free egg product,
thawed**

2 tablespoons skim milk

½ teaspoon vanilla

**6 (17 × 12-inch) sheets frozen phyllo (filo) pastry,
thawed**

Sauce

1 (12-oz.) pkg. frozen raspberries, thawed*

½ cup water

¼ cup sugar

1 teaspoon grated lime peel

1. Heat oven to 375°F. Spray six 6-oz. custard cups
with nonstick cooking spray.

2. In medium bowl, combine cream cheese, ⅓ cup
sugar, egg product, milk and vanilla; beat until
smooth. Set aside.

3. For each cup, place 1 phyllo sheet on work surface; spray with cooking spray. Fold sheet in half,
forming 8½ × 12-inch rectangle; spray again. Gently
ease center of folded phyllo into bottom and up sides
of cup. (Phyllo will hang over edges.) Repeat with
remaining phyllo sheets and custard cups.

▼ Phyllo Cheesecakes with Raspberry Sauce

4. Spoon about $1/4$ cup cream cheese mixture into each cup. Bring phyllo up over filling, loosely bunching edges together forming a ruffled top with some filling showing. Spray with cooking spray. Set custard cups in $15 \times 10 \times 1$-inch baking pan.

5. Bake at 375°F. for 12 to 15 minutes or until phyllo is golden brown. Cool slightly. Carefully remove from cups. Refrigerate at least 30 minutes or until serving time.

6. Place raspberries and water in blender container or food processor bowl with metal blade; process until smooth. Strain mixture into bowl to remove seeds. Stir in $1/4$ cup sugar and lime peel.

7. To serve, spoon $1/4$ cup raspberry sauce onto each of 6 individual dessert plates. Place 1 cheesecake on each plate. Store in refrigerator.

YIELD: 6 SERVINGS

Tip: * To thaw raspberries, place in microwave-safe bowl; microwave on HIGH for $1 1/2$ to $2 1/2$ minutes or until thawed.

Nutrition Information Per Serving
Serving Size: $1/6$ of Recipe

Calories	310	Calories from Fat	90
		% Daily Value	
Total Fat	10g		15%
Saturated	6g		30%
Cholesterol	25mg		8%
Sodium	300mg		13%
Total Carbohydrate	48g		16%
Dietary Fiber	3g		12%
Sugars	34g		
Protein	8g		
Vitamin A	8%	Vitamin C	15%
Calcium	4%	Iron	8%

Dietary Exchanges: 2 Starch, 1 Fruit, 2 Fat OR 3 Carbohydrate, 2 Fat

Phyllo *facts*

■ ■

Phyllo pastry (also spelled "filo") comes in large, tissue-thin sheets similar to strudel leaves. It's widely used in Greek and Middle Eastern baking and can encase both savory appetizers and pies and sweet desserts like baklava.

Usually, several layers are used in a recipe with melted butter brushed between each leaf. In the oven, the layers bake into flaky, crisp separate leaves. Our recipe for Phyllo Cheesecakes with Raspberry Sauce (opposite) uses nonstick cooking spray to achieve the same separate flakiness with much less fat.

Phyllo is delicate. For best results, thaw frozen phyllo overnight in the refrigerator. Thaw only as much as you will use at a time and do not refreeze. Let the phyllo, still wrapped, come to room temperature for an hour or so before using. Remove one sheet at a time from the package, making sure to keep remaining sheets covered with a clean, damp dish towel so they don't dry out.

Orange Creme Dessert with Ruby Cranberry Sauce

PREP TIME: 30 MINUTES
(READY IN 45 MINUTES)

12 chocolate-covered graham cookies, finely crushed (about 1 cup crumbs)*

2 cups fresh or frozen cranberries

¾ cup sugar

1 teaspoon cornstarch

¾ cup water

1 envelope unflavored gelatin

¼ cup orange juice

4 (5-oz.) containers (2 cups) nonfat orange yogurt

2 teaspoons grated orange peel

2 cups frozen light whipped topping, thawed

1. Heat oven to 375°F. Spray 9-inch springform pan with nonstick cooking spray. Press cookie crumbs evenly in bottom of sprayed pan. Bake at 375°F. for 7 minutes. Chill in refrigerator or freezer until completely cooled.

Low-Fat *tip*

Reduce the fat in desserts by topping them with glazes, drizzles and dustings rather than frosting.

2. Meanwhile, in medium saucepan, combine cranberries, sugar, cornstarch and water; mix well. Bring to a boil over medium heat, stirring constantly. Reduce heat to low; simmer 10 minutes, stirring occasionally. Refrigerate.

3. In small saucepan, combine gelatin and orange juice; let stand 2 minutes. Place saucepan over low heat; stir until gelatin is dissolved.

4. In blender container, combine yogurt and orange peel; blend until smooth. With blender running, add gelatin mixture. Cover; blend at high speed for 15 to 20 seconds or until combined. Spoon into medium bowl. Gently stir in whipped topping. Spoon and gently spread over cooled crust. Place in freezer for 15 minutes or until set.

5. Just before serving, top each serving with 2 tablespoons of the cranberry mixture. Store in refrigerator.

YIELD: 12 SERVINGS

Tip: * Cookies can be crushed in blender.

Nutrition Information Per Serving
Serving Size: ¹/₁₂ of Recipe

Calories	170	Calories from Fat	35
		% Daily Value	
Total Fat	4g		6%
Saturated	2g		10%
Cholesterol	0mg		0%
Sodium	55mg		2%
Total Carbohydrate	31g		10%
Dietary Fiber	1g		3%
Sugars	24g		
Protein	3g		
Vitamin A	0%	Vitamin C	6%
Calcium	8%	Iron	2%

Dietary Exchanges: 1 Starch, 1 Fruit, ½ Fat OR 2 Carbohydrate, ½ Fat

great **Garnishes**

A garnish can instantly enhance the look of an ordinary (or even extraordinary) dessert. Some easy ideas:

- **Fresh fruit.** Use a few raspberries, strawberries or blueberries to give a taste of fresh flavor and provide a nice finishing touch. For a little extra decadence, drizzle berries with melted chocolate.

- **Zesty garnish.** Use a citrus zester or fine grater to remove "zest" (the colored part of the rind) from citrus fruit. Try lime as an accent for fruit desserts, orange for chocolate and lemon to perk up vanilla treats.

- **Citrus twist.** Cut a thin, circular slice of lemon, orange or lime. Slit the circle halfway, cutting from the rind to the center. Twist the slice to form a curl.

- **Looks like snow.** Sift powdered sugar over the dessert and/or plate. To create a lacy pattern, place a doily (or create your own stencil from waxed paper) on top of the dessert and sprinkle with powdered sugar; lift off the doily carefully. This also works with cocoa powder, by itself or mixed with powdered sugar.

- **Chocolate curls.** Briefly hold a block or bar of chocolate in your hand to warm it slightly (but not melt it). Using a sharp paring knife or vegetable peeler, scrape off a long, thin strip. The chocolate should curl as you peel it. Or scrape off short pieces (or grate with a large-holed grater) to create decorative shavings. Milk chocolate works a little better than others because it's softer.

- **Chocolate leaves.** Melt semi-sweet chocolate in a double boiler over low heat, stirring constantly, until the chocolate is almost melted. Remove it from the heat and continue to stir to melt the remaining chocolate. Brush melted chocolate onto the back of washed and dried nontoxic, untreated leaves such as mint, lemon or rose leaves. (Don't use leaves from the florist—they have probably been treated with pesticides or other undesirable substances.) Refrigerate the leaves about 10 minutes or until the chocolate is set. Apply a second layer of chocolate over the first layer. Again, refrigerate the leaves until the chocolate is set. Carefully peel each leaf away from the chocolate. Store the chocolate leaves in the refrigerator or freezer until ready to use.

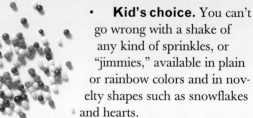

- **Kid's choice.** You can't go wrong with a shake of any kind of sprinkles, or "jimmies," available in plain or rainbow colors and in novelty shapes such as snowflakes and hearts.

Cherry-Cranberry Dessert Squares

■ ■ ■ ■ ■ ■ ■ ■ ■ ■ ■ ■ ■ ■ ■ ■ ■ ■ ■

PREP TIME: 30 MINUTES
(READY IN 1 HOUR 30 MINUTES)

1 refrigerated pie crust (from 15-oz. pkg.)

3 cups fresh or frozen cranberries

1 cup sugar

¼ cup cornstarch

½ teaspoon cinnamon

¼ cup water

1 (21-oz.) can cherry pie filling

2 (3.4-oz.) pkg. instant vanilla pudding and pie filling mix

2 cups skim milk

½ teaspoon rum extract

1 cup frozen light whipped topping, thawed

1. Heat oven to 425°F. Microwave pie crust pouch on DEFROST for 20 to 40 seconds, or let stand at room temperature for 15 minutes. Remove crust from pouch. Unfold crust; peel off plastic sheets. Press pie crust into bottom only of ungreased 13 × 9-inch pan, cutting to fit; press seams firmly to seal. Prick crust generously with fork. Bake at 425°F. for 9 to 11 minutes or until light golden brown. Cool.

2. Meanwhile, in medium nonstick saucepan, combine cranberries, sugar, cornstarch and cinnamon; mix well. Stir in water; bring to a boil. Cook and stir over medium-high heat for about 5 minutes or until cranberries pop and sauce is very thick and translucent. Add cherry pie filling; mix well. Cover surface with plastic wrap. Place in freezer for about 10 minutes to cool.

3. In medium bowl, combine pudding mix and milk. Stir in rum extract. Blend with wire whisk until thickened. Spoon over cooled baked crust. Top evenly with cranberry mixture. Refrigerate about 1 hour or until set.* Cut into squares; top with whipped topping.

YIELD: 12 SERVINGS

Tip: * To speed preparation, place in freezer for up to 30 minutes or until set.

Nutrition Information Per Serving
Serving Size: ¹/₁₂ of Recipe

Calories	310	Calories from Fat	50
		% Daily Value	
Total Fat	6g		9%
Saturated	3g		15%
Cholesterol	5mg		2%
Sodium	350mg		15%
Total Carbohydrate	63g		21%
Dietary Fiber	2g		8%
Sugars	45g		
Protein	2g		
Vitamin A	4%	Vitamin C	6%
Calcium	6%	Iron	2%

Dietary Exchanges: 1 Starch, 3 Fruit, 1 Fat OR 4 Carbohydrate, 1 Fat

■ **PRODUCE POINTERS**

Cherry *facts*

- Cherries are very perishable, so buy only what you'll use in about three days.

- Look for plump, full-colored cherries without bruises and with stems attached. If possible, ask whether you can taste the cherries before you buy them because they do not ripen further or improve in flavor after they're picked.

- Refrigerate cherries flat on a tray or in a shallow bowl, and loosely cover them with a paper towel or plastic wrap. Or freeze stemmed, pitted cherries in airtight containers for up to several months. No processing is required.

- Use the tip of a vegetable peeler to remove the pits from cherries. Or invest in a cherry pitter.

- Fresh cherries have about 80 calories per cup.

Index

■ ■

343

Conversion Chart
Equivalent Imperial and Metric Measurements

American cooks use standard containers, the 8-ounce cup and a tablespoon that takes exactly 16 level fillings to fill that cup level. Measuring by cup makes it very difficult to give weight equivalents, as a cup of densely packed butter will weigh considerably more than a cup of flour. The easiest way therefore to deal with cup measurements in recipes is to take the amount by volume rather than by weight. Thus the equation reads:

1 cup = 240 ml = 8 fl. oz.   ½ cup = 120 ml = 4 fl. oz.

It is possible to buy a set of American cup measures in major stores around the world.

In the States, butter is often measured in sticks. One stick is the equivalent of 8 tablespoons. One tablespoon of butter is therefore the equivalent to ½ ounce/15 grams.

LIQUID MEASURES

Fluid Ounces	U.S.	Imperial	Milliliters
	1 teaspoon	1 teaspoon	5
¼	2 teaspoons	1 dessertspoon	10
½	1 tablespoon	1 tablespoon	14
1	2 tablespoons	2 tablespoons	28
2	¼ cup	4 tablespoons	56
4	½ cup		110
5		¼ pint or 1 gill	140
6	¾ cup		170
8	1 cup		225
9			250, ¼ liter
10	1¼ cups	½ pint	280
12	1½ cups		340
15		¾ pint	420
16	2 cups		450
18	2¼ cups		500, ½ liter
20	2½ cups	1 pint	560
24	3 cups		675
25		1¼ pints	700
27	3½ cups		750
30	3¾ cups	1½ pints	840
32	4 cups or 1 quart		900
35		1¾ pints	980
36	4½ cups		1000, 1 liter
40	5 cups	2 pints or 1 quart	1120

SOLID MEASURES

U.S. and Imperial Measures		Metric Measures	
Ounces	Pounds	Grams	Kilos
1		28	
2		56	
3½		100	
4	¼	112	
5		140	
6		168	
8	½	225	
9		250	¼
12	¾	340	
16	1	450	
18		500	½
20	1¼	560	
24	1½	675	
27		750	¾
28	1¾	780	
32	2	900	
36	2¼	1000	1
40	2½	1100	
48	3	1350	
54		1500	1½

OVEN TEMPERATURE EQUIVALENTS

Fahrenheit	Celsius	Gas Mark	Description
225	110	¼	Cool
250	130	½	
275	140	1	Very Slow
300	150	2	
325	170	3	Slow
350	180	4	Moderate
375	190	5	
400	200	6	Moderately Hot
425	220	7	Fairly Hot
450	230	8	Hot
475	240	9	Very Hot
500	250	10	Extremely Hot

Any broiling recipes can be used with the grill of the oven, but beware of high-temperature grills.

EQUIVALENTS FOR INGREDIENTS

all-purpose flour–plain flour
coarse salt–kitchen salt
cornstarch–cornflour
eggplant–aubergine

half and half–12% fat milk
heavy cream–double cream
light cream–single cream
lima beans–broad beans

scallion–spring onion
unbleached flour–strong, white flour
zest–rind
zucchini–courgettes or marrow

Soups, Stews and Chilies ∎ Poultry ∎ Beef, Pork and Lamb

eads ∎ Desserts ∎ An Introduction to Healthier Eating ∎

eef, Pork and Lamb ∎ Fish and Seafood ∎ Meatless Entrees

althier Eating ∎ Appetizers ∎ Salads ∎ Soups, Stews and

∎ Meatless Entrees ∎ Side Dishes ∎ Breads ∎ Desserts ∎

Soups, Stews and Chilies ∎ Poultry ∎ Beef, Pork and Lamb

eads ∎ Desserts ∎ An Introduction to Healthier Eating ∎

eef, Pork and Lamb ∎ Fish and Seafood ∎ Meatless Entrees

althier Eating ∎ Appetizers ∎ Salads ∎ Soups, Stews and

∎ Meatless Entrees ∎ Side Dishes ∎ Breads ∎ Desserts ∎

Soups, Stews and Chilies ∎ Poultry ∎ Beef, Pork and Lamb

eads ∎ Desserts ∎ An Introduction to Healthier Eating

An Introduction to Healthier Eating ▪ Appetizers ▪ Salads

▪ Fish and Seafood ▪ Meatless Entrees ▪ Side Dishes ▪

Appetizers ▪ Salads ▪ Soups, Stews and Chilies ▪ Poultry

▪ Side Dishes ▪ Breads ▪ Desserts ▪ An Introduction to

Chilies ▪ Poultry ▪ Beef, Pork and Lamb ▪ Fish and Seafc

An Introduction to Healthier Eating ▪ Appetizers ▪ Salads

▪ Fish and Seafood ▪ Meatless Entrees ▪ Side Dishes ▪

Appetizers ▪ Salads ▪ Soups, Stews and Chilies ▪ Poultry

▪ Side Dishes ▪ Breads ▪ Desserts ▪ An Introduction to

Chilies ▪ Poultry ▪ Beef, Pork and Lamb ▪ Fish and Seafc

An Introduction to Healthier Eating ▪ Appetizers ▪ Salads

▪ Fish and Seafood ▪ Meatless Entrees ▪ Side Dishes